The Foundations
of Psychoanalysis

**Pittsburgh Series in
Philosophy and History
of Science**

Series Editors:

Adolf Grünbaum
Larry Laudan
Nicholas Rescher
Wesley C. Salmon

THE FOUNDATIONS
OF PSYCHOANALYSIS
A Philosophical Critique

Adolf Grünbaum

Andrew Mellon Professor of Philosophy
and
Research Professor of Psychiatry
University of Pittsburgh

UNIVERSITY OF CALIFORNIA PRESS
Berkeley   Los Angeles   London

Permission has been granted for the use of the following copyrighted material:

K. R. Eissler, M.D. "Irreverent remarks about the present and the future of psychoanalysis," *International Journal of Psycho-Analysis*, 50:461-471.

S. Freud. *Standard Edition of the Complete Psychological Works of Sigmund Freud*. James Strachey, General Editor, Vols. III, XX, and XXIII. London: Hogarth Press.

S. Freud. *Interpretation of Dreams* and *Introductory Lectures on Psychoanalysis*. London: George Allen & Unwin (Publishers) Ltd.

S. Freud. "An Autobiographical Study," Vol. XX; "Introductory Lectures," Vol. XV; "Introductory Lectures," Vol. XVI. In *Introductory Lectures on Psychoanalysis*, by Sigmund Freud. Translated by James Strachey. Copyright © 1966 by W. W. Norton & Company, Inc. Copyright © 1976, 1964, 1963 by James Strachey. Copyright 1920, 1935 by Edward L. Bery Bernays.

J. Habermas. *Knowledge and Human Interests*. Translated by Jeremy J. Shapiro. Copyright © 1971 by Beacon Press. Reprinted by permission of Beacon Press.

University of California Press
Berkeley and Los Angeles, California

University of California Press, Ltd.
London, England

Library of Congress Cataloging in Publication Data

Grünbaum, Adolf.
  The foundations of psychoanalysis.
    Bibliography: p. 287
    Includes index.
    1. Psychoanalysis.   2. Freud, Sigmund, 1856–1939.   3. Philosophy.
I. Title. [DNLM: 1. Psychoanalytic theory. WM 460 G888f]
BF173.G76   1984   150.19'52   83-9264
ISBN 0-520-05016-9
ISBN 0-520-05017-7 (pbk.)

Printed in the United States of America

1 2 3 4 5 6 7 8 9

TO
Morris Eagle
Stanley Rachman
Benjamin Rubinstein
Rosemarie Sand
who generously eased my path when I first
entered the field of this book.

Contents

Acknowledgments

In the spring of 1977, soon after I had begun to study the credentials of psychoanalytic theory, I gave a related Philosophy Department Colloquium on the Berkeley campus of the University of California. Frederick Crews, the literary critic, whom I had never met, was in the audience. During that summer, he read the embryonic draft of what was to become a book manuscript I thought I would publish. Thereupon he very kindly took the initiative of communicating his judgment of this draft to James Clark, the director of the University of California Press. Some weeks later, I was glad to receive a publication offer from the Press.

Quite independently of this development, Larry Laudan and I had proposed that the Press at the University of California become the publisher of our newly reconstituted Pittsburgh Series in the Philosophy and History of Science under our general co-editorship. We planned to enlarge this Series to include volumes by single authors, rather than only the multi-author collections of studies previously published under the auspices of our Center for Philosophy of Science at the University of Pittsburgh. When the Press accepted our proposal, Laudan urged the inclusion of my own book in the Series.

As I originally envisioned the scope of this book, it was to be a philosophical assessment of the postulational and epistemologic foundations of Freud's monumental clinical theory, as well as of its metapsychological superstructure, which was avowedly more speculative. Besides, the projected volume was to include discussion of such topics as the anti-psychiatry challenge of Thomas Szasz, psychoanalysis and theism, psychobiography and psychohistory, as well as of psychoanalysis and feminism.

Yet, as soon became clear, the lengthy preparation of a work having such a broad topical purview would needlessly delay the availability of my scrutiny of the foundations—postulational, epistemic, and heuristic—of the clinical psychoanalytic theory of unconscious motivation. Thus, once I had written that much of my scrutiny, which *includes* a critique of the hermeneutic construal of this theory, Alexander Rosenberg—a fellow philosopher—suggested that I meet the widely expressed interest in it by detaching this self-contained unit for separate publication. Hence the appearance of this book. The remainder of the work I originally envisioned, which I have yet to bring to completion, is also destined for publication by the University of California Press as a volume in the Pittsburgh Series. I am indebted to the philosophy editor of the Press, John R. Miles, for the thoughtfulness and initiative he devoted to making these arrangements.

The first impetus for my inquiry into the intellectual merits of the psychoanalytic enterprise came from my doubts concerning Karl Popper's philosophy of science, which I published in a series of four essays in 1976. As a corollary, my hunch was that his indictment of the Freudian corpus as inherently untestable had fundamentally misdiagnosed its very genuine epistemic defects, which are often quite subtle. My interest in the specific grounds on which Freud sought rational assent to his wide-ranging doctrines was piqued further by Cynthia Freeland's contributions to my seminar on "Falsifiability and Rationality," made while she was a graduate student.

As will emerge in the body of this book, I take issue with the cardinal tenets of psychoanalysis by challenging their avowed clinical credentials. For example, I shall argue in chapters 3, 4, and 5 that all of Freud's clinical arguments for his cornerstone theory of repression should be deemed to be fundamentally flawed. Yet, as shown by the above dedication, I have been the fortunate beneficiary of substantive help, and often of encouragement, not only from opponents of his legacy but also from some practicing psychoanalysts and from psychodynamically oriented clinicians. Among the latter practitioners, the psychologist Morris Eagle and the analysts Benjamin Rubinstein and Rosemarie Sand have unstintingly allowed me to avail myself of their scholarship, which is also informed by remarkable literacy in the philosophy of science.

Moreover, Philip Holzman, whose clinical experience had led him to press fundamental doubts against the scientific probity of the treatment setting (1984), gave me much encouragement by making some of my earlier writings on Freudian theory available to the psychoanalytic public in a monograph of *Psychological Issues*. Leo Goldberger, the editor of *Psychoanalysis and Contemporary Thought*, has extended the hospitality of the pages of his journal to my views. Besides, I have learned from discussions or correspondence with the analysts George Alexander, Michael Basch, David Malan, Emanuel Peterfreund, Richard Sens, Helmut Thomä and Gerhard Werner.

During my initial exploration of the literature on psychotherapeutic process and treatment outcome, Stanley Rachman, Hans Eysenck, and Edward Shoben magnanimously took the time to deal didactically with my then quite elementary questions about some of their writings. At that early stage, Professor Rachman afforded me the opportunity of a visit with him and the house staff at the Institute of Psychiatry at the University of London (Maudsley Hospital).

My more recent secondary appointment as Research Professor of Psychiatry in the School of Medicine at the University of Pittsburgh eventuated in fruitful contacts with faculty and residents of the department of psychiatry, some of whom became active participants in my seminars on philosophical issues in psychoanalysis. The colleagues in that department to whom I am especially grateful include its inspiring chairman Thomas Detre, who has been my mentor all along; Bahman Fozouni, whose generous initiatives have been a steady spur; also Margaret Cashman, Anthony Costello, Stanley Imber, Alan Kazdin, David Kupfer, and Irwin Savodnik, who have either shared their knowledge or have been encouraging. Moreover, Dr. Fozouni gave me the benefit of his extensive knowledge of the hermeneutic literature by steering me to what is most germane to my concerns.

Among philosophers, Edward Erwin, Barbara von Eckardt—the author of a forthcoming essay (1984) dealing with my writings on psychoanalysis—and Clark Glymour, whose interesting work prompted chapter 8, were a tonic to my endeavors, as were Alexander Nehamas, Wilfrid Sellars, John Watkins, the forensic psychologist Stephen Morse, the philosopher of law Michael Moore, and the historian of psychoanalysis James Blight. Peter Urbach's comments generated expository clarifications of some points in chapter 1.B.

Most recently, my cherished friends Robert S. Cohen and Larry Laudan—with the support of my prized Pittsburgh colleagues Carl Hempel, Nicholas Rescher, and Wesley Salmon—did me the honor of organizing and editing a *Festschrift* for me, entitled *Physics, Philosophy and Psychoanalysis* (Boston: Reidel, 1983). I am deeply indebted to them for this labor of love, and to the sixteen contributors, four of whom quickened my present thinking by dealing with related Freudian themes (Eagle, Glymour, Rubinstein, and Schaffner, 1983).

Elizabeth McMunn rendered invaluable research assistance by tracking down and condensing a substantial amount of relevant literature. She also bore with my various revisions while painstakingly preparing the manuscript. I thank her for these labors.

Earlier versions or portions of some of the chapters below were presented under various auspices as lectures.

The long Introduction draws on my Presidential Address to the American Philosophical Association (Eastern Division), given in December 1982, which appears in *Proceedings and Addresses of the American Philosophical Association*, vol. 57 (September 1983) pp. 5-31. Other portions of the Introduction were presented to the Rapaport-Klein Study Group in 1983 at its annual meeting in Stockbridge, Massachussets (Austen Riggs Center).

Chapter 1 derives partly from my Special University Lecture in the History of Science at the University of London (1976) and from an invited address at the International Symposium on the Philosophy of Sir Karl Popper, held at the London School of Economics (1980). It also contains material growing out of my colloquia at the Universities of Göttingen, Munich, and Düsseldorf in Germany.

Chapter 2 originated in a symposium paper, delivered at the Conference on Methods in Philosophy and the Sciences at the New School for Social Research in New York (1979). But sections B and C of this chapter incorporate ideas I presented to the Boston Colloquium for the Philosophy of Science at Boston University (1981).

Chapter 3 and the main themes of chapters 4 and 5 evolved from the invited paper I gave to the session of the Committee on Philosophy and Medicine at the meeting of the American Philosophical Association in December 1981.

But the impetus for the development of these three cornerstone chapters came from the prospect of including them—in enlarged form—in my ten *Gifford Lectures*. Addressed to the topic "Psychoanalytic Theory and Science," these Lectures are to be delivered in Scotland, at the University of St. Andrews, during the academic year 1984/85.

Chapter 8 is based on an invited paper delivered at the Conference on Confirmation, held at the Minnesota Center for Philosophy of Science in Minneapolis (1980).

I gratefully acknowledge generous research support for work on philosophic issues in psychiatry from the Fritz Thyssen Stiftung in Cologne, Germany during the period of 1977-1982.

Introduction

Critique of the Hermeneutic Conception of Psychoanalytic Theory and Therapy

The study before you is a philosophical critique of the foundations of Sigmund Freud's psychoanalysis. As such, it must also take cognizance of his claim that psychoanalysis has the credentials of a natural science. But before examining the cardinal arguments put forward by him, I need to expose a widespread exegetical myth.

It is precisely that myth, the contrived reading, which has served as the point of departure for convicting Freud of "scientistic self-misunderstanding." This demonstrably ill-founded charge was leveled by the philosophers Jürgen Habermas and Paul Ricoeur, champions of the so-called "hermeneutic" version of psychoanalytic theory and therapy. Indeed, their rendition has gained widespread acceptance in various quarters as now being at the cutting edge of the field, if not *de rigueur*. But besides resting on a mythic exegesis of Freud's writings, the theses of these hermeneuticians are based on profound misunderstandings of the very content and methods of the natural sciences.

Hence, it will be useful that I address, at the outset, not only the fabrication of the textual legend but also the multiple ontological and epistemic blunders inherent in the currently fashionable hermeneutic construal of psychoanalysis. The more so since Habermas has deemed precisely this reading of the Freudian corpus to be potentially prototypic for the other sciences of man (Habermas 1971, chapter 10). Thus, my critical scrutiny in the present Introduction may well have considerable import for hermeneutic philosophy, well beyond psychoanalysis proper.

Of course, within this study of the foundations of psychoanalysis, I do not intend to pursue these ramifications, let alone try to explain why this philosophy has achieved popularity. Yet, I hope that others who may do so will find my analysis instructive for their purpose as well.

1. The Exegetical Legend of "Scientistic Self-Misunderstanding"

Throughout his long career, Freud insisted that the psychoanalytic enterprise has the status of a natural science. As he told us at the very end of his life, the explanatory gains from positing unconscious mental processes "enabled psychology to take its place as a natural science like any other" (S.E. 1940, 23: 158). Then he went on to declare: "Psycho-analysis is a part of the mental science of psychology. . . . Psychology, too, is a natural science. What else can it be?" (S.E. 1940, 23: 282).

Five years earlier, in his 1933 lecture on *Weltanschauung*, Freud had firmly rebuffed the antinaturalism and methodological separatism that was championed by the *Geisteswissenschaften* movement as a framework for psychology and the social sciences. Its votaries deemed causal explanations to be endemic to the natural sciences in view of the general and law-like causal connections featured by these disciplines. And they rejected such nomothetic causal explanations as generically alien to the humanistic sciences. For as they saw it, the aim of the study of man ought to be the "hermeneutic" quest for idiographic understanding by such methods as empathy and intuitive self-evidence (Möller 1976: 38-62; Möller 1978: 162-211). In diametrical opposition to this delineation of the task of psychology, Freud proclaimed:

the intellect and the mind are objects for scientific research in exactly the same way as any non-human things. Psycho-analysis has a special right to speak for the scientific *Weltanschauung*. . . . If . . . the investigation of the intellectual and emotional functions of men (and of animals) is included in science, then it will be seen that . . . no new sources of knowledge or methods of research have come into being. [S.E. 1933, 22: 159]

Having thus concluded that "psychoanalysis has a special right to speak for the scientific *Weltanschauung*," the founder of this new branch of psychology deplored its reception in the scientific community. As Freud put it plaintively in 1925: "I have always felt it a gross injustice that people have refused to treat psycho-analysis like any other [natural] science" (S.E. 1925, 20: 58).

Three decades earlier, in 1895, the psychoanalytic method of clinical investigation by means of free association was only a fledgling mode of inquiry. Likewise, Freud's clinical theory of psychopathology was still nascent. At that very early juncture, he gave a neurophysiological twist to the notion of a scientific psychology and couched his then vision of a neurological underpinning for psychic processes in the reductionistic physical idiom of material particles. Thus, in the opening sentence of his 1895 manuscript "Project for a Scientific Psychology," he stated: "The intention is to furnish a psychology that shall be a natural science: that is, to represent psychical processes as quantitatively determinate states of specifiable material particles..." (S.E. 1950, 1: 295). As we learn in the next sentence, the "specifiable material particles" he has in mind are "neurones." (For clarifying commentary, see Holt 1965, Pribram and Gill 1976, Fancher 1973, Kanzer 1973, and McCarley and Hobson 1977.)

Freud's clinical work had inspired the notion of psychic repression, an idea whose theoretical elaboration was destined to become the "cornerstone" of "the whole structure of psychoanalysis" (S.E. 1914, 14: 16). Hence, in his search for a neurophysiological model of the psychic apparatus it became imperative to accommodate the cardinal hypothesis of repression. Yet, the difficulties he encountered in that endeavor generated fundamental doubts as to the sheer soundness of his neurological vision (Freud 1954: 349-350; Sulloway 1979: 123-126).

In the face of this disappointment, Freud abandoned his reductionistic program within two years of having enunciated it in the draft of his 1895 "Project" (Freud 1954: 349). Indeed, besides never publishing it, he refrained from mentioning it in his other writings. The result was that its existence was not even suspected until some years after his death. As if to allude to this failure of the "Project," Freud wrote a decade later:

every attempt...to discover a [brain] localization of mental processes, every endeavour to think of ideas as stored up in nerve-cells and of excitations as travelling along nerve-fibres, has miscarried completely. [S.E. 1915, 14: 174]

Here a caveat is in order. By 1896, I claim, Freud had despaired of foreseeably *reducing* the clinical theory *globally* to neurobiology. But I do not thereby run afoul of the well-attested *heuristic* role (Sulloway 1979: 121-123) that the neurobiological models—i.e., the purely mechanical and the organismic-evolutionary ones—retained, via analogies, in Freud's subsequent clinical and metapsychological theorizing. For my concern now is with the grounds on which he attributed *scientificity* to his evolving clinical theory. And, as I shall soon document, the heuristic role perennially enjoyed by the neuromechanical model after its collapse did not prevent that demise from ushering in the following development: Freud forsook his initial, ontologically reductive notion of scientific status in favor of a methodological, epistemic one (Grünbaum 1983a).

By the time he wrote the last chapter of *The Interpretation of Dreams* (S.E. 1900, 5: chapter vii), the legacy of the abandoned neurological model had become a postulated bipartite structure of the mind whose principal agencies were the unconscious and the preconscious. As he tells us, his "topographic" depiction of the relations of these component systems was "expressed in spatial terms, without, however, implying any connection with the actual anatomy of the brain" (S.E. 1925, 20: 32). And while pointedly eschewing the original neurological connotations of the technical vocabulary he had introduced in the "Project," he now often employed it homonymously in an avowedly mentalistic sense. Thus, the erstwhile excitation or "cathexis" of a *neuron* has now become the cathected state of an *idea* or *memory*. Likewise, a train of thought is now held to involve the *flow* of cathexes from one *idea* to another, so that *psychic energy* is invested in the mental representations of objects. And as he was stressing by 1913:

it is easy to describe the unconscious and to follow its developments if it is approached from the direction of its relation to the conscious, with which it has so much in common. On the other hand, there still seems no possibility of approaching it from the direction of physical events. So that it is bound to remain a matter for psychological study. [S.E. 1913, 13: 179]

Freud retained these mentalistic notions to the end of his life:

We assume, as other natural sciences have led us to expect, that in mental life some kind of energy is at work; but we have nothing to go upon which will enable us to come nearer to a knowledge of it by analogies with other forms of energy. We seem to recognize that nervous or psychical energy occurs in two forms, one freely mobile and another, by comparison, bound. (S.E. 1940, 23: 163-164)

The free mobility of psychic energy toward tension-discharge is supposed to be characteristic of processes associated with the unconscious system, whereas this energy is presumed to be bound against discharge for processes in which the preconscious agency is paramount (Laplanche and Pontalis 1973: 172-173). Yet he allows that there are "hyper-cathexes. . . in the course of which free energy is transformed into bound energy" (p. 164). By 1923, Freud modified his bipartite structural model, on which he had relied since 1900 (S.E. 1923, 19: 12-59; 1933, 22: 57-80). Writing in 1925, he explained:

In my latest speculative works I have set about the task of dissecting our mental apparatus on the basis of the [psycho-] analytic view of pathological facts and have divided in into an *ego*, an *id*, and a *super-ego*. The super-ego is the heir of the Oedipus complex and represents the ethical standards of mankind. [S.E. 1925, 20: 59]

These successive models of the structure and function of the psychic apparatus—propounded in 1895, 1900, and 1923—are often denominated as the "metapsychology" of Freud's theoretical edifice (Laplanche and Pontalis 1973: 250). Though the separation of the clinical theory from that metapsychology within the edifice is not always sharp, it is vital to appreciate what epistemic and logical status Freud assigned to its metapsychological part, while steadfastly claiming natural science status for his construction overall. Writing in his 1925 *Autobiographical Study*, he relegated his metapsychological notions to a "speculative superstructure of psycho-analysis" when he declared:

Such ideas as these are part of a speculative superstructure of psycho-analysis, any portion of which can be abandoned or changed without loss or regret the moment its inadequacy has been proved. But there is still plenty to be described that lies closer to actual experience. [S.E. 1925, 20: 32-33]

In the same vein, over a decade earlier he had portrayed the metapsychological hypotheses as "the top of the whole [psychoanalytic] structure," a top which "can be replaced and discarded without damaging it [the structure]" (S.E. 1914, 14: 77). Significantly, the "plenty...that lies closer to actual experience" is, of course, none other than his *clinically* based theory of personality, psychopathology, and therapy. The centerpiece of that corpus of hypotheses is the theory of repression, which features his compromise-model of neurotic symptoms, as well as of manifest dream content and of various sorts of slips. Note that these various phenomena are deemed to be "compromises" in the sense of being *substitutive gratifications* or outlets. For they are held to be conatively vicarious surrogates. Moreover, the clinical theory of repression is often couched in *personalist* language.

But in conspicuous contrast to his depiction of the metapsychology as "a speculative superstructure" which can be sloughed off, if need be, "without loss or regret," he explicitly deemed his clinical theory to be "the most essential part" of what he had wrought. For, as he told us in his own *History of the Psycho-Analytic Movement*, "The theory of repression is the cornerstone on which the whole structure of psycho-analysis rests. It is the most essential part of it" (S.E. 1914, 14: 16). Indeed, when the psychologist Saul Rosenzweig offered him alleged *experimental* evidence for this foundational doctrine in 1934, Freud replied that such evidence is superfluous in view of "the wealth of reliable [clinical] observations" on which that doctrine rests (MacKinnon and Dukes 1964: 703). Earlier, he had emphasized that "the foundation of science upon which everything rests...is observation alone" (S.E. 1914, 14: 77). Furthermore, he maintained that "Psycho-analysis is founded securely upon the observation of the facts of mental life" (S.E. 1923, 18: 266). Moreover, immediately before making this assertion, he explicitly *subordinated* the observational credentials of the metapsychology to those of the clinical theory: "It must not be supposed that these very general ideas [concerning the mental apparatus as a compound instrument, composed of an *id*, *ego*, and *super-ego*] are presuppositions upon which the work of psychoanalysis depends. On the contrary, they are its latest conclusions and are 'open to revision'." But, as for the centerpiece of the clinical theory, Freud avers: "the theory of repression is a product of psychoanalytic work, a theoretical inference legitimately drawn from innumerable observations" (S.E. 1914, 14:17)

It emerges clearly that when Freud unswervingly claimed natural science status for his theoretical constructions throughout his life, he did so first and foremost for his evolving clinical theory of personality and therapy, rather than for the metapsychology. For he had been chastened in his early reductionistic exuberance by the speedy demise of his "Project." And, once he had repudiated his ephemeral neurobiological model of the psyche after 1896, he perennially saw himself entitled to proclaim the *scientificity* of his clinical theory *entirely on the strength of a secure and direct epistemic warrant from the observations he made of his patients and of himself*. In brief, during all but the first few years of his career, Freud's criterion of *scientificity* was *methodological* and *not* ontologically reductive (S.E. 1914, 14: 77; 1915, 14: 117; 1925, 20: 32).

Yet, as we shall see, Freud's subsequent unflagging assertion of natural science status for the clinical theory has been depicted as having been parasitic on the would-be reduction of its hypotheses to a metapsychology that Freud allegedly deemed *primordially* scientific. And this doctrine of the mediated scientificity of the clinical theory is seen as a relic from the heady days of the "Project," or from the teachings of Helmholtz, Meynert, and Brücke. But, as we can already conclude, this exegesis is an arrant, if widespread, mistake. Thus, Gill (1976: 72) saddles the mature Freud of 1915 with the ontologically reductive notion of scientific status. For, as Gill would have it, Freud's positing of seemingly *psychological* hypotheses "in a natural-science framework...is a reductive attempt to convert psychological discourse to a universe alien to it—the universe of space, force and energy".

Indeed, even if Freud could be shown to have believed that he had actually effected such a reduction to the metapsychology, this would hardly establish that he had *predicated* the *scientificity* of the clinical theory upon it! For, as I have documented, he saw the natural science status of the avowed cornerstone of his edifice as anything but trickling down, so to speak, from the acknowledged speculative superstructure. On the contrary, after 1896 it was the *direct* evidential support he claimed to have for his clinical theory from his office couch—not some fancied explanatory subsumption under the abstract metapsychology— that he saw as authenticating the clinical theory. Scientifically, this authentication proceeded from the bottom up, as it were. In the same vein, the analyst Fenichel paid tribute to the Freudian corpus a few years after the demise of its creator when he said: "An understanding of the multiplicity of everyday human mental life, based on natural science, really began only with psychoanalysis" (1945: 4). Yet, at cross purposes with the mature Freud, Gill (1976: 91) insists on an ontological—rather than methodological—construal of natural science, and believes that he can conclude: "the natural-science framework is inappropriate to the data of psychoanalysis." And, as we shall see toward the end of this chapter (Section 5), the damage from Gill's ontological construal is not at all obviated by his brief, tantalizing caveat: "sciences other than the natural sciences . . . conform to the general methodological canons of the scientific method" (1976: 95).

Ironically, the leading spokesmen for the "hermeneutic" construal of Freud's clinical theory—who champion the interpretive virtues of reading texts—have given wide currency to a reading of Freud that runs afoul of just the conclusions I have documented. According to the philosophers Jürgen Habermas and Paul Ricoeur, and the late analyst George Klein, Freud claimed the status of a natural science for his clinical theory by misextrapolation from its envisaged reduction to the primordially scientific metapsychology. Thus, in an unavailing attempt to justify such an exegesis, Habermas (1971: 249) points to the fact that Freud had hypothesized various *correlations* between clinical and metapsychological concepts as typified by the following: the metapsychological concept pair "pleasure-unpleasure"—which designates libidinal energy discharge versus a damned up accumulation of excitation-tension—is associated in the theoretical system with its clinical affect-homonyms, which designate subjective pleasure and pain. Similarly, Habermas notes reprimandingly (1971: 251) that, in a paper on therapeutic technique, Freud associated the clinical concept of retrieving a repressed memory with Breuer's metapsychological notion of "'abreacting' of the quotas of affect strangulated by repression" (S.E. 1914, 12: 156).

Having imported the Hegelian idiom of "self-reflection" (1971: chapter 10), Habermas coins the term "movement of self-reflection" (p. 251) to designate the kind of psychoanalytic process that is traditionally described by speaking of the patient's "working through his(her) resistances, defenses and transference-repetitions, lifting his(her) repressions," and achieving "the return of the repressed."

But Habermas sees the self-emancipatory process that is hypothesized to occur in the psychoanalytic "movement of self-reflection" as fundamentally alien to the methodological and ontological categories featured by the natural sciences. And since he had saddled Freud with having invested the metapsychology with primordial scientificity vis-à-vis the clinical theory, he blames the correlations between the metapsychological and the clinical concepts for having trapped Freud in a far-reaching "scientistic self-misunderstanding" (pp. 246-252). Purportedly, Freud's misunderstanding was "scientistic" because he idolatrously endowed the clinical theory with natural science status by misextrapolation from the metapsychology via the stated correlations. And furthermore, his view was purportedly a "*self*-misunderstanding" to the extent that it involved a philosophical misconception of the clinical theory, a body of hypotheses which he *himself* had wrought. Finally, Freud's "scientistic" construal of the clinical theory was far-reaching, if only because it thwarted the recognition of psychoanalysis as a paradigmatically depth-hermeneutic discipline of inquiry, "as the only tangible example of a science incorporating methodical self-reflection," and as potentially prototypic for the other sciences of man (Habermas 1971: chapter 10). Hence, as the hermeneuticians would have it, it was Freud's misguided aim to confer natural science status on his enterprise by extrapolation from his metapsychological program. And this ill-fated endeavor, they tell us, issued in the "scientistic" adulteration of his entire theoretical edifice. Thus, the title of the chapter that Habermas devotes to this indictment begins with the phrase "The Scientistic Self-Misunderstanding of Metapsychology" (p. 246). Indeed, his censure of Freud is indignant and even patronizing:

> Because Freud was caught from the very beginning in a scientistic self-understanding, he succumbed to an objectivism that regresses immediately from the level of self-reflection to contemporary positivism in the mannner of Mach and that therefore takes on a particularly crude form. [P. 252]

As recently as 1981, Ricoeur again endorsed Habermas's allegation of "scientistic self-misunderstanding" (Ricoeur 1981: 259). And, in an earlier work, Ricoeur hailed the *failure* of Freud's clinical theory to qualify as an empirical or natural science by the received standards as the basis for "a counterattack" against those who deplore this failure (Ricoeur 1970: 358). Remarkably, the psychoanalyst G. S. Klein went Ricoeur one better by holding that the clinical theory and the metapsychology generate "two incompatible modes of explanation" (Klein 1976: 13), being two quite disparate theories (chapter 2). But, whereas Freud regarded the metapsychology as a "speculative superstructure," Klein rates it as an "expendable... obscurantist jargon" issuing in "the dry rot of overconceptualization" (pp. 12-13).

Habermas, Ricoeur, and Klein each give more or less detailed *arguments* for actually denying natural science status to Freud's clinical theory. In so doing, they mean to gainsay Freud's own affirmation of such status after reproaching him for having misextrapolated it from the presumed scientificity of the metapsychology. But, as I have argued, this reproach of misextrapolation is quite ill-founded. Hence, I now turn to the point-by-point scrutiny of the main additional arguments given by these hermeneuticians to sustain their various versions of the charge of "scientistic self-misunderstanding." The bill of particulars that Habermas lodged against the creator of the psychoanalytic clinical theory includes ontological considerations relating to causality as well as epistemic ones pertaining to the validation of particular and general psychoanalytic clinical hypotheses. Since his methodological claims seem to be inspired, to some extent, by his ontological theses, I shall examine the latter first.

It is to be clearly understood at the outset that, far from questioning the etiologic and therapeutic hypotheses of Freud's clinical theory, Habermas claims to take them for granted without ado. What he purportedly tried to controvert by argument are rather the tenets of the philosophical gloss that, as he sees it, Freud misguidedly grafted onto those hypotheses. Hence, in appraising Habermas's arguments and, indeed, *throughout this introductory chapter, I shall refrain from challenging the credentials of Freud's clinical hypotheses*. This challenge is deferred until chapter 2 and subsequent chapters.

2. Critique of Habermas's Philosophy of Psychoanalysis

A. Does the Dynamics of Psychoanalytic Therapy Exhibit the "Causality of Fate"?

It is a cardinal thesis of Habermas's challenge to the founding father that the *lawlike* causal nexus presumably present in the causality of nature does *not* inhere in the therapeutic dynamics of the psychoanalytic process of "self-reflection." In order to justify this denial, he takes as paradigmatic a patient's conquest of the sort of neurosis whose salient manifestation is rigidly *repetitive* behavior. Examples of this manifestation are repetitious obsessional rituals, the recurrent compulsive reenactment or recall of painful experiences, and other repetitive conduct grouped under the rubric of "the repetition compulsion." Habermas's pivotal contention is as follows: Whenever a neurotic overcomes the repetition compulsion by the lifting of his pathogenic repressions, this psychoanalytic self-reflection has actually "dissolved" and "overcome" the very *causal connection* that had previously linked the pathogen to the compulsively repetitive behavior (Habermas 1971: 271). Yet there is no counterpart to this alleged overcoming of a causal connection "as such" in the domain of the laws of nature. Hence, Habermas uses the Hegelian phrase "causality of fate" to refer to the sort of causal linkage that, he tells us, is "dissolvable," because it can purportedly be "subdued" by the therapeutic "power of reflection" (Habermas 1971: 256–257, 271; 1970: 302, 304).

But, as I shall now try to show in detail, the reasoning he uses to justify and articulate this "causality of fate" is quite mistaken. Indeed, I shall argue further that a conclusion he draws from his account *flatly repudiates* the psychoanalytic *explanation* for the patient's therapeutic transition from unconsciously driven behavior to more consciously governed conduct. Yet, paradoxically, Habermas also appears to endorse that psychoanalytic explanation.

To be specific, he uses the phrase "invariance of life history" (1971: 271) to refer to the persistent reenactment or repetition of a certain kind of conduct C, a neurotic symptom familiarly designated by the term "repetition compulsion." As Freudian theory tells us from the start, if the patient actually succeeds in lifting his own repressions, he thereby removes the pathogen *required* to sustain his affliction, and thus rids himself of his compulsion to repeat the behavior C (S.E. 1893, 2: 6). In *this* sense one can say, using Habermas's parlance, that the patient has overcome or dissolved the "invariance" *of the conduct C* that had previously been characteristic of his life history. But if that parlance is used, one must be alert to its potential to mislead by generating fallacies. To see how Habermas is victimized by his idiolectical use of this vocabulary, we need to be more precise as to the pertinent part of Freud's repression-etiology of the psychoneuroses.

In their 1893 "Preliminary Communication," Breuer and Freud drew the epoch-making conclusion that became the pillar of the clinical theory of repression. They enunciated the following etiologic hypothesis: In the pathogenesis of a psychoneurosis, repression plays the generic causal role of a *sine qua non* (S.E. 1893, 2: 6-7; 3: 29-30). The impetus for this assumption avowedly came from their belief that the therapeutic gains from their method of treatment were causally attributable to the cathartic retrieval of traumatic memories, which their patients had repressed. Once they had decided that such lifting of repressions is therapeutic, they wished to *explain* its remedial efficacy. And, as they soon realized, the desired explanation could be given deductively by the etiologic postulate that repression is causally necessary not only for the initial development of a neurotic disorder but also for its maintenance. Clearly, if a repression of type R is indeed the causal *sine qua non* for the presence of a neurosis of kind N, then it follows that the removal of R will actually issue in the obliteration of N. Hence, any patient who rids himself of R and thereupon becomes emancipated from N plainly *instantiates* that R is the causal *sine qua non* for the presence of N. Amazingly enough, Habermas claims that this very causal linkage itself is dissolved by the patient's therapeutic achievement. But surely the instantiation of a causal connection cannot possibly also qualify as the dissolution of this linkage! Hence Habermas's notion that a therapeutic achievement can "overcome" an etiologic linkage by dissolving it is incoherent.

Habermas affirms the stated etiologic hypothesis in less precise form. As he puts it, "the assumed causal connection exists between a past conflict situation [the pathogenic repression] and compulsively repeated reactions in the present (symptoms)" (1971: 272). Furthermore, he seems to have appreciated the deductive explanatory relation between the causally necessary condition asserted in the etiologic hypothesis and its therapeutic corollary. For he points out that, "the concept of a causality of the unconscious also renders comprehensible the therapeutic effect of 'analysis.'" And, in any case, he likewise affirms the therapeutic corollary that the pathological *effect* C is removed ("overcome") once the patient's "self–reflection" has terminated the further operation of its unconscious cause.

Unfortunately, however, his parlance then prompts an altogether fallacious slide from the stated therapeutic claim to the following additional conclusion: When the patient prevented the further recurrence of a pathological effect by means of terminating the ongoing operation of its psychic cause in himself, this therapeutic termination *also* dissolved (overcame) the causal connection *itself* that links the pathogenic cause etiologically to its effect (1971: 271). Yet Freud's etiologic hypothesis has told us that this causal linkage is one in which the pathogenic cause is the *sine qua non* of the neurosis. Hence, far from being "dissolved" by the therapeutic conquest of the neurosis, this very causal linkage even *entails* the therapeutic conquest! For just this sort of causal connection assures that the removal of the pathogenic cause of the neurosis will issue in the latter's elimination.

Nonetheless, Habermas slides from the therapeutic conquest of *effects* by the removal of their cause into the dissolution of the causal *linkage* between the pathogen and the neurosis. Overcoming an effect by undercutting its cause is hardly tantamount to dissolving the causal connection that links them. This illicit slide seems to have occurred in the following passage:

language and behavior are pathologically deformed by the causality of... repressed motives. Following Hegel we can call this the causality of fate, in contrast to the causality of nature. For the causal connection between the original scene, defense, and symptom is not anchored in the invariance of nature according to natural laws but only in the spontaneously generated invariance of life history, represented by the repetition compulsion, which can nevertheless be dissolved by the power of reflection. [1971: 271]

But this statement is incoherent on the face of it. For if—prior to its alleged therapeutic dissolution—there was indeed a causal connection between the repressed "original scene" and the repetition symptom, how can that repetition compulsion also have been "spontaneously generated"? And if it is spontaneously generated, how are we to understand that the stated causal connection is nonetheless "anchored" in it? Thus, one is driven to wonder at times whether Habermas himself knows just what he wishes to claim. In any case, on the same page he concludes explicitly that the patient's therapeutic achievement was nothing less than the dissolution of the causal connection codified by Freud's etiologic hypothesis. He contrasts this purported state of affairs with somatic medicine as follows:

In technical control over nature we get nature to work for us through our knowledge of causal connections. Analytic insight, however, affects the causality of the unconscious as such. Psychoanalytic therapy is not based, like somatic medicine, which is "causal" in the narrower sense, on making use of known causal connections. Rather, it owes its efficacy to overcoming causal connections themselves. [1971: 271]

But this declaration is vitiated by Habermas's failure to heed two logical facts. First, as we have previously noted, it is a *deductive consequence* of Freud's etiologic hypothesis that the removal of the repression will cause the beneficial disappearance of the neurosis. And furthermore, the patient's therapeutic achievement *instantiates* this entailed causal connection, since the patient conquers his neurosis by fulfilling its causal antecedent. Hence, the patient achieves his therapeutic gain precisely by *making use* of a causal connection rather than, as Habermas would have it, by "overcoming" such a connection!

Besides, Habermas's purported dissolution of causality in psychoanalysis boomerangs: To the detriment of his purported dichotomy between the causality of nature and the alleged psychoanalytic causality of fate, his specious reasoning can be applied to *somatic* medicine as well. For, by complete parity with it, one could deduce the inanity that a person suffering from recurrent gall colics "overcomes" the *causal linkage* between the movement of gall stones and such colics upon taking medication that dissolves the gall stones, and *thereby* terminates the colics!

He courts a further difficulty by neglecting that the therapeuticity of lifting repressions is actually an *explained* consequence of the etiologic causal connection. For by *denying* that the explanatory premise can hold at the time when its therapeutic conclusion is being instantiated, Habermas is repudiating the explanation furnished by the etiologic premise, unencumbered by his previously cited seeming acceptance of the explanation.

Despite having declared the psychoanalytic etiologies therapeutically "dissolvable," he does deem them applicable prior to the effective onset of the therapy. But, in his attempt to vindicate this *circumscribed* validity, he commits a patent causal fallacy by reasoning that repressed motives "have the status of [pathogenic] causes because they assert themselves behind the subject's back" (1970: 297; my translation). Breuer and Freud enunciated that, as a matter of empirical, logically contingent fact, repression is *causally necessary* for the pathogenesis of a psychoneurosis. And, as we recall, they pointed to the therapeuticity of lifting repressions as their evidence for this etiologic hypothesis. Freud then stressed that, as a matter of further empirical fact, repression is *not* causally sufficient for neurosis. Indeed, he hypothesized that hereditary vulnerability, no less than exposure to the repression of experiences, is a causally relevant antecedent for psychopathology (S.E. 1896, 3: 143-146, 209). Plainly, therefore, when Freudian theory postulated the pathogenic causal relevance of repression, it hardly inferred this etiologic role from the *mere* fact that the subject has no conscious awareness of what he repressed. Such a causal inference would be even more primitive than *post hoc ergo propter hoc*. But, as we just saw, Habermas does infer the causal status of unconscious motives as pathogens from the mere fact that they operate "behind the subject's back." Now, warrantedly assertible causes are sometimes said to operate from behind or *a tergo* in the *temporal* sense. Perhaps the intrusion of the latter idea prompted Habermas's causal inference. In any case, this inference makes a mockery of the epoch-making *empirical* argument given by Breuer and Freud as to why repressions should even be deemed causally relevant *at all* to the genesis of psychopathology (S.E. 1893, 2: 6-7). Indeed, as we shall see in chapter 3, despite the brilliance of *their* argument, even their avowedly inductive inference leaves much to be desired. And to this day, it is one of the great open questions of psychopathology whether its conclusion, which Habermas reaches with such abandon, is empirically true.

Furthermore, Habermas's inference of the "causality of fate" in the patient's therapeutic achievement also boomerangs. If it were legitimate, it could likewise serve to establish the following absurdity: The elementary law of thermal elongation in physics does not exhibit the nomic invariance of the causality of nature after all, because it too could be shown to be "dissolvable" by complete parity with Habermas's flawed reasoning. For consider a metal bar that is isolated against all but thermal influences. It is subject to the law $\Delta L = \alpha \Delta T \cdot L_0$, where L_0 is its length at the fixed standard temperature, ΔT the temperature increment above or below the standard temperature, ΔL the length increase or decrease due to this temperature change, and α the coefficient of linear thermal expansion characteristic of the particular material composing the metal bar. Now suppose that the bar, initially at the standard temperature, is subjected to a "pathogenic" temperature increase ΔT, which produces the elongation ΔL as its "pathological" effect. In addition to supplying this "etiology," the law of linear thermal elongation also provides a basis for a corresponding "therapy": It tells us that if the bar's temperature is reduced to its "healthy" standard value, the "pathological" effect ΔL will be wiped out. Thus, we can correlate the "therapeutic intervention" of temperature reduction with the patient's remedial lifting of his own repressions. Similarly, we correlate the bar's "neurotic symptom" ΔL with the patient's repetition compulsion.

By parity with Habermas's reasoning, we could then draw the following ludicrous conclusion: When the temperature reduction "therapeutically" wiped out the endurance of the "pathological" effect ΔL generated by the "pathogenic" temperature increase, this thermal termination also "dissolved" the stated law of thermal elongation. *Habermas has not given a scintilla of evidence for his causality of fate that could not also be adduced, equally speciously, in the thermal reductio ad absurdum argument.* In neither case can there be any question at all of "dissolving" or "overcoming" a causal connection between an initial condition I and an effect E on the strength of terminating E by a suitable alteration of I. On the contrary, it is E *itself* that is "overcome," not—as Habermas would have it—its causal linkage to I. In *any* therapy—somatic or psychiatric—overcoming an effect is hardly tantamount to dissolving the causal connection linking it to its cause. And, in *either* case, the "conquest" of E *makes use* of a causal connection by instantiating it instead of "dissolving" it. Thus, if previously repressed conflicts are consciously worked through by a patient and hence no longer issue in his repetition compulsion, this therapeutic process makes use, as we saw, of a causal connection entailed by Freud's repression-etiology. There is no therapeutic dissolution of an etiologic connection in Freud's therapy, any more than in the therapies of somatic medicine. Habermas's claim that there is causality of fate in psychoanalytic therapy but causality of nature in the somatic interventions is totally unsubstantiated.

It is quite remarkable that his causality doctrine has been rehearsed without dissent not only by his disciples but also by others who diverge from him on other topics. Among the former, Thomas McCarthy has endorsed it (1979: xiii), after giving a sympathetic account of it (1978: 201). And, in his account of psychoanalytic clinical generalizations, Schöpf (1982: 114) depicts the causal role of unconscious impulses by explicit recourse to the causality of fate.

On the other hand, the psychoanalysts Thomä and Kächele take issue with Habermas on the clinical validation of psychoanalytic interpretations. Yet, they fail to demur when paraphrasing him as follows: "The dissolution of a 'causal connection' by means of the work of interpretation [in the treatment setting] illustrates the efficacy of psychoanalytic therapy" (1973: 320). A demurrer would at least have called for scare quotes around the word "dissolution." Finally, in an article espousing a Popperian critique of hermeneutic methodological separatism, Blight first speaks of Habermas's causality of fate as "the heart of the rationale for claiming that psychoanalysis, as the prototypic form of hermeneutics, is nothing like a natural science" (1981: 172). Yet after quoting, as a single passage, the aforecited two crucial passages from Habermas (Habermas 1971: 271), Blight writes without hint of any stricture: "In this passage, Habermas, it seems to me, clearly presents his Hegelian case for psychoanalysis as hermeneutics and psychoanalysis as non-science" (1981: 172). Incidentally, in contrast to Blight's judgment that the presentation in the given excerpt is "clear," we have had occasion to deplore—for example à propos of the "spontaneously generated...repetition compulsion"—the exposition as anything but clear.

B. Are Nomological Explanations in the Natural Sciences Generically *Non*-Historical, While Causal Accounts in Psychoanalysis are Historically-Contextual?

The causality of fate is not the only causal doctrine enlisted by Habermas to contrast psychoanalysis ontologically with the natural sciences. He considers the application of psychoanalytic generalizations ("general interpretations," as in 1971: 259) to the life history of a particular analysand. This utilization generates particular interpretations that combine into a narrative. When offered to the individual patient by the analyst, particular interpretations are presumed to be stated in the *"intentional"* clinical language of desires, affects, fantasies, sensations, memories, and the like (1971: 272). Since these interpretations are couched in such motivational language, Habermas speaks of them as deriving from the "hermeneutic application" of general interpretations to the life of a particular analysand.

Now, he is concerned to contrast the logic of hermeneutic utilization with the corresponding application of lawlike principles in the nomothetic empirical sciences to particular cases. And his paradigm of the latter sort of instantiation of the antecedent of a physical law is given by: "'this stone' is considered, for example, as 'mass'" (1971: 265). Claiming that "this subsumption is unproblematic" (p. 265), he proposes to contrast it logically with an instantiation of a general interpretation in psychoanalytic practice:

> We can at first view a construction offered to the patient by the physician as an explanatory hypothesis derived from a general interpretation and supplementary conditions. . . .
> In its logical form, however, explanatory understanding differs in one decisive way from explanation rigorously formulated in terms of the empirical sciences. Both of them have recourse to causal statements that can be derived from universal propositions by means of supplementary conditions: that is, from derivative interpretations (conditional variants) or lawlike hypotheses. Now the content of theoretical propositions remains unaffected by operational application to reality. In this case we can base explanations on context-free laws. In the case of hermeneutic application, however, theoretical propositions are translated into the narrative presentation of an individual history in such a way that a causal statement does not come into being without this context. General interpretations can abstractly assert their claim to universal validity because their derivatives are additionally determined by context. Narrative explanations differ from strictly deductive ones in that the events or states of which they assert a causal relation is [*sic*] further defined by their application. Therefore general interpretations do not make possible context-free explanations. [Pp. 272-273]

Alas, Habermas did not see fit to give a single example from psychoanalysis to lend specificity to this concluding statement of his chapter "The Scientistic Self-Misunderstanding of Metapsychology: On the Logic of General Interpretation" (1971, chapter 11). But even if he had, it would have been unavailing to his thesis that—in contrast to psychoanalysis—explanations in physics are generically based on context-free, ahistorical laws. For, as I shall now show, there are telling counterexamples to it from venerable principles of physics. And these counterexamples likewise will be seen to discredit the following equally grandiose assertions by the hermeneutician H. G. Gadamer, who wrote: "It is the aim of science to so objectify experience that it no longer contains any historical element. The scientific experiment does this by its methodical procedure" (1975: 311). But how, one asks, does the scientific experiment have this ahistorical import? Gadamer reasons that the experimental method of science predicates confirmation on *repeatability to such a degree* that he feels entitled to conclude: "Hence no place can be left for the historicality of experience in science" (p. 311).

The physical theory of classical electrodynamics will now enable me to show that Habermas and Gadamer have drawn a *pseudo*contrast between the nomothetic and human sciences. For that major physical theory features laws that embody a far more fundamental dependence on the history and/or context of the object of knowledge than was ever contemplated in even the most exhaustive of psychoanalytic explanatory narratives or in any recapitulation of human history. Incidentally, Habermas's example of the stone does not even instantiate a context-free physical *law*, but only the theoretical property of mass. Hence, at best, it instantiates a *part* (the antecedent) of a physical law.

Consider an electrically charged particle having an arbitrary velocity and acceleration. We are concerned with the laws governing the electric and magnetic fields produced by this point charge throughout space at any one fixed time t. In this theory, the influence of the charge on any other test charge in space is postulated to be propagated with the finite velocity of light rather than instantaneously, as in Newton's action-at-a-distance theory of gravitation. But this *non*instantaneous feature of the propagation of the electrodynamic influence contributes to an important consequence, as follows: At any space point P, the electric and magnetic fields at a given time t depend on the position, velocity, and acceleration that the charge had at an earlier time t_0. That earlier time has the value $t - r/c$, where r is the distance traversed by the influence arriving at P at time t after having traveled from the charge to P with the velocity c of light.

Clearly, the greater the distance r that was traversed by the influence by the time t of its arrival at point P, the earlier its origination time t_0. Thus, for space points at ever larger such distances r in infinite space, the origination time $t_0 = t - r/c$ will be ever more remotely past. In short, as the distance r becomes infinitely large, the origination time goes to past infinity.

It follows that at ANY ONE INSTANT t, the electric and magnetic fields produced throughout infinite space by a charge moving with arbitrary acceleration depend on its own PARTICULAR ENTIRE INFINITE PAST KINEMATIC HISTORY! The specifics of this result are evident from the so-called "retarded" expressions for the electric and magnetic fields at a point P at time t. These equations specify the fields as functions of the aforestated kinematic attributes possessed by the charge at the appropriate earlier time (Page and Adams 1940: 144, equations

[48-7] and [48-8]). The authors of one classic treatise state the relevant upshot of these electrodynamic laws as follows: "expressions for the complete field of an element of charge [throughout space at any one time] involve a knowledge of its entire [infinite] past history" (Page and Adams 1940: 161).

Though the individual histories of each of two or more charged particles can be very different indeed, the electrodynamic laws accommodate these differences while remaining general. The generality derives from the *form* of the lawlike functional dependencies of the electric and magnetic field intensities on the earlier accelerations, velocities, and positions of the field-producing charge. But the latter's individual history consists of the infinite temporal series of the particular values of these kinematic attributes (variables).

As against Habermas, I submit that these electrodynamic laws exhibit context-dependence with a vengeance by making the field produced by a charge for any one time dependent on the particular infinite past history of the charge. And, to the detriment of Gadamer, these laws are based on replicable experiments but resoundingly belie his thesis that "no place can be left for the historicality of experience in science."

Indeed, there is a simple special case of the above very general laws whose *incomplete* statement can misleadingly suggest the context-*in*dependence of its validity: Coulomb's inverse square law for the electric field of a point charge. Being an inverse square law, it has the same dependence of the field on the distance from the field-producing entity as Newton's law of universal gravitation for point masses. Yet Newton's law is context-*free* in the sense of holding regardless of the state of motion of the gravitational masses. Besides, that law is an instantaneous action-at-a-distance law. By contrast, Coulomb's law is highly context-dependent by holding only if the field-producing charge has been *permanently* at rest for all past time. And our earlier considerations enable us to trace this important historical condition of its validity to its being a special case of a delayed action law.

There are other instructive cases of context-dependence of laws of physics that reveal further the poverty of Habermas's supposed paradigmatic example of "'this stone' is considered, for example, as 'mass'" (1971: 265). This class of cases exhibits "hysteresis" in the sense that a property of a physical system, induced by a given present influence upon it, depends not only on that present influence but also on the *past history* of variation of that influence. Thus, "hysteresis" has been defined quite generally as "that property of an element evidenced by the dependence of the value of the output, for a given excursion of the input, upon the history of prior excursions and the direction of the current traverse"

(Considine 1976: 1335). One such case is the hysteresis behavior of highly magnetizable metals (e.g., iron, cobalt, nickel, etc.), which are known as "ferromagnetic."

To be specific, let a previously unmagnetized sample of such a metal be subjected to an external magnetic field H generated by an alternating current. Then the magnetizing force H will produce an internal magnetization induction B. The value of B will increase from zero as H increases from that initial value, but B will approach and attain a limiting or saturation value with the further increase of H. Yet, the subsequent reduction of H to zero will *not* issue in the return of the internal magnetization B to zero. Thus, we can already see that the present response of the ferromagnetic material to one and the same external influence H will depend on the prior magnetization *history* of the given sample: B lags behind H, since it does not decrease to zero when H returns to zero after being nonzero.

Physicists speak of the residual internal magnetization B as "the remanence," because it betokens the influence of the sample's prior history of magnetization on its present response to the same external field H. Indeed, as shown by the pertinent law, if the last trace of this remanence is to be obliterated, the value of H will actually have to be made negative by reversing its direction. One cycle of magnetization and demagnetization can now be completed by a further decrease and then increase of H until the saturation state of B is reached again.

But, very significantly, after one such complete cycle, the dependence of the behavior of the sample on its magnetization *history* further makes itself felt as follows: After the first cycle is depicted graphically by plotting B against H, the closed curve ("hysteresis loop") representing that initial cycle will *never* be retraced by subsequent cycles of demagnetization and remagnetization (Efron 1967: 694). Another example in physics in which the response of materials to current influences is sensitive to the history of their prior exposure to like influences is furnished by solids that exhibit *elastic* hysteresis. In this case, the stress and strain (deformation) are the variables corresponding to H and B. Even rubber bands display a like behavior. Other examples include the electric hysteresis exhibited by dielectric substances in electric fields and the hysteresis of a radiation counter tube.

Some hermeneuticians may retort that these physical cases do not capture the relevant sense of "history." As if to say: "What is all-important here is *how* past states count in the determination of present behavior, not just *that* they count." Patently, it is anything but a liability to my argument that I rely on the following banal fact: The Freudian narratives adduced by Habermas are psychological, whereas my examples of context-dependence are avowedly physical. But this assumed ontological difference is itself unavailing to Habermas's thesis that there is an *asymmetry* of context-dependence, whenever general propositions are applied explanatorily to particular instances. For he rules out *simpliciter* just the sort of ingredient of history in physical laws that I have multiply documented: As he would have it (1971: 272-273), in the natural sciences, the laws are context-free *and* remain so, when applied to explain particular cases, whereas concrete psychoanalytic explanations are generically context-dependent. Thus, the stated attempt to parry my critique fails, if only because it modifies, rather than rescues, Habermas's contention. Besides, the modification is unavailing to the alleged asymmetry, since the adduced platitude—that Freudian narratives are *psychological*—is patently insufficient to sustain the asymmetry.

The context-dependent physical laws that I have adduced seem tailor-made as insuperable difficulties for the second of Habermas's alleged causal dichotomies. And I trust that the context-dependence of the physical cases I have developed adequately matches, if not surpasses, the degree of such dependence, if any, encountered when general clinical hypotheses are applied to particular patient histories.

In another connection, the analyst Wallerstein (1976: 222) illustrates such applications by reference to the psychoanalytic explanations of the idiosyncratic deployment of defense mechanisms. Such explanations are furnished, he notes, "*in terms* of the operation of particular combinations and permutations of the generally available armamentarium of possible defense mechanisms in human character." By pointing to such Freudian accounts of "the idiosyncratic patterning and deployment of defensive behaviors," Wallerstein exemplifies his conception of psychoanalysis as "truly a science which is both a general psychology, a study of the general and lawful functioning of the human mind in health and disease, and also [the study of] an idiosyncratic genetic unfolding of... the individual" (pp. 222-223).

Habermas's paradigm of the stone that has mass epitomizes the mythic universal notion of the laws of nature on which he relied to gain adherents for his dichotomy of context-dependence. And it is a commentary on our intellectual culture that by trading on such stone age physics, as it were, he and Gadamer managed to parlay the limitations of their own personal scientific horizons into a vaunted pseudocontrast between the humanistic disciplines and the natural sciences.

So much for the two theses on causality enlisted by Habermas to vindicate his reproach of "scientistic self-misunderstanding" against Freud's own construal of the clinical theory. Hence, we now turn to the appraisal of the *epistemic* allegations he puts forward in his further endeavor to sustain this indictment.

These methodological claims pertain, in the first instance, to the validation of the particular clinical hypotheses offered by the analyst to his patient. But, derivatively, his epistemic avowals also apply to the general clinical hypotheses of the theory. For, like Freud (S.E 1918, 17: 105), Habermas (1971: 259) supposes that the warrant for these general interpretations comes by conjectural induction from numerous clinically authenticated particular interpretations of the conduct of individual patients.

C. Does the Patient Have Privileged Cognitive Access to the Validation or Discreditation of Psychoanalytic Hypotheses?

The logic of validating the general hypotheses of Freud's clinical theory is one of the major themes of Habermas's hermeneutic epistemology. The pivotal claim of his account is that the patient is the ultimate epistemic arbiter of these general psychoanalytic postulates, which he calls "general interpretations" (1971: 261). Within the confines of analytic therapy, these universal hypotheses are used to generate *particular* interpretations pertaining to the individual lives of specific patients. For example, the analyst employs psychoanalytic generalizations retrodictively to construct an etiologic scenario for the pathogenesis of a patient's disorder.

In the context of the clinical setting, Habermas downgrades the doctor cognitively vis-à-vis his patient by endowing the analysand with an epistemic *monopoly* in the testing of the *particular* interpretations pertaining to his own life history. As he puts it, "analytic insights possess validity for the analyst only after they have been accepted as knowledge by the analysand himself" (1971: 261). Having claimed that the patient is thus cognitively preeminent, Habermas infers that "the success and failure [of a psychoanalytic construction] cannot be intersubjectively established" (p. 266). Thereupon, he assumes that induction from just such particular interpretations is the *sole* means for *validating* Freud's universal hypotheses, and not merely for elaborating these generalizations heuristically (p. 259). Hence, he concludes that patients enjoy privileged epistemic access as follows: "the validity of general interpretations depends directly on statements about the object domain being applied by the 'objects,' that is the persons concerned, to themselves" (p. 261). Habermas relies on this contention, in turn, to arrive at the methodological dichotomy that general interpretations are not governed by the same criteria of validation as the universal hypotheses of the empirical sciences (pp. 261-266).

It appears that the tenability of this dichotomy depends on the merits of Habermas's cognitive tribute to the patient. Note that if the analysand were actually the ultimate epistemic arbiter, as depicted by Habermas, then the patients treated by psychoanalysts would have truly formidable cognitive powers. Each patient would be not only the best judge but ultimately the *sole* judge of what was in fact the cause of his neurotic disorder, what engendered his sundry dreams, and what induced his lapses of memory, various slips of the tongue, and other bungled actions. Moreover, in Habermas's account, the cognitive monopoly of patients, taken collectively, likewise extends to *universal* psychoanalytic hypotheses. Hence, the validation of Freud's etiology of paranoia, for example, would then ultimately rest entirely on the collective verdicts of those treated for this delusional affliction. I contend that this epistemic thesis is no less untenable than Habermas's two alleged causal dichotomies.

The pillar of Habermas's account of clinical validation is that the patient is the ultimate epistemic arbiter of the general interpretations used retrodictively by the doctor to construct an etiologic scenario for the explanation of the patient's neurosis. He states this thesis of privileged epistemic access on the part of the analysand as follows:

> General interpretations occupy a singular position between the inquiring subject and the object domain being investigated. Whereas in other areas theories contain statements about an object domain to which they remain external as statements, the validity of general interpretations depends directly on statements about the object domain being applied by the "objects," that is the persons concerned, to themselves. . . . analytic insights possess validity for the analyst only after they have been accepted as knowledge by the analysand himself. For the empirical accuracy of general interpretations depends not on controlled observation and subsequent communication among investigators but rather on the accomplishment of self-reflection and subsequent communication between the investigator and his "object." [P. 261]

Thus, his more specific claim is that the application of general interpretations by patients *to themselves* makes them—to the exclusion of their analysts—the decisive epistemic arbiters of the *validity* of these general hypotheses.

But just what *argument* does he offer to show that such self-application by the patients—which occurs in the context of the application made by their analysts—confers the stated *cognitive monopoly* on the former? Why, for example, should the self-application of principles of somatic medicine made by physicians to themselves—alongside the application made by specialists who treat them—not likewise make for a corresponding cognitive monopoly on the part of the former? Habermas's case for endowing the *psychoanalytic* patient with such epistemic primacy rests entirely on his allegation that there is a "specific difference between general theories [of the received empirical sciences] and general interpretations." And he proceeds to state that purported difference as follows:

In the case of testing theories through observation (that is in the behavioral system of instrumental action), the application of assumptions to reality is a matter for the inquiring subject. In the case of testing general interpretations through self-reflection (that is in the framework of communication between physician and patient), this application becomes self-application by the object of inquiry, who participates in the process of inquiry. The process of inquiry can lead to valid information only via a transformation in the patient's self-inquiry. [P. 261]

I submit that Habermas simply begs the question. Note that in the second sentence he turns to "the case of testing general interpretations" in order to substantiate his claim as to the patient's cognitive preeminence vis-à-vis the analyst in their validation. But this opening phrase of the sentence in question is immediately followed by the *proviso* "through self-reflection." Habermas then tacitly trades on the ambiguity of this term to beg the question at issue. Obviously, the production of free associations and of various responses by the patient in the presence of the analyst—including the *reacting* to interpretations offered by the therapist—is an *intrinsic* part of the clinical testing of analytic interpretations pertaining to the patient. But this commonplace is hardly enough to yield Habermas's desired conclusion. For, if the phrase "testing through self-reflection" were to encapsulate no more than the stated platitude, it would be unavailing to the deduction of Habermas's claim. What he concludes is that the patient enjoys a *cognitive monopoly* of *appraisal* of interpretations as to their validity *vis-à-vis the analyst*. In order to manage the deduction of the latter thesis of privileged epistemic access— a thesis he states by speaking of "self-application by the object of inquiry"—Habermas relies on the ambiguity of the phrase "testing through *self*-reflection" to build into it the following sort of restriction: The *definitive appraisal* of a particular explanatory interpretation pertaining to a patient A as to truth or falsity is to be reserved *de jure* to none other than A, to the exclusion of the therapist. Though cognizant that the analyst rather than the patient may well have generated the interpretation, Habermas presupposes from the outset that probatively the therapist must *always* rely on his patient's appraisal of it. For he explicitly tells us that the testing of general interpretations *within the treatment setting* "becomes self-application by the object of inquiry" (1971: 261).

It emerges that Habermas has begged the question at issue by construing the otherwise innocuous phrase "testing through self-reflection" so as to *stipulate* that only the patient's own appraisal can carry out the application of general interpretations to his particular life situation. Of course, it then follows trivially from Habermas's proviso that the patient will be the sole or privileged epistemic arbiter of *any* such clinical hypothesis.

Indeed, note that when Habermas characterized the testing of the ordinary theories of empirical science as being effected "by observation," he studiously refrained from considering the large class of such hypotheses in which the inquiring person who tests the hypothesis is able to apply it to himself/herself in the sense of appraising it himself/herself by means of *self*-observation. Clearly, such self-application is feasible not only in, say, somatic medicine but extends also to all those hypotheses in physics, for example, whose purview includes the human body of a physicist or of some other person capable of testing the hypothesis on his or her own body. This class of self-applications can now serve to construct a reductio ad absurdum of Habermas's argument, which boomerangs. For he was concerned to contrast the testing of general theories of empirical science with the clinical appraisal of general explanatory hypotheses in psychoanalysis, and the burden of this alleged difference is that *only* in the latter validation is there an epistemic preeminence of the *object* of knowledge.

It is ironic, therefore, that by parity with his question-begging reasoning the same cognitive preeminence of the *object* of knowledge will now turn out to be deducible *in physics* for the validation of any hypothesis that is applied to the body of a person *A*. All that is needed is to proceed à la Habermas, mutatis mutandis, and to require that the very same person *A* not only be the one to whose body the hypothesis *pertains*, but also be the one who *appraises* the hypothesis as to its truth or falsity. It will be seen to be immaterial to this deduction that the *self*-observation carried out by *A* while fulfilling this cognitive assignment serves to appraise a physical hypothesis concerning his body, whereas the corresponding "self-reflective" appraisal by the patient in analysis is addressed to a hypothesis about his mental processes.

Thus, consider the physical hypothesis that in an elevator or space rocket falling *freely* in the earth's gravitational field, a weight scale on the floor will register zero for a body placed upon it. Obviously, this hypothesis of weightlessness applies equally well to the bodies of humans trapped in an elevator whose cable has been cut or to the more fortunate astronauts in their space rocket. Now, while emulating Habermas, let us require that some of these persons not only step onto the weight scale during free-fall but also be the ones who ascertain its reading after having examined the scale for defects of operation with the aid of the pertinent auxiliary hypotheses. By analogy with Habermas's initial exclusion of the analyst or other third person from the appraisal of the interpretation in favor of the patient, we have likewise excluded from ascertaining the weight scale readings any one not actually on the scale.

Clearly, under the *stipulated* initial restriction that none other than the person *A* appraise a hypothesis pertaining to himself, the conclusion reached by Habermas will follow trivially in physics no less than in psychoanalysis. The simple reason is that once his restrictive proviso has been imposed, *only* the *object of inquiry* himself/herself can carry out the *particular* sort of appraisal that has been mandated by the question-begging restriction. Thus, it then follows in physics no less than in psychoanalysis that "the application of assumptions to reality... becomes self-application by the object of inquiry." No wonder that, having traded on the ambiguity of his proviso, Habermas is then able to conclude misleadingly: "analytic insights possess validity for the analyst only after they have been accepted as knowledge by the analysand himself" (1971: 261).

McCarthy quotes the passage containing Habermas's privileged access gambit without dissent and writes: "This peculiarity of psychoanalytic inquiry has implications for the logics of application, corroboration and explanation" (1978: 204). But since the alleged "peculiarity of psychoanalytic inquiry" was deduced by begging the question, the implications McCarthy claims to draw from the purported peculiarity are ill-founded.

Besides the above flawed argument for the patient's epistemic primacy, Habermas adduces the products of the latter's memory to claim that the analyst's "interpretive suggestions... can be verified in fact only if the patient adopts them and tells his own story with their aid" (1971: 260). Yet, Habermas observes (1971: 266) that such corroboration may be *delayed* by defensive resistance. The analysand's memory allegedly affords him or her privileged epistemic access to two sorts of privy knowledge (1970: 301): (1) the historical authenticity of certain childhood events whose occurence the analyst had conjectured retrodictively by means of Freudian etiologic theory, and (2) the validity of the further hypothesis that, if authentic, these events had actually played the etiologic role of pathogens in the life of the patient. Indeed, undaunted by the imperative to furnish supporting evidence, Habermas (1971: 230-266) introduces the following postulate to justify his cognitive tribute to the analysand's recall: if a construction depicting the presumed pathogenesis of the given neurosis is actually true, then the patient's memory will corroborate it *in due course*. Habermas then relies on this sanguine expectation to conclude that, unless the patient's memory does corroborate a construction, sooner or later there is good reason *not* to accept it. As he puts it: "Only the patient's recollection decides the accuracy of the construction. If it applies, then it must also 'restore' to the patient a portion of lost life history: that is it must be able to elicit a self-reflection" (1971: 230).

Habermas insinuates, dismayingly, that these two sentences of his are a paraphrase of Freud's own view as to which of the two participants in the psychoanalytic dyad enjoys epistemic primacy over the other. He does so by introducing his own two sentences on the heels of the following 1937 statement from Freud: "the path that starts from the analyst's construction ought to end in the patient's [present] recollection" (the square bracketed word was supplied by Habermas). But, upon looking at the original of Freud's text, we find him emphasizing that, more often than not, the cognitive role of the analysand's memory is anything but the one depicted by Habermas. For immediately after saying that the analyst's construction "ought" to elicit the patient's corroborative recall, Freud declares soberingly:

but it does not always lead so far. Quite often we do not succeed in bringing the patient to recollect what has been repressed. Instead of that, if the analysis is carried out correctly, we produce in him an assured conviction of the truth of the construction which achieves the same therapeutic result as a recaptured memory [S.E. 1937, 23: 265-266]

And as we shall soon see, in the earlier two parts of the same 1937 paper Freud had invoked the confluence of various clinical inductions as the analyst's basis for achieving a trustworthy picture of the patient's forgotten years. Thus, by 1937, looking back upon a lifetime of actual practice, Freud claims in effect that "quite often" there is an epistemic asymmetry between the doctor and the analysand that is the precise *converse* of the one affirmed by Habermas. For, as Freud reports, quite often the patient's memory simply fails to supply information vital to the psychoanalytic reconstruction of the pathogenically relevant part of his early life history. Then, *in lieu* of "a recaptured memory" furnished by the patient, the analyst convinces the patient of "the truth of the construction," a conviction therapeutically equivalent to the retrieval of a pertinent memory.

Elsewhere, too, Freud stressed that, often enough, the etiologically most significant repressed experiences are brought to light by the doctor's *inferences, not* by the analysand's retrieved memories:

The patient cannot remember the whole of what is repressed in him, and what he cannot remember may be precisely the essential part of it. Thus he acquires no sense of conviction of the correctness of the construction that has been communicated to him. [S.E. 1920, 18: 18]

It appears that Habermas has used out-of-context citation of Freud tendentiously to give the reader a quite incorrect impression of Freud's own view. As Habermas would have it, the patient's memory *invariably* affords him/her privileged and hence indispensable cognitive access vis-à-vis his/her analyst to the determination of the validity of explanatory psychoanalytic interpretations. In effect, Freud rejects this epistemic asymmetry as utopian, if only because actual clinical experience with the mnemonic performance of numerous patients prompted him to give cognitive pride of place to the inferences drawn by the analyst from the totality of the patient's productions. In some of his case histories, he also offered theoretical reasons for making the doctor the ultimate epistemic arbiter, rather than the analysand. For example, in a paper on the therapeutic fiasco in his treatment of a young lesbian (S.E. 1920, 18: 147-172), Freud expressed full confidence in his own etiologic reconstruction of her sexual object choice. Yet he pointed out that she completely rejected his interpretive insights, and he attributed the rejection to her desire to punish him as a father surrogate by clinging to her neurosis.

No wonder, therefore, that some latter-day psychoanalysts as well have rejected Habermas's contrived epistemic picture of the patient's struggle to cast off the hypothesized bondage to unconscious dictates. Thus, Thomä and Kächele (1973: 315-316) adduce both the theory and practice of psychoanalysis in opposition to Habermas's claim that *no* analytic interpretation can be deemed valid until and unless the patient has confirmed it. Specifically, they point out that (1) it was precisely psychoanalytic theory itself which impugned introspection and "reflection" in the light of the evidence that they are under the governance of massive self-deceptions, (2) genuine confirmation that the patient has actually overcome the effects of his repressions—instead of just fancying himself to have done so—can be furnished exactly to the extent that this therapeutic achievement is intersubjectively ascertainable, whereas Habermas *mystifies* this therapeutic evaluation, and (3) the monopolistic validating and therapeutic role that Habermas confers on the patient's "self-reflection" is a utopian misrepresentation of the psychoanalytic process, and there is hardly any analyst who practices in accord with it or endorses it.

The clinician Morris Eagle (1973) gives a more systematic critique of the thesis of privileged epistemic access. He does so tellingly in the context of T. Mischel's—rather than of Habermas's—advocacy of acknowledgment by the patient as the touchstone of the validity of motivational attributions. As Eagle notes (p. 267), the tendency of people to disown unflattering motives and to avow flattering ones illustrates motivational self-deception. In the framework of psychoanalytic theory, one can expect the patient to deny his doctor's imputation of unconscious motives *irrespective of the evidence for them*, unless the defenses against their recognition have been successfully overcome. For example:

If the quality and circumstances of A's action and knowledge of A's character and history lead an observer to conclude that A had deceived himself about his motives, intentions, wishes, is A's acknowledgment necessary for that judgment to be valid? If self-interest (including self-esteem) is sufficiently involved and if A's capacity and willingness for self-confrontation are limited, A may never be able to acknowledge the motive attributed to him—even when his attention is called to the same things that led the outside observer to make his judgment.
. . . it is possible to act (or to reveal by quasi acts such as symptoms) as if one wanted Y and yet sincerely deny that one wants Y (that is, experiences wanting Y). [Eagle 1973: 273]

Accordingly, sometimes analysts do take the patient's denial but subsequent acceptance of some painful motivational imputation to bespeak his achievement of new insight and emotional maturation. But, as Eagle points out, if, after the analysand's initial *denial*, it is ever legitimate for the therapist to ascribe such cognitive gain and increased self-mastery to the analysand, then *this* judgment cannot itself first derive its warrant from the patient's self-confrontational assent. Instead, the doctor's verdict as to his client's attainment of new bona fide insight is predicated on a criterion of validity for interpretations that can authenticate an interpretation as a genuine (rather than fancied) insight *independently* of the patient's assent. For, in any such case, the patient's assent to the interpretation is taken to be evidence for his ability to face a conclusion about himself whose truth the analyst was able to infer validly *while the patient was still denying it*. Hence, Eagle observes cogently: "Here we see sharply a logical difficulty with avowal as a criterion. How can it serve both as a sign of ability to face the truth about oneself and as a criterion of that truth?" (1973: 267). After all, if the *analysand* were the ultimate epistemic authority—à la Habermas—why should the doctor rely on his client's assent to a given interpretation *I* but discount an earlier denial and/or the patient's avowal of a psycho-analytic conjecture *contrary* to *I*?

Eagle gives a further good reason for rejecting patient assent as a necessary condition for the validity on an analytic interpretation:

interpretive inferences about unconscious motives, wishes, etc., can (and should) be evaluated on the basis of other criteria (e.g., prediction of subsequent behavior, symptoms, associations) which have little to do with acknowledgment defined either as agreement or as conscious experience of attributed unconscious contents. If one makes inferences about certain unconscious motives on the basis of a person's verbalizations, behavior, symptoms, and developmental history, the validity of the inferences certainly does not depend ultimately on the person's avowal or acknowledgment. [P. 269]

He illustrates this epistemic moral concretely by reference to Freud's case history of his hysteric young patient Dora (see S.E. 1905, 7: 3-122):

let us suppose that Freud's interpretation that Dora was unconsciously in love with Frau K. elicited wide consensus and permitted prediction of Dora's subsequent dreams, behavior, symptoms, etc. Would Dora's acknowledgment (which was not forthcoming) be necessary before one could evaluate the validity of the interpretation? [Eagle 1973, 269]

Yet, to caution against a misunderstanding, he explains:

The point is not that acknowledgment cannot serve at all as a criterion, but that it has no privileged logical status. It is one of many possible criteria and . . . its usefulness depends upon a variety of factors including its agreement with other kinds of evidence. [P. 268]

This caveat derives further relevance from work by Rosemarie Sand (1983) in her study of "Confirmation in the Dora Case". As she illustrates by means of daydreams—such as Dora's fantasies of defloration and childbirth—there are a good many cases in which only the individual who is in a certain mental state may be privy to it and be able to attest it: "The patient is in this position when the analyst asks him: 'what are you thinking about now? what comes to mind?'" (p. 337)

For my part, I would, however, couple her salutary reminder with the further caveat that these cases of privileged epistemic access are altogether cold comfort to Habermas. For the possession of such access to the content of momentary mental states is a far cry indeed from being uniquely privy to the actual existence of a hypothesized causal nexus between, say, certain infantile experiences and specified adult personality dispositions. Yet, just such *causal* interpretations are at the heart of a whole array of psychoanalytic explanations, being central to the conjectured etiologic reconstruction of the patient's neurosis. And Habermas's thesis of cognitive asymmetry rests avowedly and crucially on the analysand's privileged access to the validity of these explanatory interpretations. Hence, it is unavailing to his case that the patient does have direct access to the object of his momentary attention, the affect he feels at the moment, and so forth, whereas the analyst and everyone else has only inferential access to these mental states.

In fact, several weighty considerations tell against Habermas's thesis that only the patient's memory-assisted "self-reflection"—to the *exclusion* of the *intersubjective* methods of an outside analytic observer—can attest the validity of analytic interpretations (1971: 266). In outline, these objections are as follows.

1. Substantial evidence recently marshaled by cognitive psychologists has shown that even in the case of *consciously* motivated behavior, a subject does not enjoy privileged cognitive access to the discernment of the motivational causes of his various actions (see Grünbaum 1980: 354-

367, for an account of the relevant studies). Though the subject often does have direct access to the individual contents of his mental states, he/she has only *inferential* access—just like outside observers—to such causal linkages as actually connect some of his own mental states. No less than in the case of causal hypotheses pertaining to physical states, the subject's avowal of causal connections between his own mental states is based either on the fallible inferences drawn by himself, or on those carried out by members of his subculture to whom he gives credence. Hence, these avowed causal linkages may be fancied or actual. In short, when a subject attributes a causal relation to some of his own mental states, he does so—just like outside observers—by invoking theory-based causal schemata endorsed by the prevailing belief-system. More often than not, a patient who seeks treatment from a Freudian doctor already brings some psychoanalytic beliefs into the therapy, or is at least receptive to etiologic interpretations of his conduct based on the analyst's theoretical stance. No wonder that analytic patients then find the rationale offered to them credible. But this credulity is hardly tantamount to privileged cognitive access.

By the same token, when a patient deems his own analysis to have issued in the alleviation of his suffering, he is no better able to certify whether this gain was actually wrought through the mediation of Freudian etiologic insights than are outside students of therapeutic *process*. Indeed, two such students, who are analysts, have issued the following disclaimer (Luborsky and Spence 1978: 360): "Psychoanalysts, like other psychotherapists, literally *do not know* how they achieve their results." If Habermas's *ipse dixit* paean to the patient's "self-reflection" is to be believed, all that these investigators need to do to dispel their avowed ignorance is ask the patient to give them the benefit of his truly formidable epistemic powers. A concrete example will now illustrate the fanciful nature of this cognitive enthronement of the patient.

For simplicity, I shall take a well-known instance of forgetting, which Freud sought to explain by pointing to a short-term repression as the cause. I discuss this case in depth in chapter 4. Hence, suffice it to say here that when a young man omitted the Latin word "aliquis" (someone) in his recitation of a line from Virgil's *Aeneid* and Freud supplied the missing word, the young man's associations issuing from this word—interspersed by some of Freud's interjections—yielded, in due course, that he had harbored a presumably repressed fear. He suspected that an Italian girlfriend had become pregnant by him. Freud then informed him that this repressed anxiety had "undeniably" produced his *"aliquis"* lapse, whereas the subject was skeptical that his worry—though genuine—had any causal bearing on his forgetting.

In chapter 4 I argue that Freud has not given any good reason at all for his attribution of this instance of forgetting to the pregnancy fear elicited by the subject's associations. But here, I must ask Habermas: how could the subject possibly know *better than Freud* or any of the rest of us whether his unconscious fear had actually caused his memory slip? *A fortiori*, how can Habermas expect us to believe in the analysand's privileged cognitive access to the validity of the far more ambitious causal claims that are central to the etiologic reconstruction of his neurotic affliction?

2. There is a second set of considerations that undermine Habermas's cognitive enthronement of the patient. Notoriously, neurotics are quite suggestible (Möller 1976: 71). By the same token, their beliefs are quite malleable. Thus, often enough, patients do claim to confirm the etiologic interpretations and sundry causal attributions made by their analysts. But, as subsequent chapters will document, such purported confirmations can be warrantedly explained by the well-attested doctrinal compliance of patients with the subtly communicated theoretical expectations of the healing authority figure to whom they have turned for help. As Freud himself appreciated all too keenly (S.E. 1917, 16: Lectures 27 and 28), even if the analyst does his best to forego overt or covert suggestion, there are myriad ways in which he can unconsciously but persuasively mold the analysand's convictions and engender a compliant pseudocorroboration. Hence, it plainly will not do to adduce the analyst's professional integrity and avowed intent not to abuse his suggestive influence as an adequate safeguard against the elicitation of *spurious confirmations* from the patient. Though Freud's writings throughout his life showed that he knew much better, he did occasionally succumb to the invocation of the therapist's integrity when he claimed that "such an abuse of 'suggestion'" had never occurred in his own practice and generally "has certainly been enormously exaggerated" (S.E. 1937, 23: 262).

The same unavailing appeal to the doctor's shunning of deception is echoed by Habermas, after enumerating the supposed theoretical "sanctions against misuse in the sense of exploiting deception." He states one such sanction and then a supposed pragmatic one as follows:

> the appropriateness of the interpretation, which is theoretically derived and applied to the particular case, requires confirmation in successful self-reflection; truth must converge with authenticity—in other words, the patient himself is the final authority. Furthermore, psychoanalysts must comply with the requirements of professional ethics and practices of a legally sanctioned association of physicians; within limits violations of professional norms and regulations can be controlled. [1973: 29]

Ricoeur (1981: 270), too, adduces the "professional code and the analytic technique itself" quite insouciantly as a bulwark against the charge of epistemic contamination by suggestion. He even terms this objection to be "crude," although Freud himself had judged it to be "uncommonly interesting" (S.E. 1917, 16: 447), if only because his confrere and one-time friend, Wilhelm Fliess, had raised it ominously.

In an earlier book, Habermas (1971: 268-269) touched on the reproach of spurious corroboration by the patient's doctrinal deference to his therapist. There he deals with this complaint in the course of citing Freud's 1937 article on "Constructions in Analysis," a paper that he had adduced quite misleadingly (1971: 230), as I have already noted. It turns out that, in this connection as well, Habermas cites tendentiously from that same paper.

There Freud explains that the patient's verbal agreement with a psychoanalytic construction is not to be taken at face value in and of itself, any more than his denial. Instead, Freud maintains (S.E. 1937, 23: 263), "there are indirect forms of confirmation which are in every respect trustworthy." On the strength of these other indicators, a construction is to be considered validated by the convergence or "consilience" of a whole array of clinical inductions, based on diverse data from the patient's various productions. I shall argue in chapter 10 that reliance on such congruence of clinical inductions from data other than patient assent or denial likewise affords no protection against suggestive adulteration of the patient's responses and the ensuing spurious corroboration. But, for argument's sake, let me nonetheless assume here, as Habermas (1971: 267-269) does, that the confluence of seemingly independent clinical inductions does have probative value, as claimed by Freud.

Then, to the grave detriment of Habermas's allegations, let me call attention to two points.

(i) On the heels of paying his tribute to the probative value of the stated convergence of clinical inductions, Freud (S.E. 1937, 23: 265-266) asserts—now that he is armed with just such inductions—that *the analyst's inference* can *reliably* fill up the serious gaps in the patient's memory. As we recall, such reliance on the analyst's inference is necessary because, as Freud emphasized, the patient's poor mnemonic performance can readily fail to supply the information vital to the reconstruction of his pathogenically crucial past. Thus, if the confluence marshaled by Freud does have probative cogency, while the patient's "yes" or "no" may be discounted, then there is good reason for according cognitive primacy to the analyst's inference over the patient's "self-reflection." And just such an epistemic elevation of the analyst's inference as the ultimate epistemic arbiter of a psychoanalytic construction is both the logical import and explicit tenor of Freud's entire paper. Hence, its conclusion obviously gainsays Habermas's bald, peremptory, though repeated, assertion that "the patient himself is the final authority." Yet Habermas studiously refrains from giving the reader any intimation of this upshot of the pertinent 1937 paper by Freud, any more than he had earlier reported Freud's remark therein about the disappointingly poor showing of the patient's recall.

(ii) As is clear from the context of Habermas's digression (1971: 266-269) into Freud's aforementioned 1937 views on the consilience of inductions, this excursion was occasioned by Habermas's concern to deny that clinical testability can be *intersubjective*. But his approving rehearsal of Freud's ideas on the consilience of clinical inductions is also patently unavailing to his contention that "the success and failure [of a construction] cannot be intersubjectively established" (1971: 266).

3. A third group of animadversions serve to discomfit even further Habermas's mystique of self-reflection: There is additional telling empirical evidence that the patient's supposed ability to achieve veridical recall of very early repressed experiences is largely a myth (S.E. 1899, 3: 322). We have already noted Freud's report of rather frequent plain failures to retrieve pathogenically crucial memories. As I have documented elsewhere (1980: 353), his writings also multiply attest the *unreliability* of purported adult memories of early childhood episodes that had presumably been retrieved by the analysis after being repressed. Besides, in chapter 6 below the reader will find an array of recent findings that militate further against regarding psychoanalytic treatment as a bona fide memory-jogging device.

As will be recalled from the aforementioned conclusions drawn by cognitive psychologists, their results undercut the subject's purportedly direct epistemic access to causal relations between his own mental states. Similarly, it turns out that recent studies of memory undermine the patient's supposed *non*inferential and reliable mnemic access to his early experiences. Earlier we saw that theoretical beliefs rather than direct introspection determine the subject's verdicts on causal relations. Similarly, the interpolative reconstruction and bending of memories by theoretical beliefs combine with the malleability of memory by suggestion to generate pseudomemories for events that never occurred. In chapter 6, there is a poignant illustration of such a pseudomemory from Jean Piaget's own early life. Yet, even the mnemonic failures reported by Freud never gave Habermas pause in his cognitive homage to the patient.

As a kind of motto for Habermas's account of the falsification of analytic interpretations, he emphasized (1971: 266) that "the [patient's] experience of reflection is the only criterion for the corroboration or failure of hypotheses." But, before giving his separate statement of how he conceives the "refutation" of clinical hypotheses, he interposes a discussion of other matters.

One of the interposed other topics is the application of a type concept of the sort encountered in general psychoanalytic hypotheses ("general interpretations") to an individual life history. Presumably, the instantiations of such notions as "oral personality" or "anal personality," and also of such nosological categories as "obsessive compulsive," are examples of what Habermas has in mind when he speaks of the "translation" of a type concept into the personal history of an analysand. Thus, we are told that, in the case of the theories of the empirical sciences, the

operational application [of their concepts and general hypotheses] necessarily proceeds within the framework of instrumental action. Consequently it does not suffice for the application of the theoretical expressions of general interpretations. The material to which the latter are applied consists not of singular events but of symbolic expressions of a fragmentary life history, that is of components of a structure that is individuated in a specific way. [1971: 265]

But why, I ask, is the use of free association in psychoanalytic investigation and therapy *not* also "instrumental action" precisely in the context of *applying* the general hypotheses of Freud's theory of repression to a given patient? After all, free association is held to yield the *particular* repressed contents harbored by a single individual! Presumably, anyone who believes in psychoanalysis *at all*, as Habermas does, credits free association with being an investigative avenue for the reliable disclosure of explanatory repressions.

Indeed, such analysts as Strachey (S.E. 1955, 2: xvi)—the translator and editor of the *Standard Edition* of Freud's works—and Kurt Eissler (1969: 461) have hailed free association as an instrument comparable to the microscope and telescope. For reasons set forth in detail in chapters 3-10 below, I do not share this epistemic valuation at all. But if psychoanalysis does have the formidable cognitive virtues that Habermas claimed for it—a *depth*-hermeneutic enterprise that can even serve normatively as a model for the humanistic sciences—then surely the *depth* with which he credits it depends on the method of free association. And, by the same token, it would seem that its use in psychoanalytic investigation plays an epistemic role quite similar to the devices of "instrumental action," even though the products it yields are, of course, mental.

Besides, it would seem that when in seismology, for example, geophysical principles are applied to particular earthquakes, these episodes—to use Habermas's words—qualify as "components of a structure that is individuated in a specific way." For note that (1) in the Lisbon earthquake of 1755, the agitation of the inland waters far beyond the limits of the disturbed area was an almost unique feature, (2) the series of 1783 quakes in southern Calabria had distinctively rapid migrations of their seismic foci, and (3) the movement engendered in the 1906 San Francisco earthquake took place along the very remarkable San Andreas fault. This simple example from the "narratives" of historical geology could be multiplied from episodes in the big bang cosmogony. Recall, too, my earlier examples from electrodynamics.

Why does Habermas presume to discuss the logic of the natural sciences *contrastingly* à propos of psychoanalysis? It would seem that he has been quite misled by his simplistic example of a stone as an instantiation of the theoretical type concept of "mass." For he introduces that example by claiming that in the concrete application of type concepts encountered in the laws of the received sciences "singular events only come into consideration insofar as they satisfy the criteria of general predicates ('this stone' is considered, for example, as 'mass')" (1971: 265). And Habermas overlooks that the analyst must use *explanatory relevance* as a criterion of *selection* from the totality of events in a patient's life history, which he could hardly encompass. Indeed, the Freudian therapist cannot even deal with *all* of the facets of such singular events as he does deem narratively relevant to his explanatory and therapeutic objectives. How then does the psychoanalyst's procedure differ from that of, say, the historical geologist in regard to reliance on "the criteria of general predicates" as a basis for selecting relevant singular events?

This brings me to the appraisal of Habermas's separate statement on the *falsification* of psychoanalytic interpretations (1970: 302; 1971: 266). His aim is to exhibit "the methodological peculiarity that general interpretations do not obey the same criteria of refutation as general theories" (1971: 266). True to form, he begins with a misdepiction of falsifications in the received empirical sciences. Habermas wrote some half century after the publication of the French original of Pierre Duhem's *The Aim and Structure of Physical Theory*. By that time, Duhem's elucidation of falsification in physics had become a staple of elementary courses in the philosophy of science. As Duhem had explained, when a hypothesis H is at issue in a given inquiry, then observational predictions p made by means of H are typically deduced not from H and some initial condition I alone, but only from their *conjunction* with some of the auxiliary hypotheses *A* of the larger theoretical system of which *H* is a part. What, then, can the physicist infer deductively from the failure of the predictions *p* under experimental test? Duhem replies:

> when the experiment is in disagreement with his predictions, what he learns is that at least one of the hypotheses constituting this group [*H*, *I*, and *A*] is unacceptable and ought to be modified; but the experiment does not designate which one should be changed. [1954: 187]

In the face of this, Habermas is either unaware of—or chooses to ignore—the typical, if not ineluctable, copresence of the collateral hypotheses *A* with *H* in the very deduction of *p*. And this untutored disregard would seem to be the basis of his case. Thus, speaking of the refutation of the general theories of the received empirical sciences, such as physics, he says (1971: 266): "If a conditional prediction [*p*] deduced from a lawlike hypothesis [*H*] and initial conditions [*I*] is falsified, then the hypothesis may be considered refuted." Oblivious to Duhem's point as to why, on the contrary, the falsity of *p* does *not* entail the falsity of *H* in physics, Habermas then deems it noteworthy that falsification is uncertain in psychoanalysis. Says he:

> if the patient rejects a construction, the interpretation from which it has been derived cannot yet be considered refuted at all. . . . there is still an alternative: either the interpretation is false (that is, the theory or its application to a given case) or, to the contrary, the resistances, which have been correctly diagnosed, are too strong. [1971: 266]

Habermas fails to note that, to the detriment of his thesis of "methodological peculiarity," precisely the same logical situation prevails in physics: The experimental failure of *p allows* that *H* be true, while the falsity of *A* (or of *I*) may be to blame for the falsity of *p*. In short, the logical situation in psychoanalysis is commonplace in any and all sophisticated theories that purport to have observable import. But by simply denying this fact, well known since Duhem, Habermas has manufactured yet another pseudoasymmetry between the methodology of the natural sciences and that of psychoanalysis. Presumably, it was his quest for yet another asymmetry that prompted him to give a separate statement on falsifiability. Be that as it may, his conclusion that, for general interpretations in psychoanalysis, "the method of falsification is not the same as for general theories" (1971: 266) is itself unsound.

As we saw, Habermas had invoked the auxiliary hypothesis of stubborn patient resistance to an unpalatable interpretation so as to allow that a construction may be true, although the patient's memory has not confirmed it. By the same token, insofar as psychoanalytic theory does expect such confirmation of a correct construction, this expectation is predicated on the corresponding auxiliary hypothesis that the patient has actually worked through and overcome his resistance. Oddly enough, on the very same page Habermas ignores this proviso of the conquest of resistance when giving the following sanguine statement of the therapeutic benefit from the analysand's mnemic confirmation: "If it [the interpretation] is correct, the patient will be moved to produce certain memories, reflect on a specific portion of forgotten life history, and overcome disturbances of both communication and behavior." Besides misrepresenting the theoretical expectation of mnemic confirmation as resting on the mere correctness of the pertinent analytic interpretation, this rosy portrayal of readily ensuing therapeutic gain is misleading. So much so that the prohermeneutic analyst G. S. Klein (1976: 36-38) denies the value of psychoanalysis as a therapy while extolling it as a method of investigation. His reason for doubting that the therapy deserves a future is sobering: "the classical psychoanalytic treatment situation is founded on dubious grounds of practicality and shaky evidence of therapeutic success" (p. 37). By "success," Klein understands "behavior change and therapeutic relief" from suffering (p. 36).

It is important to notice that, at the very outset, Habermas's treatment of the falsifiability of general interpretations in psychoanalysis is *confined* without ado to the falsifying import of one and only one kind of finding: "the patient rejects a construction." He never even considers whether there are other modes capable of discrediting general interpretations, say, by epidemiologic studies, in which the potential adverse findings even come from outside the analytic setting altogether. Habermas's peremptory and question-begging appraisal of falsifiability is in keeping with the like gambit he used, as will be recalled, to give the patient ultimate epistemic authority in the *corroboration* of interpretations.

Having imposed the requirement that *only the patient's rejection can falsify a construction,* he goes on to declare:

The criterion in virtue of which false constructions fail does not coincide with either controlled observation or communicative experience. The interpretation of a case is corroborated only by the successful continuation of a self-formative process, that is by the completion of self-reflection, and not in any unmistakable way by what the patient says or how he behaves. Here success and failure cannot be intersubjectively established, as is possible in the framework of instrumental action or that of communicative action, each in its way. [Habermas 1971: 266]

This statement is then followed by Habermas's ill-conceived attempt to buttress his denial of intersubjective testability by recourse to Freud's probative demotion of the patient's "yes" or "no" vis-à-vis other consilient clinical findings.

I maintain that Habermas's vesting of all falsifiability in psychoanalysis exclusively in the patient's self-reflection is not only cognitively myopic and arresting but also demonstrably untenable. Indeed, he did nothing to show that the patient's appraisals of interpretations need even be the principal source of falsifications. To substantiate this indictment, I shall use here one of the results I first develop in chapter 1, section B, where I shall appraise Popper's complaint of nonfalsifiability against Freud. The relevant result for my present concern with Habermas is the following: Some of Freud's etiologic postulates are potentially disconfirmable by *epidemiologic* findings, *without* any recourse at all to data from the analytic treatment setting, let alone to the experiences had by patients when their repressions are being undone in that clinical milieu.

As background, note that Habermas tacitly banished all *extra*clinical testing of general psychoanalytic hypotheses from consideration. For he simply took it for granted that the treatment setting is the sole arena for any and all validation or disconfirmation of these universal propositions. Just for argument's sake, let me assume that if one were to confine all testing to the clinical investigations carried out by the doctor-patient dyad, then the analyst can confirm an interpretation only on the authority of his patient's prior certification of its validity. Even then, it would hardly follow that the clinical setting is the principal arena for the well-designed testing of general psychoanalytic hypotheses, let alone the sole arena. But if extraclinical tests of at least some of these hypotheses are feasible, as indeed they are, then patients in analysis surely do not have the cognitive monopoly that Habermas conferred on them.

Freud's etiology of paranoia postulates that *repressed* homosexual love is *causally necessary* for being afflicted by paranoid delusions (S.E. 1915, 14: 265-266). And when the pathogenically required intensity of repression exists, it is largely engendered by the strong social taboo on homosexuality. Thus, the detailed pathogenesis of paranoia envisioned by Freud warrants the following expectation: A significant decline in the social sanctions against this atypical sexual orientation should issue in a marked decrease in the incidence of paranoia.

The recently revealed likelihood that, in 1893, Tchaikovsky was blackmailed into suicide—under threat of exposure of a homosexual liaison—is a measure of the lethal power possessed by the ban on homosexuality in the Christian world less than a century ago (Brown 1980: 626-628). This suicide occurred at the pinnacle of his career, less than a week after the Saint Petersburg premiere of his celebrated *Pathétique* symphony. Yet, for nine decades the standard biographies of him attributed his death at the age of fifty-three to cholera, probably yet another manifestation of the prevailing taboo on homosexual behavior and on suicide as well (Dorian 1981: 224-227). Since 1893, which was also the year of Breuer and Freud's momentous "Preliminary Communication," even prominent members of both sexes have publicly identified themselves as homosexuals despite the harassing agitation of Anita Bryant. Perhaps it is therefore not too early now to begin garnering appropriate statistics on the incidence of paranoia with a view to ascertaining in due course whether these epidemiologic data bear out the psychoanalytically expected decline. Failing that, the ensuing disconfirmation of the Freudian etiology will be clearly intersubjective, in contravention of Habermas's thesis. Incidentally, this example of mine, no less than others given elsewhere herein, confutes the following claim of untestability made in a well-known treatise by Kerlinger:

Some theories and theoretical statements...are untestable—at least with the means at our disposal today....A classic case is some Freudian theory....in part because it includes the construct of repression....
...the behavioral manifestations of repression are elusive. [1979: 36-37]

Returning to Habermas, let me show that not only the stated epidemiologic disconfirmability but also some of Freud's case histories furnish illustrations of falsifiability by means other than the patient's psychoanalytic self-reflection. Hence, these case histories belie the assertion that only the depth-hermeneutic construal does epistemic justice to the clinical theory. For instance, the 1909 case history of the Rat Man, which is discussed in chapter 8, served as a test of the particular sexual etiology of obsessional neurosis espoused by Freud at the time. But, to the detriment of Habermas's thesis, it was an *extra*clinical datum supplied by the patient's mother, rather than information yielded by the patient's "experience of reflection," which served crucially to *disconfirm* the 1909 etiology (S.E. 1909, 10: 206).

Whereas the case history of the Rat Man gainsays Habermas's claim of privileged access by furnishing an *extra*clinical disconfirmation of a psychoanalytic etiology, Freud's 1915 case history of a female paranoiac (S.E. 1915, 14: 263-272) does the same by means of an *intra*clinical falsification scenario. As is clear from its very title, "A Case of Paranoia Running Counter to the Psychoanalytic Theory of the Disease," it is devoted to the falsifiability of the psychoanalytic etiology of paranoia (see especially pp. 265-266). As we recall, that etiology claims *repressed* homosexual feelings to be causally *necessary* for the pathogenesis of paranoid delusions. One posited clinical scenario that Freud explicitly characterizes as disconfirming there is as follows: The patient's clinical productions show "no trace of a struggle against a homosexual attachment" (p. 265), and yet she is paranoid. Thus, we might well imagine that this person produces a copious flow of associations, and that even during many years of analysis she is characteristically nonchalant toward lesbian themes.

In our present context of logical inquiry, it is surely a legitimate extension of the clinical scenario that Freud himself deemed etiologically disconfirmatory to envision the following present-day modification of it: a paranoid woman now living in San Francisco as a self-declared lesbian comes to analysis because many of her social interactions are troubled. *Before having lifted any of her repressions*, her analyst may well become aware of both her openly lesbian life-style and of her pronounced paranoid delusions. Thus, after only *two* sessions with his 1915 patient, Freud thought he had good grounds to diagnose her as paranoid. If the analyst who is seeing the putative lesbian in San Francisco is an orthodox Freudian, he will sit up all the more and notice the following discomfiting state of affairs: although the patient is paranoid, she clearly does not harbor the minimum of repression of homosexual desires that Freud's etiology claims to be the *sine qua non* for the pathogenesis of her delusional affliction. In short, before having begun to undo such full-blown repressions as she may harbor, her doctor will realize that he has on his couch an authentic refuting instance of the received etiology (see Meissner 1978 for a recent account of the etiology). But precisely because her therapist was able to identify this disconfirming instance as such without winnowing her unconscious conflicts and defenses, she is likewise a counterinstance to Habermas's thesis that any such epistemic identification can be effected only by the patient herself.

But what of his repeated assertion that "the criterion in virtue of which false constructions fail does not coincide with either controlled observation or communicative experience" (1971: 266; 1970: 302)? As I noted, he wantonly banished all *extra*clinical disconfirmation from consideration at the outset. Hence, his denial of controlled observability here is gratuitous, even if he were to show that the dyadic psychoanalytic transaction remains refractory to controlled observation after being supplemented by videotape recordings that are studied by other trained investigators. Still more unsubstantiated is his strange denial—for the sake of claiming recalcitrance to *intersubjective* falsification—that the falsifying evidence can be subject to "communicative experience." Assume that the patient can achieve the insight of which Habermas deems him capable, and that, once achieved, it bespeaks the falsity of an analytic interpretation. Then this evidence surely need not remain bottled up solipsistically in the patient and elude articulation to the analyst. Why, then, does this articulation, which can be recorded on videotape and made available to other investigators, have to be arcane instead of qualifying as a *"communicative experience"*? Why, I ask, is the verbal *and* nonverbal communication of the analysand's newly attained mastery not as much a "communicative experience" as, say, the rendition of testimony by a witness who gives evidence acceptable in a court of law? On the other hand, let us suppose that Habermas intends the term "communicative experience" in some restricted technical sense such that the patient's communication of his newly found insight indeed fails to qualify as a "communicative experience" in the latter *idiosyncratic* sense. In that case, why should it matter for the evidential, probative purposes of falsification? Habermas would settle these various issues breezily in less than a page.

Finally, his account of falsifiability in psychoanalysis boomerangs for *two* reasons. First, because Duhem showed, before Habermas was born, that the presence of auxiliary hypotheses in the experimental testing of a major hypothesis in physics precludes a deductively conclusive refutation of the latter, despite the deductive validity of a *modus tollens* inference. By fully matching just the inconclusiveness adduced by Habermas in the light of the assumption of stubborn patient resistance, Duhem's result undercuts Habermas's purported asymmetry of falsifiability between physics and psychoanalysis. Second, the need to validate or discredit by *consilient* inductions, which Habermas likewise deems supportive of such asymmetry, has been recognized in the *natural* sciences ever since William Whewell called attention to it in the mid-nineteenth century. Thus, Freud was perceptively trying to make Whewell's notion clinically serviceable when he stressed in 1937 that the patient's assent or dissent function only as contributory pieces of evidence, because their probative value is first assessed by the requirement of consilience with other clinical inductions. By contrast, Habermas wants this reliance on confluence of evidence to count against the intersubjectivity of theory appraisal in psychoanalysis. But if Whewell's method, when applied in psychoanalysis, did have such import for Freudian theory, then why would it not have a like epistemic moral for physics? Once again, Habermas has entrapped himself in an absurdity. Yet, in this context, the analyst Jahoda (1977: 119) considers his arguments to be "powerful."

To conclude this scrutiny of Habermas's views, we are now prepared to assess his reproach that Freud deserves censure for a "particularly

crude" form of "objectivism." As we may recall, Habermas convicts him
as follows:

Because Freud was caught from the very beginning in a scientistic self-understanding, he succumbed to an objectivism that regresses immediately from the
level of self-reflection to contemporary positivism in the manner of Mach and
that therefore takes on a particularly crude form. [1971: 252]

I have argued one by one that all of the key ontological and epistemic
considerations that Habermas has marshaled to document Freud's commission of a "scientistic self-misunderstanding" have been mistaken, if
not invidious. Instead of sustaining his indictment, Habermas has
treated us to a procession of logical enormities interlaced with homiletic
ipse dixits. It should now be clear that it was not Freud but Habermas
himself who strapped the clinical theory of psychoanalysis to the Pro-
crustean bed of a philosophical ideology alien to it. Indeed, the relevant
point is not that Freud idolizes the natural sciences ("scientism"), but that
Habermas misconceives them. Thus, far from giving a philosophical
elucidation of the clinical theory, Habermas obfuscates and misdepicts it
in an exasperatingly undisciplined way.

But that is not all. In the passage I quoted last, as well as elsewhere,
Habermas has done a disservice to the exegesis of Freud's writings by a
tendentious disregard of the pertinent texts. Thus, as we shall now
illustrate by means of the opening page of Freud's "Instincts and Their
Vicissitudes," Habermas uses the epithet "positivist" indiscriminately to
derogate any conception that rejects his own methodological separatism
for psychology or the social sciences. Freud begins this paper with a brief
but pregnant disquisition on the philosophy of science (S.E. 1915, 14:
117). There he offers an account of concept formation in the sophisticated empirical sciences featuring the following interesting points,
among others:

(1) Even the initial description of phenomena that are to be explained
is—as we would say nowadays—theory-laden. Surely this is a quasi-
Kantian theme, opposed to the theory-observation dichotomy characteristic of the early days of logical empiricism. As Freud put it: "Even at the
stage of description it is not possible to avoid applying certain abstract
ideas to the material in hand, ideas derived from somewhere or other but
certainly not from the new observations alone." Indeed, he stresses that
the ideas that become the basic theoretical concepts of the given science
are—to use Poincaré's locution—free creations of the human mind rather
than Aristotelian-Thomist abstractions from sensory phenomena. Thus,
he points out that these basic postulational concepts have "in fact...
been imposed" on "the material of observation," although they "appear
to have been derived" from it.

(2) Freud recognizes that the empirical findings *underdetermine* the hypotheses used to explain them. Having noted the free postulational reign of the theoretical imagination to "impose" its high-level, abstract concepts on the observational material, Freud remarks: "Thus, strictly speaking, they [i.e., the imposed ideas] are in the nature of conventions— although everything depends on their not being arbitrarily chosen but determined by their having significant relations to the empirical material" (S.E. 1915, 14: 117).

In short, for Freud, scientific theory construction in psychology or any other modern empirical science gives full scope to the creative imagination, subject only to the proviso that such conjectural activity be informed by diligence in carrying out pertinent observations. How, I ask Habermas, does this comport with the charge of neurobiological mischief-making in metapsychological garb? How does Freud do reductively alienating violence to such concepts of the clinical theory as repression, defense, conflict, wish, fantasy, memory, cognitive-affective longing or aversion, compromise-formation, sensation, percept, and so forth? To ask these questions is to answer them, if we remain cognizant of the exegetical documentation given early in this Introduction.

It emerges that, if the hermeneutic construal of psychoanalytic theory and therapy is to be at all viable, Habermas's version will have to be forsaken. Hence, I now turn to the one offered by Paul Ricoeur.

3. Critique of Ricoeur's Philosophy of Psychoanalysis

A. Ricoeur's Truncation of the Purview of Freudian Theory

Ricoeur sets the stage for his proposed hermeneutic reconstruction by truncating the domain of occurrences to which psychoanalytic theory is to be deemed relevant. For he immures its substantive purview within the *verbal* productions of the clinical transaction between the analyst and the patient. Its subject matter, we are told, is "analytic experience [in that dyadic transaction], insofar as the latter operates in the field of speech" (1970: 375). And, thus, he stipulates at the outset that "the ultimate truth claim [of psychoanalytic theory] resides in the case histories," such that "all truth claims of psychoanalysis are ultimately summed up in the narrative structure of psychoanalytic facts" (1981: 268; see also 38 and 248).

Once the domain of relevance of Freud's theory is held to be coextensive with "a work of speech with the patient" (Ricoeur 1970: 369), even the analysand's *non*verbal productions are excluded from its scope. But, as I shall argue, Ricoeur's circumscription (1981: 248) of the domain of "facts"—or objects of knowledge—that the psychoanalytic corpus is declared to codify is a mutilation of its range of relevance. And his stated rationale for identifying the utterances made in the clinical transaction to be *the* object of psychoanalytic inquiry reveals that an extraneous philosophic aim was the intellectual motivation for his ontological amputation (1981: 248). For, as he sees it, just this circumscription enables him to draw the conclusion that—unlike the "facts" of "academic psychology" (1970: 369)—"facts in psychoanalysis are in no way facts of observable behaviour" (1981: 248). Armed with this result, he can then be confident, he believes, that scientific scrutiny cannot intrude upon his hermeneutic construal of Freudian theory.

Indeed, his entire discussion is conducted within the framework of a crude observation-theory dichotomy in which a reductively behaviorist psychology—rather than, say, a cognitive psychology that countenances intrapsychic states—serves as the paradigm of a "scientific psychology" (Ricoeur 1970: 369; Maxwell and Maxwell 1972). In any case, let me now justify my claim that the import of Freud's clinical theory defies the ontological restraint of Ricoeur's verbalistic straitjacket.

True enough, psychoanalysts generally regard their many observations of the patient's verbal and nonverbal interactions with them in the treatment sessions as the source of findings that are simply peerless *as evidence*, not only heuristically but also probatively (Jones 1959, 1: 3). But this avowed *epistemic* tribute to the evidence garnered in clinical investigations is a far cry from limiting the very purview or subject matter of the entire theory to the phenomena of the clinical transaction, let alone to "the work of speech with the patient." Nor is such stunting justified by the platitude that Freud intended the clinical findings to be *included within* the explanatory scope of his system of hypotheses. For his etiologic hypotheses purportedly explained generically why people at large acquire neuroses, *regardless of whether they are ever treated psychoanalytically or not*. Thus, Freud claimed to have given an etiologic account of why some people become paranoiacs, even if—like Judge Schreber—they are never seen by an analyst.

By the same token, he claimed to have illuminated why, even among the *unanalyzed*, the personality traits of obstinacy, orderliness, and parsimony tended to cluster together and deserved the etiologic label of "anal character." Moreover, as against Ricoeur, no less than against Habermas, it is germane that the psychoanalytic etiology of paranoia would explain an epidemiologic decrease in the incidence of paranoia by pointing to the decline of the taboo on homosexuality. And this explanation would or could be given quite apart from any concern for data from the analytic treatment setting. Indeed, just as the intersubjective epidemiologic testability of the psychoanalytic etiology of paranoia gainsays Habermas's epistemology, so also it contravenes Ricoeur's dichotomy of validation between psychoanalytic theory and academic scientific psychology. Yet Ricoeur (1974: 186) insists that "psychoanalysis does not satisfy the standards of the sciences of observation, and the 'facts' it deals with are not verifiable by multiple, independent observers. . . . there are no 'facts' nor any observation of 'facts' in psychoanalysis but rather the interpretation of a narrated history."

The therapeutic dynamics depicted in psychoanalytic theory is hardly restricted to speech acts on the analyst's couch or in his/her office. Yet, there is an obvious sense in which Freud's therapy may be and has been dubbed a "talking cure." As he has told us (S.E. 1910, 11: 13, 21), Breuer's first patient, Anna O., coined just this label for the protopsychoanalytic treatment she had received from Freud's mentor. But it is dull to be told by Ricoeur that "analysis qua 'talking cure'" is a "closed field of speech" (1970: 369). And thus, it hardly vindicates his willful impoverishment of the domain of "facts" addressed by Freud to adduce that "psychoanalysis [qua 'talking cure'] is itself a work of speech with the patient. . . it is in a field of speech that the patient's 'story' is told." Most recently, Ricoeur issued the mild disclaimer that "there is no need to insist here on the *talkcure* character of psychoanalysis" (1981: 248). But, he hastened to add that the "screening [of thoughts and feelings] through speech in the analytic situation also functions as a criterion for what will be held to be the object [of knowledge] of this science." And the verdict of that criterion is purportedly the identification of "only that part of [analytic treatment] experience which is capable of *being said*" (1981: 248) as the object of psychoanalytic knowledge.

The psychoanalytic dream theory springs the confines of Ricoeur's speech acts domain no less than Freud's etiologies do. As Ricoeur would have it, "it is not the dream as dreamed that can be interpreted, but rather the text of the dream account" (1970: 5). Without telling us just what is to be understood by the term "know," he avers: "We know dreams only as told upon awakening" (1981: 248). Does "know" here require awareness of the manifest content *and* of its being fancied? If so, why must people *verbalize* the memories of their dreams, if they are to "know" them in waking life? But even if they must do so, how would this show that the domain of psychoanalytic dream theory is devoid of dreams as actually dreamed and is confined to verbalized memories of them? Why does the domain of physical theory comprise elementary particles rather than *only*, say, the tracks they leave in Wilson cloud chambers or other registration devices, whereas the domain of the dream theory is to contain *only* verbalized memories of dreams? What, besides an imported ideological objective, prompted Ricoeur to shrink the *subject matter* of Freud's wish-fulfillment theory, which offers repressed infantile motives for dreams as dreamed during sleep, into mere verbal dream-reports during waking life?

Perhaps Ricoeur's ontological stultification of the psychoanalytic dream theory was abetted by the unsound inference that the dreamer's verbalized recollections of his/her dreams are the domain of relevance for any theory of dreams, simply because these utterances are presumed to be the *epistemic point of departure* for such a theory. Of course, Freud himself eschewed this inference, although he countenanced its premise. In his view, the epistemic *terminus a quo* of dream research was indeed an assortment of manifest dream contents, as fallibly recalled and reported by the dreamer, perhaps after some editing (S.E. 1916, 15: 84-85). Yet, while acknowledging these defects in the "data," he put them into perspective: They did not militate against the generic explanation of dreams as presumed to have been dreamed by the unanalyzed vast majority of mankind and by the analyzed alike.

It is salutary in this context to appreciate that what astronomers endeavor to explain, in the first instance, is not the visual impressions they have of celestial occurrences, but the celestial events *retrodicted* from these impressions, or the events whose earlier occurrence their impressions are taken to betoken. And just as dream reporting may well be inaccurate, so also the accuracy of astronomical observations has been lessened by the earth's atmosphere, for example. Small wonder, therefore, that what Freudian theory tries to explain, in the first instance, is not the verbal dream-*reports* made by dreamers to analysts or others, but rather the manifest dream-contents inferred from the dreamers' subsequent mnemic impressions. Nay, Freud claimed to have explained why people dream at all, in addition to purporting to illuminate generically why they dream what they dream, whether they are psychoanalyzed or not.

Similarly, according to psychoanalytic theory, the so-called "transference" phenomena become important in the treatment-transaction precisely because the encounter between the analyst and the patient poignantly *instantiates* processes that are operative in all of us, even if we never enter an analysis in our lives. Thus, the unanalyzed, no less than those who embark on a psychoanalysis, are held to *transfer* to their adult interpersonal relations unconscious conflict-laden attitudes (e.g., Oedipal feelings) originally entertained in childhood toward important figures (e.g., a parent). And by being infantile, the unwittingly transposed dispositions are inappropriate to adult life situations. Hence, by carrying them over into his/her interpersonal relations, the mature person reacts to others as if they were figures from his/her distant early past, thereby often misattributing alien motives and traits to them. In short, in all of mankind the "transference phenomena" purportedly distort interpersonal relations. And it is on the strength of being deemed universally operative that the hypothesized transference is claimed to explain the interaction of psychoanalytic patients with their doctors. Hence, the hypothesized transference furnishes yet another case against Ricoeur's contrived and tendentious attempt to shrink Freud's theory into the mold of analytic experience on the couch.

Moreover, this ideological surgery on the psychoanalytic corpus hardly coheres with Ricoeur's belated recognition of the actual scope of *causal explanation* in Freudian theory. He rightly deems causal claims to be intrinsic to this corpus of hypotheses. Yet, as we shall now see, the range of relevance of just these claims is far wider than that of "the hermeneutics of self-understanding" (1981: 264) employed within the treatment setting.

Ricoeur tells us most recently that "facts in psychoanalysis are in no way facts of observable behaviour" (1981: 248). But, in the very same chapter, he goes on to gainsay this dictum as follows:

What is remarkable about psychoanalytic explanation is that it brings into view motives which are causes.... In many ways his [Freud's] explanation refers to "causally relevant" factors.... All that is important to him is to explain... what in behaviour are "the incongruities" in relation to the expected course of a human agent's action.... It is the attempt to reduce these "incongruities" that... calls for an *explanation* by means of causes.... To say, for example, that a feeling is unconscious... is to say that it is to be inserted as a causally relevant factor in order to explain the incongruities of an act of behaviour.... From this... it follows... that the hermeneutics of self-understanding take the detour of causal explanation. [Pp. 262-264]

Here Ricoeur evidently recognized that psychoanalytic explanations are both *causal* and are intended to illuminate various sorts of behavior. If so, then their validation, if any, will have to be of a kind *appropriate* to these avowed features. But how does Ricoeur envision the appraisal of the psychoanalytic codification of a purported causal connection? As I shall argue in detail in Part II of this book, the demonstration of the *causal* relevance of various sorts of repressions cannot be effected by such clinical methods as free association, which are endemic to the Freudian enterprise. Instead, the establishment of a causal connection in psychoanalysis, no less than in "academic psychology" or medicine, has to rely on modes of inquiry that were refined from time-honored canons of causal inference pioneered by Francis Bacon and John Stuart Mill.

Now, the imperative to furnish cogent evidence of the purported causal linkages invoked to explain the patient's case history is not lessened by the injunction (Ricoeur 1981: 266-268) to fulfill the "narrativity criterion" as well. The latter requires that "the partial explanatory segments of this or that fragment of behaviour are integrated in a narrative structure" reflecting the individual analysand's etiologic life history (p. 267). But, as Ricoeur emphasizes, the psychoanalytically reconstructed scenario not only must be a *"coherent story"* (p. 267)—made "intelligible" by the explanatory (etiologic) segments—but must also aspire to being true, rather than merely persuasive and therapeutic. Quite properly, therefore, he enjoins that "we must not give up our efforts to link a truth claim with the narrativity criterion, even if this claim is validated on a basis other than narrativity itself" (p. 268).

Indeed, he elaborates (pp. 268-269) on "what makes a narration an explanation in the psychonanalytic sense of the term" as follows: "It is the possibility of inserting several stages of causal explanation into the process of self-understanding in narrative terms. And it is this explanatory detour that entails recourse to non-narrative means of proof." Significantly, he adds that the three levels over which these means of proof are spread include "the level of law-like propositions applied [*mirabile dictu*!] to typical segments of behaviour (symptoms, for example)" (p. 269). Yet, earlier in the same chapter Ricoeur had adduced "even [neurotic] symptoms" in support of his claim that "facts in psychoanalysis are in no way facts of observable behaviour" (p. 248). For there he had declared that "even symptoms, although they are partially observable, enter into the field of analysis only in relation to other factors verbalized in the 'report.'" The conscientious reader will be forgiven, I trust, for wondering whether Ricoeur himself has decided just what he wants to maintain.

At any rate, it emerges that the causal hypotheses on which psychoanalytic explanations are predicated must be appraised, after all, by none other than the methods of "academic psychology" and/or of the natural sciences! But Ricoeur had argued—in Section I of the same chapter—that just these modes of assessment ought not to be countenanced. As he told us, they are inappropriate because they differ *toto genere*, if not *toto caelo*, from the standards governing "the hermeneutics of self-understanding."

Indeed, in Ricoeur's commentary (1981: 32-40, especially 38) on the editorial introduction by J. B. Thompson, the translator of his 1981 book, he apparently endorses the methodological dichotomy enunciated there on his behalf by Thompson. Significantly, the latter declared:

In response to those critics who contend that Freud's theory does not satisfy the most elementary criteria of scientificity... Ricoeur maintains that all such contentions... betray the very essence of psychoanalysis. For the latter is not an observational science dealing with the facts of behaviour; rather it is an interpretative discipline concerned with relations of meaning between representative symbols and primordial instincts. Thus, psychoanalytic concepts should be judged, not according to the exigencies of an empirical science, but "according to their status as conditions of the possibility of analytic [treatment] experience, insofar as the latter operates in the field of speech." [Ricoeur 1981: 7]

And when speaking of "the question of proof in Freud's psychoanalytic writings," Thompson points out further that "Ricoeur's current [1981] approach to this question reveals a shift away from his earlier [1970] work," *Freud and Philosophy*: "His starting point now [in 1981] is the analytic situation, which determines what counts as a 'fact' in psychoanalysis"(Ricoeur 1981: 24).

Ricoeur's depiction of the epistemology of psychoanalysis is thus fundamentally incoherent. No wonder, therefore, that his account fails to heed the methodological import of the causal nature of psychoanalytic explanation. As he acknowledges (1981: 263), Freud gives explicitly causal explanations of "the origin of a neurosis." But once this is granted, Freud's modification of his erstwhile seduction etiology of hysteria can be shown to be quite unavailing to Ricoeur's indictment of "scientistic" psychoanalysis.

B. Are Natural Science Modes of Explanation and Validation Gainsaid in Psychoanalysis by the Pathogenicity of Seduction *Fantasies*, or by the Explanatory Role of "Meaning"?

As heralded in an admirable though pathetic 1897 letter to Wilhelm Fliess, Freud (1954: 215-218) was driven to invoke *fancied* childhood seductions after first having deemed actual ones to be the pathogens of hysteria. But even when he still thought *bona fide* seductions to have been the etiologic factor, their hypothesized pathogenicity was, of course, held to be crucially mediated causally by the *psychic* trauma of the child's *experience* of these sexual episodes. This etiologic mediation of exogenously *actuated*, yet *intrapsychic*, processes lends perspective to a Freudian passage adduced by Ricoeur (1981: 250) in the mistaken belief that it furnishes ammunition to his anti-"scientistic" cause. In the pertinent passage, Freud pays etiologic tribute to childhood seduction fantasies as follows:

It remains a fact that the patient has created these phantasies for himself, and this fact is of scarcely less importance for his neurosis than if he had really experienced what the phantasies contain. The phantasies possess *psychical* as contrasted with *material* reality, and we gradually learn to understand that *in the world of the neuroses it is psychical reality which is the decisive kind*. [S.E. 1917, 16: 369]

But Ricoeur can extract no philosophic capital from the hypothesis that the purportedly etiologic process is now held to be actuated causally by autochthonous psychic events rather than exogenously and reactively, in response to events having "*material* reality." For the fancied character of the seductions hardly obviates the imperative to validate the pathogenicity attributed to these fantasies. Yet Ricoeur overlooks in this context—just as Roy Schafer (1976: 204-205) ignores in another connection—that no matter whether the seductions are actual or only fancied, the exponent of their etiologic role cannot be absolved from giving cogent evidence for that causal attribution. And—as Part II of this book will show—the procurement of such support, in turn, requires precisely the methods of controlled inquiry decried by the hermeneuticians. In a much publicized book, J. M. Masson (1984) overlooks the same point as Ricoeur does, though Masson rejects fancied seductions as the pathogens, and instead credulously assigns that etiologic role to *actual* episodes of sexual child abuse. Hence Masson sees Freud's repudiation of his erstwhile seduction etiology as a fateful error, which grievously misdirected all of his subsequent theorizing. And he contends that a failure of nerve, rather than contrary evidence, prompted Freud's disavowal. But, whatever the merits of that accusation, Masson's rehabilitation of actual seductions as the pathogens is etiologically unfounded, as is the pathogenicity of fancied ones.

Thus, it will be a corollary of chapter 3 below that just as the method of free association is incompetent to warrant the pathogenicity of truly occurring childhood seductions, so also this method cannot attest that imagined ones were etiologic. Indeed, as chapter 8 will make clear, the relevant effect of Freud's replacement of actual childhood seductions by merely fancied ones as pathogens is only to make the task of validating their etiologic relevance much harder! Yet Ricoeur lulls himself into the ill-founded belief that by contrast to academic psychology, "psychoanalysis deals with psychical reality and not with material reality. So [*sic*!] the criterion for this reality is no longer that it is observable [however indirectly, as in physics], but that it presents a coherence and a resistance comparable to that of material reality" (1981: 251). But where in all this is there even a hint as to why we should believe that children who assumedly concoct seduction figments then become prone to developing hysteria *because* they entertain such fantasies? And may it not be that the provenance of the seduction fantasies themselves is not entirely intrapsychic but involves "material reality", much as when the death of a parent is depressogenic (S.E. 1917, 14: 239-258)?

On the other hand, if there is actually an etiologic connection between such fantasies and hysteria, then the truth of its affirmation is obviously not impugned in the least by the fictitiousness of the fabricated seductions. Ricoeur transmogrifies this patent fact into "the major difficulty facing the truth claims of psychoanalysis" (1981: 266). Let us even grant him that "what is psychoanalytically [etiologically] relevant [in this context] is what a subject makes of his fantasies," while being duly wary of the misleading locution that the patient "makes" hysteria pathogenically out of his seduction fantasies. And let us countenance, furthermore, "giving wider rein to the liberation of fantasising, to emotional development, and to enjoyment than Freud wanted to do." How then, I ask, is it "undoubtedly" the case that we are thereby "breaking the [unspecified] bond between veracity [truth-telling] and truth" (p. 266)? Not insisting on veracity does not affect whatever *bond* there is between any existing veracity and truth, does it?

When a psychiatrist allows a psychotically paranoid patient much freedom to express his delusions—or even panders to them—is the doctor thereby jeopardizing "the bond between veracity and truth"? Or is he merely not insisting on veracity? Unencumbered by such prosaic considerations, Ricoeur avers: "Nevertheless, I think that there is still something to be sought in the truth claim made from the perspective of the proper use of fantasies" (p. 266), and thereupon launches into a disquisition as to why this should be so.

Ricoeur himself seems to have conceded, albeit only implicitly and unwittingly, that etiologic hypotheses require validation qua being causal, regardless of whether the actuating pathogen is held to be an autochthonous psychic event—e.g., a seduction *fantasy*—or a response to events having "material reality," such as an actual seduction experience. As he acknowledges, any reconstruction of psychoanalysis must include its "task of integrating an explanatory stage," which "keeps psychoanalysis from constituting itself as a province of the exegetical disciplines applied to texts—as a hermeneutics" (1981: 261). And this explanatory imperative, in turn, "requires that psychoanalysis include in the process of self-understanding operations that were originally reserved for the natural sciences" (p. 261).

Indeed, the "nonnarrative" generalizations employed in psychoanalytic explanations are avowedly

already present in the ordinary explanations of individual behaviour; alleged motives—for example, hate or jealousy—are not particular events, but classes of inclinations [types of dispositions] under which a particular action is placed in order to make it intelligible. To say that someone acted out of jealousy is to invoke in the case of his particular action a feature which is grasped from the outset as repeatable and common to an indeterminate variety of individuals.... So to explain is to characterize a given action by ascribing to it as its cause a motive which exemplifies a class. [Ricoeur 1981: 269]

But, once this is recognized, as indeed it should be, its import completely undermines the hermeneutic denunciation of natural science modes of explanation in psychoanalysis. For it then becomes quite unavailing to adduce, in the words of George Klein (1976: 26), that "the central objective of psychoanalytic clinical explanation is the *reading of intentionality*; behavior, experience, testimony are studied for meaning in this sense." Instead, the hermeneutic denunciation of natural science modes of causal explanation in psychoanalysis is undercut by the *import* of the following Freudian thesis: There are, in all of us, repressed and even conscious motives that are not only first discerned to exist by analysts, but are also the *causes* of the sorts of behaviors, thoughts, feelings, and so forth purportedly explained by them. *In the context of the psychoanalytic clinical theory of psychopathology*, the ontological identity of unconscious ideation qua being mental rather than physical hardly robs it of its hypothesized causal role. For, as we saw at the outset, this Freudian theory of repression emphatically abjured an exclusively physicalistic construal of the attribute of causal relevance. Thus, within the psychic world depicted by Freud, it is simply wrongheaded to maintain that, in virtue of being mental, repressed ideation cannot function as a motivational *cause*. As well aver the inanity that because an explosion involves natural gas, this eruption cannot qualify as a cause of the collapse of a building and of the deaths of its occupants.

In the same vein, Brenner has rightly cautioned against the cognate blunder of inferring that psychoanalysis cannot employ the methods of the natural sciences merely because its subject matter is ideational, and—to that extent—differs from that of physics or even neurophysiology. As Brenner (1982: 4) has put it: "This fact [of a difference in subject matter] has misled some psychoanalysts to the conclusion that psychoanalysis is not a branch of natural science at all, but a science *sui generis*, since it has to do with language and meaning."

Yet such advocates of hermeneutic psychoanalysis as George Klein (1976: 43) and Roy Schafer (1976: 204-205) have succumbed to an equally mistaken belief. In their misconstrual of Freud's vision, the *causes* of human conduct can be, at most, *metapsychological* (in the technical sense), rather than genuinely motivational, in the mental fashion of unconscious or conscious motives. And their incongruous notion has fostered the pernicious myth that, precisely insofar as explanations in psychoanalysis are indeed motivational or supply unconscious "reasons" for our actions, they cannot be a particular *species* of causal explanations. But, as Ricoeur came to appreciate to his great credit (1981: 262-263, 269), those who draw this conclusion are in effect *repudiating* Freud's clinical explanations of neuroses, dreams, and parapraxes, although they see themselves as giving a philosophic explication of them! For in his clinical theory of repression, unconscious motives are deemed to be explanatory precisely because they are held to *engender* these various manifestations of their existence by being causally relevant to them. And the issue here so far is not whether it is sound to explain human actions causally, but only whether psychoanalysis can be reconstructed short of emasculation without doing so.

Thus, the psychoanalytic quest for the so-called "meaning" of neurotic symptoms, dreams, and slips turns out to be predicated on a crucial two-fold presupposition. First, the *concealed* "intentionality" postulated by Freud's theory does in fact exist covertly, thereby first turning these various facets of human life into targets for being psychoanalytically deciphered; after all, without the existential assumption that *there are* unconscious processes holding the key to the significance to be fathomed, it is simply illusory to investigate psychoanalytically the arcane "meaning" of the life events in question. Second—as against the stated misconceptions—the putative repressed ideation derives its *explanatoriness* in psychoanalysis from its hypothesized *causal* role, an elucidative pedigree "originally reserved for the natural sciences" (Ricoeur 1981: 261). But just this attribution of various sorts of causal efficacy to unconscious mentation cries out for cogent vindication. Hence, the very quest for the veiled "meaning," which psychoanalytic explanation is expected to disclose, *cannot redeem its avowed promise* without prior reliance on *methods of inquiry and validation* that hermeneuticians proclaim to be quite inappropriate: exactly those cognitive procedures that they are wont to categorize as endemic to the natural sciences. By the same token, insofar as these partisans do countenance causal explanations in psychoanalysis, their whole hermeneutic enterprise is tacitly parasitic on an epistemology they inveterately profess to decry.

Ricoeur is no less guilty of this legerdemain than others. For he emphatically denounces the logic of validation familiar from the natural sciences as alien to Freud's clinical theory. And he does so by misassimilating these sciences to his mythic notion of an "observational science" (1981, chap. 10, sec. I; 1970, pp. 358-375) while denying that psychoanalysis qualifies as such a science. This piece of philosophical malfeasance is not mitigated by his admission (1981: 261) that the causal explanations furnished by psychoanalysis gainsay the confinement of the Freudian edifice to a mere "province" of exegetic hermeneutics.

Nor, as we shall see further on, does George Klein come to grips with the stated import of the tacit existential and causal assumptions underlying his declaration that by seeking "the [unconscious] reasons of behavior—clinical explanation requires us, then, to identify not only [the unrecognized or even disavowed] intentionality exemplified by a configuration of experience and behavior, but the [etiologic] history of such guiding directives in a person's life (the 'genetic point of view') " (1976: 27). How, for example, would Klein justify the psychoanalytic claim that free association can serve to "identify" the allegedly operative yet unconscious "guiding directives" of behavior and the conjectured etiologic role of that repressed intentionality? Plainly, no amount of scorn heaped upon Freud's metapsychology, however justified, will supply that indispensable justification. Nor will the most elaborate articulation of heretofore arcane purported "meaning," even if brilliantly imaginative, do so. Why, for example, should any sensible person give any credence at all to an analyst's claim that the "guiding directive" of his chronic adult insomnia is his inordinate yet unacknowledged obsessive fear of death, triggered by the rather early demise of both of his parents *and* guilt because of having wished their death?

Let us now use some poignant illustrations to put into bolder relief the extent to which the entire hermeneutic enterprise is *ill-conceived* in psychoanalysis, unless it provides adequate scope for validating the causal imputations implicit in the hidden "meaning" it purports to fathom.

Suppose that the thought-fragmentation and cackling exhibited by a certain class of schizophrenic women were taken to betoken the witchcraft cunningly practiced by them and/or their unawareness of being satanically possessed. Those claiming to have acceptable grounds for such an attribution would, of course, consider themselves justified when summoning a shaman or an exorcist. By supposedly conjuring up the possessing spirits or the like, this therapist would then fathom hermeneutically the conjectured "hidden meaning" of the babble from these unfortunate women. But the rest of us will be forgiven for telling the shamans and exorcists that we deem their hermeneutic quest and ensuing revelations to be ill-conceived. For they have conspicuously failed to validate cogently the bizarre causal imputations on which their "clinical investigation" of meaning and their therapy are predicated.

True, their incantations may even favorably affect the schizophrenic symptoms, if only temporarily. But even if these therapeutic results were impressive, we would hardly credit the shamans or exorcists with having unraveled the otherwise elusive "meaning" of the witchcraft or possession symptoms. For we reject their underlying causal ontology, which determines what kind of "meaning" their quest will "uncover." And thus we dismiss their "reading of intentionality" as altogether chimerical.

Likewise, if a new school of self-styled archaeologists were to announce an array of retrodictive inferences based on exceedingly dubious causal hypotheses, we would likewise withhold our assent from their asseveration of previously elusive "archaeological meaning."

Turning to psychoanalysis, the noted analyst B. B. Rubinstein has expressed the same animadversion for the hermeneuticians in the context of dream theory. In a section on "Explanation in Terms of Meaning and Causal Explanation," Rubinstein wrote incisively:

When we interpret the meaning of a dream symbol we presuppose the actual occurrence of the very processes we posit to explain causally the production of the symbol. Clearly. . . no matter how apt an interpretation of a symbol in terms of its [purported latent] meaning, if the processes by which symbol formation is explained are improbable, we have no alternative but to discard the interpretation. . . . to an interpreter [e.g., the analyst] the *meaning* of a *dream symbol* is what the symbol, unbeknownst to the dreamer, is taken to *signify* . . . however, either the thus signified is also what has given rise to, i.e., *caused* (or contributed to cause) the occurrence of, the symbol, or the 'symbol' cannot be said to signify it. We will note that if a symbol is justifiably said to signify something then it can also be said to *represent* this something. [1975: 104-105]

One salutary corollary of this cogent statement is the following: no matter how strong the *thematic affinity* between a conjectured repressed thought and a maladaptive, neurotic action, this "meaning kinship" does not itself suffice to attest that the hypothesized repression is "the hidden intentionality" behind the given behavior. For thematic affinity alone does not vouch for etiologic lineage in the absence of further evidence that a thematically kindred repression actually *engendered* the behavior. And if there is no warrant for inferring the operation of the repression from the patient's conduct, it is only misleading to assert that the former is "the meaning" of the latter or that the latter "signifies" the former. For the behavior in question does not in fact bespeak the existence of the repression, and hence does not justify reading the latter into it. But by using the weasel word "meaning" to render what—so far as the evidence goes—is *only* a thematic affinity, the putative hermeneutician illicitly creates the semblance of having uncovered a "hidden intention" after all.

Even analysts who are not avowed hermeneuticians are prone to what might be dubbed "the thematic affinity fallacy." The diagnosis made in a case discussed in some detail at the end of chapter 4 will now serve to illustrate a cognate pitfall. As documented there, an analyst had a woman patient who had been unduly concerned about her general appearance, notably her skin. There is, of course, some thematic affinity between the dermatological deficit resented by the patient and the phallic deficit, which, according to Freud's hypothesis of female penis envy, is resented by little girls, who are held to envy their brothers the male anatomical endowment. Besides, there is also resentment in both cases. But assuming that there are grounds for attributing penis envy to little girls, this alone is a far cry from showing that their sense of anatomical "defect" is *also pathogenic*. Yet, in the case discussed late in chapter 4, the analyst diagnosed penis envy to be the hidden intentionality behind the female patient's discontent with her skin and general appearance, after having orchestrated her assent to the imputation of such envy.

Interestingly, there are also quondam behaviorists who overlooked that conversion to hermeneutic psychology does not provide absolution from the stated imperative to validate the causal hypotheses tacitly invoked by their avowed enterprise. Insouciantly endorsing psychoanalytic imputations of hidden motives, A. Gauld and J. Shotter (1977) say nothing about the grounds a hermeneutic psychologist would have—beyond thematic affinity—for claiming, for example, that unconscious aggression toward the father was the motivational cause of a patient's particular behavior. Thus, in their view, it is one mission of the hermeneutic psychologist "to elucidate by any method that he can the 'meanings' which the actions had for the agents. This task is completed when after psychotherapy the patient comes to understand that his strange action was a symbolic piece of aggression against his father" (p. 80). But what are their grounds for supposing that any of the methods countenanced by their hermeneutic doctrine have any promise to uncover "the [unconscious] 'meanings' which the actions had for the agents"?

As we already had occasion to note vis-à-vis Habermas, there is good evidence from cognitive psychology that, even in the case of *consciously* motivated behavior, the agent does not enjoy privileged epistemic access to the discernment of the motives for his/her various commonplace actions. Indeed, all too frequently the purportedly introspective ascertainment of conscious motives is demonstrably wrong. Thus, when an agent offers a motivational explanation for his own actions, he does so—just like outside observers—by invoking *theory-based* schemata endorsed by the belief-system to which he adheres. *A fortiori*, in the case of *unconsciously* engendered behavior, the patient and the analyst alike are plainly drawing on psychoanalytic theory when purporting to read the previously unrecognized "meaning" of the patient's "strange action."

How, then, can either of them be held to know—on Gauld and Shotter's showing, short of resorting to the forsaken extrahermeneutic methods of validation—that this "meaning" was unconscious aggression toward the father at all? For the purpose of effecting a change in the agent's odd behavior, it may perhaps be quite irrelevant whether the therapist's reading of the instigating unconscious motive is mythic. But Gauld and Shotter use the phrase, "the [unconscious] 'meaning' which the action had for the agent." And their use of the past tense suggests their existential assumption of a motive that was actually operative even before the patient entered therapy, rather than of a putative motive that need only become retrospectively believable for him under the influence of treatment. Yet if so, then it is anything but immaterial to their declared elucidatory objective that the analyst's motivational imputations have better credentials than mere fancy. Nonetheless, they beg the question by sidestepping this vital issue. For they conclude genially: "Once the formerly 'obscure' meanings of these various actions have been made clear, so that the actions are now as well understood as the commonplace actions which everyone can comprehend, this stage of the hermeneutical psychologist's task is over" (p. 81).

Other hermeneuticians have sought to immunize their undertaking against the risks of causal imputations by reconceptualizing, more radically than Ricoeur or Gauld and Shotter, the very aims of the psychoanalytic elucidation of "meaning." This stratagem has likewise had much appeal to a good many analysts. For, faced with the bleak import of skeptical indictments of their legacy, they are intent on salvaging it in some form. Hence, some of them will be understandably receptive to a rationale that promises them absolution from their failure to validate the cardinal hypotheses of their clinical theory, a failure I demonstrate in depth in Part II below. Be of stout heart, they are told, and take the radical *hermeneutic* turn. Freud, they learn, brought the incubus of validation on himself by his scientistic pretensions. Abjure his program of causal explanation, the more drastic hermeneuticians beckon them, and you will no longer be saddled with the harassing demand to justify Freud's causal hypotheses. One such hermeneutic advocate illustrated this repudiation of causation as follows: "the meaning of a dream does not reside in some prior latent dream [content, as Freud had claimed], but in the manifest dream and the analysand's associations to it" (Steele 1979: 400). Michael Moore has lucidly explicated this posture before vigorously rejecting it. As he puts it, the claim is

that Freud was not really explaining how the particular dream occurred...he was...not discovering its (motivational or nonmotivational) causes. On this account, the rationalizing but noncausal wishes discovered after the dream by free association have nothing to do with producing the dream; they are after-the-fact discoveries made by juxtaposing the manifest content of the dreams with the material produced by free association—an interpretive technique that may tell you something about yourself, but nothing at all of what caused your dreams. [Moore 1983: 49]

More generally, the blandishments of this renunciatory stance include the comforting assurance that the practicing analyst is immune to the taunts of critics who dispute the cost-effectiveness of his therapy. And even for the Freudian psychohistorians, the hermeneutician has the glad tidings that henceforth they can hold their heads high as protagonists of

a newly legitimated kind of humanistic discipline. In short, the claim is
that the challenge to provide validation of the causal propositions has
been obviated, and that the continuing demand for it has therefore
become an anachronism, cherished only by positivist fanatics.

I maintain, however, that the generic disavowal of causal attributions
advocated by the radical hermeneuticians is a nihilistic, if not frivolous,
trivialization of Freud's entire clinical theory. Far from serving as a new
citadel for psychoanalytic apologetics, the embrace of such hermeneuticians is, I submit, the kiss of death for the legacy that was to be saved.

Let me illustrate my case against the stated acausal hermeneutic
construal of psychoanalytic significance by reference to an allegedly
Freudian lapse of memory that has figured as a paradigmatic instance in
the literature, and to which I referred earlier in passing. To say that a slip
of the tongue, pen, ear, eye, or of memory is genuinely "Freudian" is to
say that it was engendered by a *repressed* motive. Thus, as chapter 4 will
clarify, Freud assimilated a seemingly insignificant slip of the memory to
the status of a minineurotic symptom by regarding this lapse as a
compromise between a (short-term) repressed motive that crops out in
the form of a disturbance, on the one hand, and the conscious intention
to make a certain utterance, on the other.

The pertinent paradigmatic instance of a lapse of memory involves the
forgetting of the Latin pronoun *aliquis* (someone), which a young man Y
omitted when reciting a line from Virgil's *Aeneid* (S.E. 1901, 6: chapter II).
Freud supplied the missing word and enjoined Y to use the restored
word as the point of departure for free associations. After a tortuous
chain of such associations, punctuated by some interjections from Freud,
it emerged that Y had been harboring a presumably repressed fear. An
Italian girl friend, he suspected apprehensively, had become pregnant by
him. Freud then told him that this repressed anxiety had undeniably
produced his *aliquis* lapse. But Y doubted any such causal nexus,
although he was fully aware that his worry was genuine.

Now let me contrast Freud's account of this lapse with the hermeneutic claim that Y's slip lends itself to acausal and yet psychoanalytic
interpretation.

The orthodox rationale for calling on Y to let the restored word initiate
his free associations was clear. Having deemed the lapse to be a minineurotic symptom, Freud attributed its occurrence *causally* to the operation
of some repression. And when Y asked him to *explain* how the forgetting
of the pronoun had been brought about, Freud promised to identify the
causally relevant repression by winnowing the free associations triggered in Y by the restored word *aliquis* (S.E. 1901, 6: 9). Hence, he then
used the surfacing of Y's previously repressed pregnancy worry from

these particular associations as grounds for concluding that this very fear—while as yet being repressed before the memory lapse—had caused Y to forget that word. And Freud held this inference to be licensed by the principle that a repression R present before the commission of a parapraxis by a person X qualifies as its cause, if R emerges into X's consciousness in the wake of free associations triggered by his awareness of the content of his error.

I do not profess to know at all what did cause Y's slip. But, for the reasons I give in chapter 4, I claim that if Y's repressed worry did cause him to forget *aliquis*, Freud has completely failed to supply cogent evidence for this causal nexus. And this failure to justify his causal inference deserves censure, even if one could grant him quite generally that the analyst does not inject epistemically contaminating influences into the sequence of the associations, as he contended (S.E. 1923, 18: 238). Seriously flawed though it is, Freud's account nonetheless does endeavor to offer an explanation of slips *qua slips* by purporting to have identified unconscious motives *for their occurrence*.

But I submit that the alleged interpretive meaning furnished by the acausal hermeneutic rationale is altogether insensitive to the fact that the word *aliquis* figured in a *lapse* of memory. Whatever that hermeneutic meaning, I claim that it is *not* the meaning *of a slip qua slip* at all! To be sure, the aforecited hermeneutician, no less than the orthodox analyst, sifts the free associations elicited from Y by the restoration of the forgotten word to his awareness. Yet the radical hermeneutic view now at issue demurely disclaims the postulation of causes (Steele 1979: 400), and thus forsakes the causal import of treating a slip as a minineurotic symptom. Hence, according to this construal, the interpretive meaning that is to be revealed by the winnowing of Y's associations avowedly has no *causal* relevance to the fact that *aliquis* did figure in a lapse. How, then, can the interpretive meaning revealed by the associative content of *aliquis* be held to be the significance of the *forgetting* of *aliquis*, rather than simply the associative import of that word per se, *regardless of whether it had been forgotten or not*? Indeed, on the acausal hermeneutic rationale, why should Y be asked to associate to the word *aliquis* rather than to one of the words in the line from Virgil that he had *not* forgotten? Since the emerging meaning is not the meaning of a slip *qua* slip, how can this acausal rationale provide a reason for supposing that the associations to a *forgotten* word are richer in interpretive meaning— whatever that is—than the associations to nonforgotten words, or to other associatively evocative items in the subject's life? How, then, can the drastic hermeneutician see himself as having given any reconstruction at all of Freud's theory of slips *qua* slips?

It is important to appreciate that my charge of utter emasculation here against acausal hermeneutics is *not* predicated on the soundness of the following *empirical* assumption, which Wittgenstein deemed damaging to Freud's own causal account:

> The fact is that whenever you are preoccupied with something, with some trouble or with some problem which is a big thing in your life—as sex is, for instance—then no matter what you start from, the association will lead finally and inevitably back to that same theme. [Wittgenstein 1967: 50-51]

What if the radical hermeneutician were to reply that, though the associations do not bespeak a cause of a slip, they reveal a great deal about the current psychological makeup of the person who has them? I retort by asking: On what basis does the advocate of *acausal* hermeneutics infer the psychological makeup of a person from the latter's free associations? Does the inference rely tacitly on presumed *causal* linkages between personality structure and associational output? If so, the acausalist is not entitled to invoke them, if only because the validation of causal connections would require nonhermeneutic methods that he is unwilling to license. But let us suppose that the generalizations used to draw the requisite inferences as to the associating person's makeup are not causal. Even then, it is at best unclear how they can be validated short of adopting inductive methods that the hermeneutician rejects as "scientistic."

Similar considerations warrant the conclusion that the acausal hermeneutic rationale so truncates the repression-etiology of the psychoneuroses as to trivialize that etiology *qua* theory of psychopathology. And a like verdict serves to convict the stated acausal version of the received theory of dreams, as Michael Moore has argued in his telling critique of hermeneutic "rationalization without causation" (Moore 1983: 32). Indeed, by abjuring causal claims, the radical hermeneutician forsakes not only the etiologic rationale for the presumed therapeuticity of lifting repressions, but also the causal attribution of such therapeutic efficacy. On this account, why should any troubled patient go to an analyst at all?

On the other hand, Ricoeur, as we saw, does wish to countenance reliance on causal hypotheses in psychoanalytic explanations. But, in a further effort to add a genuinely hermeneutic dimensioin to them, he proposes to *semanticize* them by means of a *semiotic* construal of symptoms. And he epitomizes this maneuver by characterizing the very subject-matter of psychoanalytic investigation and explanation as "the semantics of desire" (1970: 375). Let us be clear on the conceptual context in which Ricoeur has tried to embed his proposed assimilation of *symptoms* to *linguistic representations* of their hypothesized unconscious causes.

C. Does the Theory of Repression Furnish a "Semantics of Desire"?

In psychoanalytic theory, both full-fledged neurotic *symptoms* and minineurotic ones (e.g., manifest dream contents, Freudian slips, jokes) are seen as *compromise*-formations, products of the defensive conflict between the repressed ideas and the repressing ones (S.E. 1896, 3: 170; 1917, 16: 358-359). Qua compromise-formations, *symptoms* have traditionally also been viewed as "symbols" of the repressed, but in the altogether NON-semantic sense of being *substitutive* formations affording *replacement* satisfactions or outlets.

This nonsemiotic notion of "symbols" in psychoanalysis becomes even more explicit in Ernest Jones's major account of "The Theory of Symbolism," where he explains:

Symbolism certainly plays an important part in many neurotic symptoms; a castration complex, for instance, often results in a phobia of blindness, the eye being one of the commonest somatic phallic symbols. That symbolism arises as the result of intrapsychical conflict between the repressing tendencies and the repressed is the view accepted by all psycho-analysts.... Only what is repressed is symbolised; only what is repressed needs to be symbolised. This conclusion is the touchstone of the psychoanalytical theory of symbolism. [Jones 1938: 158]

Preparatory to articulating the psychoanalytically relevant sense of "symbolism," Jones is concerned to distinguish "*sublimations*" from "symbols":

sublimations...like symbols, come about as the result of the conflict between unconscious impulses and the inhibiting forces of repression, but they differ from symbols in that, whereas with the latter the full significance of the original complex is retained unaltered and merely transferred on to a secondary idea (that of the symbol), with the former the psychical energy alone, not the significance, is derived from the unconscious complexes and is transferred on to another set of ideas that have their own independent significance.

Finally, Jones urges that "the term 'symbolism' be reserved" for "symbolism in its most typical form," a usage already adopted by psychoanalysts:

The two cardinal characteristics of symbolism in this strict sense are (1) that the process is completely unconscious, the word being used in Freud's sense of "incapable of consciousness," not as a synonym for subconscious; and (2) that the affect investing the symbolised idea has not, in so far as the symbolism is concerned, proved capable of that modification in quality denoted by the term "sublimation." In both these respects symbolism differs from all other forms of indirect representation.

As Jones points out, symptoms that qualify as "symbols" differ from sublimations. Yet, it would be an *error* to suppose that, at least more often than not, there is thematic affinity between the ideational or affective content of a repression and the symptoms that "symbolize" it substitutively, by providing an outlet for that particular content. To be sure, Breuer's first patient, Anna O., who was severely averse to drinking water, had presumably become thus hydrophobic by strangulating and repressing the disgust she had experienced earlier at the sight of seeing a dog lapping water from a companion's drinking glass (S.E. 1895, 2: 34). But, as Breuer and Freud emphasized at the outset, "the typical hysterical symptoms" do not have any apparent thematic connection at all to their presumed pathogens:

It consists only in what might be called a "symbolic" relation between the precipitating cause and the pathological phenomenon—a relation such as healthy people form in dreams. For instance, a neuralgia may follow upon mental pain or vomiting upon a feeling of moral disgust. . . . In still other cases it is not possible to understand at first sight how they can be determined in the manner we have suggested. It is precisely the typical hysterical symptoms which fall into this class, such as hemi-anaesthesia, contraction of the field of vision, epileptiform convulsions, and so on. [S.E. 1893, 2: 5]

More generally, as Freud stressed, the products ("derivatives") of the dynamic unconscious that are thrust back into consciousness have a more or less *distant* topical connection to the primally repressed motive in which they presumably originated (S.E. 1915, 14: 149-150, 190-191). And the topical remoteness of these derivatives (symptoms, free associations, and fantasies) had been accentuated almost the moment Freud ceased his collaboration with Breuer: he soon demoted etiologically—to mere *precipitators* of neurosis—the adult repressions uncovered by his mentor's cathartic method (S.E. 1986, 3: 194-195). As recounted in chapter 3 below, the childhood repressions that then supplanted adult ones as the primogenetic pathogens of hysteria were invariably sexual, thus being further removed thematically, no less than temporally. And we need only think of the aforementioned homosexual etiology of paranoia to be struck by the topical distance between the suspicions or delusions manifesting this affliction, and repressed homosexual yearnings, which are its putative pathogen.

Similarly, obsessively conscientious performance of religious rituals is held to derive etiologically from allaying portentous diffuse anxiety, generated by carnal temptation (S.E. 1907, 9: 124). Again, the topical "distortion" (S.E. 1915, 14: 149-150) deemed characteristic of much symptom-formation is also illustrated in Ferenczi's attribution (Jones

1938: 158) of phobic blindness to repressed castration anxiety. In short, an agent unconsciously effects a "compromise" when thwarted in the pursuit of an instinctual objective: he/she settles for the substitutive satisfaction afforded by alternative conduct. And precisely when there is thematic *remove* from the original aim, this surrogate behavior would strike the agent as motivationally (causally) *unrelated* to it. All the same, due to the empathic appeal of thematic affinity, it has even been made a touchstone of the causal connection between psychic states: in Karl Jaspers's view (1973: 380-381), this connection is only a neurophysiological *epiphenomenon*, unless there is thematic affinity.

So much, then, for the conceptual context in which Ricoeur has attempted to embed his *semiotic* construal of the various outcroppings of repressed ideation. In his conception, these derivatives can be assimilated to linguistic communications, such that the subject matter of the clinical theory allegedly has the status of a veritable "semantics of desire." To gain perspective on the appraisal of this linguistic turn, let us first consider certain commonplace partial effects of purely physical states of affairs that, I submit, offer an instructive parallel—in relevant respects—to the symptoms of repressions in Freud's conative domain.

A foot-shaped configuration of the sand on a beach almost invariably originates causally from the incursion of a foot when a person or an animal walks on the beach. Hardly ever does such a beach formation result from the"chance" collocation of sand particles under the action of, say, some gust of wind. By thus being statistically linked to a prior physical interaction of the beach with a similarly shaped agency, the pedal sand structure qualifies *ontologically* as a *trace*, a mark or imprint of the past incursion (see Grünbaum 1974, chapter 9 for details). On the strength of this ontological status as a trace, the footprint can be said to derive *retrodictive significance for a human observer, who sees it*: the onlooker is *epistemically* entitled to *interpret* the sand formation as *attesting* to the prior ingress. And, in this case, the geometric isomorphism—"thematic affinity"—between a foot and the *mark* of its penetration licenses a retrodictive *inference* of the latter occurrence.

If we were now to speak loosely, though more solemnly, we could say that the sandy shape has "meaning." But this may well becloud an otherwise lucid state of affairs: qua having originated *causally* from a pedal invasion, the sand configuration is epistemically a *veridical indicator* of this inroad.

Freud often lessens the risk of a corresponding murking by using the term "meaning" abbreviatively to render a perspicuous state of affairs. Thus, note how he uses the term "meaning" in the sense of *definite causal origin*, in apposition with mention of the epistemic inferability warranted by this pedigree: "psycho-analysis...profits by the study of the numerous little slips...which people make—symptomatic actions, as they are called....I have pointed out that these phenomena are not accidental...that they have a meaning and can be interpreted, and that one is justified in inferring from them the presence of restrained or repressed impulses and intentions" (S.E. 1925, 20: 46-47). But, in the context of the footprint, there is no danger of conceptual legerdemain via *linguistic* overtones, if we were now to use a *semantic metaphor* by declaring: The pedal sand form retrodictively *"bespeaks"* or *"betokens"* the incursion event. For not even someone with Ricoeur's semantic penchant would be tempted, in *this* context, to trade on this metaphoric locution so as to assimilate the epistemic status of the trace to the *semantic* one of a *linguistic* sign.

The footprint is *not*, as such, a vehicle of communication: it is not a linguistic sign or symbol; it does *not* semantically stand for, denote, designate, or refer to the past pedal incursion. When a language-user verbalizes the inference of this event, then it is the *utterance* of this retrodiction—*not* the trace licensing it!—which has *semantic* "meaning." Whereas those "symbols" that qualify as linguistic signs do have *intension* (in the semantic sense) and extension (denotation), traces do not. And, as we shall see, what is true of traces also holds for neurotic *symptoms*, even though—when conceptualized psychoanalytically—they can also be called "symbols" in virtue of having the *conatively vicarious* function of affording substitutive gratifications or outlets and the *epistemic* function of attesting to repressed yearnings.

Even though footprints and (mini)neurotic symptoms each license alike the retrodictive inferences to their putative causes, there is, of course, one impressive difference between them: The occurrence of full-fledged or minineurotic symptoms presumably affords *vicarious conative* satisfaction for the repressed, thwarted yearnings to which they attest, whereas no kind of substitutive fulfillment of desire is implicated in the formation of physical traces as such. But this difference is as *unavailing* to Ricoeur's notion of "semantics of desire" as it is obvious. For the conatively *vicarious* status that Freud's theory attributes, for example, to manifest dream content—a minineurotic symptom—hardly bestows the *semantic* function of a linguistic vehicle of communication on such fancied wish-fulfillment. As one might therefore expect, Freud himself contrasted even the rather indefinite "ancient languages and scripts" with manifest dream contents: the former, he tells us, "are always by whatever method and with whatever assistance, meant to be understood. But precisely this characteristic is absent in dreams. A dream does not want to say anything to anyone. It is not a vehicle for communication" (S.E. 1916, 15: 231).

Ironically, Ricoeur adduces none other than dreams as his centerpiece for contriving a semantic role for symptoms by trading on their conatively vicarious nature. As he puts it: "Freud invites us to look to dreams themselves for the various relations between desire and language." In an attempt to buttress this faulty exegesis, Ricoeur makes three claims. (1) "It is not the dream as dreamed that can be interpreted, but rather the text of the [spoken] dream account," a contention which we already found to be insidiously misleading. (2) He misassimilates the *latent* dream content to "another text that could be called the primitive speech of desire," as if repressed wishes were verbal devices of communication. (3) He then concludes, "it is not desires as such that are placed at the center of the [psycho-] analysis, but rather their language" (Ricoeur 1970: 5-6). By such legerdemain, he is able to contrive his notion that the domain of psychoanalytic theory is a veritable "semantics of desire."

That the insinuations of this locution are ill-conceived becomes transparent the moment one takes a concrete case from Freud's conative realm. Thus, when a paranoiac gives verbal or nonverbal expression (e.g., by suspicious glances) to his/her persecutory delusions, this distrustful behavior is good *evidence*, for a partisan of psychoanalysis, that the afflicted person is harboring repressed homosexual longings. But, it is an arrant conceptual conflation to assimilate the vicarious paranoid outcroppings of these unconscious sexual feelings to speech acts that refer semantically to them. More generally, even when symptoms and other derivatives *are actually verbalized*, and even if they are thematically cognate to their unconscious causes, they do not linguistically designate the repressions that engender them, although they do *manifest* them!

Unencumbered by such considerations, Ricoeur construes wish-fulfillment *not* as the achievement of a desired outcome, but rather à la Husserl as the fulfillment of a "signifying intention" (1970: 30). If that were so, then Freud's theory of dreams would become a branch of the theory of descriptive semantics, which deals with natural—as distinct from formalized—languages. Indeed, as Shope (in press) has noted, Ricoeur endorses Lacan's obfuscating view that a symptom is like a language whose speech must be realized, whatever that is. If this characterization were appropriate for neurotic symptoms, why would it not also be applicable to psycho*somatic* and even somatic symptoms?

For example, if a person afflicted by an as yet undiagnosed subdural hematoma has severe headaches, why could one not extrapolate to this somatic symptom Ricoeur's referential account of all neurotic behavior? One might then say that the headaches hint darkly at the patient's intracranial pressure, because they are a kind of indirect language whose hidden reference it is the task of *interpretation* to articulate. Hermeneutically "unenlightened" neurologists refer to such interpretations as "diagnoses," just as physicists who seek a theoretical identification of the particles producing particular cloud chamber tracks, for example, do not see any point in speaking of their activity as "deciphering track texts hermeneutically." For it would be insipid to foist a semantic role on somatic symptoms by calling them "*telltale*," for example, with a view to then seeing them as an indirect language. Yet Ricoeur insists on contriving a linguistic construal for dreams as dreamed: "It must be assumed . . . that dreams in themselves border on language, since they can be told, analyzed, interpreted" (Ricoeur 1970: 15). But all manner of physical occurrences—e.g., solar flares, barometric drops, and the productions by quasars or pulsars—can be, and are, reported, *interpreted*, or analyzed, though not of course *psycho*analyzed.

In any case, it is spurious to assimilate to one another the following two sets of relations: (1) the way in which the effect of a cause *manifests* it and hence can serve *epistemically* as evidence for its operation, and (2) the manner in which a linguistic symbol represents its referent semantically or designates the latter's attributes. To be an effect *E* of a certain cause *C*, so that *E* manifests *C* and is evidence for it, and to be *furthermore* a *conative surrogate*, is plainly quite different from being any kind of linguistic representative: Paranoid *behavior* may well be a *vicarious outlet* for repressed homosexuality, but in no case is it a verbal label for it! Thus, as we saw, etiologically that behavior is the afflicted person's attempt to cope with the anxieties generated by his unconscious sexual urges, *not* his/her attempt to *communicate* these yearnings by means of persecutory delusions and behavior. Yet Ricoeur has left no stone unturned to insinuate the assimilation of epistemic inferability and conative vicariousness, on the one hand, to semantic reference, on the other. And he does so on the unavailing ground that analysts speak of symptoms as "symbols" when they are concerned to convey that symptoms qualify as *conative surrogates* qua compromise formations. Once this logical state of affairs is articulated, the hollowness of Ricoeur's "semantics of desire" becomes apparent.

Robert Shope (1973; in press) has contributed a painstaking textual examination of Freud's several uses of the term "meaning," and of those passages from Freud that Ricoeur adduces to support a semantic construal of symptoms. In a telling rebuttal of that exegesis, Shope successfully controverts a reading according to which "Freud thought that mental phenomena such as dreams have meaning in the manner in which a language or speech signifies something" (1973: 284). The manifest content of a dream "points to" the latent content, Shope rightly avers, *not* by designating it semantically, but "only in the sense in which a clue points toward something" (1973: 285). As illustrations, he mentions (1) rock strata that serve as clues to the past for the geologist, "but not through any intentionality" (p. 302), (2) physical symptoms that indicate the presence of viral disease, and (3) a rise in prices betokening a change in some other economic variable (p. 293). Hence, Shope sums up lucidly:

Freud views the relation between these mental phenomena [dreams, symptoms, or parapraxes] and their meaning as similar to the relation between the symptoms of measles and its cause. They are signs only in the sense that organic symptoms are signs of a diseased organism, or dark clouds signs of rain to come. Symptoms are signs to the investigator, and may arouse his expectations about finding their source, as dark clouds may arouse expectations of rain. If the investigator chooses, he may make these phenomena or representations of them into signs, in Ricoeur's sense, in the investigator's sign language. But to the patient symptoms do not yet designate or intend their underlying sources, any more than the darkness of a cloud designates or intends rain to the cloud or to any person before an observer devises a sign language. Rather, the symptoms of neuroses stand for their psychic sources in the sense of being stand-ins, that is, they appear in consciousness in place of the appearance of their hidden meaning; they are substitutes for it. [p. 294]

And in his more recent paper, Shope put the cogent upshot of his earlier study as follows:

to say something is a stand *in*, i.e., something that occurs because a wish is not consciously admitted, or, in Ricoeur's words, something that occurs in place of "what the desire would say could it speak without restraint" (1970: 15), is not to say that the symptom stands *for* the (content of) the wish in the sense of referring to it. [Shope: in press]

D. Ricoeur's Disposal of "The Question of Proof in Freud's Theory"

We can now conclude our scrutiny of Ricoeur's chapter on "The Question of Proof in Freud's Writings." In its last pages (Ricoeur 1981: 268-273), he develops the import, as he sees it, of his earlier arguments for the answer to the following query: "What sort of verification or falsification are the statements of psychoanalysis capable of?" But, as we saw, he speciously sets the stage for his reply by the following stratagem: (1) He mutilates the purview of the psychoanalytic theoretical corpus by peremptorily deeming it coextensive with "a work of speech with the patient" (1970: 369), thereby excluding even the analysand's nonverbal productions. (2) Having restrained the domain of psychoanalysis by his verbalistic straitjacket, he opines that "there are no 'facts' nor any observation of 'facts' in psychoanalysis but rather the interpretation of a narrated history" (1974: 186). (3) He contrives a pseudodichotomy between psychoanalysis and "academic psychology," after misequating the latter with a crudely conceived behaviorism, and derives a spurious moral from the thesis that "psychoanalysis deals with psychical reality and not with material reality" (1981: 251). (4) He carries out a misassimilation of neurotic symptoms qua compromise-formations to *linguistic* representations of their hypothesized unconscious causes.

No wonder, therefore, that his treatment of the problem of validation of psychoanalytic theory turns into a question-begging parody of what it ought to be, as I shall now illustrate.

(1) He offers nothing toward the validation of the *causal* hypotheses with which, he acknowledges (1981: 262-264, 269-270), Freud's clinical theory is replete! For example, Ricoeur's first criterion of "the validation apt to confirm the truth claim belonging to the domain of psychoanalytic facts" is altogether *self*-validating and stale: "a good psychoanalytic explanation must be coherent with the theory or, if one prefers, it must conform to Freud's psychoanalytic system" (1981: 271).

His evasion of the corroboration of the causal efficacy of analytic treatment furnishes another instance. On the one hand, he tells us that a psychoanalytic explanation offered to the patient "is itself [held to be] a causally relevant factor in the [therapeutic] work—the working through—of analysis" (1981: 263). But, when offering his third criterion of validation for Freudian theory, he remains altogether silent as to how—short of resort to the eschewed methods of the empirical sciences— he proposes to fulfill the following demand: "A good psychoanalytic explanation must...become a therapeutic factor of amelioration.... therapeutic success...constitutes in this way an autonomous criterion of validation" (1981: 272-273).

(2) He offers a naive, if not smug, dismissal of the completely unsolved problem of epistemic contamination by suggestion, which he sees as arising from a "crude" objection:

> I shall leave aside the crude...objection, namely, that the analyst *suggests* to his patient that he accept the interpretation which verifies the theory. I am taking for granted the replies which Freud opposes to this accusation of suggestibility. They are worth what the measures taken at the level of the professional code and the analytic technique itself against the suspicion of suggestion are worth. [1981: 270]

As Part I of this book will show in detail, Freud valiantly, yet unsuccessfully, struggled throughout his life to hold just this epistemic objection at bay, after deeming it "uncommonly interesting" (S.E. 1917, 16: 447). And, as I already remarked vis-à-vis Habermas, Freud himself (ibid.: Lectures 27 and 28) appreciated all too keenly that even if the analyst does his best to forego overt or covert suggestion, there are myriad ways in which he can unconsciously but persuasively mold the analysand's convictions and engender a compliant pseudocorroboration. Hence, it plainly will not do to adduce the analyst's professional integrity and avowed intent not to abuse his suggestive influence, as an adequate safeguard against the elicitation of *spurious confirmations* from the patient.

(3) Ricoeur concludes by invoking the probatively synergistic, cumulative character of his proposed criteria of validation. He does concede that this purported "proof apparatus of psychoanalysis...is...highly problematical." Yet the fact remains that we are left completely in the dark as to how any *one* of his criteria of validation can be met at all within the avowed *confines* of (1) the purely verbal *intra*clinical "facts" countenanced by him as constituting the purview of Freud's theory, and (2) the renunciation of natural science modes of causal validation in favor of purely hermeneutic devices of some sort. Hence, it would seem that, under these restrictions, his criteria are, collectively no less than severally, quite unhelpful.

It emerges that Ricoeur's hermeneutic construal of psychoanalysis is no more cogent than the one offered by Habermas.

4. Are Repressed Motives *Reasons But Not Causes* of Human Thought and Conduct?

Some of the appeal of a hermeneutic construal of psychoanalysis does not derive from the specific arguments given by Ricoeur or Habermas. Instead, this purported reconstruction gains plausibility from assorted cognate theses that pertain to the role of intentionality in human action. As we are told in some quarters, explanation of action by *reasons* is *incompatible* with explanation by *causes* (Gauld and Shotter 1977: 12-13).

Thus, George S. Klein has claimed that Freudian metapsychology and clinical theory "derive from two different philosophies of inquiry and explanation" (1976: 26; also 1-2). And after disparaging the former, Klein commended the clinical theory for its attempt "to state reasons rather than causes" (p. 56; also pp. 12,21). In a similar vein, von Wright has characterized explanations of human action as "making phenomena teleologically intelligible rather than predictable [or explainable] from knowledge of their efficient causes" (von Wright 1977: 8).

We need to bear in mind that the thesis of reasons *versus* causes—hereafter "R *vs*. C"—pertains to the role of reasons in the *explanation* of action, as distinct from their function in either *deliberation* before acting or in *justification* afterward. For, as K. Baier has noted:

In explanation, the word "reason"...is...used to claim that some fact (which is declared to be *the* reason) has actually moved the agent to act as he did....In explanation, it is indeed true that no factor can be *the reason* why the agent did something or can be *the agent's reason for* doing something, unless the agent actually was moved to act in this way by that factor....in deliberation and in justification, [however,] a fact may be said to be a reason for doing something, although the agent was not moved by it to do that thing, or although he knows that he will not be moved by it. [Baier 1958: 149]

In short, explanatory reasons are *motivating* reasons, while other sorts of reasons may well not be motivating. These distinctions are important for psychoanalysis, if only because of their role in Ernest Jones's notion of the defense mechanism of "rationalization." The latter pertains to an agent's construction of a false rationale for what he/she did. In such situations, (1) the desire/belief set avowed by the agent as his motives ("reasons") for what he did are quite *different* from the actually operative, true motives, and (2) the agent offers the false rationale to *justify* his conduct to others, and even to himself, being (unconsciously) aware that his true motives could not legitimate it.

R *vs*. C develops its case by reference to the so-called "practical syllogism," which has the following form: an action *A* is held to be carried out, because the agent aims to achieve a goal *G and* believes that *A* will issue in the attainment of *G*. And, pointing to these stated reasons for doing *A*, R *vs*. C *denies* that an agent's state of having a reason for action (in the *explanatory* sense) can belong to a species of the genus "cause."

Yet, it is perfectly clear that—whether rightly or wrongly—Freud, the determinist, championed just such an inclusion. For he deemed explanatory reasons to be a species of motive, and motives—whether conscious or unconscious—in turn, a species of the genus of cause. Moreover, he *allowed* that some "motives" might not even be mental. Thus, he characterizes the psychoanalyst's quest for "sufficient motives" as a refined implementation of our "innate craving for causality" (S.E. 1910, 11: 38). Indeed, sometimes he speaks *interchangeably* of motives and causes. For example, he hypothesized an obsessive patient's "flight into [psychological] illness" such that the patient's mental *anticipation* of being incapacitated by the illness was actually "the *cause* or *motive* of falling ill [psychologically]" (S.E. 1909, 10: 199, italics in original; in the *German* original [*Gesammelte Werke* 7: 420, London: Imago, 1941], the wording is "die Ursache, das Motiv des Krankenwerdens"). More generally, as Robert Shope has carefully documented exegetically, "Freud does not maintain that dreams, errors, or symptoms are motivated or express motives in an everyday sense" (Shope 1973: 291). Instead, Shope points out (in press, section 2; 1973: 290-292), Freud employs "motive" in a technical sense akin to the *etymological* one: in his parlance, a "motive" is an exciting, instigating cause that *moves* us to action. But nevertheless, Freud does not overlook that ideational causes of human behavior—conscious or repressed—have properties *over and above* those of purely *generic* causes!

In sum, Shope gives several citations (S.E. 1900, 5: 541-542, 560-561, and 4: 81-82) to support the following conclusions:

The sense which Freud gives to the expression "motive for" is indicated by his willingness to speak of the "motive force" behind the dream as the "dream-instigator."...He is concerned...with the sense in which the motor supplies the motive power and force behind the motion. Freud thus finds it natural to speak of wishes as the only things which can "set the apparatus in motion" or "at work" (S.E. 1900, 5: 567, 598). This reference to forces as exciting causes is built into the very meaning of the term "motive" as Freud uses it. [Shope 1973: 292]

It is therefore unavailing for Stephen Toulmin to invoke none other than the psychoanalytic dream theory as support for the following contention: "The kernel of Freud's discovery is the introduction of a technique in which the psycho-therapist begins by studying the *motives for*, rather than the *cause of* neurotic behaviour" (Toulmin 1954: 138; italics in original). To prepare the ground for this dubious exegesis, Toulmin had offered the following purportedly paradigmatic case of causal explanation of human conduct: a person acts in a certain way "because he was given an injection of cocaine twenty minutes ago" by someone else (p. 134). Toulmin contrasts this supposed model of explaining action causally with instances in which *wanting* to go home is offered as the *reason* for some behavior. The issue posed was whether motivational explanations in psychoanalysis qualify as a species of causal explanations. And the intended moral of Toulmin's comparison is that no motivational explanation of an action can qualify as being *causal*.

But, qua paradigm of a causal explanation of conduct, Toulmin's example of the cocaine injection *begs the question* at issue in the present context. For in this illustration, the explanatory physical injection of cocaine *automatically* excludes, at the outset, the agent's conation and ideation—such as desiring and believing—be it conscious or unconscious. Evidently, Toulmin has illicitly traded on the common nontechnical uses of the terms "reason," "motive," and "cause" in ordinary discourse about human behavior. By means of such question-begging reliance on the parlance of daily life, he believes to have established that "The success of psychoanalysis...should re-emphasize the importance of 'reasons for action' as opposed to causes of action'" (p. 139). And, in this way, he believes to have vindicated his initial contention that "troubles arise from thinking of psycho-analysis too much on the analogy of the natural sciences" (p. 134).

The purported hermeneutic reconstruction of psychoanalytic explanations within the framework of the R *vs.* C thesis seems to be predicated on a grievous mistake. Those who regard this reconstruction to be feasible, and indeed illuminating or even vital, have made an *ontologically reductive* physicalistic error as follows: they have unfortunately overlooked that the *causal relevance* of an antecedent state X to an occurrence Y is *not* at all a matter of the *physicality* of X; instead, the causal relevance is a matter of whether X—be it physical, mental, or psycho-physical—MAKES A DIFFERENCE to the occurrence of Y, or AFFECTS THE INCIDENCE of Y. Why, one is driven to ask, is the ontological neutrality of X as between being physical or ideational (conative) not a banality among any and all students of psychoanalysis? If a repression R is, indeed, the psychic pathogen of a neurosis N, then the presence of R is *causally relevant* to the incidence of N in the class of those who harbor R, precisely because it *makes a difference* to becoming afflicted by N. And R is held to affect the incidence of N in the same sense as a bona fide carcinogen affects the somatic incidence of cancer, or as certain psychic dispositions are held by some investigators to affect psychosomatically the incidence of ulcerative colitis. Hence, those who operate under the myth that a cause must be a *physical agency* of one sort or another run afoul of a simple fact: when the motives of agents qualify as causes of their actions, this causal relevance has the same ontological grounds as in the case of physical antecedents that cause, say, astronomical events, i.e., the antecedents *make a difference* to the outcome.

Clearly, if an agent is actually moved to do A by having a certain reason or motive M—so that his having M explains his action A—then this very presence of M made a difference to his having done A. But, in that case, the agent's having M qualified as being *causally relevant* to what he did, *regardless of whether M is conscious or repressed*. And—as will be apparent from later illustrations—especially when the motives are repressed, it is clearly *logically contingent* rather than logically necessary that an ideational motive *does make a difference* to the actual overt behavioral occurrence of an action. Thus, in the case of conscious motives, paraplegics and other sorts of paralytics need no convincing on this score. For, as they know, even when an action is intended, the willing of its performance hardly renders it logically necessary that its successful execution will actually materialize.

To take a pedestrian example of conscious action, consider a person who desires to read a book that he believes to be normally available at some library. If that combination of desire and belief actually prompts him/her to go there to borrow the book, then his reason (motive) *M* for doing so qualifies as explanatory just because *M* makes a difference to going: when the agent neither needs a book nor has any other business at the library, i.e., when he has no motive (reason) for going there, then he indeed refrains from going. Plainly, by affecting the incidence of visits to a library, having a reason that prompts one to go there qualifies as *causally relevant* to making such visits. *Mutatis mutandis*, the same conclusions apply to more sophisticated instances of acting from reasons, e.g., in the case of an agent who, motivated by family bonds, deliberately gives nepotistic preference to a relative in authorizing a promotion. Hence, it emerges that the analysis I have offered does vindicate the view expressed by Robert Holt, who wrote: "For years, I have operated on the assumption that a reason is one kind of cause, a *psychological* cause, and that various types of causes can be handled in the same study without confusion" (Holt 1981: 135). And, in a comprehensive chapter "Recent Work on the Free-Will Problem," Ofstad (1983: 48-49) points out that even when the term "reason" is *not* used to label a causal factor, "the statement that an action was done for a reason does not imply that it was not caused" (p. 49).

In his full-length book on Freud, Ricoeur (1970: 359-360) endorses Toulmin's claim that psychoanalytic explanations are *not* causal, just *in virtue* of being motivational. As Ricoeur saw it then, in psychoanalysis "an explanation through motives is irreducible to an explanation through causes. . . . a motive and a cause are completely different," instead of the former being a species of the latter. Hence, one must welcome that, under the influence of Michael Sherwood (1969), Ricoeur did have second thoughts in his later work (1981: 262-263) and, commendably enough, repudiated the ordinary language approach to Freudian explanations along with the "dichotomy between motive and cause."

Some proponents of R *vs*. C (e.g., R. Schafer 1976: 204-205, and Gauld and Shotter 1977: 9-10) have secured spurious plausibility for their tenets by ignoring that—in psychology, no less than in physics and somatic medicine—*causal relevance* is a less demanding, logically weaker relation than either being causally sufficient or being causally necessary. In medicine, for example, there is evidence that heavy tobacco smoking is indeed causally relevant to cardiovascular disease and to lung cancer. But it is a commonplace that such smoking is neither causally necessary nor causally sufficient for acquiring these illnesses. Familiar as these facts are, Roy Schafer tries to make philosophical capital out of taking no cognizance of the properties of causal relevance as such. For he claims falsely that every cause is even *both* necessary *and* sufficient for the occurrence of the outcome to which it is causally relevant. And he notes that, in the psychoanalytic explanation of a case of male impotence on the basis of castration anxiety, the adduced motives ("reasons") neither *assure* the occurrence of the impotence they serve to explain, nor are they *required* for its occurrence. Having used a false premise, he is then able to conclude that unconscious "reasons" cannot belong to the genus of "cause." Thus, as Schafer would have it:

we rely on reasons—reasons that are, in essence, redescriptions that make actions comprehensible. We do not rely on causes—causes that are the conditions regularly antecedent to the actions in question. Causes are the conditions in the absence of which the specific action would not be performed and in the presence of which it must be performed. [Schafer: 204-205]

But as Freud explained in 1896 (S.E. 1896, 3: 209), the tubercle bacillus is not disqualified from being the specific cause of tuberculosis merely because many carriers of this bacillus do not develop this disease. And Freud made just this point in order to *disabuse* people of the notion that infantile seduction episodes cannot be the specific causes of adult hysteria merely because many people have had such childhood experiences *without* becoming hysterics.

Moreover, in their *Studies on Hysteria*, Breuer (S.E. 1895, 2: 212) and Freud (S.E. 1893-1895, 2: 173, 263, 287-288, 290) introduced the so-called principle of causal "overdetermination" (see also Freud S.E. 1895, 3: 131; 1896, 3: 216; 1905, 7: 60) which Freud also called much more lucidly *"the principle of the complication of causes"* (S.E. 1901, 6: 60-61; italics in original). According to this principle, clinical phenomena are normally attributable to a conjunction and/or temporal succession of causes, *each* of which is only a *partial* cause, precisely because—*at best*—these causally relevant factors are only *jointly* rather than singly causally sufficient for the production of the given clinical phenomenon. I submit that Schafer's account is simply oblivious of this fundamental principle of causal explanation in the psychoanalytic clinical theory. For, as we saw, he maintains that this theory lends support to his R *vs.* C thesis. And one of his key grounds for claiming that a motive cannot qualify as a cause of behavior, but only a "reason", is that a motive is typically not *sufficient* for the occurrence of the ensuing action.

More generally, one must wonder—within Schafer's scheme of causality—in what current theories of the natural sciences his notion does have a bona fide use. Surely not in statistical physics, such as the theory of radioactive decay, or in somatic medicine. In the former branch of the natural sciences, the causally relevant antecedents featured in its explanations are surely *not* both sufficient and necessary for the occurrences they explain, as demanded by Schafer's depiction of causation. In medicine, syphilis is causally necessary for paresis but hardly sufficient, since only a minority of syphilitics become victims of paresis. Seemingly unaware that his largely quixotic requirements for causality go unfulfilled in the theories and applications of the contemporary natural sciences, Schafer invokes these requirements to claim that Freudian theory is *barred* from using the concept of causality "in any rigorous and untrivial sense" (1976: 205).

Moreover, believing that he is administering the coup de grâce to the idea of motivational causation, Schafer commits the inveterate reductive error that I have been at pains to exorcise. For he claims that only antecedent events in the external or *meta*psychological worlds, but *not* our *ideational representations* of such antecedents nor our ensuing motives, can play a causal role worthy of the name. Once this mistaken premise is granted, Schafer infers that since motives are "features" of an agent's "personal world of meaning and goals," they "can exist only as the agent's reasons," to the exclusion of also being causes (1976: 205). Apparently, like so many others, Schafer has relied on a mythological conception of the natural sciences to erect a pseudo-contrast between them and psychoanalysis.

Regrettably, Gauld and Shotter's entire hermeneutic case is vitiated by at least the following notions: (1) The same simplistic construal of the causal relation as Schafer's, (2) the straw man that the ontology of stimulus-response behaviorism is paradigmatic for any psychological theory of human action that aspires to meet scientific standards, and hence (3) the myth that the explanatory standards of the natural sciences are intrinsically comitted to a physicalistic reductionism such that psychic states (e.g., intentions, fears, hopes, beliefs, desires, anticipations, etc.) are held to be, at best, epiphenomena, having no causal relevance of their own.

The practical syllogism as such can be coherently applied, at least to consciously motivated action or behavior, by those who deem motives to be a species of cause (e.g., Michael Moore 1983), no less than by proponents of R *vs*. C. Yet, the doctrine put forward by R *vs*. C takes as its point of departure the explanatory applicability of the practical syllogism to any behavior that is to be explained by "reasons," i.e., by a desire/belief set. Hence, the attempt to reconstruct psychoanalytic explanations of conduct hermeneutically *within* the framework of R *vs*. C—as exemplified by the British school of ordinary language analysis—is basically undercut if important classes of psychoanalytic explanations simply defy assimilation to the practical syllogism. Let me give some of the grounds for claiming just such intractability, although we saw earlier that R *vs.* C was invalidated, without any recourse to such refractoriness, by an account of causal relevance.

The aforementioned etiology of paranoia provides a telling counterexample to the presumed applicability of the practical syllogism. As we recall from my proposal for an epidemiologic test of that etiology, it postulates that *repressed* homosexual love is *causally necessary* for being afflicted by paranoid delusions (S.E. 1915, 14: 265-266). This very postulate itself is, of course, incompatible with the R *vs.* C claim that neither unconscious nor conscious motives can be a species of cause. But I am now concerned to show that the explanatory role of repressed ideation in Freud's etiology of paranoia is *refractory* to the practical syllogism.

Freud postulates a kind of *causal microstructure as mediating* between the hypothesized repressed homosexuality and the engendered paranoid delusions (S.E. 1911, 12: 63). As we shall have occasion to note in another context (chapter 1, section B), the mediating causal dynamics operates as follows: Given the social taboo on male homosexuality, the failure to repress homosexual impulses may well issue in feelings of severe anxiety and guilt. And this anxiety could then be eliminated by converting the love emotion "I love him" into its opposite "I hate him," a type of transformation that Freud labeled "reaction formation." Thus, the pattern of reaction-formation is that once a dangerous impulse has been largely repressed, it surfaces in the guise of a far more acceptable *contrary* feeling, a conversion which therefore serves as a *defense* against the *anxiety* associated with the underlying dangerous impulse. When the defense of reaction-formation proves insufficient to alleviate the anxiety, however, the afflicted party may resort to the further defensive maneuver of "projection" in which "I hate him" is converted into "He hates me." This final stage of the employment of defenses is then the full-blown paranoia. Thus, this rather epigrammatic formulation depicts reaction-formation and projection as the repressed defense mechanisms that are actuated by the postulated specific pathogen of paranoia.

Hence, the question is: In the psychoanalytic explanation of a paranoiac's delusional conduct, can the afflicted agent be warrantedly held to have "reasons" for his/her behavior such that he/she unconsciously believes it to be a means of attaining the fulfillment of his/her homosexual longings? Can the paranoiac be warrantedly said to have unconsciously *intended* his delusional persecutory thoughts and comportment to accomplish his erotic objectives?

Just for argument's sake, postulate the existence of clinical evidence such that the paranoid agent could be held to regard his persecutory thoughts unconsciously as a means of coping with his homosexually engendered anxiety. And suppose further that this belief was unencumbered by the realization that this anxiety-reduction is purchased at the cost of generating other anxieties by the negative responses of those who are victimized by his ill-founded suspicions. Even then, such a putative unconscious belief would hardly be tantamount to the quite different belief that these suspicions conduce to the realization of his homosexual goals.

Indeed, as Shope has argued in detail (1970; 1973: 290-292), Freud does *not* regard psychopathological symptoms, slips (parapraxes), and manifest dream contents as forms of *intentional actions*. Yet, quite compatibly, he did hypothesize the *causes* of these phenomena to be repressed "intentions," and hence took symptoms, etc. to attest to the presence of unconscious strivings. Moreover, as Shope documents further, "It is extremely difficult, in fact, to find an analyst who reports that a patient recalls not just the presence of an unconscious wish or intention but an intentional or voluntary connection it had with a symptom or error" (Shope 1973: 292-293, n. 11)! Finally, Shope (1973: 290 n.9) calls attention to the fact that, whereas Freud's German original speaks of the intention *in whose service* ("in deren Dienst") an obsessive woman behaved compulsively, the *Standard Edition* renders this in English as "the intention with which she was performing the obsessional action" (S.E. 1917, 16: 277). In this way, the English rendition *obscures* the fact that Freud "usually refuses to say that the person intended the act to accomplish the suppressed or repressed intention," though he claims, of course, that the intention *produces* the action.

Thus, take Freud's aforementioned report of the memory-slip of forgetting the Latin word *aliquis*, which he attributed to the subject's repressed pregnancy fear (see chapter 4 for details). This well-known case fails to conform to the practical syllogism. For there is not a shred of evidence that the male subject underwent his memory lapse in the unconscious belief—however foolish—of thereby realizing his desire (hope) that his paramour is *not* pregnant. Therefore, the proponent of R *vs.* C has no basis for claiming that the subject unconsciously *intended* his own mnemonic failure as a means of achieving the much desired freedom from pregnancy, even if his desire itself is deemed to qualify as an "intention." As Morris Eagle (1980: 368-369) has stressed, there is a major gap between a mere wish and a plan to realize it. But without a plan, the agent's conduct cannot be held to have been envisaged by him as a means to the fulfillment of his wishes. Nor, as Eagle points out further (p. 371), can the stated gap be bridged by Roy Schafer's purely *verbal* device of *calling* such conduct "disclaimed actions." Such semantic baptism does nothing toward assimilating Freud's motivational explanations to those in which the motives qualify as "reasons for action" in the sense of the practical syllogism. In short, there was no unconsciously planned action, based on a belief in a means-ends connection. And without it, Freud's example cannot be held to instantiate the practical syllogism.

Robert Shope (1973: 301) usefully calls attention to another illustration of the poignant absence of evidence for the operation of an unconscious belief in a means-ends connection: Lacking this sort of evidence, Freud effectively disavowed the role of such a belief in favor of a mere *"mechanism"* of *hysterical conversion*. For, in his case history of Elizabeth von R., he hypothesizes that "in place of the mental pains which she avoided, [hysterical] physical pains made their appearance." The patient's "motive was that of defence," an escape from an intolerable mental condition, whereas "the mechanism was that of conversion." Significantly, Freud *disavows* any role of *intended*, voluntary action in the operation of conversion:

I cannot, I must confess, give any hint of how a conversion of this kind is brought about. It is obviously not carried out in the same way as an intentional and voluntary action. It is a process which occurs under the pressure of the motive of defence. [S.E. 1895, 2: 166]

Furthermore, it would be an error of moment to invoke Freud's likening of repressed mental states to conscious ones in an endeavor to assimilate psychoanalytic explanations to the practical syllogism after all. He did tell us that

latent [repressed] states of mental life...with the help of a certain amount of work [free association]...can be transformed into, or replaced by, conscious mental processes.

And, furthermore, he declared that

all the categories which we employ to describe conscious mental acts, such as ideas, purposes, resolutions and so on, can be applied to them. Indeed, we are obliged to say of some of these latent states that the only respect in which they differ from conscious ones is precisely in the absence of consciousness. [S.E. 1915, 14: 168]

Yet it would be a major error to take this avowal as license for the assimilation of a typical psychoanalytic explanation to the practical syllogism. Relying on Freud's likening of repressed mentation to conscious ideation here, this assimilation would take the following *subjunctive* form: If the agent who harbors certain repressed aims (desires, goals, or "intentions") *were* made conscious of them, then he/she would *believe* his/her neurotic conduct to be a means to their fulfillment *and* would engage in that maladaptive conduct. For example, on this construal of the psychoanalytic explanation of paranoid comportment, the attribution of such thought and behavior to repressed homosexual impulses would be held to license a subjunctive conditional as follows: If the homosexual feelings *were* conscious, they would combine with an instance of the stated putative means-ends belief to yield *motivating reasons* for the agent's paranoia, just as is required by the practical syllogism.

But, to the detriment of R *vs.* C, this envisaged attempt to vindicate the psychoanalytic applicability of the practical syllogism boomerangs altogether, because Freud's theory *denies* the subjunctive conditional that was called to the rescue. For its repression-etiology makes the repressed state of the homosexual aims causally *necessary* for the agent's delusional persecutory affliction. Thus, far from assuring that the transformation of these erotic desires into conscious ones would provide the agent with a motivating rationale for the continuation of his/her pathological behavior, psychoanalytic theory teaches that such lifting of the sexual repression would *dissipate* the disorder. Besides, according to Freud's etiology, the homosexual impulses—even while still repressed—were only causally necessary rather than sufficient for the paranoia. True, Freud would countenance speaking of these erotic desires as "intentions" even in their repressed state. All the same, we see that *this* assimilation of latent mental states to conscious ones *compatibly forbids*—rather than licenses—the corresponding subjunctive assimilation of his explanation of paranoid conduct to the practical syllogism.

Thus, the advocate of R *vs.* C has failed anew to show that the paranoiac *intended* his/her deluded conduct as a means to the fulfillment of his/her sexual yearnings ("intentions")! No amount of vague general talk about "the meaning" or "directional aims" (Klein 1976: 39) of the paranoiac's behavior should be allowed to gloss over this failure. For "the meaning" of this pathological conduct that is disclosed by psychoanalysis in this context is simply the repressed homosexuality, which is hypothesized to be the relevant pathogen. And such "intentionality" as inheres in that "meaning" has turned out to be quite insufficient for making the engendered deluded behavior into a voluntary action, *intended by* the agent as a means to his/ her erotic objective. Yet, unless the agent's conduct is thus intended, its psychoanalytic explanation is devoid of the motivating reasons essential to R *vs.* C.

It emerges that, in psychoanalysis, the notion of *intentionality* appropriate to the explanation of premeditated actions—intended because of the agent's belief in their conduciveness to his goals—typically applies at best in *only a Pickwickian or metaphorical sense*, if at all. Unconsciously, the agent is conatively *intent* upon a certain desideratum, but he is hardly intent upon the behavior that is causally engendered by this yearning *as an action toward that desideratum*. There even are *consciously* caused actions whose explanation spells a salutary *caveat* with a like moral. Michael Moore has given an illuminating example to make this point:

Suppose X is a prisoner who wants very much to get out of prison. He rattles the bars of his cell "because he wants out." His rattling the cage is an action he performs, and his desire causes it; yet he doesn't rattle the bars *in order* to get out because he does not believe for an instant that he can shake loose the bars. [Moore 1980: 497; 1983: 35]

Thus, X *expresses* his desire for freedom by rattling the cell bars. But— given X's lack of the pertinent belief—*this* desire does not qualify as his "reason for" his action in the sense of the practical syllogism, although a secondary *desire-to-express* the first desire may so qualify.

In a last ditch effort, the champion of R *vs*. C might try to fall back on the thesis that the connection between motivating reasons and actions is logically necessary rather than logically contingent, regardless of whether the motives are conscious or repressed. If this tenet could be sustained in the context of psychoanalytic explanations, it would indeed gainsay the causal role of repressed motives to the benefit of R *vs*. C. For if the connection between such motives and the conduct explained by them is to be causal, it must be logically *contingent*. But, as I have already animadverted above, the thesis is hardly convincing even when applied to consciously motivated action (see Sellars 1973 for a detailed defense of this conclusion). Moreover, its application to psychoanalytic explanations of conduct is demonstrably unsound.

For consider our earlier example of the micro- and macrostructure of Freud's etiology of paranoia. Is it not clear that the hypothesized transformation of reaction-formation—in which "I love him" is supplanted by "I hate him"—is no less logically contingent than, say, Newton's inverse square law of gravitation? Since Freud did not even claim universality for such reaction-formation on the part of the homosexually repressed, how could that transformation of affect be deemed logically necessary? The universality he did claim was the *converse* one that every paranoiac had undergone reaction-formation to his/her repressed motives. Equally plainly, the further transformation of projection, in which "I hate him" is superseded by "He hates me" is logically contingent. *A fortiori*, it would be *absurd* to claim that the contingently mediated connection between the repressed homosexuality and the paranoiac's delusional behavior is logically necessary: Evidently, that linkage is fully as logically contingent as the fact that there is conservation of linear momentum, a connection exemplified by the motions of two colliding billiard balls. The same conclusion is reached upon considering further cases, such as other examples of Freudian reaction-formation like the following: "an exaggerated sympathy can be a defense against an impulse to cruelty" (Wallerstein 1976: 220). Hence, the hermeneutic advocate of R *vs*. C. cannot salvage his doctrine by claiming a logically necessary connection between Freudian motives and the conduct they are supposed to explain.

Nonetheless, just for argument's sake, let us suppose that the psychoanalytic explanations furnished by Freud's *clinical* theory could be well reconstructed hermeneutically within the framework of R *vs*. C. Even then, this would not be enough to sustain the hermeneutic construal of the psychoanalytic enterprise. For the adequacy of this approach hinges on whether the clinical theory is explanatorily *autonomous*. And such autonomy turns on the ability of the clinical theory to give an account of the "provenance and aetiology" of the agent's "reasons" for his actions (Eagle 1980: 341) *without* recourse to causes of a sort not invoked in the clinical theory. Yet significantly, B. B. Rubinstein (1976) and Morris Eagle (1980: 331, 333, 341-342, 344, 346, 356-357) have argued cogently that the clinical theory indeed fails to be explanatorily autonomous in just this way. True, Freud's own metapsychology was egregiously and multiply flawed (Holt 1976). Nonetheless, its animating quest for needed explanations going beyond those provided by the clinical theory is hardly discredited by its own notorious miscarriage (Holt, 1981). Hence, it is unfortunate that such analysts as George Klein, Roy Schafer, and even Merton Gill, as distinct from his co-author Pribram (Pribram and Gill 1976), have so overreacted to their legitimate dissatisfactions with the metapsychology as to eschew—or at least despair of—widened explanatory objectives that inspired its vision. Resigned encapsulation within the explanatory horizons of the clinical theory—by making it the be-all and end-all of psychoanalysis—forecloses the wider vision for which the phenomena do cry out (Holt, 1982).

In the conclusion of his illuminating essay on "Freud's Early Theories of Hysteria," the noted psychoanalyst Benjamin B. Rubinstein has tellingly and succinctly put the limitations of the clinical theory vis-à-vis the metapsychology into just the sobering perspective relevant here:

The theory of hysteria is not all of psychoanalysis. But it epitomizes a number of the problems that beset this discipline.... Critical psychoanalysts are in the habit of blaming Freud's metapsychology for all the difficulties inherent in the theory. Metapsychology, however, presents a comparatively minor problem. Although we may be far from a solution, it need not disturb us once we recognize its proper function which is to remind us of the fact that mind cannot exist without a body and that, accordingly, the mental operations that interest psychoanalysis can also be viewed as physiological processes and sometimes, for proper understanding, have to be viewed that way.

It is the clinical part of psychoanalysis that is really disturbing. It is top-heavy with theory but has only a slim evidential base. [Rubinstein 1983: 187]

Since hermeneuticians have often pointed to Freud's theory of dreams as the centerpiece of their case, it is particularly instructive that this part of Freud's edifice does not bear out their contention at all. We have already noted Shope's documentation that generally Freud himself did not regard manifest dream contents as forms of intended action, any more than he viewed symptoms or slips as such action, although he spoke of their presumed *causes* as "intentions." But, quite apart from Freud's own explicit views, Michael Moore (1980; 1983) has perceptively argued in detail that, on Freud's evidence, the dreaming of manifest dream contents simply does not pass muster as an intended action. For it turns out that, despite the linguistic regalia of "intention" in which he clothed his explanations of various dreams, conceptual examination of these explanations reveals that "dreams are not productions we stage for [unconscious] reasons, but are events caused by wishes" (Moore 1980: 538; 1983: 64)

Among the array of grounds given by Moore for this conclusion, the following two deserve special mention:

(1) In the case of Freud's "Irma Injection Dream," a specimen dream discussed in depth below in chapter 5:

Freud did not actively bring about the dream of Irma's injection.... His dream happened to him in the same way that the death of his father happened to him— in neither case did he bring about the occurrence (which is not to deny, in either case, that he might have had some wishes related to each event). Dreaming is like nondirectional thinking—sudden inspiration, revelation, or images and the like— in that it just happens without the will or agency of the subject. [1983: 49-50]

(2) The minor premise of the practical syllogism, asserting the agent's conscious *or unconscious* belief that his ensuing conduct is a means to his goal, does not apply when wishes are *fantasized* as fulfilled in a dream:

There are no *beliefs* by the dreamer that his "action" of dreaming would be a means to achieving the object of his wish.... Freud reports no memory of such a belief, either as part of his dream or as part of his waking belief set. Nor is free association said to produce a memory of such a belief. Yet without such a belief, a crucial element of practical reasoning is missing which leads one to conclude that the "action" is not to be understood on the model of practical reasoning... at all. [1980: 523; 1983: 53-54]

More generally:

> For almost all other specimens of dreams which Freud analyzes, no...belief about the dream being a means to the actual attainment of the object of desire can be made out. [1980: 524; 1983: 54]

And the invention of such a rationale would fail to be explanatory by being a matter of "rationalization without causation" (1980: 492-495; 1983: 32-34).

In the same vein, Morris Eagle has lucidly issued a clarifying animadversion:

> The assumption is that because dreams appear personally meaningful and appear to reflect our innermost preoccupations, concerns, and desires, they are motivated [by reasons for having dreamt, in the sense of the practical syllogism]. But the fact that dream contents are made up of our most pressing preoccupations and desires (and let us assume that they are) does not mean that we *wanted* to dream these contents or that these contents were dreamt in order to fulfill certain desires and wishes. It could simply mean that pressing preoccupations and desires continue to influence thought (or perhaps even especially influence thought) in the dream state. . . . Dreams are not the carrying out of intentions and aims. Rather, they are happenings which *reflect* intentions and aims. [Eagle 1980: 363-364]

5. Critique of George S. Klein's Version of Hermeneutic Psychoanalysis.

It remains to examine George Klein's version of hermeneutics more systematically than above. Yet an exegetical *caveat* is in order, because Klein's sudden death prevented him from putting his *Psychoanalytic Theory* (1976) into finished form. Instead, this book owes its posthumous publication to the editorial labors of Merton Gill and Leo Goldberger. Hence, had he lived, Klein might well have revised some of the formulations that form the basis of my critique. It therefore should be borne in mind that my attributions to him are subject to this qualification.

George Klein's philosophy of psychoanalysis starkly exhibits several of the key defects of the hermeneutic construal that I have been at pains to set forth. This is not surprising, for the moral he drew from the differences between the metapsychology and the clinical theory was avowedly indebted (Klein 1976: 26) to Ricoeur, as well as to the sort of ordinary language philosophy exemplified by Toulmin's notion of psychoanalysis.

It is now germane to recall, from the opening pages of this chapter, my objections there to the exegesis of Freud on which Habermas and Ricoeur rested the charge of "scientific self-misunderstanding" against him. There I documented from the mature Freud—as distinct from the pre-1897 young Freud—that the following contrary reading is exegetically faithful:

(1) The mature Freud termed the clinical theory of repression "the cornerstone on which the whole structure of psychoanalysis rests. It is the most essential part of it" (S.E. 1914, 14: 16). To boot, he explicitly deemed the metapsychology *epistemologically expendable* as compared to the clinical theory.

(2) After the demise of his 1895 "Project," Freud's criterion of scientificity was avowedly *methodological* or *epistemic* and *not* ontologically reductive. And having stressed that the clinical theory "lies closer to actual experience" with patients than the "speculative [metapsychological] superstructure" (S.E. 1925, 20: 32-33), he claimed natural science status first and foremost for his evolving clinical theory of personality and therapy. Yet, he did not disparage, let alone disclaim, the metapsychology scientifically. Thus, Robert Holt spoke not only for himself but also, I submit, for the mature Freud, when he aptly declared: "science is defined by its methods, not its subject matter" (Holt 1981: 133).

(3) Whatever his long-term hopes for a partial reduction of the clinical theory to the metapsychology, the mature Freud surely did *not* regard the latter as *primordially scientific* vis-à-vis the former. By the same token, after 1896, he hardly considered the scientificity of the clinical theory to be *parasitic* on its would-be reduction to metapsychological hypotheses.

(4) Hence, far from seeing the scientificity of his avowed clinical cornerstone as trickling down, so to speak, from the acknowledged speculative superstructure, he saw the clinical theory as authenticated scientifically from the bottom up, as it were, by the cumulative evidence garnered in his office and from his self-analysis.

Yet, as we saw, unencumbered by the contrary textual evidence, Habermas contrived the exegetical myth that the mature Freud had deemed the metapsychology primordially scientific on ontological grounds, as a presumed lifelong relic from the heady 1895 days of the "Project." And furthermore, under the long-term influence of the teachings of Helmholtz, Meynert, and Brücke, the mature Freud allegedly had *predicated* the scientific status of the clinical theory on its would-be reduction to the metapsychology. Having gone this far in mythmaking, Habermas maintained that the envisioned reduction is a sham, so that Freud's attribution of scientificity to the clinical theory is a *misextrapolation* from the primordially scientific metapsychology. Freud is then given the supposed philosophical *coup de grâce*: He is indicted as having scientistically misunderstood his own clinical theory.

Klein (1976: 42-43, 46) espoused much of this independently, or echoed it from Ricoeur. Indeed, along with a number of others, Klein (pp.

2, 28-29, 42-49) apparently succumbed to a reductive error that is as inveterate as it is dreary: the thesis that the scientific status of a theory in any domain of phenomena turns on its *ontological reduction* to the *physicalistic* entities of the received natural sciences. Thus, in the case of psychoanalysis, he concluded that it could lay claim to natural science status only on the strength of being ontologically reduced to the *non*mentalistic hypotheses of neurology and physiology, if not to physics. And this mistaken notion then led Klein to the following incorrect supposition: Since Freud perennially claimed scientific status for his enterprise, even the mature Freud aspired to such a physicalistic reduction *in order to vindicate* just this avowal of scientificity (pp. 42-46). Oddly enough, Klein seems to have been unaware that Freud had long since repudiated his early reductively ontological hallmark of scientificity in favor of an epistemic or methodological one.

Thus, Klein (pp. 43,46) would have us believe that Freud demeaned *as unscientific* any explanations based on the concepts of his own clinical theory! Indeed, amazingly, Klein saddles Freud's "philosophy of science" not only with the scientific denigration of the clinical theory, but with the aspiration to achieve its explanatory supplantation and ultimate extinction by purging the psychoanalytic edifice of all of its conative ("purposive") categories. As Klein would have it:

Freud's philosophy assumed: (1) that concepts of purposefulness and meaning are unacceptable as terms of *scientific* explanation; (2) that an acceptable *explanation* must be purged of teleological implications; (3) that regularities described with purposivistic concepts will ultimately be explainable through the use of purely psychological models, which disclose the causes of which the purposive principle is simply a descriptive expression.
...Freud was brought up in the by now well-documented tradition of the Brücke-Meynert scientific value system, which held it as axiomatic that no phenomenon was to be considered "explained" except in physical-chemical terms, "neurophysiological" being within this classification....There is little reason to believe that Freud disputed this. [pp. 43-44]

And, speaking of "contemporary psychoanalysts" (p. 45), Klein complains:

They do not, I believe, sufficiently realize the extent to which Freud's philosophy of science, which motivated the "Project," persisted throughout his lifetime, the extent to which it determined what we call metapsychology, and the fact that the economic point of view is simply a veiled extension of the physiologizing effort. [p. 46]

But ironically, in addition to the textual evidence I have already adduced, one of Freud's 1915 papers on metapsychology, for example, makes it unambiguous that he had outgrown the reductive philosophy which had animated his early "Project." For, in his paper on "The Unconscious" he tells us:

It is clear in any case that this question—whether the latent states of mental life, whose existence is undeniable, are to be conceived of as conscious mental states or as physical ones—threatens to resolve itself into a verbal dispute. We shall therefore be better advised to focus our attention on what we know with certainty of the nature of these debatable states. As far as their physical characteristics are concerned, they are totally inaccessible to us: no physiological concept or chemical process can give us any notion of their nature. On the other hand, we know for certain that they have abundant points of contact with conscious mental processes; with the help of a certain amount of work they can be transformed into, or replaced by, conscious mental processes, and all the categories which we employ to describe conscious mental acts, such as ideas, purposes, resolutions and so on, can be applied to them. Indeed, we are obliged to say of some of these latent states that the only respect in which they differ from conscious ones is precisely in the absence of consciousness. Thus we shall not hesitate to treat them as objects of psychological research, and to deal with them in the most intimate connection with conscious mental acts. [S.E. 1915, 14: 168]

One can only surmise that the actual inspiration for Klein's portentous misreading of the mature Freud's philosophy of science is not to be sought in the writings of the founding father. Instead, the impetus seems to have derived from the ideological stresses within the psychoanalytic community of Klein's time, occasioned by the idolatrous insistence on the probity of the extant metapsychology in some of these quarters. This motivational conjecture insinuates itself from his complaint against the explanatory downgrading of clinical concepts at the hands of many of his analytic colleagues. As he declared ruefully.

Yet, as analysts came to formulate their ideas systematically, they abandoned this [clinical] level and assumed the aims and mannerisms of natural scientists talking about energies, forces, cathexes, systems, layers, mechanisms, and physical analogies, rather than meanings. [1976: 42-43]

The myth that Freud perennially disparaged the clinical theory explanatorily vis-à-vis the metapsychology is of-a-piece with the previously exposed blunder that the relation of *causal relevance* is inherently physicalistic, a notion apparently shared by Klein (1976: 26-29). That Freud constructively envisioned the biochemical *enlargement* of the clinical theory rather than the latter's physico-chemical replacement is attested by the *conjoint* role he assigned to clinical and presumably biophysical factors in the etiology of the neuroses. Thus, he held (S.E.

1896, 3: 210; also 191, 201) that traumatic experiences were causally necessary rather than sufficient as pathogens. For he thought he had reason to believe that within the class of those who had psychologically suffered such pathogenic experiences, antecedent hereditary vulnerability determines which individual does become neurotic and which one does not. And he allowed or conjectured presciently that hereditary vulnerability may well be a matter of biochemical attributes. This important feature of the psychoanalytic theory of neurosogenesis strongly militates in favor of the tenet, espoused above, that the clinical theory ought not to be deemed explanatorily autonomous.

Klein's flawed reading of Freud is not confined to philosophical matters, but extends to his account of Freud's developmental hypotheses, which include the etiologies of the neuroses. For, as early as 1895 (S.E. 1895, 3: 136), Freud introduced the notion of the "specific" etiology of a particular nosologic entity N (e.g., obsessional neurosis, anxiety neurosis). And one of the defining characteristics of the specific pathogen P of a given N is that P is causally *"necessary"* for the genesis of N, a feature it shares with the so-called etiologic *"preconditions"* (S.E. 1895, 3: 136). Hence, in all of the specific etiologies, Freud claimed that the genesis of N had to have been *invariably preceded* by the presence of P. Yet Klein writes: "In the clinical theory the genetic point of view refers to the fact that aims [the subject's dispositions] have a history, not in the sense of trying to specify invariable and unconditional antecedents, but in the sense of specifying an inner logic of development" (Klein 1976: 29-30). Whatever "an inner logic of development" may be, all of the specific etiologies—such as the homosexual etiology of paranoia, or the seduction theory of hysteria—did "specify invariable...antecedents." For they all licensed the universal retrodictive inference of P from N.

Klein lodges additional philosophical reproaches against Freud. Regrettably, he saw fit (pp. 43 and 45) to denominate Freud a lifelong "positivist," a bugaboo word in his vocabulary. But, like Habermas, he never documented the appropriateness of applying this *technically preempted* philosophic term to the mature Freud in either its Comtean or Machian senses. Klein thought that Freud deserves the intended censorious overtones because of yet another objectionable long-term tenet that Klein had foisted on him: the view that the clinical theory is a mere temporary expedient, a heuristic way-station en route to a metapsychology that will render all motivational explanations superfluous by reducing the clinical theory to genuinely scientific categories (Klein 1976: 46-49). Having thus supposed that Freud perennially debased the clinical theory as a merely protoscientific crutch, Klein felt entitled to declare:

Freud's philosophy of science implies a stand on the mind-body problem: that mentalistic concepts are temporary expedients, to be ultimately reduced to the terms of physiological mechanism. For Freud, teleology was anathema. He felt that descriptive concepts formulated in terms of purpose had no status as explanations of behavior. [p. 46]

On this depiction, the mature Freud is alleged to have held that if the clinical theory *B* is actually reduced—in a sense that, alas, Klein leaves quite vague—to a scientifically respectable physicalist theory *A*, then *B* thereby *forfeits* any explanatory and/or scientific merit it may have initially possessed. But, to my knowledge, neither Klein nor the hermeneuticians who influenced him have produced any *cogent* textual evidence that there was any time at all after 1896 when Freud held that view, let alone that his theoretical work was permanently animated by it. For example, such a reading derives no support from Freud's statement that "all our provisional ideas in psychology will presumably some day be based on an organic substructure." (S.E. 1914, 14:78). For he illustrates such an anchorage by a state of affairs in which "the sexual function differs from other bodily processes in virtue of a special chemistry" (S.E. 1914, 14: 125). Nay, the ungenerous nature of the latter reading becomes apparent upon applying the reasoning that Klein imputes to Freud, mutatis mutandis, to some cases in the history of physics.

Consider, for example, the approximative probabilistic reduction of classical thermodynamics—with its concepts of temperature, quantity of heat, pressure, etc.—to the statistical mechanics of the constituent particles of thermodynamic systems. What physicist would say that this sort of explanatory subsumption of thermodynamic theory under statistical mechanics robbed the former of its explanatory value in its circumscribed macroscopic domain, thereby rendering it scientifically altogether superfluous? Surely classical thermodynamics did not become scientifically defunct because of the explanatory virtues of the statistical microtheory that turned out to undergird it as a probabilistic approximation. Instead of redounding to the explanatory oblivion of macrothermodynamics, the merits of the microtheory served to limit but hardly abolish the scientific license and explanatory purview of the reduced macrotheory. Again, the derivation of Kepler's laws of planetary motion as specified approximations from Newton's laws of motion and gravitation hardly issued in the explanatory sterilization or the utter scientific banishment of Kepler's theory. Nor yet would Newton have regarded his inverse square law of gravitation as having been rendered explanatorily otiose if he had succeeded in finding "the cause" of such gravitation. Why then suppose with Klein that the mature Freud actually aimed the metapsychological and/or biophysical enlargement of the clinical theory at its total explanatory extinction? No such considerations gave Klein pause when he reiterated: "Bear in mind that Freud needed to escape teleological [conative] explanation" (1976: 48), since Brücke-Meynert physico-chemical reductionism purportedly held lifelong sway over him. And furthermore: "Thus, metapsychology was...an expression of his philosophy of science.... It is simply a philosophical stance regarding what is true explanation and what is really 'real'" (p. 49).

Indeed, as we recall, Klein (1976: 13) opines that the clinical theory ("CT") and the metapsychology ("M") constitute "two incompatible modes of explanation." And, of-a-piece with this antithesis is Gill's (1976) doctrine that "Metapsychology is not Psychology." Thus, Gill reasons (pp. 85-86) that since M and CT belong to different universes of discourse, any and all envisioned reductions of the latter to the former must be "pseudo-explanations" (p. 86). But prima facie in physics, classical electromagnetic theory and the ray optics of lenses also pertain to "different universes of discourse." Yet in a triumphant unification of theoretical understanding, the reduction of the latter to the former qualified as a bona fide explanatory subsumption. Alas, Freud has not been well served philosophically by some of the most distinguished contemporary protagonists of his clinical theory. This is a pity all the more, since Gill makes allowance for the potential explanatory *value* of suitable reductions as follows: "I assume there is a material substrate for an unconscious wish—or for a conscious wish, for that matter," and "the recognition that many drive propositions are biopsychological...does not mean that clinical psychoanalytic discoveries about sexuality are being discarded" (1976: 95).

But what of the merits of Klein's positive articulation of the explanations furnished by the clinical theory? As we have already seen, he commended it for its alleged attempt "to state reasons rather than causes" (p. 56) when seeking "the reasons of behavior" (p. 27), praising it for "the reading of intentionality" (pp. 23, 26, 71), and for "*unlocking meanings*" (p. 48; see also 53, 70-71). More explicitly, he opines:

The central objective of psychoanalytic clinical explanation is the *reading of intentionality*; behavior, experience, testimony are studied for meaning in this sense, as jointly exemplifying directive "tensions," avowed, disavowed, repressed, defended.... Applied to the understanding of symptoms, for example, such explanation consists in going back from a symptom not to the workings of a mechanism which is itself actually or potentially observable, but a life-history context in which the symptom becomes intelligible as exemplifying an aimful solution. [p. 26]

This declaration calls for several critical comments:

(1) As we have already seen, in the psychoanalytic context of repressed ideation it is illegitimate to trade, as Klein does, on the action-vocabulary of *"intentionality,"* "aimful," "purpose," and so forth in the received sense of the practical syllogism. For, as we saw, in the context of premeditated conscious action, the agent believes his conduct to be conducive to the realization of his aims. And the presence of this belief plays a crucial role in the explanation of human action by *motivating reasons*. Hence, the apparent *absence* of a corresponding belief in the case of unconsciously engendered conduct permits at best a merely *Pickwickian* application of the adjectives "intended" or "intentional" to such comportment. Therefore, Klein's loaded use of the received vocabulary of action cannot validly serve his objective of widening the conceptual chasm between the clinical theory and the metapsychology beyond the dimensions acknowledged by Freud. In particular, his key phrase "the reading of intentionality" is a weasel locution. It functions misleadingly, on a par with the tricky word "symbol" when used to denote substitutive outlets for repressed impulses, though not as egregiously as Ricoeur's enormity, "the semantics of desire."

(2) As an important corollary to the foregoing criticism, it has become patent that Klein drew a pseudocontrast when he commended the clinical theory for its concern "to state reasons rather than causes" (1976: 56). The explanatory repressions turned out not to qualify as motivating *reasons*. There can therefore be no question of these repressions being such reasons *as opposed* to causes. And, in any case, these latent contents hardly forfeit their *causal relevance* in virtue of being unconscious desires. Thus, there was nothing illicitly physicalistic, metapsychological, or otherwise alien to the clinical theory in Freud's thesis that the explanatory unconscious ideation of that theory in a species of the genus "cause." Nor did such speciation impoverish this ideation, since he fully allowed it to possess endlessly fascinating properties (e.g., "primary process" attributes) over and above those of mere generic causes. In short, Klein's reading of "intentionality" or of "latent meaning" is none other than the use of Freud's clinical postulates to interpret behavior theoretically in individual cases by inferring its unconscious causes. For particular psychoanalytic interpretations *articulate the psychic contents* to which the general clinical hypotheses attribute particular symptoms, slips, and dreams—repressed contents that were purportedly distorted by the defensive operations of censorship, displacement, condensation, and so on.

But physicists, too, "read" phenomena in the sense of interpreting them theoretically by hypothesizing explanatory causes for them. And such physical cosmogonies as the big bang model of the universe are historical or narrative, as is historical geophysics. Similarly, Darwinians "read" biogeographical distributions by offering explanatory historical narratives for them. Furthermore, every beginning student knows that the generic *identity* of the phenomena interpreted by the psychoanalyst is ideational, and therefore differs in *identity* from the phenomena "read" by the physicist. Hence, in addition to being potentially misleading, it is just turgid to inflate this utter banality by designating the psychoanalyst's *interpretive* stock-in-trade as being "hermeneutic." Nor is there any need to label the *meta*interpretative *philosophy* of psychoanalysis as "hermeneutic," any more than it is illuminating to so designate, say, the metainterpretive philosophy of physics. True, it was Dilthey rather than Ricoeur, Habermas, Klein et al., who grafted the term "hermeneutics" from its original philological context (biblical exegesis) onto psychology. But whatever the verdict on its appropriateness to Dilthey's idiographic, antinomothetic conception of psychology, I have argued that its extrapolation to Freud's *nomothetic* clinical theory begets conceptual mischief. For its *nontrivial* applicability to this body of hypotheses is predicated on the philosophical theses of the latter-day hermeneuticians, which have turned out to be quite alien to psychoanalytic theory.

(3) Klein sees himself as having exorcised Freud's metapsychology while articulating or elaborating Freud's clinical theory. But Eagle has shown illuminatingly that Klein likewise repudiated central notions and tenets of the latter set of hypotheses. For example, Klein "redefines repression" (Eagle 1980a: 180, 188). Similarly for Freud's concept of sexuality:

What is distinctively Freudian is a conception in which all behavior—including patently non-drive behavior—is seen to be, directly or indirectly, in the service of drive gratification. Klein essentially reverses this position by arguing that sexual gratification is in the service of maintaining unity of self. Thus, his formulations entail a rejection not only of the libido or drive-discharge components of the Freudian theory of sexuality, but of the Freudian proposition that sexuality has a special, central, and ubiquitous motivating role in behavior.
. . . in short, what permits one to see sexuality as a central motivation in a wide range of behaviors—is precisely the assumptions contained in instinct theory and libido theory. Without such assumptions, sexuality takes its place as only one among many motives. [1980a: 186]

Finally, like Ricoeur, Klein failed to face the import of the requirements for the *validation* of the clinical theory. Laudably and refreshingly enough, he avers:

The logic and dependability of inferences from phenomenology [i.e., from the "observational data of the psychoanalytic situation"] crucially influence the validity of the extraphenomenological concepts. Unless those inferences are valid, the concepts refer to witches and unicorns. [Klein 1976: 51]

In the spirit of this injunction, he declared his readiness to heed it, but under the condition that, among other things, "psychoanalytic explanation...aims at specifying the subject's own vantage point...[a reconstruction that] is more a process of seeing pattern or 'fit' than detecting causes" (p. 27). Though having thus reiterated his refusal to regard clinical explanation as a species of causal explanation, he hastened to add: "Questions of validation and rules of evidence are no less critical for this orientation to explanation in terms of meanings perceived by an observer and lived out by a subject. They are in fact a matter of great and neglected importance in psychoanalysis, but pursuit of this topic would get us off the track I have set for myself" (pp. 27-28).

Understandably, Klein was not able to pursue that *pivotal* issue there. But since the returns on such a crucial inquiry were hardly in, it was gratuitous for him to shower *epistemic* praise on the psychoanalytic method of clinical investigation qua method of validation (pp. 36-38). In fact, his panegyric goes well beyond any deserved recognition of the *heuristic* value of clinical inquiry:

Here I wish to stress that the induction of lawfulness from data obtained in the psychoanalytic situation can be conducted with a systematic rigor comparable to experimentation. Some say that the data of the analytic situation can only generate hypotheses, not "prove" them. But there is no basis in principle for denying that rigorous standards of demonstration can apply to the nonexperimental occurrences of the psychoanalytic situation. [1976: 66]

On the contrary, as chapters 3-5 and 8 in Part II will show, even if the data garnered in the analytic treatment setting could be taken at face value epistemically as uncontaminated, that ambience simply does not command the probative resources to authenticate the cardinal explanatory hypotheses of the clinical theory. As I have pointed out earlier, embracing Klein's, Ricoeur's, or Habermas's versions of hermeneutics cannot provide escape from the cognitive imperativeness of such validation. Yet, by insisting on intraclinical testing, just these doctrines disallow adequate methods for the requisite investigation. H. Thomä and H. Kächele (1973: 206, 219, 221, 224) also go so far as to claim probative autonomy for intraclinical testing as the *sole* epistemic avenue for validation. And the untenability of this contention is not lessened by their rejection of Habermas's extreme complaint of scientistic self-misunderstanding against Freud.

Besides, it will emerge from the aforementioned chapters of Part II that it is ill-conceived and counterproductive for Klein (1976: 36-38) to disclaim, as he does, the *therapeutic* efficacy of psychoanalytic treatment while extolling the epistemic capabilities of the method of clinical investigation. For, as we shall see, ever since Freud collaborated with Breuer, therapeutic achievements furnished the *sole* clinical warrant for the method of free association as a trustworthy avenue for certifying pathogens, as well as the purported agencies of dream-formation and of generating "slips."

Though, to my knowledge, Klein did not explicity espouse hermeneutics under its label, it is clearly appropriate to regard him as a leading, articulate spokesman for that movement within the psychoanalytic community, as I have done.

6. The Collapse of the Scientophobic Reconstruction of Freud's Theory

What, then, is the upshot of my scrutiny here of the cardinal tenets of Habermas, Ricoeur, and Klein? First, their proposed philosophical reconstruction of the clinical theory rests on a mythic exegesis of Freud's own perennial notion of scientificity. And, of-a-piece with this contrived reading, their paradigm of the natural sciences is wildly anachronistic. Second, they have traded misleadingly on the "intentionality" appropriate to psychoanalytic motivational explanations by misassimilating it—in one way or another—either to the practical syllogism or to the symbolic function of a *language*. Indeed, such Pickwickian intentionality as characterizes human conduct if explained psychoanalytically does not have either the ontological or the epistemic import claimed by their philosophical theses. Thirdly, once the hermeneutic construal is robbed of its scientophobic myths, its sterility for the constructive utilization of the Freudian legacy in psychology and psychiatry becomes apparent. The residue from Dilthey's original version of hermeneutics toward the fruition of research has turned out to be merely a negativistic ideological battle cry. The more recent hermeneutic gloss on psychoanalysis similarly has all the earmarks of an investigative *cul-de-sac*, a blind alley rather than a citadel for psychoanalytic apologetics.

Flawed as Freud's own arguments will turn out to be in the succeeding chapters, their caliber will be seen to be astronomically higher, and their often brilliant content incomparably more instructive than the gloss and the animadversions of Freud's hermeneutic critics, who so patronizingly chide him for scientism. So much for their unjustified demand that we abjure the very standards of validation by which Freud himself wanted his theory to be judged.

Avowedly, his criteria of validation are essentially those of hypothetico-deductive inductivism (S.E. 1914, 14: 77; 1915, 14: 117; 1925, 20: 32). And he took adherence to them to be the hallmark of the scientific probity that he claimed for his theory. Hence, it behooves me to appraise Freud's *arguments* for his monumental clinical theory of personality and therapy by his own standards. Therefore, the verdict that I shall reach on this basis will surely not be predicated on the imposition of some extraneous methodological purism. Nor does my application of his avowed norm of scientific rationality to psychoanalysis imply that I deem this touchstone to be *the* criterion of demarcation between science and nonscience. In short, I shall grant Freud his own canon of scientific status in addressing the following key question: Did his clinical arguments vindicate the knowledge claims he made for his evolving theory by labeling it "scientific"?

My answer will be twofold. The reasoning on which Freud rested the major hypotheses of his edifice was fundamentally flawed, even if the probity of the clinical observations he adduced were not in question. Moreover, far from deserving to be taken at face value, clinical data from the psychoanalytic treatment setting are themselves epistemically quite suspect.

Insofar as I developed some of the latter criticisms in earlier publications (Grünbaum 1977; 1979b; 1980), such leading orthodox analysts as Brenner (1982: 4-5) have not come to grips with them, although he did address certain objections by others (Brenner 1968; 1970: 34-45). Similarly, the critiques offered from a philosophy of science perspective by the clinicians Möller (1978) and Perrez (1979) seem to have been disregarded by traditional Freudians. Yet the more heterodox analyst Edelson has recently urged (1983) the imperativeness of dealing with the challenge I am posing. It remains to be seen to what extent, if any, his hopes for the program envisaged by him materialize. Until and unless they do, his queries do not, I claim, cogently impugn my animadversions in Part I below, let alone those in Part II.

Despite my opening remarks, the reader may at first have wondered why I chose to present a scrutiny of hermeneutics as a lengthy introduction to my own critique of Freud. I trust that the desirability of doing so may now be more readily appreciated. Indeed, I hope that, at this point, those who had been convinced by the hermeneutic construal of psychoanalysis may be open to my appraisal of the psychoanalytic enterprise from a perspective they may have heretofore judged anachronistic. Be that as it may, I now turn to an examination of the clinical foundations of psychoanalysis in their received form.

PART I

THE CLINICAL METHOD OF PSYCHOANALYTIC INVESTIGATION: PATHFINDER OR PITFALL

1.

Is Freud's Theory Empirically Testable?

A. CLINICAL VERSUS EXPERIMENTAL TESTABILITY: STATEMENT OF THE CONTROVERSY.

Hans Eysenck (1963: 220) has maintained that "we can no more test Freudian hypotheses 'on the couch' [used by the patient during psycho-analytic treatment] than we can adjudicate between the rival hypotheses of Newton and Einstein by going to sleep under an apple tree." And, in Eysenck's view, although clinical data from the couch may be heuristi-cally fruitful by suggesting hypotheses, only suitably designed *experi-mental* studies can perform the *probative* role of *tests*. Against this denial of clinical testability, Clark Glymour (1974: 304) has argued that "the theory Sigmund Freud developed at the turn of the century was strong enough to be tested [cogently] on the couch." Furthermore, Glymour proposes to illuminate Eysenck's disparagement of clinical data, but then to discount it, in the following dialectical give-and-take:

It stems in part, I think, from what are genuine drawbacks to clinical testing; for example, the problem of ensuring that a patient's responses are not *simply* the result of suggestion or the feeling, not without foundation, that the "basic data" obtained from clinical sessions—the patient's introspective reports of his own feelings, reports of dreams, memories of childhood and adolescence—are less reliable than we should like. But neither of these considerations seems sufficient to reject the clinical method generally, although they may of course be sufficient to warrant us in rejecting particular clinical results. Clinicians can hopefully be trained so as not to elicit by suggestion the expected responses from their patients; patients' reports can sometimes be checked independently, as in the case of memories, and even when they cannot be so checked there is no good reason to distrust them generally. But I think condemnations like Eysenck's derive from a belief about clinical testing which goes considerably beyond either of these points: the belief that clinical sessions, even cleansed of suggestibility and of doubts about the reliability of patients' reports, can involve no rational strategy for testing theories. [1974: 287]

I think that Eysenck's claim is wrong. I think there is a rational strategy for testing important parts of psychoanalysis, a strategy that relies almost exclusively on clinical evidence; moreover, I think this strategy is immanent in at least one of Freud's case studies, that of the Rat Man. Indeed, I want to make a much bolder claim. The strategy involved in the Rat Man case is essentially the same as a strategy very frequently used in testing physical theories. Further, this strategy, while simple enough, is more powerful than the hypothetico-deductive-falsification strategy described for us by so many philosophers of science. [1974: 287-288]

Despite this epistemological tribute to Freud's couch, Glymour issues a caveat:

I am certainly not claiming that there is good clinical evidence for Freud's theory; I am claiming that if one wants to test psychoanalysis, there is a reasonable strategy for doing so which can be, and to some degree has been, effected through clinical sessions. [1974: 288]

More recently, Glymour (1980) told us more explicitly why we should countenance the rationale that animated Freud's clinical investigation of psychoanalytic hypotheses during the treatment of his Rat Man patient Paul Lorenz. Glymour points to at least three important specific episodes in the history of physical science in which he discerns just the logical pincer-and-bootstrap strategy of piecemeal testing that he also teased out from Freud's analysis of Paul Lorenz. Thus, he says, "unlikely as it may sound...the major argument of the Rat Man case is not so very different from the major argument of Book III of Newton's *Principia*" (1980: 265). And he stresses that this argument employs a logical *pincer* strategy of more or less *piecemeal* testing *within* an overall theory, instead of the completely global theory appraisal of the hypothetico-deductive method, which altogether abjures any attempt to rate different components of the theory individually as to their merits in the face of the evidence.

Precisely because he sees the piecemeal procedure as thus able to *allocate* praise or blame *within* the total theory, Glymour considers this method a salutary and effective antidote to the intratheoretic epistemological promiscuity that is endemic to the fashionable holism championed by Duhem and Quine (Glymour 1980: 145-152). If you have been smarting under the holist dogma, which has it that intratheoretic epistemic bewilderment is the inevitable fate of rational man, Glymour beckons you to be undaunted and of stout heart: the logical pincer method affords deliverance by *vindicating* the actual contrary conduct of science and common sense, which is to accept or reject those particular component hypotheses that are at issue in scientific debate or daily life at a given time.

Yet Glymour (1980: 151) acknowledges that there is a "kernel of truth" in holism's emphasis on the *network* character of the linkages between the component hypotheses of a theory. And this kernel is such that the pieces of a theory must be *assessed* together prior to selecting particular ones for acceptance or rejection, because this selection "must depend on what else we believe and what else we discard" (p. 152). In short, one lesson drawn by Glymour from the pincer strategy is that the viable residue of the holist legacy need not saddle us with philosophical defiance of scientific practice and good sense.

Besides commending Freud's clinical study of the Rat Man for its rationale, Glymour likewise attributes a fair degree of scientific rigor to a *few* of Freud's other investigations. But he couples these particular appreciative judgments with a largely uncomplimentary overall evaluation, deploring the very uneven logical quality of the Freudian corpus. Indeed, Glymour (1980: 265) thinks he is being "gentle" when he deems Freud's 1909 case study of Little Hans to be "appalling." He finds that "on the whole Freud's arguments for psychoanalytic theory are dreadful," marred by the frequent—though by no means universal—substitution of "rhetorical flourish" for real argument, and a "superabundance of explanation" rather than cogent evidence (p. 264). Yet clearly these quite fundamental dissatisfactions with Freud's all too frequent lapses do not militate against Glymour's espousal of the clinical testability of such central parts of psychoanalytic theory as the specific etiology of the psychoneuroses, at least in the etiological versions that Freud enunciated before 1909.

Just this championship of the *probative* value of data from the analytic treatment sessions is philosophical music to the ears of those who echo Freud's own emphatic claim that the bulk of psychoanalytic theory is well founded empirically. For, as Ernest Jones reminded everyone in his "Editorial Preface" to Freud's *Collected Papers*, the clinical findings are "the real basis of Psycho-analysis. All of Professor Freud's other works and theories are essentially founded on the clinical investigations" (Jones 1959, 1: 3). Thus most advocates of this theoretical corpus regard the analyst's many observations of the patient's interactions with him in the treatment sessions as the source of findings that are simply *peerless*, not only heuristically but *also* probatively. We are told that during a typical analysis, which lasts for some years, the analyst accumulates with each patient a vast number of variegated data that furnish evidence relevant to Freud's theory of personality no less than to the dynamics and outcome of his therapy. The so-called "psychoanalytic interview" sessions are claimed to yield genuinely probative data because of the alleged real-life nature of the rich relationship between the analyst and the analysand. Even an analyst who recently declared it to be high ·time that Freudians "move from overreliance on our hypothetical discoveries to a much-needed validation of our basic theoretical and clinical concepts" (Kaplan 1981: 23) characterizes "the naturalistic observations within the psychoanalytic treatment situation" as "the major scientific method of psychoanalysis" (p. 18). Hence, the clinical setting or "psychoanalytic situation" is purported to be the arena of *experiments in situ*, in marked contrast to the contrived environment of the psychological laboratory with its superficial, transitory interaction between the experimental psychologist and his subject. Thus, the analysts A. M. Cooper and R. Michels (1978: 376) tell us that "increasingly this [psychoanalytic] inquiry has recognized the analytic situation itself as paradigmatic for all human interactions" (p. 376). Indeed, the psychoanalytic method is said to be uniquely suited to first eliciting some of the important manifestations of the unconscious processes to which Freud's *depth* psychology pertains (Brenner 1982: 3), and this method of investigation allegedly achieves great superiority over "the methods of academic psychology," because it *also* "makes possible an independent, objective appraisal of those [important] aspects of mental life." Hence when skillfully handled, its results will be "scientifically reliable" (p. 2). Nay, as Brenner (1970: 42) would have it, as against analytically untutored introspection and impoverished academic psychology, "The psychoanalytic method is the only method so far available which has made possible the scientific observation of the major motivational forces of man's mental life."

This superior *investigative value* of the analyst's clinical techniques is thus held to make the psychoanalytic interview at once the prime testing ground and the heuristic inspiration for Freud's theory of personality as well as for his therapy. Some leading orthodox analytic theoreticians have been concerned to *exclude* the so-called "metapsychology" of Freud's psychic energy model, and *a fortiori* its erstwhile neurobiological trappings, from the avowed purview of clinical validation. Therefore, it is to be understood that the term "psychoanalytic theory of personality" is here construed to *exclude* the metapsychology of psychic energy with its cathexes and anticathexes. In any case, most analysts have traditionally been quite skeptical, if not outright hostile, toward attempts to test Freudian theory experimentally *outside* the psychoanalytic interview.

Just such an assessment was enunciated again quite recently by Lester Luborsky and Donald Spence (1978). They do issue the sobering caveat that "psychoanalysts, like other psychotherapists, literally *do not know* how they achieve their results" (p. 360). But they couple this disclaimer with the tribute that analysts "possess a unique store of clinical wisdom." Moreover, Luborsky and Spence emphasize that *"far more is known now* [in psychoanalysis] *through clinical wisdom than is known through quantitative* [i.e., controlled] *objective studies* [emphasis in original]" (p. 350). In short, they claim that—in this area—clinical confirmation is presently superior to experimentally obtained validation. And they deem findings from the psychoanalytic session to have such epistemic superiority not only therapeutically but also in the validation of Freud's general theory of unconscious motivation (pp. 356-357). Similarly, clinical validation is claimed for Heinz Kohut's currently influential variant of psychoanalysis, which supplants Freud's Oedipal conflict by the child's *pre*-Oedipal narcissistic struggle for a cohesive self as the major determinant of adult personality structure (Ornstein 1978; Goldberg 1978).

Having extolled "clinical wisdom" vis-à-vis experimental studies, Luborsky and Spence (1978: 356) declare that "Freud was probably right" in his terse negative response to the psychologist Saul Rosenzweig, when the latter sent him experimental results that Rosenzweig took to be supportive of Freud's theory of repression (Rosenzweig 1934). Though Freud was then in his late seventies and ill with cancer, he took only a short time to react to this unsolicited claim of confirmation. Quite soon thereafter, he wrote Rosenzweig with almost patronizing disenchantment:

I have examined your experimental studies for the verification of the psychoanalytic assertions with interest. I cannot put much value on these confirmations because the wealth of reliable observations on which these assertions rest make them independent of experimental verification. Still, it can do no harm. [quoted in MacKinnon and Dukes 1964: 703; the German original is reproduced on p. 702]

Just what was Freud's rationale for feeling entitled to dismiss Rosenzweig's experimental investigation in the way he did?

Note at once that Freud's dissatisfaction was *not* that Rosenzweig's experiment failed to qualify logically as a genuine test of the psychoanalytic conception of repression. Thus, Freud's objection was *not* that sheer evidential *irrelevance* rendered the experimental results probatively unavailing. Nor did he level the weaker charge that Rosenzweig's findings failed to pass muster *logically* as confirmations. On the contrary, he did refer to them as "confirmations" (*Bestätigungen*). Rather what disenchanted Freud was that in his view, these results were *probatively superfluous* or *redundant*, albeit harmless as such. But *why* did Freud look upon them as superfluous? As he stated, he regarded psychoanalytic hypotheses as already abundantly well established clinically by "a wealth of reliable observations." Hence, he saw no need for further substantiation by experiments conducted outside the psychoanalytic situation.

Three years after Freud's dismissive reply, Rosenzweig (1937: 65) commented on it by writing: "many analysts today would not agree with Freud's view. . . and . . . possibly Freud himself has in the interim changed his mind." Some psychoanalysts did indeed dissent from Freud's appraisal of Rosenzweig's claim of experimental confirmation. But while doing so, these other analysts *indicted* rather than endorsed Rosenzweig's contention that his findings support Freud's theory of repression. For they objected vehemently that, far from yielding harmlessly superfluous confirmations, Rosenzweig's work was fundamentally unsound, because his experiment simply did not qualify logically as a test of the *psychoanalytic* notion of repression (MacKinnon and Dukes 1964: 703-709). I concur completely with these other analysts that whatever relevance Rosenzweig's findings may have to *non*psychoanalytic accounts of forgetting, they patently have no evidential bearing on Freudian repression as that notion is articulated in Freud's classic 1915 paper (S.E. 1915, 14: 146-158). Indeed, it is most puzzling that this fact was not evident to Rosenzweig before others pointed it out. For in the aforecited 1934 article, Rosenzweig himself states explicitly at the outset (p. 248) what he takes to be the pertinent construal of Freud's 1915 paper. And I submit that the probative *irrelevance* of Rosenzweig's laboratory findings is immediately perspicuous from that very formulation. For our purposes, however, the details of this logical malfeasance need not concern us.

Despite their strong differences, both of the parties to the above dispute about the probative value of *clinical* data for the empirical appraisal of psychoanalytic theory do agree that at least part of the Freudian corpus is indeed cogently testable by empirical findings of *some* sort: the Freudians have the support of Glymour, for example, in contending that *actually realizable* observations made within the confines of the treatment setting do afford epistemically sound testability, and such anti-Freudian protagonists as Eysenck make the contrary claim that epistemically well-conceived tests are actually realizable, at least in principle, but *only* in the controlled environment of the laboratory or in other *extra*clinical contexts. And clearly, the assumption of actual empirical testability shared by the disputants is likewise affirmed by someone who maintains that *both* clinical and extraclinical findings are suitable, at least in principle, for testing psychoanalysis.

Yet this shared assumption of actual testability has again been denied simpliciter by Popper, who has even denied the *logical* possibility of testing psychoanalysis empirically. As recently as when he replied to his critics in 1974 (Popper 1974, 2: 984-985), he reiterated his earlier claim that Freud's theory, as well as Adler's, are "simply non-testable, irrefutable. There was no conceivable human behaviour which would contradict them" (Popper 1962: 37). It is then a mere corollary of this thesis of nontestability that *clinical* data, in particular, likewise cannot serve as a basis for genuine empirical tests. But when Popper claims that his falsifiability criterion of demarcation between science and nonscience bars psychoanalysis from the pantheon of the bona fide empirical sciences, his *principal* concern is not with Freudian theory as such, important though it is. Thus in 1974 he stressed the quite general role of his demarcation criterion within his overall philosophy, when he wrote:

my criterion of demarcation... is more than sharp enough to make a distinction between many physical theories on the one hand, and metaphysical theories, such as psychoanalysis, or Marxism (in its present [as distinct from its original] form), on the other. This is, of course, one of my main theses; and nobody who has not understood it can be said to have understood my theory. [1974: 984]

But our concern is with why Popper is so emphatic to be understood as claiming that, *unlike* Marxism, "psychoanalysis was immune [to falsification by any logically possible empirical findings] to start with, and remained so" (1974: 985). In the footnote that he appends to this very sentence, he steers us to his *Conjectures and Refutations* (1962). On turning to this earlier work (chap. 1, sections 1 and 2; pp. 156-157, 255-258), we find that not so much psychoanalysis itself (or present-day Marxism) is the prime target of his charge of nonfalsifiability, but rather its role as a *centerpiece* of his castigation of *inductivism* qua method of scientific theory-validation and/or criterion of demarcation. For, as I read it, we are told (pp. 33-38) that inductivism does countenance the claims of ubiquitous empirical confirmation of Freud's theory that are made by its adherents. And similarly, inductivism gives sanction, we learn, to the purported validations of Adler's revisionist version of psychoanalysis and of contemporary Marxism. Thus by 1919, Popper had convinced himself both that inductivism does not have the methodological resources to challenge the scientific credentials of psycho-analysis *and* that Freud's theory—as well as Adlerian revisionism and Marxism—is in fact empirically irrefutable. On this basis, Popper argued that the inductivist method of confirmation and its criterion of demarcation are *unacceptably permissive.*

Hence, the real philosophical villain of his story was inductivism rather than psychoanalysis or Marxism as such, although he deplored them in their own right. Having found to his dismay in 1919 that inductivism still held sway as a criterion of demarcation, Popper adduced psychoanalysis—Freudian and Adlerian—as the *pièce de résistance* of his case against it. He therefore concluded: "Thus there clearly was a need for a different criterion of demarcation" (1962: 256). In short, psychoanalysis was and—at least as of 1974—has remained Popper's prime illustration of the greater stringency that he claims for the falsifiability criterion he enunciated. But, clearly, if he were right that Freud's theory is simply untestable altogether, then it would be pointless to inquire whether this theory can be cogently tested *clinically.* Hence, it now behooves us to address Popper's stated challenge.

B. THE PURPORTED UNTESTABILITY OF THE PSYCHOANALYTIC THEORY OF PERSONALITY

In earlier publications, I have argued that neither the Freudian theory of personality nor the therapeutic tenets of psychoanalysis are untestable in Popper's sense (Grünbaum 1976, 1977, 1979*a*). Furthermore, there I contended in detail that Popper's portrayal of psychoanalysis as a theory entitled to claim good *inductivist* credentials is predicated on a caricature of the requirements for theory validation laid down by such arch-inductivists as Bacon and Mill. Thus, I pointed out that Freud's theory is replete with *causal* hypotheses and that the evidential conditions that must be met to furnish genuine inductive support for *such* hypotheses are very demanding. But I emphasized that precisely these exacting inductivist conditions were pathetically *unfulfilled* by those Freudians who claimed ubiquitous confirmation of the psychoanalytic corpus, to Popper's fully justified consternation.

My epistemological scrutiny of psychoanalysis as a scientific theory in some of these earlier articles elicited a very encouraging laudatory response from John Watkins (1978: 351-352; but see also p. 140 for the *context* of Watkins's response that is provided by the editors). He did not challenge my conclusion that psychoanalysis is actually falsifiable. Yet he questioned the *bearing* of this claim on Popper's demarcation criterion itself. As he put it, "suppose (with Grünbaum) that psychoanalytic theory is testable; then Popper was wrong about Freudian theory: it is better than he thought." Why, asks Watkins (1978: 351), would one presume that Popper's "demarcation-criterion was in trouble because it actually included something which Popper himself had mistakenly excluded"? And he objects that "Grünbaum seems to take the unscientific status of Freudian theory as a datum against which that demarcation-criterion should be judged, rather than the other way around" (p. 352). David Miller demurred in a similar vein (private communication).

But their objection overlooks the cardinal point I was concerned to make when I discussed Freud's theory in the context of Popper's philosophy of science. For the title of the relevant section of the earliest essay in which I dealt with this topic was "Popper's Historiography of Inductivism and the Test Case of Freudian Psychoanalytic Theory" (Grünbaum 1976: 215). Neither there nor elsewhere thereafter did I offer the refutability of psychoanalysis as a counterexample to Popper's falsificationist demarcation criterion as such. Instead, I adduced the falsifiability of Freudian theory against Popper's contention that this influential theory provides a centerpiece illustration of the following major thesis espoused by him: the falsifiability criterion of demarcation is *more restrictive* than the inductivist one, and hence ought to supersede it! There is no basis in my writings, I submit, for the depiction of my views given by Watkins (1978: 351) when he wrote: "Grünbaum claims that Popper's demarcation criterion is...too weak because, contrary to Popper's intention, it fails to exclude Freud's psychoanalytical theory." Rather, on the pertinent page (Grünbaum 1976: 227), I explicitly addressed what I called "Popper's demarcation *asymmetry*" (p. 214), which is the *contrast* drawn by Popper between his criterion of scientificality and the inductivist one. What I did maintain concerning this contrast was that it is "unsound" to ascribe *greater stringency* to Popper's falsifiability criterion, at least "with respect to psychoanalysis."

That my focus was on the *comparative* stringency of the two demarcation criteria when I discussed Freud vis-à-vis Popper—and *not* on the adequacy of Popper's criterion *as such!*—is further apparent in that I went on to assess the strictness of the inductivist criterion in the very next sentence. Speaking there of advocates of eliminative inductivism as distinct from the enumerative inductivism that Bacon disparaged as "puerile," I declared: "the mere fact that...inductivists try to use supportive instances to 'probabilify' or credibilify hypotheses does NOT commit them to granting credible scientific status to a hypothesis *solely* on the strength of existing positive instances, however numerous" (1976: 227-228). When I then gave "the upshot of my comparison of inductivist conceptions of scientificality with Popper's," I wrote that

> the moral I draw is the following: Popper was seriously mistaken in claiming that IN THE ABSENCE OF NEGATIVE INSTANCES, all forms of inductivism are necessarily committed to the (probabilified) scientific credibility of a theory, merely because that theory can adduce numerous positive instances.

Finally, upon applying this import to "psychoanalysis in particular," I concluded:

> Thus, the inductivist's willingness to either probabilify or somehow credibilify theories which *can* marshal genuinely supportive positive instances does *not* render the inductivist helpless to dismiss the positive instances adduced by psychoanalysts as non-probative. [1976: 229]

Hence, I think that Watkins's complaint against taking the unscientific status of Freudian theory "as a datum" by which to judge the falsifiability criterion of demarcation should not have been laid at my door at all. Indeed, I wonder whether Popper's own account of the logical role played by Freudian theory when he evolved his demarcation criterion (1962: chap. 1) would not justify directing Watkins's complaint against the reasoning then employed by Popper himself. Thus, as I read the first four pages of this chapter, Popper started out from the following premise: psychoanalysis, like astrology and the Marxist theory of history, "does not come up to scientific standards," but it *is* countenanced as such by the "*inductive*" empirical method of theory validation. He then saw his task, he tells us, as one of devising a criterion of demarcation more stringent than inductivism, at least to the extent of *excluding* psychoanalysis (besides Marxism) as being nonscientific: "My problem perhaps first took the simple form, 'What is wrong with Marxism, psychoanalysis, and individual [Adlerian] psychology? Why are they so different from physical theories, from Newton's theory, and especially from the theory of relativity?'" (1962: 34).

To Peter Urbach's mind, I have misread Popper's epistemic rejection of the ubiquitous confirmations claimed by the Freudians he encountered. For on Urbach's reading, Popper pointed to these alleged validations *not* as an indictment of the permissiveness of the confirmation criteria countenanced by inductivism; instead, as Urbach would have it, Popper was concerned to expose the *delusion* of the Freudians that the purported confirmations satisfy inductivist canons. But I submit that, besides straining charity, Urbach's reading boomerangs, for it completely undercuts Popper's avowed purpose to adduce psychoanalysis as a prime illustration of his thesis that the inductivist criterion of demarcation is unacceptably permissive, and that his falsificationist alternative is more stringent (Popper 1962: 33-36; 1974: 984).

Thus, when speaking of psychoanalysis, Adlerian psychology, and Marxism, Popper (1962: 36) declared: "it was practically impossible to describe any human behaviour that might not be claimed to be a verification of these theories," an assertion immediately followed by his falsificationist manifesto whose first contention states: "It is easy to obtain confirmations, or verifications, for nearly every theory—if we look for confirmations" (p. 36). Evidently Popper's complaint is not that the abundant confirmations claimed by Freudians are actually devoid of inductivist warrant; instead, his charge is precisely that inductivist criteria are helpless to disavow the credentials that Freudians had claimed for their theory!

In earlier articles, I have devoted attention to Popper's views on psychoanalysis. But there are further philosophical reproaches that he lodged against Freud (and Adler) that I have not examined heretofore. These additional strictures comprise both emphatic arguments for the untestability of psychoanalytic theory, and a censorious utilization of some purported textual exegesis of Freud's 1923 paper on the theory and practice of dream interpretation. I believe that Popper's further complaints call for critical scrutiny. But since my overall concern in the present essay is with the *clinical* credentials of psychoanalysis, I shall consider Popper's additional objections to Freud in a different subdivision as follows: (1) those that do *not* focus on *clinical* observations in particular, and (2) those offered to deny the probative relevance of *clinical* findings as such.

Let me now deal with the first of these two sets of additional Popperian indictments of psychoanalysis. I shall then defer the scrutiny of the second group until after I have argued in much detail that by *inductivist* standards, the clinical validation of Freudian theory is very largely spurious, despite the *heuristic* value of clinical data.

In his replies to critics, Popper (1974: 985) wrote:

Marxism was once a science, but one which was refuted by some of the facts which happened to clash with its predictions.

However, Marxism is no longer a science; for it broke the methodological rule that we must accept falsification, and it immunized itself against the most blatant refutations of its predictions.

Psychoanalysis is a very different case. It is an interesting psychological metaphysics (and no doubt there is some truth in it, as there is so often in metaphysical ideas), but it never was a science. There may be lots of people who are Freudian or Adlerian cases: Freud himself was clearly a Freudian case, and Adler an Adlerian case. But what prevents their theories from being scientific in the sense here described is, very simply, that they do not exclude any physically possible human behaviour. Whatever anybody may do is, in principle, explicable in Freudian or Adlerian terms. (Adler's break with Freud was more Adlerian than Freudian, but Freud never looked on it as a refutation of his theory.)

The point is very clear. Neither Freud nor Adler excludes any particular person's acting in any particular way, whatever the outward circumstances. Whether a man sacrificed his life to rescue a drowning child (a case of sublimation) or whether he murdered the child by drowning him (a case of repression) could not possibly be predicted or excluded by Freud's theory; *the theory was compatible with everything that could happen—even without any special immunization treatment.*

Thus while Marxism became nonscientific by its adoption of an immunizing strategy, psychoanalysis was immune to start with, and remained so.

This important passage prompts me to make the following series of critical comments:

1. Even a casual perusal of the mere *titles* of Freud's papers and lectures in the *Standard Edition* yields two examples of falsifiability. The second is a case of acknowledged falsification, to boot. The first is the paper "A Case of Paranoia Running Counter to the Psychoanalytic Theory of the Disease" (S.E. 1915, 14: 263-272); the second is the lecture "Revision of the Theory of Dreams" (S.E. 1933, 22: 7-30, especially pp. 28-30). Let us consider the first.

The "psychoanalytic theory of paranoia," which is at issue in the paper, is the hypothesis that *repressed* homosexual love is *causally necessary* for affliction by paranoid delusions (S.E. 1915, 14: 265-266). The patient was a young woman who had sought out a lawyer for protection from the molestations of a man with whom she had been having an affair. The lawyer suspected paranoia when she charged that her lover had gotten unseen witnesses to photograph them while making love, and that he was now in a position to use the photographs to disgrace her publicly and compel her to resign her job. Moreover, letters from her lover that she had turned over to the lawyer deplored that their beautiful and tender relationship was being destroyed by her unfortunate morbid idea. Nonetheless, aware that truth is sometimes stranger than fiction, the lawyer asked Freud for his psychiatric judgment as to whether the young woman was actually paranoid.

The lover's letters made "a very favorable impression" on Freud, thereby lending some credence to the delusional character of the young woman's complaints. But, assuming that she was indeed paranoid, Freud's initial session with her led to a theoretically disconcerting conclusion: "The girl seemed to be defending herself against love for a man by directly transforming the lover into a persecutor: there was no sign of the influence of a woman, no trace of a struggle against a homosexual attachment" (S.E. 1915, 14: 265). If she was indeed delusional, then this seeming total absence of repressed homosexuality "emphatically contradicted" Freud's prior hypothesis of a homosexual etiology for paranoia. Thus, he reasoned: "Either the theory must be given up or else, in view of this departure from our [theoretical] expectations, we must side with the lawyer and assume that this was no paranoic combination but an actual experience which had been correctly interpreted" (S.E. 1915, 14: 266). Furthermore: "In these circumstances the simplest thing would have been to abandon the theory that the delusion of persecution invariably depends on homosexuality" (p. 266). In short, Freud explicitly allowed that if the young woman *was* paranoid, then her case was a *refuting* instance of the etiology he had postulated for that disorder. Alternatively, he reckoned with the possibility that she was not paranoid.

As it turned out, during a second session the patient's report on episodes at her place of employment not only greatly enhanced the likelihood of her being afflicted by delusions but also accorded with the postulated etiology by revealing a conflict-ridden homosexual attachment to an elderly woman there. But the point is that the psychoanalytic etiology of paranoia is empirically falsifiable (disconfirmable) *and* that Freud explicitly recognized it. For, as we saw, this hypothesis states that a homosexual psychic conflict is causally necessary for the affliction. Empirical indicators can bespeak the absence of homosexual conflict as well as the presence of paranoid delusions so as to discredit the stated etiology.

Hence, this example has an important general moral: whenever empirical indicators can warrant the *absence* of a certain theoretical pathogen P as well as a differential diagnosis of the *presence* of a certain theoretical neurosis N, then an etiologic hypothesis of the strong form "P is causally necessary for N" is clearly empirically falsifiable. It will be falsified by any victim of N who had not been subjected to P. For the hypothesis *predicts* that anyone not so subjected will be spared the miseries of N, a prediction having significant prophylactic import. Equivalently, the hypothesis *retrodicts* that any instance of N was also a case of P. Hence, if there are empirical indicators as well for the *presence* of P, then this retrodiction can be empirically instantiated by a person who instantiates both N and P.

Being a strict determinist, Freud's etiological quest was for *universal* hypotheses (S.E. 1915, 14: 265). But he believed he had empirical grounds for holding that the development of a disorder N after an individual I suffers a pathogenic experience P depended on I's hereditary vulnerability. Hence, his universal etiologic hypotheses typically asserted that exposure to P is *causally necessary* for the development of N, *not* that it is causally sufficient.

Indeed, by claiming that P is the *"specific"* pathogen of N, he was asserting not only that P is causally necessary for N but also that P is never, or hardly ever, an etiologic factor in the pathogenesis of any other nosologically distinct syndrome (S.E. 1895, 3: 135-139). Robert Koch's specific etiology of tuberculosis, i.e., the pathogenic tubercle bacillus, served as a model (S.E. 1895, 3: 137). By the same token, Freud pointed to the tubercle bacillus to illustrate that a pathogen can be quite explanatory, although its mere presence does not guarantee the occurrence of the illness (S.E. 1896, 3: 209). And Freud was wont to conjecture *specific* etiologies for the various psychoneuroses until late in his career (S.E. 1925, 20: 55). Hence, as illustrated by the above example of paranoia, these etiologies evidently have a high degree of empirical falsifiability whenever empirical indicators can attest a differential diagnosis of N, as well as the absence of P. For the hypothesis that P is the specific pathogen of N entails the universal prediction that every case of non-P will remain a non-N, and equivalently, the universal retrodiction that any N suffered P, although it does not predict whether a given exposure to P will issue in N. Thus, Glymour's account (1974) of Freud's case history of the Rat Man makes clear how Freud's specific etiology of the Rat Man's obsession was falsified by means of disconfirming the retrodiction that Freud had based on it.

Let us return to our paranoia example. As I pointed out in an earlier article (Grünbaum 1979*a*: 138-139), the etiology of paranoia postulated by psychoanalysis likewise makes an important "statistical" prediction that qualifies as "risky" with respect to any rival "background" theory that denies the etiologic relevance of repressed homosexuality for paranoia. By Popper's standards, the failure of this prediction would count against Freud's etiology, and its success would corroborate it. In the *"Introduction,"* I already had occasion to adduce this result against Habermas in outline.

To be specific, originally Freud (S.E. 1911, 12: 63) hypothesized the etiology of male paranoia (Schreber case) along the following lines. Given the social taboo on male homosexuality, the failure to repress homosexual impulses may well issue in feelings of severe anxiety and guilt. The latter anxiety could then be eliminated by converting the love emotion "I love him" into its opposite "I hate him," a type of transformation that Freud labeled "reaction formation." Thus, the pattern of reaction formation is that once a dangerous impulse has been largely repressed, it surfaces in the guise of a far more acceptable *contrary* feeling, a conversion that therefore serves as a *defense* against the *anxiety* associated with the underlying dangerous impulse. When the defense of reaction formation proves insufficient to alleviate the anxiety, however, the afflicted party may resort to the further defensive maneuver of "projection," in which "I hate him" is converted into "He hates me." This final stage of the employment of defenses is then the full-blown paranoia. Thus, this rather epigrammatic formulation depicts reaction formation and projection as the repressed defense mechanisms that are actuated by the postulated *specific* pathogen of paranoia. But if repressed homosexuality is indeed the specific etiologic factor in paranoia, then the decline of the taboo on homosexuality in our society should be accompanied by a decreased incidence of male paranoia. And, by the same token, there ought to have been relatively less paranoia in those ancient societies in which male homosexuality was condoned or even sanctioned. For the reduction of massive anxiety and repression with respect to homosexual feelings would contribute to the removal of Freud's *conditio sine qua non* for this syndrome.

Incidentally, as Freud explains (S.E. 1915, 14: 265), before he enunciated universally that homosexuality is the specific pathogen of paranoia, he had declared more cautiously in his earlier publication that it is "perhaps an invariable" etiologic factor (S.E. 1911, 12: 59-60, 62-63, especially p. 59). When I first drew the above "statistical" prediction from Freud's etiology (Grünbaum 1979a: 139), I allowed for Freud's more cautious early formulation. There I predicated the forecast of decreased incidence as a concomitant of taboo decline on the *ceteris paribus* clause that no other potential causes of paranoia become operative. But, by making repressed homosexuality the *conditio sine qua non* of the syndrome, Freud's specific etiology clearly enables the prediction to go through *without* any such proviso.

But even assertions of pathogenic causal relevance that are logically *weaker* than the specific etiologies can be empirically disconfirmable. They can have testable (disconfirmable) predictive import, although they fall short of declaring P to be causally necessary for N. Thus, when pertinent empirical data fail to bear out the prediction that P positively affects the incidence of N, they bespeak the causal *irrelevance* of P to N. Consequently, the currently hypothesized causal relevance of heavy cigarette smoking to lung cancer and cardiovascular disease is disconfirmable, as is the alleged causal relevance of laetrile to cancer remission, which was reportedly discredited by recent findings in the United States.

The etiology that Freud conjectured for one of his female homosexual patients furnishes a useful case in point. He states its substance as follows:

It was just when the girl was experiencing the revival of her infantile Oedipus complex at puberty that she suffered her great disappointment. She became keenly conscious of the wish to have a child, and a male one; that what she desired was her *father's* child and an image of *him*, her consciousness was not allowed to know. And what happened next? It was not *she* who bore the child, but her unconsciously hated rival, her mother. Furiously resentful and embittered, she turned away from her father and from men altogether. After this first great reverse she forswore her womanhood and sought another goal for her libido. [S.E. 1920, 18: 157]

But later on, he cautions:

We do not, therefore, mean to maintain that every girl who experiences a disappointment such as this of the longing for love that springs from the Oedipus attitude at puberty will necessarily on that account fall a victim to homosexuality. On the contrary, other kinds of reaction to this trauma are undoubtedly commoner. [S.E. 1920, 18: 168]

Thus, he is disclaiming the predictability of lesbianism from the stated pubescent disappointment *in any one given case*. Yet the frustration does have disconfirmable predictive import, although its causal relevance is not claimed to be that of a specific pathogen. For by designating the stated sort of disappointment as *an* etiologic factor for lesbianism, Freud is claiming that occurrences of such disappointment *positively affect* the incidence of lesbianism.

This predictive consequence should be borne in mind, since Freud's case history of his lesbian patient occasioned his general observation that the etiologic explanation of an already existing instance of a disorder is usually not matched by the predictability of the syndrome *in any one given case* (S.E. 1920, 18: 167-168). An apologist for Popper was thereby led to conclude that the limitation on predictability in psychoanalysis thus avowed by Freud is tantamount to generic nonpredictability and hence to nondisconfirmability. But oddly enough this apologist is not inclined to regard the causal relevance of heavy smoking to cardiovascular disease as wholly nonpredictive or nondisconfirmable, although chain smoking is not even held to be a specific pathogen for this disease, let alone a universal predictor of it.

The comments I have made so far in response to Popper's aforecited 1974 statement have focused largely on Freud's 1915 paper on paranoia, whose very title announces an instance of empirical falsifiability. Besides, Freud's 1933 "Revision of the Theory of Dreams" presents an acknowledged falsification by the recurrent dreams of war neurotics. But we shall have occasion to discuss the clinical credentials of the psychoanalytic dream theory in chapter 5. Hence, it will suffice to have merely mentioned Freud's 1933 revision here before proceeding to the second set of comments that are prompted by Popper's 1974 declaration.

2. At the 1980 Popper Symposium, I asked what *proof* Popper has offered that *none* of the *consequences* of the theoretical Freudian postulates are empirically testable, as claimed by his thesis of nonfalsifiability. One of Popper's disciples in effect volunteered the reply that this untestability is known by direct inspection of the postulates, as it were. To this I say that the failure of some philosophers of science to identify testable consequences by such inspection may have been grounds for suspecting untestability, but is hardly adequate to furnish the required proof of nonfalsifiability.

Indeed, the examples of falsifiability that I have already adduced have a quite different moral: the inability of certain philosophers of science to have discerned *any* testable consequences of Freud's theory betokens their insufficient command or scrutiny of its logical content rather than a scientific liability of psychoanalysis. It is as if those with only a rather cursory exposure to physics concluded by inspection that its high level hypotheses are not falsifiable, just because *they* cannot think of a way to test them. For instance, both expertise and ingenuity made it possible recently to devise tests capable of falsifying the hypothesis that neutrinos have a zero rest mass (Robinson 1980). By the same token, I reject the hubristic expectation that if high-level psychoanalytic hypotheses are testable at all, then almost any intellectually gifted academic ought to be able to devise potentially falsifying test designs for them. Failing that, some Popperians rashly suggest that the presumption of inherent nontestability is strong.

Hence, let me return to my stated question: what proof, if any, did Popper actually offer for his aforecited emphatic reiteration that the Freudian theoretical corpus is wholly devoid of empirically testable consequences? To furnish such a proof, it would be necessary to establish the *falsity* of the claim that there exists at least one empirical statement about human behavior among the logical consequences of the psychoanalytic theoretical postulates. But as Popper has admonished elsewhere, an existential statement asserting that an *infinite* class A has at least one member that possesses a certain property P cannot be deductively falsified by any finite set of "basic" evidence sentences, each of which *denies* that some individual in A has P. Yet Popper has committed himself *tout court* to the *falsity* of the following *existential* statement: the infinite Tarskian consequence class of the psychoanalytic theoretical corpus does contain at least one member that qualifies as an empirical statement about human behavior.

Hence, I must ask: what *argument* has Popper given to sustain his denial of this existential statement? How did he manage to convince himself that the infinite consequence class of Freud's theory contains no testable members at all? Indeed, what would it be like to give a *proof* of this denial that is consonant with the requirements of a deductivist? Would one first try to axiomatize all of Freud's theory, perhaps with a view to availing oneself of Craig's method of re-axiomatization for the purpose of trying to eliminate all of the prima facie theoretical terms, and to determining whether all of the remaining theorems must somehow still be *generically* "*non*observational"? I do not profess to know the answer, but the problem is Popper's, not mine.

What he does offer in lieu of anything like such a *general* argument is a procedure that has at least the appearance of reliance on his methodological *bête noire*: induction by enumeration. For in the above citation and elsewhere, he invokes mere examples. Thus, he points to the quite different behavior of two men toward a child, one of whom would try to rescue it from drowning, the other who would attempt to kill it by drowning. Popper had also adduced this supposed illustration with a little more detail in his earlier writings (1962: 35). He gives no indication whatever whether he drew this example from any actual case history or publication of Freud's (or Adler's). Yet if Freud and Adler did play fast and loose with the ascription of dispositions to people in the manner of Popper's example, then their case histories surely ought to be rich in actual illustrations of such malfeasance. As the example stands, however, it appears grossly contrived. And I contend that, in any case, it is unavailing.

But here we can forego a detailed statement of my reasons for this judgment, for I have previously set them forth elsewhere (1979a: 134-135). There I did so by reference to Popper's more detailed original statement of his example.

Let me say here, however, that if Popper's case of the drowning child is to have any cogency at all, he would need to show that Freud's theory grants unrestricted *license* to postulate *at will* whatever potentially explanatory initial conditions we may fancy as to the motivation or dispositions of a given person in particular external circumstances. One looks in vain for Popper's documentation of such utter license in psychoanalysis. Yet in the aforecited passage, he again implicitly assumes it by simply telling us that "whatever anybody may do is, in principle, explicable in Freudian or Adlerian terms." This, in the face of the fact that Freud scorned the attribution of such universal explanatory power to his theory as a vulgar misunderstanding, when he referred to psychoanalysis and wrote: "It has never dreamt of trying to explain 'everything'" (S.E. 1923, 18: 252).

Hence, in an earlier article (1979*a*: 135) I asked concerning psycho-analysis: "Is it clear that the postulation of initial conditions *ad libitum* without any *independent* evidence of their fulfillment is quite generally countenanced by that theory to a far greater extent than in, say, physics, which Popper deems to be a bona fide science?" I claim that Freud's writings warrant a negative answer to this question. Moreover, William Goosens has made my evaluation of the case of the drowning child succinct by pointing out that Popper's use of this example to support his charge of nonfalsifiability boomerangs. For by gratuitously assuming unbridled freedom to postulate initial conditions in the manner of the example, it could be adapted, *mutatis mutandis*, to do the following: one would simply say that Newton's physics "does not exclude any particular particle's acting in any particular way," after having made just such gratuitous use of the failure of Newton's *laws* of motion themselves to restrict the direction in which a particle may move through a given point.

On the heels of saying that Freud's and Adler's theories do not exclude any physically possible human behavior, Popper told us that "whatever anybody may do is, in principle, explicable in Freudian or Adlerian terms." But if a theory *does not exclude* any behavior at all, no matter what the initial conditions, how then can it deductively *explain* any *particular* behavior? To explain deductively is to exclude: as Spinoza emphasized, to assert *p* is to deny every proposition incompatible with it. I can use two notions introduced by Michael Martin (1978: 10-16) to refine the statement of the relevant connection between the falsifiability of psychoanalysis, on the one hand, and its ability to explain facets of human thought or conduct, on the other. As Martin noted, the consequences of a theory may be empirically vague, and/or it may be unclear just what empirical statements the theory entails. Thus, he speaks respectively of "consequence vagueness" and of "deductive indetermi-nacy," and he points out that either of these two properties adversely affects the testability of a theory. Using these locutions, I maintain that insofar as consequence vagueness and/or deductive indeterminacy do militate against the empirical falsifiability of Freud's theory, they under-cut its *explanatory capability* as well as its *inductive confirmability*, and vice versa. For if a theory *T* fails to explain, either deductively or probabilistically, any particular behavior *b*, then *b* cannot confirm or support *T* by inductivist standards, notwithstanding Popper's caricature of these criteria of confirmation.

3. In the 1974 passage cited above, Popper seems to have made a parenthetical gesture in the direction of documentation from Freud by trying to *illustrate* the nonfalsifiability of psychoanalysis and/or Freud's inhospitality to falsifications as follows: "Adler's break with Freud was

more Adlerian than Freudian, but Freud never looked on it as a refutation of his theory." I submit that qua illustration of Freud's purported inhospitality to refutation, Popper's aside about the rift between Freud and Adler is unavailing and rather frivolous.

When Adler was still a Freudian, he reportedly told Freud that it was hardly gratifying for him to spend his entire life being intellectually overshadowed by Freud (Colby 1951: 230). Hence, it has been conjectured that Adler's doctrinal break with Freud was at least partly motivated by the desire to be a recognized innovative thinker in his own right. In his own psychological theory, Adler then went on to subordinate the sexual drive to the drive to assert oneself and to overcome a sense of inferiority even in sexual encounters. Perhaps Popper was referring to Adler's declared desire *not* to be Freud's understudy, when Popper said that "Adler's break with Freud was more Adlerian than Freudian." I myself do *not* see that the phenomenon of Adler's dissent does qualify as a *disconfirming* instance for Freud's theory. But *if* it does so qualify—as Popper seems to suggest here—then why does Popper feel entitled to claim that its falsifying force is lessened just because "Freud never looked on it as a refutation of his theory"?

In contrast, if Freud's theory is indeed as empirically *empty* as claimed by Popper by reference to his example of the drowning child, then how can Popper claim to *know*—as he does in the citation—that "Freud himself was clearly a Freudian case, and Adler an Adlerian case"? For, if psychoanalysis and Adlerian psychology are each thus devoid of empirical import, as alleged by Popper, how can even Freud's self-analysis and Adler's "masculine protest" defiance of Freud sustain Popper's assertion here that their respective personalities instantiated their respective theories?

More fundamentally, if Freud's theory is a mere "psychological metaphysics" or "myth," which only the future might see transformed into a testable theory—much as Empedocles' theory of evolution was a mere myth for a long time (Popper 1962: 38)—how, then, could Popper claim to know in 1974, by his own standards of factual empirical knowledge, that "there is some [nontautological] truth in it"? Unfortunately, he gives us no details. Far from being *unable*, like a myth, to make falsifiable predictions, psychoanalytic theory even makes predictions that qualify as "risky" by Popper's standards. Our discussion of "symptom substitution" in chapter 2, section C, will furnish another illustration of such a prediction. The reader will recall our earlier example of the expected decline in the incidence of paranoia as homosexuality becomes more accepted.

4. Freud made a major retraction in regard to the *distinctive* therapeutic merits he had claimed emphatically for his own modality of psychiatric treatment. Thus, in his fullest account of the dynamics he postulated for his version of analytic therapy (S.E. 1917, 16: 448-463), he had contended that, unlike other therapies—which substitute cosmetics for the extirpation of the pathogens that keep neuroses alive—analysis acts "like surgery" (p. 450) by overcoming resistances to the patient's educative insight into the role of these pathogens (see also S.E. 1925, 20: 43). And on this basis, he maintained in that 1917 account, as well as a few pages earlier (pp. 444-445), that psychoanalytic treatment has the uniquely *prophylactic* power of not only averting the patient's relapse into his prior affliction but also preventing his becoming ill with a different, fresh neurosis. Yet in his famous paper "Analysis Terminable and Interminable" (S.E. 1937, 23: 216-254), Freud repudiated both of these prophylactic capabilities. (The editors of the *Standard Edition* point out [23: 214-215], however, that Freud *seems* to have reinstated the durability of the therapeutic conquest of a *prior* neurosis in a paper that he wrote only a year later, but which was published posthumously [S.E. 1940, 23: 179].) Incidentally, throughout this essay, the term "analytic therapy" will be used to refer to *Freud's* own pioneering conception and/or practice of Breuer's therapeutic legacy, unless explicitly indicated otherwise.

F. J. Sulloway (1979), in a lengthy historical account of the evolution of Freud's theories under the influence of their initial biological moorings, and R. E. Fancher (1973), in an earlier depiction of the development of psychoanalytic psychology, give ample evidence that Freud's successive modifications of many of his hypotheses throughout most of his life were hardly empirically unmotivated, capricious, or idiosyncratic. What reconstruction, I ask, would or could Popper give us of Freud's rationale for these repeated theory changes, and still cling to his charge of nonfalsifiability and/or to his charge that Freud was inhospitable to adverse evidence? I see no escape from the conclusion that this charge ought never to have been leveled in the first place, or at least should not have been repeated by Popper as late as 1974. To have reached this conclusion, one need only to have read Freud's letters to Wilhelm Fliess, which were available in print two decades earlier than Popper's last statement on this matter (Freud 1954). Thus, to take a dramatic example, we learn from a letter that Freud wrote in 1897 how adverse evidence that he himself had uncovered drove him to repudiate his previously cherished seduction etiology of hysteria (Freud 1954, letter #69: 215-218). And even his at least occasional *intellectual hospitality* to refutation by others is apparent from the concluding sentence of a letter to Fliess in which he privately outlined the substance of his first 1895 paper on anxiety neurosis (Freud 1954, draft E: 88-94). The last sentence of this letter reads: "Suggestions, amplifications, *indeed refutations* and explanations, will be received with extreme gratitude [emphasis added]." In fact, as we shall now see, that 1895 paper offered a falsifiable etiology.

5. In his instructive 1895 "Reply to Criticisms of My Paper on Anxiety Neurosis" (S.E. 1895, 3: 123-139), Freud stated explicitly what sort of finding he would acknowledge to be a *refuting* instance for his hypothesized etiology of anxiety neurosis. Indeed, this reply, as well as the original paper defended in it, throw a great deal of light on Freud's understanding of the standards that need to be met when validating causal hypotheses. An account of his argument in these two 1895 papers on anxiety neurosis will illuminate just how the early Freud functioned as a *methodologist*, even though his theory of anxiety neurosis is not part of *psychoanalytic* theory proper.

And why is Freud's theory of anxiety neurosis not part of psychoanalytic theory proper? He hypothesized that no repressed ideas are the pathogens of anxiety neurosis, a syndrome that he detached as a distinct nosologic entity from neurasthenia, after the American neurologist Beard had singled out the latter as a clinical object. Since unconscious ideation is thus not implicated in the etiology of anxiety neurosis, the *psychoanalytic* method is not able, let alone necessary, to uncover its pathogenesis. By the same token, analytic *therapy* is not only unavailing for it but inapplicable to it. Indeed, the very etiology Freud conjectured for it entailed that only an alteration in the patient's current sexual life—not the probing of the unconscious legacy of his childhood—can remove its presumed *somatic* pathogen.

As Freud tells us, he had detached anxiety neurosis from Beard's neurasthenia as a distinct clinical entity because the symptoms of the former "are clinically much more closely related to one another" than to the typical symptoms of neurasthenia: "they frequently appear together and they replace one another in the course of the illness." And he labeled the underlying theoretical syndrome "anxiety neurosis," because all of its manifestations can be grouped around its chief nuclear symptom of anxiety (S.E. 1895, 3: 91). Thus, having enumerated the members of this *cluster* of symptoms and their incidence in specified life situations, Freud saw himself able to make fallible differential diagnoses of the presence of this cluster.

When proceeding to offer, in quite theoretical terms, his hypothesis as to the underlying etiology of this syndrome, he exempts two sorts of cases from its purview: (1) patients who give evidence that their affliction is a matter of "a grave hereditary taint," and (2) avowedly *very rare* and hence *negligible* cases in which "the etiology is doubtful or different" (S.E. 1895, 3: 99, 127). As for the first case type, he emphasizes that if "no heredity is to be discovered" in a given instance of the syndrome, he will "hold the case to be an acquired one," and will claim that his hypothesized etiology does apply to it (S.E. 1895, 3: 135). But what did Freud count as evidence for the presence of "a grave hereditary taint"?

Although he does not tell us in this particular paper, Breuer and he gave some indication of his answer in the same year on the opening page of the foundational case history of Anna O. Increased incidence of the disorder among "more distant relatives" is the criterion they give there for a neuropathic heredity (S.E. 1895, 2: 21). Yet as Freud noted in his "Heredity and the Aetiology of the Neuroses," "a retrospective diagnosis of the illnesses of ancestors or absent members of a family can only very rarely be successfully made" (S.E. 1896, 3: 144). The importance he presumably attached to the stated requirement that the relatives showing higher-than-average incidence of the symptoms be "more distant" can be gauged from his admonition not to infer hereditariness carelessly from mere increased incidence among siblings or cousins who lived together. As he emphasizes, the latter increased incidence could well be a matter of *"pseudo-heredity"* (S.E. 1896, 3: 209, 156).

Nowadays, when determining whether heredity enhances vulnerability to an affective disorder, investigators would seek such information as the comparative incidence of the disorder among separated monozygotic and dizygotic twins, as well as the incidence in the general population (Winokur 1975). *A fortiori* quite stringent probative demands would be made, if those suffering from a given disorder were to be subdivided into hereditary and acquired cases, as proposed by Freud. But even during his own time, Freud surely was all too aware that his decision to count a case of anxiety neurosis as "acquired" on the mere strength of not being *demonstrably* hereditary was fraught with the risk of misclassifying a bona fide hereditary case as "acquired" from sheer lack of information. By not fulfilling the antecedent pathogenic conditions required by Freud's specific etiology, such a *pseudo*acquired case can then *spuriously falsify* that etiologic hypothesis, which is restricted to *acquired* cases. Though Freud presumably appreciated this risk of spurious falsification no less than we do, the fact remains that he was willing to run it. And apparently, he was likewise willing to chance that the test cases he would face when being challenged by his critics would not happen to be the very rare etiologically anomalous ones, whose existence he had acknowledged at the outset. For as we shall see, he explicitly called on his critic Löwenfeld to confront him with cases of the syndrome in which the antecedent required by his specific etiology was *missing*. Thus, he was committing himself to accept such a finding as falsifying.

He had postulated that the psychically unassimilated neurophysiological effect of unrelieved or aborted, purely somatic sexual excitation is the specific pathogen of anxiety neurosis. For example, the forfeiture of the relief of sexual tension by either partner in coitus interruptus or reservatus often issues in the creation of the very condition he had thus hypothesized to be etiological. Freud explains how he tested his hypothesis in these cases by a procedure akin to J. S. Mill's joint method of agreement and difference, and found that it stood up well under such testing. But, as Benjamin Rubinstein has remarked, we do not know what sampling method Freud used, nor whether his findings were statistically significant.

What matters for us now is just how Freud dealt, in his second 1895 paper on anxiety neurosis (S.E. 1895, 3: 123-139), with the critique of his postulated etiology offered by the psychiatrist Leopold Löwenfeld, who claimed to have refuted it by clinical findings.

To recapitulate, Freud had made the strong quasi-*universal* claim that unless the etiology of the anxiety syndrome is easily seen to be *purely* hereditary in a given patient, the stated impairment of sexual life is the "specific cause" of this syndrome in the following twofold sense: this sexual impairment is well-nigh causally *necessary* for the occurrence of the syndrome, and furthermore, this sexual deficit is never (or hardly ever) an etiologic factor in any *other* distinct syndrome (S.E. 1895, 3: 99, 127, 134-139). Thus, Freud was claiming, among other things, that the stated abnormality of the sexual life had to have been present in practically *every* person who suffers from *acquired* (rather than purely hereditary) anxiety neurosis. Accordingly, he pointedly declared (S.E. 1895, 3: 128) that if Löwenfeld were to refute this claim, Löwenfeld would have to confront him with cases of the acquired syndrome in which Freud's postulated specific pathogen is missing. Freud makes clear that he regards an observably normal sex life to be an *empirically sufficient* indicator for the *absence* of this hypothesized pathogen, for he challenged Löwenfeld to confront him "with cases in which anxiety neurosis has arisen after a psychical shock although the subject has (on the whole) led a *normal vita sexualis.*" Furthermore, he noted that Löwenfeld had not fulfilled this condition when adducing the case of a woman patient whose anxiety neurosis Löwenfeld had attributed to a single frightening experience (S.E. 1895, 3: 129). Hence, speaking of anxiety neurosis also as "phobia," Freud provided a summary statement that would do any falsificationist proud:

The main thing about. . . phobias seems to me to be that *when the vita sexualis is normal*—when the specific condition, a disturbance of sexual life in the sense of a deflection of the somatic from the psychical, is not fulfilled—*phobias do not appear at all.* However much else may be obscure about the mechanism of phobias, my theory can only be refuted when I have been shown phobias where sexual life is normal. [S.E. 1895, 3: 134]

It has been objected that Freud's challenge to Löwenfeld was empty after all. For suppose that, in a given patient, they both agree that the differential diagnosis is anxiety neurosis. And assume further that, by all accounts, the patient's sex life is normal. Then the complaint is that everyone's sex life can be held to be abnormal in *some* respect, so that Freud could always escape refutation by pleading some such abnormality. But I should point out that, in a later paper, Freud explicitly disavowed such an evasive maneuver: "Since minor deviations from a normal *vita sexualis* are much too common for us to attach any value to their discovery, we shall only allow a serious and long-continued abnormality in the sexual life of a neurotic patient to carry weight as an explanation" (S.E. 1898, 3: 269). Besides, even in the above citation from his 1895 paper, he had barred such an escape by allowing parenthetically that a refuting instance would be present, even if the anxiety neurotic's sex life is normal only "on the whole."

But what of repudiating the differential diagnosis to evade falsification when the phobic patient's sex life is blissful? At *first* sight, one can get the quite mistaken impression that the retraction of a differential diagnosis for the sake of upholding an etiology *must* be illicit, and that Freud was guilty of just that. True, he did preserve the etiology of neurasthenia, though not of anxiety neurosis, by repudiating initial differential diagnoses. As he reports:

So far as the theory of the sexual aetiology of neurasthenia is concerned, there are no negative cases. In my mind, at least, the conviction has become so certain that where an interrogation has shown a negative result, I have turned this to account too for diagnostic purposes. I have told myself, that is, that such a case cannot be one of neurasthenia. [S.E. 1898. 3: 269]

It is immaterial that this report pertains to neurasthenia rather than anxiety neurosis, for it is safe to assume that Freud was not loath to follow the same procedure with respect to the etiology of anxiety neurosis. And since our concern is with the latter, I shall make this assumption, at least for expository purposes. But then I must point out that on the heels of reporting his retraction of a differential diagnosis to preserve his etiology, Freud hastened to emphasize the following: his retractions soon turned out to be supported by *independent* evidence for an *alternative* diagnosis (S.E. 1898, 3: 269-270). To provide perspective for gauging the merits of Freud's detailed handling of this independent confirmation, let us first see how non-Freudians deal with similar problems today.

Nowadays, just as in Freud's day, the differential diagnosis of anxiety neurosis presents at least two sorts of problems: (1) to differentiate it as a primary syndrome from organic diseases that often *mimic* many of the same symptoms, (2) to discriminate between anxiety neurosis and other psychiatric afflictions, notably depression. As for the first problem, even if the patient presents a typical cluster of anxiety-related symptoms, it is essential to rule out such physical disorders as ischemia (e.g., coronary insufficiency), hyperthyroidism, caffeinism, paroxysmal atrial tachycardia, psychomotor epilepsy, hypoglycemia, drug abuse, and drug withdrawal syndrome, among others. And in regard to the second problem, note that the symptoms of the two psychiatric disorders always overlap, at least in regard to disturbances of sleep, appetite, and sexuality. It is generally recognized that unless a symptom cluster is pathognostic for one particular disease, it is typically very difficult indeed to make a unique diagnosis by exclusion of potential diagnostic pitfalls (Slater and Roth 1977: 96-97).

Now suppose that an initial differential diagnosis classified some patients as belonging to a certain nosologic category C. But assume further that, thus classified, their prior histories are incompatible with a previously hypothesized etiology of C that had been accepted. Or that, when the patients classified as C underwent a treatment t previously deemed effective for C, they responded poorly, thereby impugning the therapy t. Then the very fallibility of differential diagnoses may make it reasonable to retract the initial differential diagnosis and preserve previously accepted etiologic or therapeutic hypotheses, provided that independent evidence for an alternative diagnosis is then forthcoming. Just such a procedure is illustrated in a recent book of psychiatry whose authors are anything but Freudians (Slater and Roth 1977: 96-97).

As they point out in effect (p. 97), when patients who are prima facie depressives react by acute exacerbation of their symptoms to treatments that are deemed effective for depression, the latter claim of therapeutic effectiveness is not rejected; instead, the treatment fiasco is taken to be good grounds for then making a new differential diagnosis of anxiety neurosis. Thus, when particular patients initially classified as depressives get worse after treatment by presumably antidepressant tricyclic compounds or by electroshock, the therapeuticity of these treatments for bona fide depressives is not impugned; rather, it is then inferred that the given patients ought to be reclassified as suffering from anxiety neurosis. Independent evidence to sustain the reclassification is not easily procured: modern statistical methods were needed to achieve a satisfactory degree of differentiation between depression and anxiety neurosis (Slater and Roth 1977: 226).

With this perspective, let us ask: when Freud preserved his etiologies by the retraction of initial differential diagnoses, did he make his continued adherence to this inference contingent on the production of *independent* evidence for the unsoundness of the initial diagnoses? As he reports, when a number of prima facie neurasthenics turned out to have personal histories incompatible with his postulated sexual etiology of neurasthenia, he was driven to reclassify them as victims of progressive paralysis. And, Freud maintains, "The further course of those cases later confirmed my view" (S.E. 1898, 3: 269). In another case, the alternative diagnosis that a physical ailment is aping the symptoms of neurasthenia received independent confirmation (pp. 269-270).

But the procurement of independent evidence for an alternative differential diagnosis became more murky when it just called for reliance on the psychoanalytic method. The etiologies Freud had enunciated for both anxiety neurosis and neurasthenia *excluded* repressed ideation from their pathogenesis. Hence, the diagnostic identification of patients suffering from these so-called "actual" neuroses provided no scope for the use of the psychoanalytic method of clinical investigation, whose hallmark was the exposure of repressions. Breuer's work on hysterics, however, had led Freud to postulate repression etiologies for the "psychoneuroses" of hysteria and obsessional disorder. Hence, when there was a need to *confirm* that a patient's presenting symptoms ought to be rediagnosed as betokening one of the psychoneuroses rather than one of the "actual" neuroses, reliance on the psychoanalytic method became essential in order to find etiologic corroboration.

Just this need for independent confirmation by the psychoanalytic method arose when Freud resorted to an alternative diagnosis of psychoneurosis to prevent the refutation of the etiologies he had enunciated for the actual neuroses:

Sometimes an interrogation discloses the presence of a normal sexual life in a patient whose neurosis, on a superficial view, does in fact closely resemble neurasthenia or anxiety neurosis. But a more deep-going investigation regularly reveals the true state of affairs. Behind such cases, which have been taken for neurasthenia, there lies a psychoneurosis—hysteria or obsessional neurosis. . . .

Falling back on psychoneurosis when a case of neurasthenia shows a negative sexual result, is, however, no cheap way out of the difficulty; the proof that we are right is to be obtained by the method which alone unmasks hysteria with certainty—the method of psycho-analysis. [S.E. 1898, 3: 270]

In short, Freud's procedure was to invoke the etiologies of the psychoneuroses—which he had evolved by means of the psychoanalytic method—as a basis for independently confirming alternative diagnoses required to preserve his etiologies of the actual neuroses. For when prima facie cases of anxiety neurosis or neurasthenia did not fulfill the antecedents demanded by Freud's etiologies, he then *rediagnosed* them as cases of psychoneurosis. Unless the psychoanalytic method is fundamentally flawed and/or there is reason to doubt the etiologies predicated upon it, Freud is entitled to claim that this procedure is indeed not a "cheap way out of the difficulty."

It is one central thesis of this essay that the clinical psychoanalytic method and the causal (etiologic) inferences based upon it are fundamentally flawed epistemically, but for reasons *other than* nonfalsifiability. What is now relevant, instead, to the appraisal of Freud's reliance on *psychoanalytic* rediagnoses of prima facie neurasthenics is a matter of personal scientific integrity raised by Glymour (private communication): we know from Freud's private 1897 letter (number 69) to Fliess that, by the time he *denied* having used a "cheap way out," he had good reason to be quite diffident about *such* rediagnoses, because his seduction etiology of hysteria lay in shambles. Indeed, we know from one of his 1898 letters to Fliess that Freud was fairly cynical about the entire 1898 article in which he espoused rediagnoses: "You must promise me to expect nothing from the chit-chat article. It really is nothing but tittle-tattle, good enough for the public, but not worth mentioning between ourselves" (Freud 1954, letter #81: 243). Yet, having started his self-analysis in the summer of 1897 (see S.E., 3: 262), and having thereby been led to postulate the Oedipus complex by October 1897 (Freud 1954, letter #71: 223), perhaps Freud entertained hopes by early 1898 of vindicating the psychoanalytic method after all.

In any case, a proper appraisal of Freud's methodology even during the formative years of psychoanalysis defies Popper's crude categories. But deplorably, the simplistic verdicts Popper was able to generate by his obliviousness to Freud's actual writings have not only gained wide currency but are still in vogue. One need only turn to such very recent books as those by Stannard (1980: chaps. 3, 4) and Clark (1980). Yet I trust it will become clear from the scrutiny of clinical validation I shall offer in this essay just why Popper's application of his falsifiability criterion is too insensitive to exhibit the most *egregious* of the epistemic defects bedeviling the Freudian etiologies, interpretation of dreams, theory of parapraxes, etc. Indeed, as I shall argue, time-honored inductivist canons for the validation of causal claims have precisely that capability.

6. In 1937, two years before his death, Freud published his "Constructions in Analysis" (S.E. 1937, 23: 257-269). This methodologically crucial paper is devoted to the logic of clinical disconfirmation and confirmation of psychoanalytic interpretations and reconstructions of the patient's past, which are the epistemic lifeblood of Freud's entire theory. In chapter 10, I shall argue for the spuriousness of the *consilience* of clinical inductions espoused by Freud in that 1937 paper. But this spuriousness does not make it any less odd that anyone should have pen in hand and charge Freud with total insensitivity to falsifiability without even allowing for the following opening paragraph of that key paper:

A certain well-known man of science...gave expression to an opinion upon analytic technique which was at once derogatory and unjust. He said that in giving interpretations to a patient we treat him upon the famous principle of "Heads I win, tails you lose." That is to say, if the patient agrees with us, then the interpretation is right; but if he contradicts us, that is only a sign of his resistance, which again shows that we are right. In this way we are always in the right against the poor helpless wretch whom we are analysing, no matter how he may respond to what we put forward. Now...it is in fact true that a "No" from one of our patients is not as a rule enough to make us abandon an interpretation as incorrect.... It is therefore worth while to give a detailed account of how we are accustomed to arrive at an assessment of the "Yes" or "No" of our patients during analytic treatment—of their expression of agreement or of denial. [S.E. 1937, 23: 257]

7. Although Popper did not mention ambivalence in the 1974 statement quoted earlier, let me comment here on his rhetorical question of whether the psychoanalytic concept of ambivalence is not typical of a whole family of Freudian notions, "which would make it difficult, if not impossible, to agree" (Popper 1962: 38, n. 3) on criteria for falsifying the explanatory relevance of such concepts. Incidentally, Popper combines this rhetorical question with the tantalizing parenthetical caveat that he does not deny the existence of ambivalence. But I submit that insofar as there is actual agreement on definite *criteria* for falsification in those theories that Popper does deem "scientific," I do not see why such agreement should be, in principle, more elusive in the case of ambivalence, *modulo* Duhemian excursions into the quite elastic Lakatosian protective belts. For let us turn to Freud's ascription of ambivalence to Little Hans or more generally, say, to children (Laplanche and Pontalis

1973: 26-28), where there is testability, I suggest, for the following reason: to predicate ambivalence of children toward their parents is to say that there will be *some* behavioral manifestations of hostility as well as some overt expressions of affection, and *one* of these two contrary affects may be largely unconscious or covert at any one time. If there were no such mixed behavioral orientation at all, the ascription of ambivalence would be disconfirmed. Of course, Freud's theory of child ambivalence does not predict which one of the two polar affects a child will display on a given occasion. But *such* nonpredictability is not tantamount to untestability.

So much for my scrutiny of those Popperian objections to Freud that were *not specifically* aimed at impugning the probative relevance of the *clinical* data from analytic treatment sessions. Chapter 11 will deal with Popper's strictures on such data.

2.
Did Freud Vindicate His Method of Clinical Investigation?

I should remind the reader that "clinical data" are here construed as findings coming from *within* the psychoanalytic treatment sessions. When I am concerned with contrasting these data from the couch with observational results secured from *outside* the psychoanalytic interview, I shall speak of the former as *"intra*clinical" for emphasis.

It will be useful to provide some advance perspective on the issues to be treated in the present chapter. Hence I shall now outline those of my theses that will emerge from them and from their ramifications in either the present or later chapters.

1. Freud gave a cardinal epistemological defense of the psychoanalytic method of clinical investigation that seems to have hitherto gone entirely unnoticed. I have dubbed this pivotal defense "The Tally Argument" in earlier publications (Grünbaum 1979b, 1980). It was *this* defense—or its bold lawlike premise—I maintain, that was all at once his basis for five claims, each of which is of the first importance for the legitimation of the central parts of his theory. These five claims are the following:

    (i) Denial of an irremediable epistemic contamination of clinical data by suggestion

    (ii) Affirmation of a crucial difference, in regard to the *dynamics* of therapy, between psychoanalytic treatment and all rival therapies that actually operate entirely by suggestion

    (iii) Assertion that the psychoanalytic method is able to validate its major causal claims—such as its specific sexual etiologies of the various psychoneuroses—by essentially *retrospective* methods without vitiation by *post hoc ergo propter hoc*, and without the burdens of prospective studies employing the controls of experimental inquiries

(iv) Contention that favorable therapeutic outcome can be warrantedly attributed to psychoanalytic intervention *without* statistical comparisons pertaining to the results from untreated control groups

(v) Avowal that, once the patient's motivations are no longer distorted or hidden by repressed conflicts, credence can rightly be given to his or her introspective self-observations, because these data then do supply probatively significant information (cf. Kohut 1959; Waelder 1962: 628-629)

2. The epistemological considerations that prompted Freud to enunciate his Tally Argument make him a sophisticated scientific methodologist, far superior than is allowed by the appraisals of friendly critics like Fisher and Greenberg (1977) or Glymour (1980), let alone by very severe critics like Eysenck.

Yet evidence accumulating in the most recent decades makes the principal premise of the Tally Argument well-nigh empirically untenable, and thus devastatingly undermines the conclusions that Freud drew from it. Indeed, no empirically plausible alternative to that crucial discredited premise capable of yielding Freud's desired conclusions seems to be in sight.

3. Without a viable replacement for Freud's Tally Argument, however, there is woefully insufficient ground to vindicate the intraclinical testability of the cardinal tenets of psychoanalysis (especially of its ubiquitous causal claims)—a testability espoused traditionally by analysts, and more recently by Glymour on the strength of the pincer-and-bootstrap strategy. This unfavorable conclusion is reached by the application of neo-Baconian inductivist standards, whose demands for the validation of causal claims can clearly not be met intraclinically unless the psychoanalytic method is buttressed by a powerful substitute for the defunct Tally Argument. Moreover, in the absence of such a substitute, the epistemic decontamination of the bulk of the patient's productions on the couch from the suggestive effects of the analyst's communications appears to be quite utopian. But, just for the sake of argument, let us suppose that we *can* take the patient's clinical responses at face value as epistemically uncontaminated. As the six chapters of Part II will show, *even then* Freud's cardinal clinical arguments for his entire cornerstone theory of repression would still remain fundamentally flawed.

4. Insofar as the credentials of psychoanalytic theory are currently

held to rest on clinical findings, as most of its official spokesmen would have us believe, the dearth of acceptable and probatively cogent clinical data renders these credentials quite weak. Thus, lacking a viable alternative to the aborted Tally Argument with comparable scope and ambition, the future validation of Freudian theory, if any, will have to come very largely from *extra*clinical findings (Masling, 1983).

5. Two years before his death, Freud invoked the *consilience* of clinical inductions (in the sense of William Whewell) to determine the probative cogency of the patient's assent or dissent in response to the interpretations presented by the analyst (S.E. 1937, 23: 257-269). But such a reliance on consilience is unavailing until and unless there emerges an as yet unimagined trustworthy method for epistemically decontaminating each of the *seemingly* independent consilient pieces of clinical evidence. For, as I shall argue, the methodological defects of Freud's "fundamental rule" of free association (S.E. 1923, 18: 238; 1925, 20: 41; 1940, 23: 174) ingress *alike* into the interpretation of several of these prima facie independent pieces of evidence (e.g., manifest dream content, parapraxes, waking fantasies). This multiple ingression renders the seeming consilience probatively spurious. But even if the consilient emergence of a repression were genuine, this would still not show that repressions *engender* neuroses, dreams or "slips."

6. Given the aforementioned dismal inductivist verdict on clinical testability, that traditional inductivist methodology of theory appraisal no more countenances the *clinical* validation of psychoanalysis than Popper does (1962: 38, n. 3). Hence, the specifically clinical confirmations claimed by many Freudians but abjured as spurious by inductivist canons are unavailable as a basis for Popper's charge of undue permissiveness against an inductivist criterion of demarcation. And, as I have already argued in chapter 1, section B, the actual falsifiability of psychoanalysis undercuts Popper's reliance on Freud's theory as a basis for claiming greater stringency for his criterion of demarcation.

Finally, Popper's astonishing omission of Freud's explicit reference to the Tally Argument from a passage that Popper adduced against him renders Popper's exegesis of Freud highly unfair and misleading. It was only by simply ignoring and omitting mention of Freud's reference to the Tally Argument when citing the passage in question that Popper was able to indict Freud for being incredibly oblivious to the contaminating effects of suggestion. Indeed, Freud's concern with these effects was always unflagging.

Let me begin with my account of Freud's rationale for putting clinical confirmation on an epistemic throne.

A. ARE CLINICAL CONFIRMATIONS AN ARTIFACT OF THE PATIENT'S POSITIVE "TRANSFERENCE" FEELINGS TOWARD THE ANALYST?

Despite Freud's fundamental epistemic reliance on clinical testing, he did indeed acknowledge the challenge that data from the couch ought to be discounted as being inadmissibly contaminated. Even friendly critics like Wilhelm Fliess charged that analysts induce their docile patients by suggestion to furnish the very clinical responses needed to validate the psychoanalytic theory of personality (Freud 1954: pp. 334-337). Freud himself deemed it necessary to counter decisively this ominous charge of *spurious* clinical confirmation. For he was keenly aware that unless the methodologically damaging import of the patient's compliance with his doctor's expectations can somehow be neutralized, the doctor is on thin ice when purporting to mediate veridical insights to his client rather than only fanciful *pseudo*insights persuasively endowed with the ring of verisimilitude. Indeed, if the probative value of the analysand's responses is thus negated by brainwashing, then Freudian therapy might reasonably be held to function as an emotional corrective *not* because it enables the analysand to acquire bona fide self-knowledge, but instead because he or she succumbs to proselytizing *suggestion*, which operates the more insidiously under the pretense that analysis is *non*directive.

After Freud had practiced analysis for some time by communicating his interpretations of the patient's unconscious motivations, he felt himself driven to modify the dynamics of his therapy by according the role of a catalyst, vehicle, or ice-breaker to the patient's positive feelings for the analyst. For Freud had to mobilize these positive feelings to overcome the analysand's resistances with a view to eliciting confirmation from the latter's memory, whenever possible (S.E. 1920, 18: 18). And depending on whether the analysand's feelings toward his doctor were positive or negative, Freud spoke of the emotional relationship as a positive or negative "transference" (S.E. 1912, 12: 105). When thus acknowledging the vehicular therapeutic role of the positive transference relationship and attributing it to the doctor's authority qua parent surrogate, Freud knew all too well (S.E. 1917, 16: 446-447) that he was playing right into the hands of those critics who made the following complaints: clinical data have no probative value for the confirmation of the psychoanalytic theory of personality, and any therapeutic gains from analysis are *not* wrought by true insightful self-discovery but rather are the placebo effects induced by the analyst's suggestive influence. Thus, Freud gave ammunition to just these critics when he acknowledged the following: in order to overcome the patient's fierce resistances to the analyst's interpretations of his unconscious conflicts, the analyst cannot rely on the patient's intellectual insight but must decisively enlist the patient's need for his doctor's approval qua parental surrogate (S.E. 1917, 16: 445; 1919, 17: 159). In fact, Freud himself points out that precisely this affectionate help-seeking subservience on the part of the analysand "clothes the doctor with authority and is transformed into belief in his communications and explanations" (S.E. 1917, 16: 445). In this vein, Freud asks the patient to believe in the analyst's theoretical retrodictions of significant happenings in the client's early life when the patient himself is *unable to recall* these hypothesized remote events (S.E. 1920, 18: 18-19). For, as Freud tells us: "The patient cannot remember the whole of what is repressed in him, and what he cannot remember may be precisely the essential part of it. Thus he acquires no sense of conviction of the correctness of the construction that has been communicated to him" (S.E. 1920, 18: 18).

Thus, despite his best efforts, the analyst may well be stymied when seeking confirmation of his reconstructions of the patient's childhood by retrieving the latter's repressed memories. In such situations, Freud justifies his demand for the patient's faith in his retrodictions by the assumption that the analysand has a "compulsion to repeat" or re-enact prototypic conflictual childhood themes with the doctor: "He [the patient] is obliged to *repeat* the repressed material as a contemporary experience instead of, as the physician would prefer to see, *remembering* it as something belonging to the past" (S.E. 1920, 18: 18). The repeated themes are held to derive from infantile sexual yearnings once entertained by the patient toward his parents (S.E. 1925, 20: 43). Now the main evidence that Freud adduces for his repetition-compulsion postulate is that the adult realities at the time of the analytic transaction show the patient's positive feelings toward his analyst to be extravagant in degree as well as grotesque in character (S.E. 1914, 12: 150; 1917, 16: 439-444). Yet this very state of mind clearly heightens the patient's suggestibility via intellectual and psychological subordination to his doctor. And this suggestibility is not lessened, especially in regard to genetic transference interpretations, in an analysis employing the technique recommended by Merton Gill (1980: 287), who accords a role to genetic transference interpretations but urges that "the bulk of the analytic work should take place in the transference in the here and now" (p. 286).

Moreover, ever since Freud had studied with Charcot in 1885 and had then used prohibitory suggestion to order hypnotized patients to shed their symptoms, he had appreciated the power of pure suggestion to effect impressive even if only temporary remissions (S.E. 1905, 7: 301-

302). Thus, in 1893, when Breuer and he published their joint Preliminary Communication on Breuer's cathartic method for treating hysteria
(S.E. 1893, 2: 3-17), they pointedly *argued* that *not* suggestion but rather
the cathartic release of strangulated affect associated with a traumatic
memory is responsible for the therapeutic gains of hysterics who had
been treated by that method (S.E. 1893, 2: 7). Freud was wont to repeat
this disavowal of prohibitory suggestion in later years when speaking of
Breuer's original hypnotic version of the cathartic method (e.g., in S.E.
1904, 7: 250). And once Freud had modified Breuer's method so as to
transform it into full-fledged psychoanalysis, he was at pains again and
again—even before his 1917 landmark paper "Analytic Therapy"—to
dissociate the dynamics of his therapy from the prohibitory suggestion
devices of other treatment modalities, just as Breuer and he had thus
dissociated the cathartic method itself (S.E. 1895, 2: 99, 305; 1904,
7: 250, 260-261, 301; 1910, 11: 146-147; 1912, 12: 105-106; 1913,
12: 125-126; 1913, 12: 143-144; 1914, 12: 155-156).

Indeed, Breuer and Freud *predicated* their *etiologic* identification of
repressed traumatic memories as being *pathogens* on precisely their
"observation" that the therapeutic successes of the cathartic method are
wrought by the hypnotized patient's abreactive recall of the forgotten
traumatic experience, and not by prohibitory suggestion. Thus, therapeutic recall of a repressed memory emerged as a kind of proto insight
into the pathogen of the patient's psychoneurosis. Once Freud had
replaced hypnosis by free association in the psychoanalytic method of
treatment and investigation, the moral he drew from the cathartic
method was that any genuine therapeutic gain attained by his patients
requires insight into the actual pathogens of their affliction. Hence, the
durable achievement of substantial therapeutic progress could be held to
betoken the correctness of the etiology inferred by means of the psychoanalytic method of inquiry.

So far, we have been tacitly assuming that the hypnotized patient's
recall of a traumatic event is veridical. But recent experimental studies of
hypnotic recall (Dywan and Bowers 1983) have cast much doubt on the
authenticity of hypnotically enhanced remembering. These investigations have shown that hypnotic hypermnesia is achieved largely at the
expense of veridicality: When highly hypnotizable subjects recalled
twice as many new items hypnotically as the control subjects, they
introduced *three* times as many new errors, despite their intense conviction that the new memories were trustworthy! Thus, hypnotic memory is
less, not more, reliable than normal pre-hypnotic recall. It would seem
that, by being more suggestible, the hypnotized person translates some
of his own beliefs and/or those of the hypnotist into *pseudo*-memories.

By 1900, Wilhelm Fliess had objected (Freud 1954: 334-335) that a cognate doctrinal compliance with the analyst's interpretations occurs, when the patient is asked to retrieve memories via free association rather than hypnotically.

No wonder, therefore, that Freud saw the clinical confirmations of his *etiologic* hypotheses placed in some jeopardy when critics seized on the avowed *catalytic* remedial role of the patient's transference relationship to his analyst. Critics adduced the role of transference to *deny* that veridical insight into the pathogens of the analysand's neurosis is the therapeutically effective ingredient of an analysis. Thus, at the end of his 1917 lecture "Transference," which beautifully set the stage for the crucial next one, "Analytic Therapy," Freud squarely addressed the portentous challenge of suggestibility as follows:

It must dawn on us that in our technique we have abandoned hypnosis only to rediscover suggestion in the shape of transference.

But here I will pause, and let you have a word; for I see an objection boiling up in you so fiercely that it would make you incapable of listening if it were not put into words: "Ah! so you've admitted it at last! You work with the help of suggestion, just like the hypnotists! That is what we've thought for a long time. But, if so, why the roundabout road by way of memories of the past, discovering the unconscious, interpreting and translating back distortions—this immense expenditure of labour, time and money—when the one effective thing is after all only suggestion? Why do you not make direct suggestions against the symptoms, as the others do—the honest hypnotists? Moreover, if you try to excuse yourself for your long detour on the ground that you have made a number of important psychological discoveries which are hidden by direct suggestion—what about the certainty of these discoveries now? Are not they a result of suggestion too, of unintentional suggestion? Is it not possible that you are forcing on the patient what you want and what seems to you correct in this field as well?"

What you are throwing up at me in this is uncommonly interesting and must be answered. [S.E. 1917, 16: 446-447]

This thoroughgoing recognition of the double bombshell of suggestibility *and* the careful 1917 argument Freud then offered in an attempt to defuse it stands in refreshing contrast to the manner in which typical contemporary analysts insouciantly ignore the heart of the matter or make light of it.

Thus, Linn A. Campbell (1978: 1, 8-9, 20-21) maintains that the *deliberate* use of suggestion with a view to obtaining an *uncritical* or unreflective response from the patient is antithetical to the *exploratory aims* of analytic therapy. But Campbell does not even consider how the therapist's good intention to let the patient be critical can be expected to provide prophylaxis against compliant yet reflective patient responses that issue in spurious clinical confirmations. The closest Campbell comes to entertaining that the elicitation of such patient responses might actually be unavoidable is as follows: he acknowledges the risk of *inadvertent* covert suggestion by the analyst when the latter has an unconscious neurotic need for a shortcut to the patient's gratitude (pp. 19-20). Yet Campbell soothingly assures us that, in any such case, truth will out: any symptom relief ensuing from such an unconscious misalliance between patient and therapist will be transient, since the patient will be left vulnerable to later stresses. Thus, by the end of Campbell's article the central issue has been successfully sidetracked.

In another recent article on psychoanalysis and suggestion, the German analyst Helmut Thomä (1977: 51) claims that the patient's skepticism counteracts the analyst's suggestive influences, especially when the analysand has hostile feelings toward his doctor, But it is a commonplace among analysts that even patients who have angrily abandoned their initial therapist and enter re-analysis with another, turn out to retain notions they acquired from their first analyst. Yet on the strength of patient skepticism, Thomä does not adequately come to grips with the problem to which his entire article is presumably addressed.

As a last illustration of the epistemic laxity of respected present-day analysts, I quote from the senior Chicago analyst Michael Basch (1980: 70-71), who wrote:

Only the hope of fulfilling infantile wishes can mobilize a patient for the therapeutic task. In adulthood, as in childhood, only the hope for love and the fear that love will be withdrawn can overcome the resistance to examining defensive patterns that have, after all, been established to avoid anxiety.

A patient who has a positive transference to the therapist wants to please him and will talk about what she thinks will interest him. . . . A patient lets himself be known, even though he fears exposing himself to humiliation and punishment, because he wants the therapist's affection and approval, not simply because he wants to get well. To know this about a patient is to be alert to the dangers of the transference relationship. The patient in a positive transference will, unconsciously, do his best to conform to the therapist's wishes as he, the patient, understands them. If the therapist wants to talk in terms of the Oedipus complex and incestuous sexuality, the patient will do his utmost to bring out material in such a way that it will fit that set; if another therapist approaches the same patient in a different framework, the latter will oblige that therapist in turn.

But when Basch points to the latter compliance as an illustration of the dangers inherent in the patient's eagerness to please his analyst, he cheerfully disregards the *epistemic* ravages of that compliance; for he tells us that "all is well" so long as the therapy sessions do not stagnate or become boring, and the patient's behavior changes. If such stagnation is avoided, we are told, the patient may safely be presumed to be acquiring bona fide insights. Only the stated kind of stagnation is held to bespeak that "the therapist's focus was not accurate and that he must lead the patient's introspection in a different direction" (p. 71). But this ignores that the patient may be undergoing brainwashing and may embrace mythological analytic interpretations even as his symptoms improve and as he finds the sessions interesting.

I shall be concerned to discuss just how Freud himself brilliantly, albeit unsuccessfully, came to grips with the full dimensions of the mortal challenge of suggestibility, which he himself stated so eloquently. When he picked up this gauntlet in his 1917 lecture, "Analytic Therapy," he gave us his cardinal epistemological defense of the psychoanalytic method of clinical investigation and testing, a pivotal vindication whose import had gone completely unnoticed in the literature, as far as I know, until I called attention to its significance in two recent papers (Grünbaum 1979b, 1980). There I dubbed Freud's fundamental 1917 defense of his clinical epistemology "The Tally Argument."

B. FREUD'S RELIANCE ON THE HYPOTHESIZED DYNAMICS OF THERAPY AS A VINDICATION OF HIS THEORY OF UNCONSCIOUS MOTIVATION

Freud begins his 1917 "Analytic Therapy" lecture by recalling the question that he is about to address. As he puts it:

You asked me why we do not make use of direct suggestion in psycho-analytic therapy, when we admit that our influence rests essentially on transference [which amounts to the utilization of the patient's personal relationship to the analyst]—that is, on suggestion; and you added a doubt whether, in view of this predominance of suggestion, we are still able to claim that our psychological discoveries are objective [rather than self-fulfilling products of *unintentional* suggestion]. I promised I would give you a detailed reply. [S.E. 1917, 16: 448]

The careful reply he then proceeds to give falls into two parts.

First, he tries to explain meticulously that in *hypnosis*, suggestion serves the *pivotal* role of simply ceremonially *forbidding* the symptoms to exist, whereas in the dynamics of psychoanalytic therapy, the function of suggestion is that of being a *catalyst* or "vehicle" in the *educative* excavation of the repressed underlying etiology of the symptoms. And as he stressed nearly a decade later, "it would be a mistake to believe that this factor [of suggestion] is the vehicle and promoter of the treatment throughout its length. At the beginning, no doubt" (S.E. 1926, 20: 190). Second, far from begging the question by just *asserting* this epistemically wholesome role for suggestion in analysis, he justifies his assertion by enunciating the following premise: the veridical disclosure of the patient's hidden conflicts, which are the pathogens of his or her neurosis, is causally necessary for the durable and thoroughgoing conquest of his or her illness. But the disclosure thus requisite for therapeutic success will occur, in turn, *only* if incorrect analytic interpretations, spuriously confirmed by *contaminated* responses from the patient, have been discarded in favor of correct constructions derived from clinical data *not* distorted by the patient's compliance with the analyst's communicated expectations. In short, in the second part of his reply to the stated charge of contamination, Freud gives an *argument* for deeming the therapeutically favorable outcome of an analysis to be adequate reason for attributing the following probative merit to such a successful analysis: "Whatever in the doctor's conjectures is inaccurate drops out in the course of the analysis" (S.E. 1917, 16: 452).

Let us now look at Freud's more detailed statement of his twofold reply to the basic question posed by him at the start of his 1917 lecture. As he points out (S.E. 1917, 16: 449-450), the elimination of symptoms by hypnosis is usually only temporary and hence requires a quasi-addictive repetition of the treatment. In the course of thus forbidding the symptoms, the doctor learns nothing as to their "sense and meaning." Thus, he tells us:

In the light of the knowledge we have gained from psycho-analysis we can describe the difference between hypnotic and psycho-analytic suggestion as follows. Hypnotic treatment seeks to cover up and gloss over something in mental life; analytic treatment seeks to expose and get rid of something [footnote omitted]. The former acts like a cosmetic, the latter like surgery. The former makes use of suggestion in order to forbid the symptoms; it strengthens the repressions, but, apart from that, leaves all the processes that have led to the formation of the symptoms unaltered. Analytic treatment makes its impact further back towards the roots, where the conflicts are which gave rise to the symptoms, and uses suggestion in order to alter the outcome of those conflicts. Hypnotic treatment leaves the patient inert and unchanged, and for that reason, too, equally unable to resist any fresh occasion for falling ill. An analytic treatment demands from both doctor and patient the accomplishment of serious work, which is employed in lifting internal resistances. Through the overcoming of these resistances the patient's mental life is permanently changed, is raised to a high level of development and remains protected against fresh possibilities of falling ill [footnote omitted]. This work of overcoming resistances is the essential function of analytic treatment; the patient has to accomplish it and the doctor makes this possible for him with the help of suggestion operating in an *educative* sense. For that reason psycho-analytic treatment has justly been described as a kind of *after-education* [footnote omitted]. [S.E. 1917, 16: 450-451]

After a theoretical interlude to which we shall turn shortly, Freud completes his account of the difference between the *therapeutic* employment of suggestion in hypnosis, on the one hand, and in analysis, on the other. Thus, he explains further:

We endeavour by a careful technique to avoid the occurrence of premature successes due to suggestion; but no harm is done even if they do occur, for we are not satisfied by a first success. We do not regard an analysis as at an end until all the obscurities of the case are cleared up, the gaps in the patient's memory filled in, the precipitating causes of the repression discovered. We look upon successes that set in too soon as obstacles rather than as a help to the work of analysis; and we put an end to such successes by constantly resolving the transference on which they are based [which is to analyze the patient's emotional attachment to the analyst *and* to wean him from the dependence engendered by it]. It is this last characteristic which is the fundamental distinction between analytic and purely suggestive therapy, and which frees the results of analysis from the suspicion of being successes due to suggestion. In every other kind of suggestive treatment the transference is carefully preserved and left untouched; in analysis it is itself subjected to treatment and is dissected in all the shapes in which it appears. At the end of an analytic treatment the transference must itself be cleared away; and if success is then obtained or continues, it rests, not on suggestion, but on the achievement by its means of an overcoming of internal resistances, on the internal change that has been brought about in the patient.

The acceptance of suggestions on individual points is no doubt discouraged by the fact that during the treatment we are struggling unceasingly against resistances which are able to transform themselves into negative (hostile) transferences. [S.E. 1917, 16: 452-453]

But note that, as Freud himself emphasizes, the doctor makes it possible for the patient to overcome resistances "with the help of suggestion operating in the *educative* sense" (S.E. 1917, 16: 451). And, as we recall, he had acknowledged that the patient's transference attachment to the analyst "clothes the doctor with authority and is transformed into belief in his communications" (S.E. 1917, 16: 445). Hence, it can readily be objected that precisely because the doctor is thus leading the patient—much as a lawyer may be leading a witness in the courtroom— the asserted *therapeutic* differences between hypnosis and analysis boomerang, since an avowedly *educative* use of suggestion provides even more scope for indoctrinating the patient to become an ideological disciple than the prohibitory kind of suggestion, which is essentially confined to the symptoms.

Characteristically, Freud is alert to the legitimacy of this challenge, and he addresses it head-on in what I regard as epistemologically perhaps the most pregnant single passage in his writings:

But you will now tell me that, no matter whether we call the motive force of our analysis transference or suggestion, there is a risk that the influencing of our patient may make the objective certainty of our findings doubtful. What is advantageous to our therapy is damaging to our researches. This is the objection that is most often raised against psycho-analysis, and it must be admitted that, though it is groundless, it cannot be rejected as unreasonable. If it were justified, psycho-analysis would be nothing more than a particularly well-disguised and particularly effective form of suggestive treatment and we should have to attach little weight to all that it tells us about what influences our lives, the dynamics of the mind or the unconscious. That is what our opponents believe; and in especial they think that we have "talked" the patients into everything relating to the importance of sexual experiences—or even into those experiences themselves—after such notions have grown up in our own depraved imagination. These accusations are contradicted more easily by an appeal to experience than by the help of theory. Anyone who has himself carried out psycho-analyses will have been able to convince himself on countless occasions that it is impossible to make suggestions to a patient in that way. The doctor has no difficulty, of course, in making him a supporter of some particular theory and in thus making him share some possible error of his own. In this respect the patient is behaving like anyone else—like a pupil—but this only affects his intelligence, not his illness. After all, his conflicts will only be successfully solved and his resistances overcome if the anticipatory ideas he is given tally with what is real in him. Whatever in the doctor's conjectures is inaccurate drops out in the course of the analysis [footnote omitted]; it has to be withdrawn and replaced by something more correct. [S.E. 1917, 16: 452]

Note at once that Freud acknowledges the patient's *intellectual* docil-ity. But he emphasizes that while the doctor therefore "has no difficulty, of course, in making him . . . share some possible error of his own . . . this only affects his intelligence, not his illness." Thus, Freud is clearly relying on the alleged refractoriness of the neurosis to dislodgment by the mere pseudoinsights generated by incorrect conjectures on the part of the analyst. And he depends on that purported refractoriness to serve as nothing less than the epistemic underwriter of the clinical validation of his entire theory. For Freud allows that the objection most often raised against psychoanalysis is as follows: epistemologically, therapeutic success is *non*probative, because it is achieved *not* by imparting veridical insight but rather by the persuasive suggestion of fanciful pseudoin-sights that merely ring verisimilar to the docile patient. He leaves no doubt as to the utter devastation that would be wrought by this objection if it could not be overcome. As he explains, "If it were justified, psycho-analysis would be nothing more than a particularly well-disguised and particularly effective form of suggestive treatment and we should have to attach little weight to all that it tells us about what influences our lives, the dynamics of the mind or the unconscious" (S.E. 1917, 16: 452].

Let us now articulate systematically the *argument* he uses to counter the charge of epistemic contamination of clinical data by suggestion, and his attempt to avert the ominous import of that charge. His counterargument does invoke *therapeutic* success. Hence, let us be mindful that the successful therapeutic conquest of the analysand's neurosis is held to consist in an adaptive restructuring of the intrapsychic personality dispositions such that there is concomitant lasting overt symptom relief without symptom substitution. The intrapsychic restructuring is deemed crucial to safeguard the quality and durability of overt symptomatic improvement.

Immediately after asserting that the doctor's theoretical stance, *if erroneous*, can persuasively affect the patient's intelligence but *cannot* dislodge his illness, Freud gives us the fundamental premise on which he rests this imperviousness of the patient's neurosis: "After all, his conflicts will only be successfully solved and his resistances overcome if the anticipatory ideas [i.e., interpretative depictions of analytic meaning] he is given tally [both objectively and subjectively] with what is real in him" (S.E. 1917, 16: 452). This bold assertion of the *causal indispensability* of psychoanalytic insight for the conquest of the patient's psychoneurosis is a terse enunciation of the thesis that Freud had previously formulated more explicitly in his 1909 case history of Little Hans, where he wrote:

In a psycho-analysis the physician always gives his patient (sometimes to a greater and sometimes to a less extent) the conscious anticipatory ideas by the help of which he is put in a position to recognize and to grasp the unconscious material. For there are some patients who need more of such assistance and some who need less; but there are none who get through without some of it. Slight disorders may perhaps be brought to an end by the subject's unaided efforts, but never a neurosis—a thing which has set itself up against the ego as an element alien to it. To get the better of such an element another person must be brought in, and in so far as that other person can be of assistance the neurosis will be curable. [S.E. 1909, 10: 104]

The assumptions that Freud actually invokes in this context can be stated as a conjunction of two causally necessary conditions as follows: (1) only the psychoanalytic method of interpretation and treatment can yield or mediate to the patient correct insight into the unconscious pathogens of his psychoneurosis, and (2) the analysand's correct insight into the etiology of his affliction and into the unconscious dynamics of his character is, in turn, *causally necessary* for the therapeutic conquest of his neurosis. I shall refer to the *conjunction* of these two Freudian claims as his "Necessary Condition Thesis" or, for brevity, "NCT." I have been careful to formulate this thesis with respect to the "psychoneuroses," as distinct from the so-called "actual" neuroses. For, as we shall see further on, Freud denied that NCT holds for the *actual* neuroses, and I ask that this important restriction be borne in mind even when I omit the qualification for brevity. Clearly, NCT entails not only that there is no spontaneous remission of psychoneuroses but also that, if there are any cures at all, psychoanalysis is *uniquely* therapeutic for such disorders as compared to any *rival* therapies. In view of the importance of NCT, I have also dubbed it "Freud's Master Proposition" (Grünbaum 1983*a*: 17).

Armed with his daring NCT, Freud promptly uses it to legitimate probatively the clinical data furnished by psychoneurotic patients whose analyses presumably had been successful. Nay, upon asserting the existence of such therapeutically successful patients *P*, as well as Freud's NCT, *two* conclusions follow in regard to any and all patients *P* who emerged cured from their analyses:

Conclusion 1. The psychoanalytic interpretations of the hidden causes of *P*'s behavior given to him by his analyst are indeed correct, and thus—as Freud put it—these interpretations "tally with what is real" in *P*.

Conclusion 2. Only analytic treatment could have wrought the conquest of *P*'s psychoneurosis.

In view of Freud's use of the appealing phrase "tally with what is real," I have used the label "Tally Argument" for the argument whose two premises and two conclusions I have just stated. And this designation has since been adopted by other writers.

It is of capital importance to appreciate that Freud is at pains to employ the Tally Argument in order to justify the following epistemological claim: actual *durable* therapeutic success guarantees *not only* that the pertinent analytic interpretations *ring* true or credible to the analysand *but also* that they *are* indeed veridical, or at least quite close to the mark. Freud then relies on this bold intermediate contention to conclude nothing less than the following: collectively, the successful outcomes of analyses do constitute *cogent* evidence for all that general psychoanalytic theory tells us about the influences of the unconscious dynamics of the mind on our lives. In short, psychoanalytic treatment successes as a whole vouch for the truth of the Freudian theory of personality, including its specific etiologies of the psychoneuroses and even its general theory of psychosexual development.

As a further corollary, the psychoanalytic probing of the unconscious is vindicated as a method of etiologic investigation by its therapeutic achievements. Thus, this method has the extraordinary capacity to validate major causal claims by essentially retrospective inquiries, *without* the burdens of prospective longitudinal studies employing (experimental) controls. Yet these causal inferences are not vitiated by *post hoc ergo propter hoc* or other known pitfalls of causal inference. Magnificent, if true!

Thus, Freud thought his theory of personality ought to command the assent of the scientific public. After all, the first conclusion of the Tally Argument had, in effect, absolved the psychoanalytic method of investigation from cognitive vitiation by the fact that the imperious analyst subjects the hapless patient to *educative* suggestion. And as we saw in his "Analytic Therapy" lecture, which is number 28 of his 1917 Introductory Lectures, he had predicated this vindication on the existence of genuinely successful treatment outcomes from analysis by claiming that the analyst *can* indoctrinate the patient erroneously but cannot thereby dislodge his illness.

Yet in an earlier lecture (number 16) of the same series, he simply ignored the pivotal role that therapeutic success was to play in his Tally Argument. For in the earlier lecture he declared:

Even if psycho-analysis showed itself as unsuccessful in every other form of nervous and psychical disease as it does in delusions, it would still remain completely justified as an irreplaceable instrument of scientific research. [S.E. 1917, 16: 255]

But in the face of the suggestibility challenge, this statement is a gratuitous piece of salesmanship, unworthy of the Freud who gave us the Tally Argument. In fact, Freud emphasizes (S.E. 1917, 16: 438-439, 445-446) that within the class of psychoneuroses, the subclass of so-called "narcissistic neuroses"—as distinct from the "transference neuroses" (Laplanche and Pontalis 1973: 258, 462)—are simply *refractory* to his therapy. Hence, in the case of the former subclass of disorders, the Tally Argument is, of course, unavailable to authenticate his clinically inferred etiologies by means of therapeutic success. Yet, in another lecture (number 27), he explicitly gave the same epistemic sanction to the clinical etiologies of the two subclasses of psychoneuroses (S.E. 1917, 16: 438-439). And presumably he did so by *extrapolating* the therapeutic vindication of the psychoanalytic method of etiologic investigation from the transference neuroses to the narcissistic ones.

I have called attention to *two* conclusions that follow from the premises of Freud's Tally Argument. One of them asserts the truth of the
psychoanalytic theory of personality; the other claims unique efficacy
for analytic therapy. But Freud himself explicitly deduced only the first of
these two conclusions, and stated the second quite separately in the same
1917 paper, as if it needed to stand on its own feet epistemically.

Thus, well after having inferred the first claim, he tells us (S.E. 1917,
16: 458) that the therapeutic successes of analysis are not only "second to
none of the finest in the field of internal medicine" but also that
psychoanalytic treatment gains "could not have been achieved by any
other procedure," let alone spontaneously. The latter assertion of unique
therapeutic potency is a reiteration of the equally sanguine claim he had
made in 1895 when evaluating his therapeutic results from the cathartic
precursor of analysis. For at that much earlier time, he had declared,
"I . . . have accomplished some things which no other therapeutic procedure could have achieved" (S.E. 1895, 2: 266). Small wonder, therefore,
that Freud concluded his 1917 "Analytic Therapy" paper by blithely
dismissing doubts as to the therapeutic efficacy of analysis, after merely
alluding to the difficulties of statistical comparisons of treatment outcome with results from untreated control groups, let alone with the
results from rival therapies. The very same complacent position is taken,
for example, by Erich Fromm (1970: 15), who does not hesitate to tell us
that "many patients have experienced a new sense of vitality and
capacity for joy, and no other method than psychoanalysis could have
produced these changes."

In short, if psychoanalytic treatment does have the therapeutic
monopoly entailed by the Tally Argument, then it can warrantedly take
credit for the recoveries of its patients *without* statistical comparisons
with the results from untreated control groups, or from controls treated
by rival modalities (cf. S.E. 1917, 16: 461-462). Moreover, when analytic
therapy does score remedial triumphs, these gains are *not* placebo
effects. For if the second conjunct of NCT is to be believed, the working
through of the patient's unconscious conflicts is the decisive remedial
factor. And this quintessential therapeutic role is not compromised by
the analyst's function as parent-surrogate and catalytic icebreaker in the
earlier stages of treatment (S.E. 1926, 20: 190).

Note that *if* Freud is warranted in postulating his NCT, and if psychoanalytic treatment outcome does bespeak its therapeutic efficacy, then he
is surely entitled to *dissociate* the remedial insight dynamics of his
treatment process from the mechanisms of the purely suggestive therapies. In thus setting his therapy apart from mere or prohibitory suggestion, he can then be undaunted by the catalytic, vehicular role he had

been led to accord to the transference relationship. Indeed, he focuses on the role of the transference in the patient's achievement of insight when he explicitly sets forth the fundamental characteristic that, in his view, "frees the results of analysis from the suspicion of being successes due to suggestion" (S.E. 1917, 16: 453). Freud does acknowledge, of course, that "the special personal influence of the analyst... exists and plays a large part in analysis" (S.E. 1926, 20: 190), but as he points out at once, "it would be a mistake to believe that this factor is the vehicle and promoter of the treatment throughout its length. At the beginning no doubt" (S.E. 1926, 20: 190); for it is a cardinal therapeutic aim of an analysis to afford the patient insight into his unconscious conflicts. Yet ironically the patient's transference of his infantile conflicts onto the analyst is activated and functions *obstructively* as a diversion just when the most sensitive repressed material is threatened by exposure: "in analysis [positive and negative] transference emerges as *the most powerful resistance* to the treatment" (S.E. 1912, 12: 101).

Hence, if the patient is to "work through" and overcome the resistances that obfuscate his access to the desired insight, his transference attachment must be dissected and *resolved*, whereas it is left untouched and *preserved* in the suggestive therapies (S.E. 1917, 16: 453). An analysis is intended to issue in the patient's emotional *independence* from the doctor; merely suggestive treatment, however, preserves the dependence on the therapist. Freud deems just this difference in dealing with the transference to be "the fundamental distinction between analytic and purely suggestive therapy" (S.E. 1917, 16: 453; see also 1914, 12: 155-156). As he put it:

it is perfectly true that psycho-analysis, like other psycho-therapeutic methods, employs the instrument of suggestion (or transference). But the difference is this: that in analysis it is not allowed to play the decisive part in determining the therapeutic results. It is used instead to induce the patient to perform a piece of psychical work—the overcoming of his transference-resistances—which involves a permanent alteration in his mental economy. The transference is made conscious to the patient by the analyst, and it is resolved by convincing him that in his transference-attitude he is *re-experiencing* emotional relations which had their origin in his earliest object-attachments during the repressed period of his childhood. In this way the transference is changed from the strongest weapon of the resistance into the best instrument of the analytic treatment. Nevertheless its handling remains the most difficult as well as the most important part of the technique of analysis. [S.E. 1925, 20: 42-43]

By the same token, he differentiates between transference remissions and analytic cures:

Often enough the transference is able to remove the symptoms of the disease by itself, but only for a while—only for as long as it itself lasts. In this case the treatment is a treatment by suggestion, and not a psycho-analysis at all. It only deserves the latter name if the intensity of the transference has been utilized for the overcoming of resistances. Only then has being ill become impossible, even when the transference has once more been dissolved, which is its destined end. [S.E. 1913, 12: 143]

Astonishingly, the *analysis* and resolution of the patient's transference subordination to his analyst has *itself* been invoked to *discredit* the following reproach: because of the epistemically confounding effects of the patient's doctrinal acquiescence to the analyst's quasi-parental authority, the ensuing clinical data are liable to furnish only *spurious* confirmations of psychoanalytic hypotheses. But what is the basis for the alleged capability of the analysis of the transference to purge psychoanalytic investigation of self-fulfilling bogus findings? It is that the patient's childlike doctrinal compliance with his therapist is *itself* formally part and parcel of the targets of the resolution of his "transference neurosis." Yet I cannot emphasize strongly enough that such an invocation of the analysis of the transference to rebut the charge of self-validation is logically a viciously circular bootstrap operation.

For clearly, the psychoanalytic dissection of the patient's deferential submission to his doctor already presupposes the empirical validity of the very hypotheses whose spurious confirmation by the analysand's clinical responses was at issue from the outset! As Freud told us explicitly, "The transference is made conscious to the patient by the analyst, and it is resolved by convincing him that in his transference-attitude he is *re-experiencing* emotional relations which had their origin in his earliest object-attachments during the repressed period of his childhood" (S.E. 1925, 20: 43). But the etiologic hypotheses employed to furnish just these purported insights and convictions to the patient are themselves avowedly predicated on clinical data, and all of these data have been admittedly suspect all along as being confounded by indoctrination.

Hence, it is plainly altogether question begging and self-validating to maintain by way of rebuttal that the analysis of the transference precludes spurious confirmation by guaranteeing the patient's emancipation from compliance with the analyst's communicated expectations. This specious disposition of the stated complaint of spurious clinical confirmation is hardly remedied upon heeding a recent injunction from Merton Gill (1980: 286), who declares: "the bulk of the analytic work should take place in the transference in the here and now." For obviously, analytic work having the latter focus rests on hypotheses whose validation is no less in question than the credentials of the *genetic* transference interpretations whose role Gill wishes to reduce.

But let us return to Freud's own account of the analysis of the transference. Toward achieving its resolution, he remarks "it is the analyst's task constantly to tear the patient out of his menacing illusion [of loving the analyst] and to show him again and again that what he takes to be new real life [i.e., realistic affection] is a reflection of the past" (S.E. 1940, 23: 177). Quite naturally, therefore, it is a recurring theme in Freud's writings that his therapy extirpates the pathogens of the patient's symptoms in surgical fashion, whereas the basic pathology is left intact by the suggestive treatments, which are thus merely cosmetic (S.E. 1917, 16: 450, 459; 1910, 11: 52, 146; 1905, 7: 260-261). Incidentally, this contrast between psychoanalytic treatment and mere suggestion is not retracted at all by Freud's 1921 reiteration that suggestibility is a "riddle." He then professed anew his lifelong agnosticism regarding the causal mechanism of individual suggestibility whereby group suggestion effects illogical psychological dominance over individuals and results in a change of their behavior (S.E. 1921, 18: 88-90).

A caveat recently issued by a contemporary analyst exemplifies the continuing allegiance, in at least some quarters, to Freud's distinction between (1) transference-induced symptom remissions, which are deemed ephemeral or fragile under new stresses, and (2) the analytic eradication of the underlying pathogens. In an article on transference, Brian Bird (1972: 285-286) writes:

One of the most serious problems of analysis is the very substantial help which the patient receives directly from the analyst and the analytic situation. For many a patient, the analyst in the analytic situation is in fact the most stable, reasonable, wise, and understanding person he has ever met, and the setting in which they meet may actually be the most honest, open, direct, and regular relationship he has ever experienced.... Taken altogether, the total *real* value to the patient of the analytic situation can easily be immense. The trouble with this kind of help is that if it goes on and on, it may have such a real, direct, and continuing impact upon the patient that he can never get deeply enough involved in transference situations to allow him to resolve, or even to become acquainted with, his most crippling internal difficulties. The trouble, in a sense, is that the direct nonanalytical helpfulness of the analytic situation is far too good! The trouble also is that we as analysts apparently cannot resist the seductiveness of being directly helpful.

Despite Freud's theoretical disavowal of mere suggestion as a remedial tool, he was not above making therapeutic promises to patients that, by his own account, were at best just hopes at the time. Thus, in 1910 he tells us that even "when I alone represented psycho-analysis...I assured my patients that I knew how to relieve them permanently of their sufferings" (S.E. 1910, 11: 146). Yet on the next page, he allows that these assurances may well be unjustified. For after pointing out that even rival therapies deriving suggestive force from being fashionable are unable "to get the better of neuroses," he says, "time will show whether psychoanalytic treatment can accomplish more."

As long as Freud saw himself entitled to adduce his NCT, he felt able—with a *single* stroke—to rebuff the twin suggestibility attacks on the dynamics of his therapy as well as on the cognitive reliability of the clinical data gathered by psychoanalytic investigation. Precisely because the crucial NCT premise of his Tally Argument declared correct *etiologic* insight to be *therapeutically* indispensable, this argument legitimated Freud's confidence in the following proposition: his *retrospective* clinical ascertainment of the etiologies of the psychoneuroses and of the causes of normal personality development *by the psychoanalytic method* was not vitiated by pitfalls of causal inference such as *post hoc ergo propter hoc*, but rather was methodologically sound. No wonder he felt justified in saying, "In psycho-analysis there has existed from the very first [i.e., even in the original cathartic method] an inseparable bond between cure and research.... Our analytic procedure is the only one in which this precious conjunction is assured" (S.E. 1926, 20: 256). Indeed, as Freud had told us as early as 1893, "Breuer learnt from his first patient that the attempt at discovering the determining cause of a symptom was at the same time a therapeutic manoeuvre" (S.E. 1893, 3: 35). Thus, he maintained that in psychoanalysis, "scientific research and therapeutic effort coincide" (S.E. 1923, 18: 236). One is therefore dumbfounded by the statement of analyst Judd Marmor (1968: 6): "I suspect that it was largely the historical accident that Freud was attempting to earn a living as a psychiatric practitioner that drove him to utilize his investigative tool simultaneously as a therapeutic instrument." As against this claim, chapter 3 will show in detail that the "inseparable bond between cure and research," which existed "from the first" (S.E. 1926, 20: 256) took the form of making the therapy primary as follows: the attribution of *therapeutic* efficacy to the lifting of repressions was indeed the epistemic basis for endowing Freud's method of free associations with the ability to certify causes (e.g., pathogens).

The explicit conclusion that Freud drew from his Tally Argument has essentially been reiterated in recent decades by prominent analysts. One of the more articulate endorsements is given by the Freudian Robert Waelder. In his review article on Sidney Hook's well-known symposium (1959), Waelder (1962: 629-630) writes:

Whenever a psychoanalyst is satisfied that he has untied the Gordian knot of a neurosis and has correctly understood its dynamics and its psychogenesis, his confidence is based on two kinds of data, one of outside observation of events, the other of the patient's self-observation. The first is the experience, repeated countless times during the working-through period of the analysis and again countless times during the person's later life, that this particular interpretation, or set of interpretations, and no other, can dispel the symptoms when they reappear, that they alone are the key that opens the lock; because particularly in the more serious neurosis of long standing, successful analytic therapy often does not bring about an ideal "cure" in the sense of our utopian desires, a traceless disappearance of disturbances without any price to be paid for it, but rather the ability to conquer them and to maintain a good, though contrived rather than stable, balance by vigilance and effort.

Then... there is an inner experience; what had been unconscious can now be consciously felt.

Waelder contrasts psychoanalysis with "a purely physicalistic discipline" by characterizing it epistemically as "largely, though by no means entirely, a matter of introspection and empathy" (pp. 628-629). Hence, he *also* invokes confirmation of the analyst's interpretations by the patient's *introspections* to espouse Freud's Tally Argument claim that "whatever in the doctor's conjectures is inaccurate drops out in the course of the analysis" (S.E. 1917, 16: 452). Thus, Waelder (1962: 629) elaborates on the contribution made by "the patient's self-observation" to the analyst's confidence in having "correctly understood" the psychogenesis and dynamics of his client's neurosis:

The interpretations offered by the psychoanalyst to his patient point out inner connections that can be fully experienced. Of course, any individual interpretation that is suggested in the course of an analysis may or may not be correct; the patient may or may not accept it, and his acceptance or rejection may be caused by realistic estimates or by emotional prejudices. But as analysis proceeds, mistaken interpretations will gradually wither away, inaccurate or incomplete interpretations will gradually be amended or completed, and emotional prejudices of the patient will gradually be overcome. In a successful analysis, the patient eventually becomes aware of the previously unconscious elements in his neurosis: he can fully feel and experience how his neurotic symptoms grew out of the conflicts of which he is now conscious; and he can fully feel and experience how facing up to these conflicts dispels the symptoms and, as Freud put it, "transforms neurotic suffering into everyday misery"; and how flinching will bring the symptoms back again.

Incidentally, as I have shown elsewhere in detail (Grünbaum 1980: pp. 354-367), just this accolade to the epistemic reliability of the analysand's introspections when validating etiologic and therapeutic claims is gainsaid by the recent conclusions of the cognitive psychologists Nisbett and Wilson. In the *"Introduction,"* I adduced their results against Habermas's cognitive tribute to the patient's "self-reflection." The upshot there was, as the reader will recall, that just like outside observers, the subject has only *inferential*—rather than direct or privileged—access to such causal linkages as actually connect some of his mental states. And in carrying out such inferences, the analysand is under his doctor's tutelage.

Very recently, the analyst Michael Basch (1980: 171) echoed Freud's NCT:

"Insight," "psychoanalytically oriented" or "depth" psychotherapy...is based on Freud's recognition that psychological problems are developmental, and that only by obtaining [veridical] insight into the process that gives rise to them can a resolution based on cause [as distinct from a shallow and fragile symptom remission] be reached.

Like Waelder, Basch (p. 83) points to the "repeated experience" of failing to achieve the desired change in the patient's behavior in response to some entirely plausible interpretation, but then scoring a therapeutic breakthrough after offering some *particular* interpretation. And, just like Waelder, Basch takes this finding to be *evidence* for the correctness and insightfulness—rather than the mere *persuasiveness* for the patient—of the *one* interpretation that issued in significant therapeutic gain. But can any such therapeutic episode actually count in favor of Freud's NCT? Surely not until and unless there are good grounds for claiming that the "repeated experience" adduced by Basch may indeed be taken to bespeak the truth—*not* just the *congeniality!*—of the therapeutically distinguished interpretation, as well as the falsity of the therapeutically barren analytic conjectures. Yet neither Basch nor Waelder have supplied such grounds.

What clues does Freud himself give us as to the evidence that led him to champion his NCT until at least 1917? Clearly, this question is imperative, because the *empirical tenability* of this cardinal premise of his Tally Argument is the pivot on which he rested his generic tribute to the probative value of the clinical data obtainable by the psychoanalytic method of inquiry. It would seem that until at least 1917, Freud regarded NCT as supported by the *dynamics* he avowedly felt driven to postulate in order to make intelligible the *patterns* of therapeutic success *and* failure resulting from the use of the following two treatment modalities: (1) Josef Breuer's cathartic method of abreaction, which still employed hypnosis on hysterics, and (2) Freud's own innovative psychoanalytic version of Breuer's method, which replaced hypnosis by the technique of free association to treat psychoneurotics. Indeed, the pioneering reasoning by which Freud responded to his therapeutic successes and failures countenanced the sort of inferences that we already encountered in the aforecited writings by the analysts Waelder and Basch. Let us see how Freud was presumably led to that reasoning without, however, countenancing it on our part.

Breuer's findings seemed to betoken the therapeuticity of the patient's abreactive and articulate recall of the repressed traumatic experience during which a particular hysterical symptom presumably first appeared. The positive therapeutic results that Breuer and Freud first obtained by means of such catharsis then served as their *evidence* for identifying that repressed traumatic experience etiologically as the specific cause, or *pathogen*, of the given symptoms (S.E. 1893, 2: 6-7; 1893, 3: 29-30; 1896, 3: 193). In this way, Breuer had concluded, for example, that his patient Anna O.'s strong aversion to drinking water had been caused by strangulated and repressed disgust at the sight of seeing a companion's dog drink water from a glass (S.E. 1895, 2: 34-35). Once the etiology of the patient's hydrophobic behavior has been thus inferred, it can serve to explain Breuer's "cure", as will be seen in chapter 3 in detail. (Hereafter, brevity will be served by not always saying explicitly that the traumata deemed pathogenic by Breuer and Freud were indeed *repressed* experiences.)

But quite *apart* from therapeutic success, Freud lays down two generic necessary conditions of adequacy that must be met by any traumatic experience, *if* that trauma is to furnish a *satisfactory etiologic explanation* of the given symptom by qualifying as its "specific cause." Freud gives the following example to motivate these conditions of adequacy:

Let us suppose that the symptom under consideration is hysterical vomiting; in that case we shall feel that we have been able to understand its causation (except for a certain [hereditary] residue) if the analysis traces the symptom back to an experience which *justifiably produced a high amount of disgust*—for instance, the sight of a decomposing dead body. But if, instead of this, the analysis shows us that the vomiting arose from a great fright, e.g., from a railway accident, we shall feel dissatisfied and will have to ask ourselves how it is that the fright has led to the particular symptoms of vomiting. This derivation lacks *suitability as a determinant*. We shall have another instance of an insufficient explanation if the vomiting is supposed to have arisen from, let us say, eating a fruit which had partly gone bad. Here, it is true, the vomiting *is* determined by disgust, but we cannot understand how, in this instance, the disgust could have become so powerful as to be perpetuated in a hysterical symptom; the experience lacks *traumatic force*. [S.E. 1896, 3: 193-194]

Accordingly, he enunciates his generic requirements:

Tracing a hysterical symptom back to a traumatic scene assists our understanding only if the scene satisfies two conditions; if it possesses the relevant *suitability to serve as a determinant* and if it recognizably possesses the necessary *traumatic force*. [S.E. 1896, 3: 193]

Yet, in fact, any and *every* repressed traumatic experience satisfying these two conditions of explanatory adequacy might well be *etiologically irrelevant* to hysteria, if only because Breuer's and Freud's fundamental hypothesis of a *repression etiology* may be generically false! And, *if* so, then Breuer was surely mistaken in attributing crucial pathogenic significance to the *particular* traumatic experience that occasioned the *onset* of a given hysterical symptom, an experience I shall hereafter call "occasioning trauma" for brevity. But for quite different reasons, Freud was persuaded to downgrade the etiologic role of the occasioning trauma from a "specific" cause to a mere precipitating (releasing) cause (S.E. 1895, 3: 135-136).

As Freud explains (S.E. 1896, 3: 193-197), his reasons were the following: (1) with overwhelming frequency, the occasioning trauma violated at least one of Freud's two stated requirements for etiologic adequacy, and (2) whenever his psychoanalytic procedure uncovered a repressed occasioning trauma that violated both of these adequacy conditions, the undoing of *this* repression was altogether useless therapeutically. In all such cases, "we also fail to secure any therapeutic gain; the patient retains his symptoms unaltered" (S.E. 1896, 3: 195)!

We must appreciate why Freud took this therapeutic fiasco to cast additional doubt on the pathogenic potency of the occasioning trauma. It was because he expected therapeutic success once the patient was no longer repressing an *etiologically essential* memory. This expectation was based on the general moral of Breuer's cathartic method, which Freud still took seriously and which he had rendered concisely as follows: "Breuer learnt from his first patient that the [successful] attempt at discovering the [psychically sequestered] determining cause of a symptom was at the same time a therapeutic manoeuvre" (S.E. 1893, 3: 35).

Though Freud therefore demoted the *occasioning* trauma etiologically, he insisted that the *generic* postulation of a repression etiology for hysteria was empirically warranted. This warrant came from the psychoanalytic disclosure of a much *earlier* sexual trauma which, in his view, did have impressive pathogenic earmarks (S.E. 1896, 3: 193). As he put it:

We finally make our way from the hysterical symptom to the scene which is really operative traumatically and which is satisfactory in every respect, both therapeutically and analytically. . . . If the first-discovered scene is unsatisfactory, we tell our patient that this experience explains nothing, but that behind it there must be hidden a more significant, earlier, experience; and we direct his attention by the same technique to the associative thread which connects the two memories—the one that has been discovered and the one that has still to be discovered [footnote omitted]. A continuation of the analysis then leads in every instance to the reproduction of new scenes of the character we expect. [S.E. 1896, 3: 195-196]

The most important finding that is arrived at if an analysis is thus consistently pursued is this. Whatever case and whatever symptom we take as our point of departure, *in the end we infallibly come to the field of sexual experience*. So here for the first time we seem to have discovered an aetiological precondition for hysterical symptoms. [S.E. 1896, 3: 199]

In short, Freud had inferred a substantial difference in pathogenic significance between the occasioning trauma, on the one hand, and the presumed earlier sexual trauma, on the other. And he related that difference to his own emendation of the etiologic assumption governing Breuer's cathartic therapy: "Thus a sexual trauma [during childhood] stepped into the place of an ordinary [occasioning] trauma [from later life] and the latter was seen to owe its aetiological significance to an associative or symbolic connection with the former, which had preceded it" (S.E. 1923, 18: 243).

We are engaged in developing the sorts of findings that Freud presumably deemed collectively supportive of his NCT. To gauge the probative value of his evidence, however, we must not overlook that he avowedly coaxed, coached, and even browbeat the patient in the quest for the theoretically expected data. Thus, as we saw, he relates just how he "*infallibly*" arrived at the purported early sexual traumata: "If the first-discovered scene is unsatisfactory, we tell our patient that this experience explains nothing, but that behind it there must be hidden a more significant, earlier experience; and we direct his attention by the same technique to the associative thread which connects the two memories—the one that has been discovered and the one that has still to be discovered" (S.E. 1896, 3: 195–196). Numerous other statements by Freud (e.g., S.E. 1895, 2: 293; 1898, 3: 269; 1905, 7: 58-59; 1909, 10: 179-180) show that he felt entitled on theoretical grounds to hector the patient relentlessly for not having retrieved the desired sort of memory. Indeed, as he reports (S.E. 1896, 3: 204), "Before they come for analysis the patients know nothing about these scenes. They are indignant as a rule if we warn them that such scenes are going to emerge." Clearly, the analysand is admonished beforehand as to what is expected of him. And this avowed brain washing is conducive to yielding only spurious confirmations of etiologic hypotheses. For Freud's inquisitorial methods could not even reliably authenticate the bare occurrence of the doctrinally desired early experience. But an event that never happened could hardly have been the pathogen. Yet patently, he thought that his ensuing findings were anything but bogus.

Thus, in the 1896 paper from which we have been citing, Freud reported therapeutic failures and successes, respectively, as follows: (1) psychoanalytic treatment issued in a therapeutic fiasco whenever the patient was clearly left without any insight into the actual specific etiology of his neurosis, which had remained sequestered in his unconscious while the shallow analysis was uncovering only a *precipitating* cause of his affliction; and (2) cases in which the psychoanalytic undoing of the patient's repression of a trauma was "satisfactory in every respect both therapeutically and analytically," these therapeutically successful cases being instances in which the patient achieved bona fide etiological insight, since the pertinent trauma had all the earmarks of being "really operative" pathogenically (S.E. 1896, 3: 195). Note that Freud's two conditions for etiologic adequacy are avowedly only necessary rather than sufficient conditions for identifying a trauma as being etiologically essential for hysteria. Yet he seems to take it for granted here that the concrete features of a repressed trauma can collectively vouch for its pathogenic potency, *independently* of any *therapeutic benefit* engendered by its mnemic restoration to the patient's consciousness (S.E. 1896, 3: 202-203). As Edward Erwin has remarked to me, if such direct etiologic identifiability were indeed granted, then Freud could have spared himself the circuitous detour of trying to vindicate it via NCT.

But perhaps Freud thought that such *direct* identifiability is feasible in *some* cases and not possible in others. If so, then the etiologic inferences in the *latter* cases would first be vindicated via NCT, once its bold second conjunct can claim evidential support. This conjunct asserts that correct insight into the essential etiology of the patient's neurosis is causally necessary for his therapeutic conquest of it. Evidential support for this assertion would be provided, in turn, once the purported cases of direct etiologic identifiability are invoked to buttress the stated two correlations as to therapeutic outcome; for the aforementioned concomitances bespeak the kind of causal relevance of insight to therapeutic outcome that is avowed by NCT. In any case, it would seem that, even in the remainder of the same 1896 paper, Freud did not hesitate to adduce just this daring NCT claim, as I shall now show.

When reporting that the vast majority of *occasioning* traumatic scenes *violated* at least one of his two conditions for etiologic adequacy, Freud recorded some rare exceptions: "The traumatic scene in which the symptom originated [i.e., the occasioning trauma] does in fact occasionally possess both the qualities—suitability as a determinant and traumatic force—which we require for an understanding of the symptom" (S.E. 1896, 3: 194). Then he declared emphatically that the pathogenesis of hysteria can *never* be effected by the occasioning trauma without the etiologic contribution of *earlier* painful experiences, no matter what other qualities that later trauma possesses. Immediately after enunciating this proposition, he reverts to those avowedly *rare* occasioning traumata that *do* satisfy his two etiologic adequacy conditions:

You might suppose that the rare instances in which analysis is able to trace the symptom back direct [*sic*] to a traumatic scene [i.e., occasioning trauma] that is thoroughly suitable as a determinant and possesses traumatic force, and is able, by thus tracing it back, at the same time to remove it (in the way described in Breuer's case history of Anna O.)—you might suppose that such instances must, after all, constitute powerful objections to the general validity of the proposition [of the etiologic *parasitism* of the occasioning traumata] I have just put forward. It certainly looks so. But I must assure you that I have the best grounds for assuming that even in such instances there exists a chain of [etiologically] operative memories which stretches far back behind the first [occasioning] traumatic scene, *even though* the reproduction of the latter alone may have the result of removing the symptom. [S.E. 1896, 3: 197]

Here Freud is acknowledging that prima facie his proposition of etiologic parasitism faces "powerful objections" from those rare *occasioning* traumata that satisfy his two *necessary* conditions for etiologic adequacy *and* whose restoration to the patient's consciousness issues in symptom removal. He then uses the italicized words *even though* to single out this *therapeutic* outcome as a special challenge to the proposition that he had enunciated just before.

But why should he suppose at all that symptom removal, engendered by the patient's recall of occasioning traumata that satisfy his two necessary conditions, would prima facie gainsay the etiologic parasitism that his proposition attributed to every occasioning trauma? I submit that *his rationale* for this supposition *is furnished by none other than his NCT*, which declared insight into the *essential* etiology of a neurosis to be causally necessary for a cure. For clearly the fulfillment of the two *necessary* conditions of etiologic adequacy by some occasioning traumata is entirely compatible with the etiologic parasitism of *all* such traumata, since these necessary conditions are not also jointly sufficient. Instead, as is patent from Freud's use of the words *even though*, the etiologic parasitism of occasioning traumata *seems* to run counter to the symptom removal that did ensue in some cases when the analysis retrieved *only* an *occasioning* trauma!

Hence, I ask anew: even prima facie, why should this positive therapeutic outcome not be achieved in the wake of insight into an etiologically *marginal* trauma? And I answer: because—if the resulting symptom removal *were* tantamount to the conquest of the underlying neurosis—then the remission would violate NCT's demand for insight into the *essential* etiology of the neurosis as a condition requisite for its conquest.

Fortunately, after having presented the tantalizing challenge posed by the symptom remissions, Freud does not leave us wondering indefinitely whether and how he does reconcile his NCT with this positive treatment outcome from etiologically marginal insight. Later in his paper (S.E. 1896, 3: 206), he cautions that the patient's symptom removal need not be tantamount to his "radical cure," if only because the analysand may be prone to relapses. Aware that a *symptom* cure may actually *not* betoken the conquest of the *underlying* neurosis, he explicitly deems fragile any symptom cure occurring in the wake of the *failure*, on the part of the patient's etiologic insight, to penetrate beyond the occasioning trauma to the "specific aetiology" (S.E. 1896, 3: 209-210) of his affliction. Hence, he has preserved compatibility with NCT. As he explains:

In a number of cases therapeutic evidence of the genuineness of the [traumatic] infantile scenes can also be brought forward. There are cases in which a complete or partial cure can be obtained without our having to go as deep as the infantile experiences. And there are others in which no success at all is obtained until the analysis has come to its natural end with the uncovering of the earliest traumas. In the former cases we are not, I believe, secure against relapses, and my expectation is that a complete psycho-analysis implies a radical cure of the hysteria. [S.E. 1896, 3: 206]

But Freud leaves unclear here *on what grounds* he takes the stated therapeutic results to be "evidence" for his seduction etiology. Could he be invoking NCT, no less than he surely seems to have done earlier in the same paper? The same exegetical question as to the role of NCT is posed by his reliance on "therapeutic success" to "confirm" his analytically inferred sexual etiology of hysteria, when avowedly submitting the credentials of that etiology "to the strictest examination":

If you submit my assertion that the aetiology of hysteria lies in sexual life to the strictest examination, you will find that it is supported by the fact that in some eighteen cases of hysteria I have been able to discover this connection in every single symptom, and, where the circumstances allowed, to confirm it by thera-peutic success. [S.E. 1896, 3: 199]

When reading these passages, we must be mindful of his etiological ranking of the earliest traumata vis-à-vis the later ones.

All the events subsequent to puberty to which an influence must be attributed upon the development of the hysterical neurosis and upon the formation of its symptoms are in fact only concurrent causes—"*agents provocateurs.*"... These accessory agents are not subject to the strict conditions imposed on the specific causes; analysis demonstrates in an irrefutable fashion that they enjoy a pathogenic influence for hysteria only owing to their faculty for awakening the unconscious psychical trace of the childhood event. [S.E. 1896, 3: 154-155]

While thus stressing the causal ranking among the etiological factors, Freud called attention to their cumulativity (S.E. 1895, 3: 214, 216). Moreover, in one of his 1895 case histories (Fräulein Elisabeth von R.), Freud had not only downgraded the occasioning trauma etiologically but had asserted the bold second conjunct of NCT even with respect to *symptom removal*:

Indeed, in the great majority of instances we find that a first trauma has left no symptom behind, while a later trauma of the same kind produces a symptom, and yet that the latter could not have come into existence without the cooperation of the earlier provoking cause; nor can it be cleared up without taking all the provoking causes into account. [S.E. 1895, 2: 173]

In another 1895 case history, Freud had adumbrated the role he attributed to the patient's inherited constitution in the auxiliary etiology of hysteria:

Frau von N. was undoubtedly a personality with a severe neuropathic heredity. It seems likely that there can be no hysteria apart from a disposition of this kind. But on the other hand disposition alone does not make hysteria. There must be reasons that bring it about, and, in my opinion, these reasons must be appropriate: the aetiology is of a specific character. [S.E. 1895, 2: 102]

In this way, he gave a partial answer to the question about the *causally sufficient* condition for this disorder, a question he put as follows: "What can the other factors be which the 'specific aetiology' of hysteria still needs in order actually to produce the neurosis?" [S.E. 1896, 3: 210]

Incidentally, in recent years there have been allegations that cases of classical hysteria of the sort seen by Freud have since disappeared. Clearly, if there is no temporal stability in the diagnostic criteria used to identify patients as hysterics, then the *reported* secular decline in the prevalence of this disorder hardly bespeaks an actual decrease in its incidence. As the analyst Kaplan (1981: 15) explains illuminatingly:

The diagnosis of hysteria, however, was applied to a diverse group of patients with not only conversion, but with phobic and other symptoms paralleling the development of our psychoanalytic theories and new preformed conceptions about hysteria.

There is also evidence that the classically described hysteria is still commonly seen today, more often in less sophisticated patients, but in all social classes, not necessarily by psychoanalysts, but by psychiatrists and other physicians [footnote omitted]. Now as we look back, many of the patients previously seen as suffering from hysteria would no longer be so diagnosed.

Cognizant of Freud's distinction between a symptom cure and a radical one, analysts have perennially prided themselves on treating the causes of neuroses, rather than the mere symptoms, by means of undoing repressions psychoanalytically. But in his 1917 lecture "Transference," Freud qualified the sense in which analysis can claim to be a "causal therapy." For there he pointed out that much as lifting repressions is a more thoroughgoing attack on a neurosis than mere symptom removal, it is not an attack on those *earlier* roots of the etiological series in the patient's constitution, which first make the patient at all *vulnerable* to pathogenic experiences (S.E. 1917, 16: 435-436). The latter kind of assault on the pathogenic dispositions—perhaps "by some chemical means," he tells us—"would be a causal therapy in the true sense of the word" (p. 436). But until and unless Freud's etiologies do have adequate credentials, his therapy has no claim to being *any* kind of "causal therapy."

As we have seen, his distinction between a symptom cure, perhaps induced by the transference relationship, and a cure of the underlying neurosis serves to obviate a spurious counterexample to his NCT, which is generated by failure to allow for this distinction. That this caveat is salutary is further illustrated by its relevance to the proper construal of a cryptic statement in his 1917 "Analytic Therapy" lecture. There (S.E. 1917, 16: 449), only a few pages before making use of NCT in the Tally Argument, he recalls his disappointments when he practiced both Bernheim's and Breuer's versions of hypnotic therapy. The procedure could be used with some patients but not with others, was unaccountably quite helpful with some while achieving little with others, and even when successful, the resulting improvement was not durable. This lack of permanence necessitated an addictive repetition of the treatment, which deprived the patient of his self-reliance (see also S.E. 1905, 7: 301). Having registered these complaints, Freud nonetheless punctuated them by the following cryptic demurrer: "Admittedly sometimes things went entirely as one would wish: after a few efforts, success was complete and permanent. But the conditions determining such a favourable outcome remained unknown" (S.E. 1917, 16: 449). A footnote appended to the term "permanent" by the editors of the *Standard Edition* steers the reader to an instance of this kind in Freud's paper "A Case of Successful Treatment by Hypnotism" (S.E. 1892 1: 117-128), which appeared in two parts in December 1892 and January 1893.

But when we turn to this paper, it becomes clear that Freud expressed himself misleadingly by describing the success of the hypnotic treatment reported there as "permanent," and that this success consisted of symptom removals that do *not* gainsay NCT. The patient was a woman whose various hysterical symptoms prevented her from breast-feeding her first child. Two sessions of prohibitory hypnotic suggestion à la Bernheim did suffice to remove all of her symptoms. But this removal was "permanent" only until she had a second child a year later, when her symptoms returned and had to be removed hypnotically once again. That Freud regarded such hypnotic symptom removals as shallow, ephemeral transference cures is evident from the following 1904 statement by him, which is much less cryptic than the aforecited 1917 demurrer:

I gave up the suggestive technique, and with it hypnosis, so early in my practice because I despaired of making suggestion powerful and enduring enough to effect permanent cures. In every severe case I saw the suggestions which had been applied crumble away again; after which the disease or some substitute for it was back once more. [S.E. 1905, 7: 261]

He reiterated his distinction between a psychoanalytic "radical cure" of a full-fledged neurosis and a shallow one by "more convenient methods of treatment" (S.E. 1905, 7: 262-263), and allowed for "slighter, episodic cases which we see recovering under all kinds of influences and even spontaneously." And, as we recall, as part of his 1909 enunciation of NCT, he again allowed that "slight disorders may perhaps be brought to an end by the subject's unaided efforts, but never a neurosis" (S.E. 1909, 10: 104).

It will be recalled that in 1896, Freud had marshaled both therapeutic and other clinical findings that he regarded as evidence for the pathogenic role of the inferred infantile seduction scenes (S.E. 1896, 3: 199, 206). But in the same 1896 paper, he took special pains to address doubts as to whether these episodes had occurred at all, not merely whether—if genuine—they were also the specific pathogens of hysteria. Though Freud privately repudiated even the very occurrence of the seductions only a year and a half later (Freud 1954, letter #69 to Wilhelm Fliess: 215-217), it is instructive to see just what doubts he canvassed, and how he rebuffed them in 1896.

Ever mindful of the challenge of suggestibility, he asked rhetorically:

Is it not very possible either that the physician forces such scenes upon his docile patients, alleging that they are memories, or else that the patients tell the physician things which they have deliberately invented or have imagined and that he accepts those things as true? [S.E. 1896, 3: 204]

And he replies to the first doubt:

I have never yet succeeded in forcing on a patient a scene I was expecting to find, in such a way that he seemed to be living through it with all the appropriate feelings. [S.E. 1896, 3: 205]

Here Freud is undaunted, although he himself had mentioned earlier in the paper that if the occasioning trauma is etiologically unsatisfactory, "we tell our patient that his experience explains nothing, but that behind it there must be hidden a more significant, earlier, experience" (S.E. 1896, 3: 195-196). Even twenty-eight years after his repudiation of the seduction etiology, he is unrelenting on this point: "I do not believe even now that I forced the seduction phantasies on my patients, that I 'suggested' them" (S.E. 1925, 20: 34). Yet, at that later time, he did retract his 1896 reply to the charge that his patients had manufactured the seduction scenes and had duped the analyst. His confident reply in 1896 had been that there is "conclusive proof" to the contrary:

The behaviour of patients while they are reproducing these infantile experiences is in every respect incompatible with the assumption that the scenes are anything else than a reality which is being felt with distress and reproduced with the greatest reluctance....
Why should patients assure me so emphatically of their unbelief, if what they want to discredit is something which—from whatever motive—they themselves have invented? [S.E. 1896, 3: 204]

But as he explains in 1925:

When, however, I was at last obliged to recognize that these scenes of seduction had never taken place, and that they were only phantasies which my patients had made up or which I myself had perhaps forced on them, I was for some time completely at a loss. My confidence alike in my technique and in its results suffered a severe blow; it could not be disputed that I had arrived at these scenes by a technical method which I considered correct, and their subject-matter was unquestionably related to the symptoms from which my investigation had started. [S.E. 1925, 20: 34]

And in an earlier historical account, he reports that the mistaken etiology "might have been almost fatal to the young science" of psychoanalysis:

When this aetiology broke down under the weight of its own improbability and contradiction in definitely ascertainable circumstances...I would gladly have given up the whole work, just as my esteemed predecessor, Breuer, had done when he made his unwelcome discovery. Perhaps I persevered only because I no longer had any choice and could not then begin again at anything else. [S.E. 1914, 14: 17]

Though the seduction etiology debacle thus jeopardized the psycho-analytic enterprise in general, it did *not* refute the bold second conjunct of NCT in particular. Clearly, NCT would have been strongly discon-firmed *if* there had been cases of patients who had been genuinely cured after being given *pseudo*insight by their analysis into episodes of sexual abuse that had presumably never occurred in *their* childhood, though probably in others. But the very first of the four reasons that Freud gave Fliess in 1897 for abandoning the seduction theory was precisely that no such therapeutic conquests of the underlying neurosis materialized. Indeed, as he pointed out, such remedial gains as he did achieve were of the sort that could readily have been wrought by suggestion:

The first group of factors were the continual disappointment of my attempts to bring my analyses to a real conclusion, the running away of people who for a time had seemed my most favourably inclined patients, the lack of the complete success on which I had counted, and the possibility of explaining my partial successes in other, familiar, ways [i.e., suggestion]. [Freud 1954: 215]

But these therapeutic disclaimers are second thoughts, since he had twice adduced therapeutic results in support of his seduction etiology only the year before, as we saw. If Freud's more considered, unfavorable therapeutic inventory is assumed, then his replacement of actual by fancied seductions as the pathogens of hysteria did not serve to gainsay his NCT. Thus, the compatibility of NCT, including its first conjunct, with the collapse of the seduction etiology shows that this debacle, at any rate, provides no basis for judging Freud to have been intellectually dishonest when he explicitly enunciated NCT in 1909 and 1917. None-theless, his scientific candor does appear questionable in the light of the nine years he permitted to elapse before even *publicly intimating* his change of view (S.E. 1906, 7: 274-275).

C. WAS FREUD'S ATTEMPTED THERAPEUTIC VINDICATION OF THE PSYCHOANALYTIC THEORY OF PERSONALITY SUCCESSFUL?

The capacity of Freud's 1917 Tally Argument to *warrant* the actual truth of its conclusions depends, of course, on the empirical tenability of its two premises. As noted before, NCT is the pivot that gave any therapeu-tic triumphs achieved by analysis the leverage to vouch for the authen-ticity of its clinical data. Hence, to the extent that Freud disavowed one or both of these premises in later years, he forfeited his erstwhile reliance on this argument to vindicate the psychoanalytic method of inquiry and/or the conclusions he had reached by means of it. Again, to the extent that analytic treatment nowadays continues not to effect real cures of neuroses, and NCT is rendered dubious by currently available empirical information, Freudian theory is now devoid of this vindication in the face of the remaining twin challenge from suggestibility. As we saw in Section A, Freud himself had acknowledged (S.E. 1917, 16: 446-447) that he must try to nullify the following two-fold indictment: Suggestion is at once the decisive agent in his therapy, and the cognitive bane of the psychoanalytic method of investigation.

For a number of decades, Freud did claim empirical sanction for both of the premises in his Tally Argument. But ironically, in his later years he himself undermined this argument by gradually renouncing or significantly weakening each premise. Thus, in an important 1937 paper (S.E. 1937, 23: 216-254), his disparagement of the quality and durability of actual psychoanalytic treatment outcome bordered on a repudiation of treatment success. As Freud reported ruefully, a satisfactory psychoanalysis is not even prophylactic against the recurrence of the affliction for which the analysand was treated, let alone immunizing against the outbreak of a different neurosis. Thus, far from holding out hope for cures, Freud essentially confined the prospects to palliation. But the import of this therapeutic pessimism is shattering. For, even if NCT were true, it would need the existential premise of documented cures in order to vouch for the etiologies inferred by means of free association. But even when Freud was not quite that pessimistic about the caliber of therapeutic outcome (S.E. 1926, 20: 265), he gainsaid his erstwhile NCT in 1926 by conceding the existence of spontaneous remission as follows: "As a rule our therapy must be content with bringing about more quickly, more reliably and with less expenditure of energy than would otherwise be the case the good result which in favourable circumstances would have occurred of itself" (S.E. 1926, 20: 154). Of course, the label "spontaneous remission" is to convey that gains made by an afflicted person were caused entirely by extraclinical life events rather than by professional therapists, not that these benefits were uncaused. Notably, Freud grants that neuroses yielding to analytic therapy would, in due course, remit spontaneously anyway. In this way, he demoted his own treatment from being therapeutically indispensable to the status of a mere expediter of otherwise expectable recoveries. Hence, even Freud's own evidence placed his NCT premise in serious jeopardy. And once that proposition became defunct, even spectacular therapeutic triumphs became probatively unavailing for the validation of his hypotheses by means of the Tally Argument.

Other analysts have likewise made concessions to spontaneous remission and have acknowledged that "all pervading" psychic improvements or cures can be effected without psychoanalytic insight by theoretically rival treatment modalities such as behavior therapy (Malan 1976: 172-173, 269, 147). It is to be understood that various treatment modalities are held to be "rivals" of one another in the sense that there is a divergence between their *theories* of the rationale, dynamics, methods, or techniques of the therapeutic process. Notably in psychoanalysis and behavior therapy, but perhaps also in some of the other modalities, the underlying theoretical rationale also comprises hypotheses pertaining to personality development, etiology, and the current dynamics of pathological behavior. Thus, the divergences between the rival therapies naturally extend to *these* causal hypotheses as well. Notoriously, there is a plethora of such rival therapeutic modalities, at least well over 125.

In recent decades, comparative studies of treatment outcome from rival therapies have failed to reveal any sort of superiority of psychoanalysis within the class of therapeutic modalities that exceed the spontaneous remission rate gleaned from the (quasi-)untreated controls (Smith, Glass, and Miller 1980; Rachman and Wilson 1980; Strupp, Hadley, and Gomes-Schwartz 1977). But, if analytic treatment is thus not superior to its rivals in the pertinent diagnostic categories, it becomes quite reasonable—though *not* compelling—to interpret its therapeutic achievements as placebo effects. And, if so, then the therapeutic successes of psychoanalysis are *not* wrought after all by the patient's acquisition of self-knowledge, much to Socrates' sorrow. In this vein, the psychiatrist Jerome Frank has contended that the analyst, no less than his competitor, heals neurotics by supportively counteracting their demoralization, not by excavating their repressions. Indeed, Frank's hypothesis even allows rival therapies to have differential effects in virtue of their differential abilities to mobilize agencies common to all of them. The shared techniques for such mobilization usually include well practiced rituals, a special vocabulary, a knowledgeable manner, and the therapist's charisma (Grünbaum 1980; 341-351). To be sure, it is still arguable that psychoanalytic treatment gains are *not* placebogenic. But, the damaging fact remains that NCT has become quite doubtful. Moreover, even the evidence for treatment gains from analytic and nonanalytic psychotherapy, which was adduced by Smith, Glass and Miller (1980), has just been deemed incapable of sustaining their conclusion. As Prioleau, Murdock, and Brody (1983) have pointed out, the findings used by Smith et al. do not show that the benefits from psychotherapy exceed those yielded by treatments designed to be placebos.

Ironically, in the case of some psychoanalytic theoreticians, the willingness to countenance the existence of spontaneous remission of full-fledged neuroses in *contravention* of NCT was prompted by the need to cope with a difficulty posed by behavior therapy for the *received* Freudian theory of the origin *and* maintenance of neurotic symptoms. To articulate the pertinent difficulty, note what would be expected to happen, according to this received account of symptom formation, when a symptom is extinguished by a direct attack on it, while its underlying neurosis is left intact. A neurotic symptom is held to be a compromise, *formed* in response to an unresolved conflict between a forbidden unconscious impulse and the ego's defense against it. The symptom is held to be *sustained* at any given time by a *coexisting*, ongoing unconscious conflict, which—as claimed by NCT—does not resolve itself without psychoanalytic intervention. Hence, if the repression of the unconscious wish is not lifted psychoanalytically, the underlying neurosis will persist, even if behavior therapy or hypnosis, for example, extinguishes the particular symptom that only *manifests* the neurosis at the time. As long as the neurotic conflict does persist, the patient's psyche will call for the defensive service previously rendered by the banished symptom. Hence, typically and especially in severe cases, the unresolved conflict ought to engender a *new* symptom. And incidentally, this expectation qualifies as a "risky" prediction in Popper's sense, since such rival extant theories as behavior intervention disavow just that expectation.

Thus, when Freud explained his disappointments with hypnotic therapy, he claimed, as we saw, that in every severe case he had treated suggestively, the patient either relapsed or developed *"some substitute"* for the original symptoms (emphasis added; S.E. 1905, 7: 261). But is such so-called "symptom substitution," which is the *replacement* of an extinguished symptom by a new one, in fact a normal occurrence? Fisher and Greenberg (1977: 370) have summarized empirical studies of the incidence of *new* symptoms, construed as "behaviors judged socially or personally maladaptive":

The evidence is consistent and solid that in many types of cases, symptoms can be removed by behavioral treatments with no indication that the patient suffers any negative consequences. . . . In fact, many of the investigations find signs of generalized improvement in functioning after the removal of an incapacitating symptom.

More recently, in a long-term follow-up of agoraphobic patients who had received behavior therapy, these patients were not only "much better at follow-up than they had been before treatment" but there was also no evidence of any symptom substitution (Munby and Johnston

1980: 418). This, then, is the difficulty posed for the analytic dynamics of symptom maintenance by behavioristic symptom extinction without relapse.

As Edward Erwin (1978: 161) has noted, some pro-Freudian writers have proposed to accommodate this dearth of symptom substitution, and they have done so by postulating that there are indeed remissions of neuroses *without* benefit of psychoanalytically mediated insight as follows: though all symptoms are *initially* generated defensively, in a good many cases their underlying conflicts are resolved by spontaneous ego maturation, and in such instances the sheer inertia of an acquired habit may well preserve the symptoms as "ghosts" of the erstwhile neurosis. Hence, when a symptom is only a relic of a spontaneously conquered neurosis, the behavioristic extinction of the latter's "ghost" ought *not* to issue in any substitute for it. Such replacement by a new symptom ought to occur only when the vanished one was a manifestation of an *ongoing* conflict, rather than a ghost. Rhoads and Feather (1974: 17) claim to be able to tell whether a given symptom is a ghost symptom or not. Furthermore, they report having "found that classical [behavioristic] desensitization proceeds quickly and rapidly when used to treat 'ghost' symptoms," whereas such therapy does not have this effect in the case of *non*ghost symptoms.

But clearly, this proposed division of existing symptoms into "ghosts" and "nonghosts" invokes the spontaneous remission of neuroses. Thus, the postulate of vestige symptoms repudiates NCT—a veritable pillar of Freudian therapeutic doctrine—as well as the received psychoanalytic dynamics of symptom maintenance (S.E. 1893, 2: 6), for the sake of accommodating the sparsity of symptom substitution. And, as I shall now show, by rejecting the received analytic view that *present* symptoms are manifestations of coexisting and ongoing repressed conflicts, the ghost-symptom theorists unwittingly effect an *epistemic subversion* of the Freudian etiology of *initial* symptom *origination*, which they are anxious to retain. This epistemic undercutting results because the hypothesis of symptom maintenance repudiated by the ghost-symptom theorists has been the major avenue for the purported clinical inferability of symptom *formation* ever since Breuer and Freud had enunciated it (S.E. 1893, 2: 6).

In order to *justify* their etiologic identification of an original act of repression as the specific pathogen responsible, at the outset, for the initial formation of the symptom, the founders of psychoanalysis extrapolated backward from the maintenance dynamics they postulated for the continuing existence of the symptom. The evidence they marshaled, in turn, to justify this dynamics was that therapeutic symptom removal ensued from the abreactive lifting of a *coexisting* repression. In this way, they inferred etiologies via symptom maintenance from cathartic treatment success. The importance of the role they assigned to this ongoing repression as the cause of the current existence of a symptom is betokened by the pains they take to *reject* the notion that the symptom "leads an independent existence" as a mere vestige, once it has been engendered by an initial and subsequently forgotten trauma. Thus, they declare: "We must presume rather that the psychical trauma—or more precisely the [repressed] memory of the trauma—acts like a foreign body which long after its entry must continue to be regarded as an agent that is still at work" (S.E. 1893, 2: 6).

Clearly then, in order to certify the etiologic identification of the original repression as the prime pathogen on the basis of the therapeutic results they adduce, Breuer and Freud rely on their causal account of symptom maintenance. Even long after Freud had introduced free association as the key to fathoming repressions—as, for example, in the interpretation of manifest dream content—that venerable account of symptom maintenance remained the principal epistemic avenue for the inferability of etiology by means of the clinical data obtained from psychoanalytic investigation! Yet precisely that time-honored explanation of why symptoms persist when they do is incompatible with the "ghost thesis" that while they persist, there is frequent spontaneous dissipation of the initial repression, which purportedly engendered the symptoms to begin with.

It emerges, therefore, that Freudians who espouse the ghost-symptom hypothesis (e.g., Weitzman 1967: 307) do so on pain of severing a vital inferential link that has been paradigmatic for the clinical validation of Freud's etiologies. Hence, the resort to ghost symptoms for the sake of accommodating the sparsity of symptom substitution boomerangs: the cost of this accommodation is the epistemic subversion of the psychoanalytic etiology of original symptom formation, an etiology that the Freudian ghost theoreticians avowedly wish to preserve. This cost must then be added to the epistemic sacrifice incurred by the disavowal of NCT, which we have already tallied.

Furthermore, note that the ghost-symptom hypothesis explains the low incidence of symptom substitution by the high prevalence of ghost symptoms. For just this reason, the hypothesis ironically provides theoretical grounds for deeming psychoanalytic therapy very largely superfluous, at least for all those nosologic categories of patients which featured the sparsity of symptom substitution. Indeed, on that hypothesis, the presenting symptoms of the typical patient who is accepted for analysis are likely to be ghost symptoms, since people of high ego-strength presumably have a good chance of spontaneous ego-maturation. Hence, the permanent removal of these presenting symptoms without risk of being replaced by others hardly requires the pain, time, and expense exacted by psychoanalysis. If such symptoms yield to treatment at all, their short-term nonanalytic extinction will do. Analysis is then reduced to being the treatment of choice for only that small minority of psychoneurotics who are now presumed to be afflicted by *non*ghost symptoms. In the great majority of cases, psychoanalysis must then be deemed a *placebo* therapy (Grünbaum 1980: 325-350; 1983*b*). Yet Freud had insisted that the working through of the patient's conflicts is the crucial therapeutic factor in treatment, and indeed the ingredient "which distinguishes analytic treatment from any kind of treatment by suggestion" (S.E. 1914, 12: 155-156).

In short, opting for ghost symptoms gainsays NCT, undermines the received clinical epistemology of Freud's etiologies of the psychoneuroses, and makes analytic therapy largely superfluous to boot. This is a high price to pay.

Did Freud himself ever countenance the possibility of spontaneous erosion of the pathological repressions, while the symptoms persist as mere vestiges of the repressions? Late in his career, in a footnote to his disappointingly fuzzy 1926 essay on anxiety, Freud entertained, even if he did not espouse, this ghost-symptom hypothesis (S.E. 1926, 20: 142, n. 1). There he explained that the 1923 advent of his *second* topographic model of the mind—which featured the id, ego, and superego as agencies—prompted him to question his erstwhile view of symptom maintenance. At least in the case of psychoanalytically untreated victims of neurotic symptoms, he had believed in the continuing unconscious survival of initially repressed instinctual impulses. It seems "ready to hand and certain," he tells us, "that the old, repressed wishes must still be present in the unconscious since we still find their derivatives, the symptoms, in operation." Yet by 1926, "we begin to suspect that it is not self-evident, perhaps not even usual, that those impulses should remain unaltered and unalterable in this way." Hence, by that time, he had come to deem his entrenched view unduly restrictive: "It does not enable us to decide between two possibilities: either that the old wish is now operating only through its derivatives, having transferred the whole of its cathectic energy to them, or that it is itself still in existence too." This is Freud's plea for entertaining, if not embracing, the ghost-symptom hypothesis.

Weitzman (1967: 307) calls attention to this plea in order to make two points: (1) "successful symptomatic treatment may be taken as evidence" for the ghost-symptom hypothesis, and (2) this hypothesis "might be extended and elaborated in ways entirely compatible with analytic theory." Evidently Weitzman is quite unaware that, for the reasons I have given, the incorporation of the ghost postulate in analytic theory devastatingly undermines it epistemically. Besides, it largely negates such relevance as analysts have been wont to claim for Freud's therapy.

So far, I have not mentioned the existence of more recent findings that blur the widely reported absence of symptom substitution after behavioristic extinction of a primary symptom. For I wished to show to what lengths analytic writers were willing to go in order to accommodate the reportedly clear-cut failure of their initial expectations of new symptoms. Hence let me now call attention to the careful work of Kazdin and Herson (1980: 290 and 292-293), who relate the results of further evaluation of behavioral treatment: "it is clear that treatment effects are not necessarily restricted to the target behavior focused upon in treatment. . . . not all of the changes that accompany improvements in the target behavior are positive. . . . several behaviors may emerge as a function of behavioral treatment, some of which are adaptive or desirable, others of which are regarded as new problems. . . . it is clear that behavior therapy does not invariably result in beneficial effects for those behaviors not focused upon in treatment" (pp. 292-293). But, by the same token, these findings do *not* furnish clear-cut corroboration for the psychoanalytic expectation of substitutive manifestations of a hypothesized underlying neurotic conflict upon the behavioristic extinction of the undesirable target conduct.

The difficulties besetting NCT and/or the Tally Argument that I have set forth augment the already massive ones I had recently developed elsewhere *in detail* (Grünbaum 1980: 319-354; pp. 326-342 of this reference are amplified in Grünbaum 1983*b*). And since the Tally Argument is thus gravely undercut, any therapeutic successes scored by analysts, even if spectacular, have become *probatively* unavailing to the validation of psychoanalytic theory via that argument. Indeed, as I took pains to show (Grünbaum 1980: 343-352), not only is NCT discredited but no empirically warranted *alternative* premise that could take its place and yield the desired sanguine conclusions seems to be in sight. Hence, currently no viable surrogate for the defunct Tally Argument appears on the horizon. But this leaves unanswered the gravamen of the reproach that the psychoanalytic method of inquiry issues in bogus confirmations; for Freud had placed cardinal reliance on the Tally Argument to counter the indictment that clinical data are inauthentic as a result of suggestibility. In fact, Freud saw this argument as having redeemed, with one stroke, his 1917 promise (S.E. 1917, 16: 446-447) to nullify the two-fold indictment that suggestion is at once the decisive agent in his therapy and the cognitive bane of his method of clinical investigation.

The vital legitimating role that NCT would have played epistemically if it were viable points up a *linkage* between Freud's therapy and the attempted clinical validation of his general theory of unconscious motivations that was intrinsic to the psychoanalytic enterprise from the start. As he emphasized: "In psycho-analysis there has existed from the very first an inseparable bond between cure and research" (S.E. 1926, 20: 256). Indeed, we saw that in the cathartic method the epistemic dependence of the inferred etiology on therapeutic results was a crucial one: it was the therapy that enabled Breuer and Freud at all to propel the patients' various clinical responses under hypnosis into repression etiologies.

Thus, psychoanalytic hypotheses that do *not* themselves pertain at all to either the dynamics or the outcome of analytic therapy nonetheless have been *epistemically parasitic* on therapeutic results, partly to legitimate the probity of nontherapeutic clinical data, and partly to support the etiologies directly in the manner of the "Preliminary Communication" by Breuer and Freud. Yet Freud's essential reliance on positive therapeutic outcome to vindicate the probity of clinical data via NCT in the face of suggestibility is being widely overlooked. Those who have made it fashionable nowadays to dissociate the clinical credentials of Freud's theory of personality—the "science"—from the credentials of his therapy ought to face that they are stepping on very thin ice indeed. But before I turn to taking the measure of this thinness, I need to juxtapose two major sets of prima facie divergent methodological injunctions to which Freud adhered; for this juxtaposition will permit a reappraisal of Freud as a methodologist.

The first of the two methodological directives is to use the psychoanalytic method for the clinical ascertainment of the specific etiologies of the *psycho*neuroses, and more generally to validate *causal* hypotheses pertaining to unconscious motivations intraclinically *without* experimental controls. Freud considered this injunction to be vindicated by his Tally Argument. The second injunction pertained to the etiologic investigation of disorders such as anxiety neurosis, to which the psychoanalytic method of inquiry *and* therapy is avowedly *inapplicable*, because repressed ideation is held to play no role in their pathogenesis. In regard to probing the etiology of such afflictions, Freud gave the explicit admonition against victimization by *post hoc ergo propter hoc* and other pitfalls of causal inference, a caveat that he issued and applied devastatingly in his 1895 reply to Löwenfeld. I shall now set forth Freud's handling of the second of these two injunctions in order to put into still bolder relief his reliance on his NCT to legitimate the psychoanalytic method of clinical investigation as a means of validating hypotheses pertaining to unconscious motivations. As a corollary, I shall then challenge the unduly disparaging verdicts that even friendly critics have reached on him as a methodologist.

Freud's explicit warning against victimization by the pitfalls of causal inference in etiological inquiry is set forth in his searching 1895 "Reply to Löwenfeld" (S.E. 1895, 3: 123-139), which we had occasion to adduce against Popper in chapter 1, section B. Near the end of this reply, Freud articulates an admirably rich and lucid typology of the different senses in which diverse etiological factors may be causally relevant to a neurosis (pp. 135-136). It will be recalled that Löwenfeld had offered a critique of Freud's specific etiology of anxiety neurosis, a syndrome that Freud had been concerned to distinguish from neurasthenia, both clinically and etiologically. Löwenfeld claimed to have evidence that the psychical shock of a suddenly frightening experience—rather than any sexual disturbance—was the pathogen of anxiety neurosis. But Freud upheld his thesis that the specific etiology of this syndrome is sexual, and he did so in a two-part argument as follows: (1) he chided Löwenfeld for having fallaciously inferred the rival *non*sexual etiology that fright is the pathogen of anxiety neurosis by illicit causal reasoning based on *post hoc ergo propter hoc*, and (2) he referred to the investigation he himself had carried out in his first paper on anxiety neurosis (S.E. 1895, 3: 90-115) to validate the specific sexual etiology he had postulated for that syndrome. As for the first part of his argument, note Freud's keen appreciation of methodological pitfalls that are commonly laid at his door by critics:

About the facts themselves, which Löwenfeld uses against me, there is not the slightest doubt.

But there *is* doubt about their interpretation. Are we to accept the *post hoc ergo propter hoc* conclusion straight away and spare ourselves any critical consideration of the raw material? There are examples enough in which the final, releasing cause has not, in the face of critical analysis, maintained its position as the *causa efficiens*. One has only to think, for instance, of the relationship between trauma and gout. . . . It is clear to the meanest capacity that it is absurd to suppose that the trauma has "caused" the gout instead of having merely provoked it [i.e., provoked its *onset*]. It is bound to make us thoughtful when we come across aetiological factors of this sort—"stock" factors, as I should like to call them [footnote omitted]—in the aetiology of the most varied forms of illness. Emotion, fright, is also a stock factor of this kind. . . . I am justified in drawing the following conclusion: if the same specific cause can be shown to exist in the aetiology of all, or the great majority, of cases of anxiety neurosis, our view of the matter need not be shaken by the fact that the illness does not break out until one or other stock factor, such as emotion, has come into operation.

So it was with my cases of anxiety neurosis. [S.E. 1895, 3: 127]

But what *positive* reasons had Freud adduced in support of the specific sexual etiology he had inferred for anxiety neurosis? He reasoned essentially in the fashion of J. S. Mill's joint method of agreement and difference, using the particular case in which the inferred specific etiologic factor was realized by the practice of coitus interruptus. But note that Freud was careful (S.E. 1895, 3: 114) to distinguish between the underlying factor in the nervous system, which he had hypothesized to be specifically etiologic for a given syndrome, on the one hand, and the kinds of overt activities (or inactivities) that often—though not always!—*realize* this factor, on the other.

The English translation of the pertinent passage is unfortunately misleading. It renders Freud's German word *Vorkommen*—which means "incidence"—as "onset." The word *onset* is likely to mislead the reader into misidentifying a state that is likely to *contain* the underlying *specific* etiologic factor (e.g., coitus interruptus) with a mere "precipitating or releasing cause," which Freud was at pains to distinguish from the "specific cause" (S.E. 1895, 3: 135-136).

Two major points in Freud's argument for his specific sexual etiology of anxiety neurosis deserve notice: (1) he was careful to guard against the inferential pitfall of *post hoc ergo propter hoc* by producing a variety of instances in which the *absence* of the presumed cause issued in the *absence* of the anxiety attacks; and (2) the "*therapeutic* proof" of his hypothesized etiology is furnished, as he tells us, by the results produced upon the patient's alteration of his or her sexual practices (S.E. 1895, 3: 104); for his cases of anxiety neurosis *cured themselves* when coitus interruptus was suspended in favor of normal intercourse. Thus, far from claiming that *only* psychoanalysis can cure anxiety neurosis, Freud drew on the specific etiology he had inferred for it from *non*psychoanalytic clinical data to provide theoretical grounds for concluding that anxiety neurosis is *not even amenable* to psychoanalytic treatment. As he explains, "Anxiety neurosis...is the product of all those factors which prevent the somatic sexual excitation from being worked over psychically" (S.E. 1895, 3: 109), an assertion he reaffirmed as late as 1926 (S.E. 1926, 20: 141). Hence, in anxiety neurosis, "the affect does not originate in a repressed idea but turns out to be *not further reducible by psychological analysis, nor amenable to psychotherapy* [emphasis in original]" (S.E. 1895, 3: 97). Clearly, anxiety neurosis, and any other neurosis in whose pathogenesis repression is held to play no role, is excluded from the purview of NCT.

As Freud emphasizes here, no repressed idea and no "psychic working over" play any etiological role in anxiety neurosis, which results from the *direct* transformation of *somatic* sexual excitation into the symptoms (S.E. 1895, 3: 81, 124). Therefore, analytic treatment cannot remove its specific cause by means of psychoanalytic insight into the significance of its symptoms. It follows that the very etiology of anxiety neurosis that Freud had inferred by causal inquiry à la J. S. Mill provided theoretical reasons for concluding that this specific etiology could never have been disclosed, let alone validated, by the *intra*clinical devices of psychoanalytic investigation. Moreover, the pathogenic events specific to anxiety neurosis occur during the patient's adult life rather than during infancy or childhood and are therefore essentially contemporary or "actual."

This array of etiological and therapeutic results pertaining to this neurosis—and also to neurasthenia—contrasts sharply with the corresponding ones that Freud believed to have established for hysteria, obsessional neurosis, and paranoia by means of the *psychoanalytic* method of investigation and therapy. He therefore separately classified anxiety neurosis and neurasthenia as "actual neuroses," and distinguished them from the psychoanalytically tractable "psychoneuroses" (S.E. 1898, 3: 278-279; but see also the 1896 statement in 3: 167-168). It is now clear why I was concerned to formulate Freud's NCT initially as pertaining to the *psycho*neuroses and to exclude the actual neuroses from its purview.

As shown by his 1895 debate with Löwenfeld on anxiety neurosis, Freud obviously had a keen appreciation of the methodological safeguards afforded by controlled prospective causal inquiry, no less than of the pitfalls of *post hoc ergo propter hoc* inferences in the validation of the specific *contemporary* etiologies of the actual neuroses. But in 1895, Freud published not only his two papers on anxiety neurosis but also the *Studies on Hysteria*, which he had coauthored with Breuer. How, then, could that same Freud have forsaken the methodological safeguards of prospective causal inquiry, and have been content to employ the purely *intra*clinical psychoanalytic method to discover and validate the *infantile* etiologies of the psychoneuroses retrospectively? I trust I have shown why I claim that, at least as long as he was inclined to try to meet the challenge of suggestibility, Freud would very probably have given the following answer: *in the case of the psychoneuroses, the Tally Argument is the epistemic underwriter of clinical validation* by means of the psychoanalytic method of etiologic investigation, whereas no such underwriter is available to permit dispensing with the prospective methods of controlled causal inquiry in the case of the *actual* neuroses. Thus, as long as he felt able to rely on the Tally Argument, he felt quite justified when he expressed a sovereign patronizing serenity in the face of the following *dismissal* of his scientific credibility: the therapeutic successes of psychoanalysis as an emotional corrective are *not* achieved by imparting veridical self-knowledge, but rather by using suggestion to induce the compliant production of just those clinical data required to validate its theory, which therefore derives only *spurious* confirmation from these data.

The methodological vindication that Freud had put forward was apparently overlooked by his friendly critics Fisher and Greenberg, who judged him to be epistemologically uncritical on exactly this score as follows: "While therapist suggestion may lead to patient changes, therapist suggestion does not lead to data acceptable for validating hypotheses about personality. Freud never really came to terms with the differences involved in trying to learn about people as opposed to trying to change them" (Fisher and Greenberg 1977: 363). True, after the empirical demise of NCT, Freudians are no longer entitled to adduce therapeutic success as evidence for the veridicality of the analyst's interpretations. But since Freud did offer the Tally Argument, it would seem that, at one stage, he did come to terms, *albeit unsuccessfully*, "with the differences involved in trying to learn about people as opposed to trying to change them." For there, he addressed head-on the challenge: "What is advantageous to our therapy is damaging to our researches" (S.E. 1917, 16: 452).

A similar conditional exoneration of Freud applies, I believe, to Fisher and Greenberg's reaction to the admission made by Freud when he said: "Quite often we do not succeed in bringing the patient to recollect what has been repressed. Instead of that, if the analysis is carried out correctly, we produce in him an assured conviction of the truth of the construction which achieves the same therapeutic result as a recaptured memory" (S.E. 1937, 23: 265-266). After citing this passage, Fisher and Greenberg comment:

The retreat from confidence in the analyst's ability to establish "what really happened" in childhood to a method emphasizing "this is what must have happened to you" is an open acknowledgment of suggestion occurring in the treatment. It also, of course, raises some serious questions about how a theory of infantile sexuality could be validated solely on the basis of information obtained from psychoanalytic therapy. [Fisher and Greenberg 1977: 367]

Here again, these sympathetic critics seem to have overlooked that precisely in this context, Freud—at an earlier stage of his career, when he still espoused NCT—would have pointed to his Tally Argument, in which he at least tackled, though unsuccessfully, just the issue they raise.

To my knowledge, writers on Freud have simply failed to appreciate that he offered this argument and have even typically taken no cognizance of the pertinent part of his 1917 lecture (number 28). The psychologist N. S. Sutherland (1977: 114-115) is the one author known to me who did cite and criticize precisely this portion. It is therefore quite disappointing that the significance of Freud's enunciation of the NCT premise was completely lost on him. As will be recalled, the issue posed by Freud at the very start of the passage in question is whether it is true of analysts—as charged by their opponents—that "the influencing of our patient may make the objective certainty of our findings doubtful" (S.E. 1917, 16: 452). As I have argued, the question thus posed by Freud is *addressed* rather than begged when he responds by adducing NCT to claim that it is not damaging, though reasonable: "After all, his conflicts will only be successfully solved and his resistances overcome if the anticipatory ideas he is given tally with what is real in him" (p. 452). Yet Sutherland complains of question begging by commenting as follows:

> Note the skill with which Freud makes concessions to his opponents—"the objection...cannot be rejected as unreasonable"—only to trounce them at the expense of taking for granted the very point he is trying to prove. "After all, his conflicts will only be successfully solved and his resistances overcome if the anticipatory ideas he is given tally with what is real in him." [Sutherland 1977: 115]

I have juxtaposed the causal reasoning that Freud displayed in his reply to Löwenfeld with his concern to *vindicate* psychoanalytic investigation as a probatively cogent method of inquiry by means of the Tally Argument. And I have argued that once cognizance is taken of this argument, his stature as a scientific methodologist appears in a rather more favorable light than even friendly critics like Fisher and Greenberg have been prepared to allow.

Yet once Freud gave up NCT, he seems to have simply disregarded his own 1917 avowal that the authenticity of clinical data is epistemically parasitic on therapeutic achievements. Thus, in the very year in which he acknowledged that neuroses do remit spontaneously in due course (S.E. 1926, 20: 154), he proclaimed himself "a supporter of the inherent [scientific] value of psychoanalysis and of its independence of its application to medicine" (S.E. 1926, 20: 254). Hence, he demanded: "I only want to feel assured that the therapy will not destroy the science." But by precisely the account he gave in his "Analytic Therapy" lecture, once intraclinical validation is bereft of the legitimation that he drew from therapeutic success via the Tally Argument, the menacing suggestibility problem, which he had held at bay by means of this argument, comes back to haunt data from the couch with a vengeance. Therefore, unless analytic treatment is the paragon of the therapies as claimed in the Tally Argument, Freud himself has acknowledged that he cannot be assured of the inherent scientific value of psychoanalysis, no matter how devoutly he desires it.

A host of epistemic liabilities other than suggestibility intermingle with it to bedevil clinical validation. An account of the range and depth of these further pitfalls will now serve to undermine the cornerstone repression etiology. Moreover, the major pillars of the theory of repression will turn out to be ill-founded, *even if clinical data could be taken at face value as being uncontaminated epistemically.*

PART II

THE CORNERSTONE OF THE PSYCHOANALYTIC EDIFICE: IS THE FREUDIAN THEORY OF REPRESSION WELL FOUNDED?

Freud's method of free association has been hailed as the master key to unlocking all sorts of repressed ideation (S.E. Editor's Introduction, 2: xvi-xviii). Its products have been claimed to be uncontaminated excavations of buried mentation precisely because the flow of associations generated when the patient adheres to the governing "fundamental rule" is allegedly "free." As Freud maintains, it was "confirmed by wide experience" that the *contents* of all the associations that flow in the patient's mind from a given initial content do stand in an *internal causal connection* to that initial content (S.E. 1923, 18: 238). By avowedly being purely *internal*, this causal relatedness rules out the mediation of externally injected content in the strictly deterministic linkages that Freud postulates to exist between the initial mental content and the ensuing associations. And *if* there actually is no such external mediation, then the patient's flow of associations is indeed immune to contamination by distorting influences emanating from the analyst's suggestions! Thus, the analyst could then be held to function as a neutral catalyst or expeditor of the flow of his patient's free associations, even when he prompts the analysand to continue them after he suspects that they are being censored by internal resistances. In this way, the chain of the patient's associations is purported to serve as a pathway to the psychoanalytic unmasking of his repressions.

Freud recognized, it is true, that "free association is not really free," *to the extent* that "the patient remains under the influence of the analytic situation even though he is not directing his mental activities on to a particular subject. We shall be justified in assuming that nothing will occur to him that has not some reference to that situation" (S.E. 1925, 20: 40-41). But he makes it quite clear on the same page that this acknowledgment of a *global* influence by the analytic situation is *not* tantamount to admitting epistemic contamination of the products of free association by the analyst's influence: "it [free association] guarantees to a great extent that...nothing will be introduced into it by the expectations of the analyst" (p. 41). Thus, unencumbered by the stated qualifications, Freud deems free association to qualify as the "open sesame" for entry into the thoughts and feelings sequestered in the unconscious by repression.

For argument's sake, let us grant just for now that the patient's adherence to the fundamental rule of free association does safeguard the uncontaminated emergence of actually existing *repressed* wishes, anger, guilt, fear, or what have you. Why should the disclosure of these unconscious states be so very important? Clearly, it is because repressed ideation is held to have central *dynamic* significance in psychoanalytic theory. As Freud explains, "The theory of repression is the cornerstone on which the whole structure of psycho-analysis rests. It is the most essential part of it" (S.E. 1914, 14: 16). Hence, the cardinal epistemic value that is claimed for free association depends on the credentials of the theory of repression. It therefore behooves us now to examine the logical foundations of this theory in some detail. The upshot of that scrutiny will be that the reasoning by which Freud sought to justify the very foundation of his theory was grievously flawed. Thereupon we shall be able to appraise the probative value of free association.

Freud had emphasized that Breuer's "cathartic method [of therapy and clinical investigation] was the immediate precursor of psychoanalysis; and, in spite of every extension of experience and of every modification of theory, is still contained within it as its nucleus" (S.E. 1924, 19: 194). Josef Breuer used hypnosis to revive and articulate the patient's memory of a *repressed* traumatic experience that had presumably occasioned the first appearance of a particular hysterical symptom. Thereby Freud's mentor induced a purgative release of the pent-up emotional distress that had been originally bound to the trauma. Since such cathartic reliving of a repressed trauma seemed to yield relief from the particular hysterical symptom, Breuer and Freud hypothesized that repression is the *sine qua non* for the pathogenesis of the patient's psychoneurosis (S.E. 1893, 2: 6-7; 1893, 3: 29-30).

This *etiologic* role of repressed ideation then became prototypic for much of Freud's own theory of unconscious motivations. Repressed *wishes* were postulated to be the motives of *all* dreaming. Sundry repressed mentation was deemed to cause the *bungling* of actions at which the subject is normally successful ("parapraxes," such as slips of the tongue or pen, instances of mishearing or misreading, cases of forgetting words, intentions, or events, and the mislaying or losing of objects) (S.E. 1916, 15: 25, 67). Thus, even in the case of "normal" people, Freud saw manifest dream content and various sorts of "slips" as the telltale symptoms of (temporary) *mini*neuroses, engendered by repressions.

Freud arrived at the purported sexual repression-etiologies of the psychoneuroses, as well as at the supposed causes of dreams and parapraxes, by lifting presumed repressions via the patient's allegedly "free" associations. At the same time, excavation of the pertinent repressed ideation was to remove the pathogens of the patient's afflictions. Hence, scientifically, Freud deemed the psychoanalytic method of investigation to be both heuristic *and* probative, over and above being a method of therapy. And he claimed that clinical evidence furnishes compelling support for his theoretical edifice.

Therefore, we can scrutinize the logical foundations of psychoanalytic

theory by examining Freud's clinical arguments for the repression etiology of the psychoneuroses and for the cardinal causal role of repressed
ideation in committing "Freudian slips" and in dreaming. Chapters 3, 4,
and 5 of this book are devoted to just such a scrutiny, and their upshot
will be that the reasoning by which Freud sought to justify the very
foundation of his theory was grievously flawed.

3.

Appraisal of Freud's Arguments for the Repression Etiology of the Psychoneuroses

The central causal and explanatory significance enjoyed by unconscious ideation in the entire clinical theory rests, I submit, on two cardinal inductive inferences drawn by Breuer and Freud. As we are told in their joint "Preliminary Communication" of 1893 (S.E. 1893, 2: 6-7), they began with an observation made after having administered their cathartic treatment to patients suffering from various symptoms of hysteria. In the course of such treatment, it had turned out that, for each distinct symptom S afflicting such a neurotic, the victim had *repressed* the memory of a trauma that had closely preceded the onset of S and was thematically cognate to this particular symptom. Besides repressing this traumatic memory, the patient had also strangulated the affect induced by the trauma. In the case of each symptom, our two therapists tried to lift the ongoing repression of the pertinent traumatic experience, and to effect a release of the pent-up affect. When their technique succeeded in implementing this twin objective, they reportedly observed the dramatic disappearance of the given symptom. Furthermore, the symptom removal *seemed* to be durable.

Impressed by this treatment outcome, Breuer and Freud drew their first momentous *causal* inference. Thus they enunciated the following fundamental therapeutic hypothesis: The dramatic improvements observed after treatment were produced by none other than the cathartic lifting of the pertinent repressions. But before the founders of psychoanalysis credited the undoing of repressions with remedial efficacy, they

177

had been keenly alert to a rival hypothesis, which derived at least prima facie credibility from the known achievements of the admittedly suggestive therapies. On that alternative explanation of the positive outcome after cathartic treatment, that benefit was actually wrought by the patient's credulous expectation of sympton relief, not by the particular treatment ritual employed to fortify his or her optimistic anticipation. Breuer and Freud believed that they could rule out such an account of the treatment gains, an account to which I shall refer as "the hypothesis of *placebo effect*" (Grünbaum 1981). In an attempt to counter this challenge, they pointed out that the distinct symptoms had been removed *separately*, such that any one symptom disappeared only after lifting a *particular* repression (S.E. 1893, 2: 7). Thereupon they were ready for a *second* major causal inference. Thus, Breuer and Freud explicitly adduced the separate *therapeutic* removal of particular neurotic symptoms, by means of undoing repressions having a thematic and associative affinity to these very symptoms, as their *evidence* for attributing a cardinal *causal* role in *symptom formation* to the repression of traumatic events. Let us look at the intermediate reasoning on which the founders of psychoanalysis relied to claim therapeutic support for their etiologic identification of an original act of repression as the specific pathogen initially responsible for the formation of the neurotic symptom.

Breuer and Freud extrapolated this account of the origination of the symptom backward from the dynamics they had postulated for the subsequently continuing existence of the symptom. They had been led to attribute the *maintenance* of the symptom, in turn, to a *coexisting* ongoing repression of the traumatic *memory*, which "acts like a foreign body which long after its entry must continue to be regarded as an agent that is still at work." But what is their basis for this attribution? As they explain at once: "we find the evidence for this in a highly remarkable phenomenon," which they describe as follows: "*each individual hysterical symptom immediately and permanently disappeared when we had succeeded in bringing clearly to light the memory of the event by which it was provoked and in arousing its accompanying affect* [emphasis in original]" (S.E. 1893, 2: 6). Yet, as they also reported, "Recollection without affect almost invariably produces no result."

What, then, is the evidence they give for their etiologic identification of the repressed experience of a particular traumatic event E as the pathogen—avowedly *not* as the mere precipitator!—of a given symptom S that first appeared at the time of E? Plainly and emphatically, they predicate their identification of the repression of E as the pathogen of S on the fact that the abreactive lifting of that repression issued in the durable *removal* of S. And, as their wording shows, they appreciate all too well that *without* this symptom removal, neither the mere painfulness of the event E, nor its temporal coincidence with S's first appearance, nor yet the mere fact that the hysteric patient had *repressed* the trauma E could justify, even together, blaming the pathogenesis of S on the repression of E. Thus, the credibility of the repression etiology is crucially dependent on the reportedly durable separate removal of various particular symptoms, a therapeutic outcome deemed supportive because it appears to have been wrought by *separately* lifting particular repressions!

This epistemic dependence of the repression etiology on the presumed cathartic dynamics of effecting positive therapeutic outcome is further accentuated by the pains that Breuer and Freud take promptly to argue that their symptom removals are the result of the lifting of repressions rather than of suggestion: "It is plausible to suppose that...the patient expects to be relieved of his sufferings by this procedure, and it is this expectation...which is the [therapeutically] operative factor. This, however, is not so....The symptoms, which sprang from separate causes were separately removed" (S.E. 1893, 2: 7). Thus, the separate symptom removals are made to carry the vital probative burden of discrediting the threatening rival hypothesis of placebo effect, wrought by mere suggestion (cf. Grünbaum, 1983*b*).

Believing to have met this challenge, Breuer and Freud at once reiterate their epoch-making repression etiology. Let us now recapitulate the essential steps of the reasoning that prompted them to postulate this etiology. First, they attributed their positive therapeutic results to the lifting of repressions. Having assumed such a *therapeutic connection*, they wished to *explain* it. Then they saw that it would indeed be explained deductively by the following etiologic hypothesis: the particular repression whose undoing removed a given symptom S is *causally necessary* for the initial formation *and* maintenance of S. Thus, the nub of their inductive argument for inferring a repression etiology can be formulated as follows: the *removal* of a hysterical symptom S *by means of lifting* a repression R is *cogent evidence* that the repression R was *causally necessary* for the formation of the symptom S (S.E. 1893, 2: 7). For if an ongoing repression R is causally necessary for the pathogenesis *and* persistence of a neurosis N, then the removal of R must issue in the eradication of N. Hence the inferred etiology yielded a deductive explanation of the supposed remedial efficacy of undoing repressions.

Moreover, the founders of psychoanalysis appreciated that the threat posed by the rival hypothesis of placebo effect could be ominous. For, unless they could meet it convincingly, it would totally abort their bold inference of a repression-etiology from their fundamental therapeutic tribute to the undoing of repressions, a tribute incompatible with the placebo hypothesis. Indeed, as will become increasingly clear from chapters 3-5, to this day the *whole* of the clinical psychoanalytic enterprise is haunted by the mortal threat from the very live possibility of placebo effect. The continuing failure of psychoanalytic research to discredit this altogether reasonable challenge jeopardizes the very foundations of Freud's entire clinical theory. As chapters 4 and 5 will make clear, the compromise-models of manifest dream content and of sundry sorts of "Freudian" slips are endemic to this theory, no less than the stated etiologic and therapeutic hypotheses.

In any case, at the time, Breuer and Freud believed that their therapeutic results *had* ruled out the dangerous rival hypothesis of placebo effect by suggestion. And this belief did figure, as we saw, in their reasoning, when they concluded the following: (1) An *ongoing*, coexisting repression is causally necessary for the *maintenance* of a neurosis *N*, and (2) an *original* act of repression was the causal *sine qua non* for the *origination* of *N*. But their argument suffers from two key difficulties:

(a) Their appeal to the separate removal of a distinct symptom *S* by retrieving the traumatic experience of a particular event *E* actually did not rule out the rival hypothesis of placebo effect after all. For even under hypnosis, the patient was well aware that the therapist was *intent* upon uncovering a thematically particular *E* when focusing the former's attention upon the initial appearance of the distinct *S*. Thus, it was communicated to the patient that Breuer and Freud attached potential therapeutic significance to the recall of *E* with respect to *S*. To discredit the hypothesis of placebo effect, it is essential to have comparisons with treatment outcome from a suitable control group whose repressions are *not* lifted. Hence the attribution of remedial efficacy to the abreactive lifting of repressions was devoid of adequate evidential warrant.

(b) Assume, for argument's sake, the cogency of their evidence for concluding that the cathartic undoing of particular repressions was causally sufficient for the various symptom removals. This would then have furnished support, in the sense of J. S. Mill's methods, for inferring that the cognitive or affective repression of *E* was a causal *sine qua non* for the *maintenance* of *S*. But the granted therapeutic premise would not have warranted Breuer's and Freud's *extrapolation* that the repression of *E* was also a causally necessary condition for the *origination* of *S*. For, as Morris Eagle has remarked, their therapeutic conclusion does comport with the following *contrary etiologic hypothesis*: The *conscious* traumatic experience itself—as distinct from its ensuing repression—was responsible for the *initial formation* of *S*, whereupon the displeasure (anxiety) from the trauma actuated the repression of *E*, which is causally necessary for the mere *maintenance* of S. Chapter 8 will highlight the significance of this failure to offer cogent evidence for the initiating pathogenic role of repression. Such evidence would be furnished by data militating *against* the rival hypothesis that repression is etiologically irrelevant to the initial formation of the symptoms.

Note that the affect attached to a traumatic experience E can be *suppressed* (strangulated) but such that there is still conscious awareness of this pent-up affect. Thus, the affect attached to E can be suppressed without also being repressed. For example, Breuer's pioneering patient Anna O. felt disgust at the sight of seeing a dog drinking water from a glass, but she "said nothing as she wanted to be polite" toward the dog's owner (S.E. 1895, 2: 34). Furthermore, the *affect* attached to E can be repressed without cognitive repression of E as a whole. Yet, when E as a whole is repressed, this repression includes its accompanying affect *qua being attached to E*.

By the same token, the cognitive *restoration* of the forgotten E as a whole does also lift the repression of the affect attached to it. But the cognitive repression of E can be *lifted without* undoing E's affective *suppression*. Indeed, as Breuer and Freud report, the implementation of just this latter scenario was almost always therapeutically unavailing: "Recollection without [release of the attached pent-up] affect almost invariably produces no [therapeutic] result" (S.E. 1893, 2: 6). Thus it would be empirically false to deem the *mere* lifting of the cognitive repression of E *without* catharsis causally sufficient for the removal of the symptom S.

Hence, we must endeavor to construe the Breuer-Freud etiology of psychoneurosis such that it does *not* entail this empirical falsehood. Yet, it would have this untoward consequence if it were taken to assert that *both* cognitive repression *and* affective suppression of E are causally *necessary* for neurosogenesis.

On the other hand, just the undesirable false consequence is averted— as Carl Hempel and Morris Eagle have each remarked to me—by articulating the founding etiology of psychoanalysis as follows: Either cognitive repression or affective suppression of E, i.e., *at least one* of the two, is causally necessary for neurosogenesis, rather than both. And this version of the etiology would explain the reported therapeutic finding that the *cathartic* lifting of the repression—i.e., the undoing of the affective suppression as well as of the cognitive repression—is causally sufficient for symptom-removal. Yet this same version would *not explain*, but only allow the observation, made by Breuer and Freud, that mere recall without release of pent-up affect is "almost invariably" unavailing therapeutically.

Though the discharge of pent-up affect is thus deemed *therapeutically* essential, to accompany the cognitive retrieval of the repressed memory of *E*, it would be cumbersome to say so whenever one speaks of the presumed therapeutic role of lifting repressions. Therefore, brevity is served by the expository practice of simply crediting the therapeutic gain to the restoration of repressed memories, but with the understanding that affect-release is to be co-present.

Clearly, the attribution of *therapeutic* success to the undoing of repressions—rather than to mere suggestion—was the foundation, both logically and historically, for the central dynamical significance that unconscious ideation acquired in psychoanalytic theory: without reliance on the presumed dynamics of their *therapeutic* results, Breuer and Freud could never have propelled clinical data into repression etiologies. This is not at all to deny that the psychiatric *Zeitgeist* had already paved the way for such a theory of psychopathology. But it *is* to say that, as they tell us (S.E. 1893, 2: 6), "the evidence" for their epoch-making etiologic postulate was furnished by the remedial efficacy of lifting adult repressions having the specified affinity to the symptoms.

As we saw, they had argued pointedly that the therapeutic gains made by their cathartically treated patients were *not* wrought by suggestion. Instead, they attributed these remedial results to the abreactive recall of those *repressed* traumata during which the distressing symptoms had first appeared. Since these traumata occasioned the onset of the hysterical symptoms, I shall refer to them as "occasioning" traumata. Hence, we can say that Breuer and Freud had credited the patient's improvements to the *lifting* of the particular repression by which he had sequestered the memory of the *occasioning* trauma in his unconscious. Yet, when Freud himself treated additional patients by Breuer's cathartic method, this treatment failed to achieve *lasting* therapeutic gains. Indeed, the ensuing correlation of symptom relapses and intermittent removals, on the one hand, with the vicissitudes of his personal relations to the patient, on the other, led him to *repudiate* the *decisive* therapeutic role that Breuer and he had attributed to undoing the repression of the *occasioning* trauma!

The evidence and reasoning that had driven Freud to this repudiation by 1896 are poignantly recalled by him in his 1925 "Autobiographical Study":

Even the most brilliant [therapeutic] results were liable to be suddenly wiped away if my personal relation with the patient became disturbed. It was true that they would be reestablished if a reconciliation could be effected; but such an occurrence proved that the personal emotional relation between doctor and patient was after all stronger than the whole cathartic process. [S.E. 1925, 20: 27]

Hence, by 1896, it had become painfully evident to Freud that Breuer and he had been all too hasty in rejecting the rival hypothesis of placebo effect. And, ironically, he began to be haunted by the possibility that lifting repressions may not be therapeutically efficacious after all.

Freud's therapeutic repudiation of abreactively retrieving the memory of the *occasioning* trauma also had a momentous corollary: he likewise renounced the major *etiologic* significance that he and Breuer had originally attributed to the *repression* of *this* trauma (S.E. 1896, 3: 194-195). Yet he adhered undauntedly to the research program of seeking the pathogens of neuroses among *some* repressed traumata or *other* (S.E. 1896, 3: 195-199). And, though the disappointments of cathartic treatment outcome had undercut the very basis for giving decisive remedial credit to the lifting of repressions, he unflinchingly clung to the therapeutic view that the excavation of *some* repression or *other* would remove the pathogen of the patient's affliction. But, as I shall now argue, the empirical rationale that Breuer and Freud had used for postulating a *repression* etiology *at all* was altogether undermined by just the findings that induced Freud himself to repudiate the attribution of therapeutic gain to the undoing of the repression of the occasioning trauma.

The aforementioned symptom *relapses*, which ensued after Freud had lifted the patient's repression of the occasioning trauma, showed him that the undoing of this repression failed to uproot the *cause* of the neurotic symptoms. Moreover, the fragile, ephemeral symptom remissions achieved by patients who received Breuer's cathartic treatment could hardly be credited to the lifting of this repression. By Freud's own 1925 account, giving such therapeutic credit had very soon run afoul of a stubborn fact: "The personal emotional relation between doctor and patient was after all [therapeutically] stronger than the whole cathartic process" (S.E. 1925, 20: 27). For even *after* the patient's repression of the occasioning trauma had indeed been undone cathartically, the alternation between his remissions and relapses still depended *decisively* on the ups and downs of how well he got along emotionally with his doctor.

Yet, as we saw earlier, the 1893 postulation of a repression etiology of neurosis in Breuer and Freud's foundational communication had rested *crucially* on the premise that the patient's symptom removals had actually been wrought by lifting his repression of the memory of the occasioning trauma. Thus, Freud's own abandonment of just this therapeutic premise completely negated the very reason that Breuer and he had invoked for postulating the pathogenicity of repression at all. In short, I claim that *the moral of Freud's therapeutic disappointments in the use of the cathartic method after 1893 was nothing less than the collapse of the epoch-making 1893 argument for the repression etiology of neurosis,* which Breuer and he had propounded.

Why, I ask, did Freud adamantly retain the generic repression etiology instead of allowing that this etiology itself had simply become baseless? And why, in the face of this baselessness, was he content with his mere etiologic demotion of the repressed *occasioning* trauma, while clinging to the view that the pathogen is bound to be some other earlier repressed trauma of a sexual nature, to be excavated via free associations (S.E. 1896, 3: 195-199)? Whatever his reason, he seemingly did not appreciate that the etiologic fiasco suffered by Breuer's account in the wake of the disappointingly fragile therapeutic results had made a shambles of the very cornerstone of this psychoanalytic edifice; for such an appreciation would have been tantamount to his realization that the etiology of neurosis still posed the same fundamental challenge as it had *before* Anna O. enabled Breuer to stumble upon the alleged "talking cure." Instead, Freud avowedly committed himself to a "prolonged search for the traumatic experience from which hysterical symptoms appeared to be derived" (S.E. 1923, 18: 243), just when the initially plausible traumatic etiology had been found to be baseless after all.

I have stressed the collapse of the 1893 therapeutic argument on which Breuer and Freud rested their originally hypothesized repression etiology of neurosis. Yet I need to forestall a possible misunderstanding of my methodological complaint against Freud's tenacious search for evidence that might have warranted the *rehabilitation* of the repression etiology in a *new* version. Hence, let me emphasize that I do *not* fault the pursuit of this research program per se after the demise of the cathartic method. What I do find objectionable, however, is Freud's all too ready willingness—once he was no longer collaborating with Breuer—to claim pathogenicity for purported childhood repressions on evidence *far less cogent* than the *separate* symptom removals that Breuer and he had pointedly adduced in 1893. In short, having embarked on the program of retaining the repression etiology *somehow*, Freud was prepared to draw etiologic conclusions whose credentials just did not live up to Breuer's initial 1893 standard. Even that higher original standard, I contend, was still not high enough.

Indeed, I maintain that the repression etiology of neurosis would have lacked adequate empirical credentials, even if the therapeutic gains from cathartic treatment had turned out to be both durable and splendid. For, even such impressive results may well not be due at all to the lifting of pathogenic repressions; instead, they may be a *placebo effect* (Grünbaum 1980: 325-343), as we saw earlier. And even if the therapeutic gains were actually wrought by the lifting of repressions, there would be grounds for attributing the *maintenance* of the symptoms to these repressions, but not their *initial formation*.

Moreover, as I shall argue in chapter 8 in detail, the retrospective validation of repression as the initial pathogen lacks the sort of controls that are needed to attest *causal relevance*, and there is doubt about the reliability of purported memories elicited under the suggestive conditions of hypnosis. Incidentally, despite the innovative replacement of hypnosis by free association to recover repressed mentation in psychoanalytic treatment, Freudian therapy has retained an important tenet of its cathartic predecessor: "Recollection without affect almost invariably produces no [therapeutic] result" (S.E. 1893, 2: 6).

As we saw above, Freud's own subsequent (1917) *therapeutic* defense of his sexual version of the repression etiology by means of the Tally Argument has fared no better empirically than the original reliance on cathartic treatment success as evidence for the pathogenicity of repression. And, as chapter 8 will show, proposed *clinical* vindications of this etiology *without* reliance on the presumed dynamics of the therapy are epistemically quite hopeless. Hence, whatever his own evidential or personal motivations for retaining the repression etiology, I claim that it should now be regarded as *generically* devoid of clinical evidential support, no less than Breuer's particular version of it, which Freud repudiated as clinically unfounded. By the same token, I maintain that the demise of the therapeutic justification for the repression etiology fundamentally impugns the *investigative cogency* of lifting repressions via "free" associations in the conduct of etiologic inquiry. In short, the collapse of the therapeutic argument for the repression etiology seriously undermines the purported *clinical research* value of free associations, which are given pride of place as an epistemic avenue to the presumed pathogens! After all, Freud had enunciated his fundamental rule of free association as a maxim of clinical research, because he thought that associations governed by it had reliably *certified* the unconscious pathogens of the neuroses.

Yet, though it is widely overlooked, *the attribution of therapeutic success to the removal of repressions not only was but remains to this day, the sole epistemic underwriter of the purported ability of the patient's free associations to certify causes.* Thus, these associations are still deemed to be a reliable *investigative* avenue leading to the detection of the pathogens of neuroses *and* authenticating them as such.

Analysts such as Strachey (S.E. 1955, 2: xvi) and Eissler (1969: 461) have hailed free association as an instrument comparable to the microscope and the telescope. And it is still asserted to be a trustworthy means of etiologic inquiry in the sense of licensing the following *causal infer-*

ence: Let a causal chain of the analysand's free associations be initiated by his neurotic symptoms, and thereupon issue in the emergence of previously repressed memories; then, we are told, this emergence qualifies as *good evidence* that the prior ongoing repression of these memories was actually the *pathogen* of the given neurosis. Whereas all Freudians champion this causal inference, a number of influential ones have explicitly renounced its *legitimation* by the presumed therapeutic dynamics of undoing repressions.

To them I say: Without this vindication or some other as yet unknown epistemic underpinning, not even the tortures of the thumbscrew or of the rack should persuade a rational being that free associations can *certify* pathogens or other causes! For, without the stated *therapeutic* foundation, this epistemic tribute to free associations so far rests on nothing but a glaring causal fallacy. Therefore, it is unavailing to extol the method of clinical investigation by free association as a trustworthy resource of etiologic inquiry, while issuing a modest disclaimer as to the therapeutic efficacy of psychoanalytic treatment. And one is dumbfounded to find that noted psychoanalysts such as George S. Klein have done just that (1976: 36-38). Also, amazingly, the renowned analyst Judd Marmor conjectured, as we recall, that it was the accidental need to earn his livelihood as a psychiatric practitioner which drove Freud "to utilize his investigative tool [of free association] simultaneously as a therapeutic instrument" (1968: 6). In brief, we see anew that those who have made it fashionable nowadays to dissociate the credentials of Freud's repression-theory of personality—the so-called "science"—from the merits of psychoanalytic therapy are stepping on thin ice indeed. How very thin will become even more apparent from our impending scrutiny of the psychoanalytic theory of "slips" and of dreams. To avoid a serious misunderstanding, let me point out that I assert a dependence of the *clinical* credentials of Freud's theory of personality on therapeutic results. But, as will be recalled from Section 2C of the Introduction, I *deny* that the treatment setting is the principal arena, let alone the sole arena for the *well designed* testing of the theory of repression. And chapter 8 will furnish my systematic reasons for this contention.

One is all the more disappointed that David Rapaport tries to parry the epistemic challenge to the method of free association by (1) overlooking that the *causal connectedness* of the sequence of emerging free associations as such has far better epistemic credentials than *post hoc ergo propter hoc*, (2) completely *begging the question* as to whether the causal dynamics of unconsciously engendered thought and behavior is *in fact* of the following sort: a repression which emerges at the end of a chain of free associations—as its *terminus ad quem*—was actually the original cause of the symptom that initiated the chain as its *terminus a quo*, (3) simply declaring that modes of causal inference which are normally taken to be patently unsound do become legitimate when used to infer the *unconscious* causes of human conduct. For, as Rapaport put it:

Adopting the method of free association, however, binds us, to a far-reaching degree, in respect to what kind of rules, what type of logic, there are in the unconscious. For example, if one idea follows another in a chain of free associations, the analyst will assume *post hoc ergo propter hoc* (after it thus because of it). I believe that this rule goes without an explanation. What is the justification for psychoanalysis taking such a stand? Perhaps the *propter* is somewhat too narrow a term, because frequently the causal relationship just referred to is reversed like this: "The cause of it, therefore after it."...Let us remind ourselves that these are the abhorrent examples our logic teachers gave us in school to show us how not to think. In the logic of free association, in the logic of the unconscious, they have as eminent a place as the rules of the syllogism have in ordered thinking. [1967: 216-217]

Clearly, Rapaport begs the very question as to the reliability of free association as a means of *certifying* emerging repressions to be pathogens. Just this vital question was also lost on Macmillan (1977: 224-226), who devotes a section on "Symptoms, Memories, Logic and Causes" to showing that Freud's notion of symptom formation was based on T. Meynert's 1885 physiological associationism. For one is left in the dark on whether Freud thought that Meynert's assumptions can *underwrite* precisely the crucial causal inference of pathogenicity, which he claimed to be licensed by his method of free association. Thus, Rapaport has plainly supplied no cogent reason for supposing that Freud's "logic of free association" has at all *discerned* the etiologic "logic of the unconscious."

Though the repression etiology of psychoneurotic disorders was thus itself in grave jeopardy from lack of cogent clinical support, Freud extrapolated it by postulating that repressions engender "slips" (parapraxes) and dreams no less than they spawn full-blown neuroses. For example, he assimilated a slip of the tongue to the status of a mini-neurotic symptom by viewing the slip as a *compromise* between a repressed motive that crops out in the form of a disturbance, on the one hand, and the conscious intention to make a certain utterance, on the other. But as against this generalized explanatory reliance on repressed mentation, I shall argue for the following thesis: even if the original *therapeutic* defense of the repression etiology of neuroses had actually turned out to be empirically viable, Freud's compromise models of parapraxes and of manifest dream content would be *misextrapolations* of that etiology, precisely because they lacked any corresponding therapeutic base at the outset. For in 1900 Freud defended the heuristic and probative use of free association in *interpreting dreams* by pointing to its primary use in *etiologic* inquiry. And he explicitly adduced *therapeutic* results, in turn, to legitimate free association as a reliable means of certifying the pathogens etiologically. As he put it: "We might also point out in our defense that our procedure in interpreting dreams [by means of free association] is identical with the procedure by which we resolve hysterical symptoms; and there the correctness of our method is warranted by the coincident emergence and disappearance of the symptoms" (S.E. 1900, 5: 528).

Before turning to an examination of the psychoanalytic theory of slips, it behooves me to call attention to some highly misleading recent depictions of both the content and validity of the distinctively Freudian theory of repression.

Plainly, the very occurrence of repression—in the psychoanalytic sense of banishing a thought from consciousness and/or denying it entry (S.E. 1915, 14: 147)—is a *necessary* condition for the cardinal and protean *causal role* that Freud attributed to it. Yet, it must not be overlooked that the bare *existence* of the psychic mechanism of repression—which was asserted speculatively before Freud by Herbart and Schopenhauer (S.E. Editor's Introduction, 2: xxii; Ellenberger 1970: 209)—is still a far cry from its Freudian role as a generic pathogen, as a dream-instigator, and as a begetter of parapraxes.

Yet Paul Kline (1981: 196 and 436), Seymour Fisher (1982: 680), as well as Matthew Erdelyi and Benjamin Goldberg (1979) gloss over or ignore the momentous epistemic gap between attesting to the bare *occurrence* of repression, and providing cogent support for its alleged role in neurosogenesis, etc. Correlatively, the locution "theory of repression" is used in a seriously ambiguous way. Thus, the dust jacket of Kline's book announces misleadingly that "there is...incontrovertible experimental support...for the theory of repression." Then, inside the book, when giving the *definition* of *"Repression proper,"* Kline includes in it the claim that "repression [is] a pathogenic or unsuccessful mechanism of defence" (Kline 1981: 196). But this definitional inclusion of an etiologic role begs the causal question as to whether mental acts of repression are, in fact, neurosogenic.

For the experimental evidence that Kline (ibid.: 226 and 436) proceeds to adduce relates to the *existence* of the mechanism of repression, but does *not* bespeak any etiologic role at all. Hence, none of the experimental support invoked by him can serve to buttress the Freudian causal role of repression! Incidentally, Kline (ibid.: vii) sees his own mustering of experimental results as a rebuff to the wholesale rejectionism of Eysenck and Wilson (1973), on the one hand, and as an improvement on Fisher and Greenberg's (1977) uncritical acceptance of methodologically dubious results, on the other.

These comments on alleged experimental support for "the theory of repression" prompt me to issue an important caveat. For I am concerned to forestall a potential misunderstanding of a central thesis of this book. I do claim to substantiate herein the poverty of the *clinical* credentials of the foundations on which Freud's edifice avowedly rests. Yet I emphatically *allow* for a weighty possibility: Future *extra*clinical evidence (e.g., epidemiologic or experimental findings) *may* turn out to reveal after all that Freud's brilliant intellectual imagination was quite serendipitous for psychopathology and other facets of human conduct, despite the clearcut failure of his clinical arguments. Thus, contrary to Seymour Fisher's (1982: 681) most recent verdict that "Freud is scientifically alive and well," I maintain that psychoanalysis is thus alive, but—at least currently—hardly well, as it were.

I shall develop further major doubts in succeeding chapters (especially in chapters 4, 5, 6, 8, and 10). Yet the poverty of clinical confirmations I have already documented so far shows how hollow and evasive it was on Brenner's part (1982: 4) to have lodged the following recent complaint: "there are philosophers of science who are critical of psychoanalytic theories, and who mistakenly characterize psychoanalysis as speculation rather than as a branch of science. This they do despite the fact that they are themselves without experience in using the method that provides the basis for the theories they criticize." Neither I nor many of the other critics I know gainsay that the psychoanalytic method equips its practitioners with a *heuristically* fecund basis for propounding hypotheses, especially in the hands of a soaring mind like Freud's. But if the practice of psychoanalysis does make for the *cogency* of the clinical *arguments* offered by its advocates, why is it—I ask—that there is as yet no such viable argument for the repression etiology of psychoneurosis in, say, Brenner's (1982) conflict-version, let alone for the use of free association to *certify* pathogens? Would Brenner say that unless Francis Galton had himself engaged in petitionary prayer—or had conducted prayer services ecclesiastically for others—the statistical doubts he raised (Galton 1872) as to its remedial efficacy need not be addressed by theologians? If my critique is unsound, then those who, like Brenner, do have "experience in using the method" ought to be able to discredit it *other than* by pointing to my *lack* of practical experience with it.

4.

Examination of the Psychoanalytic Theory of Slips—of Memory, the Tongue, Ear, and Pen

One of Freud's paradigm cases of a slip of the memory will now serve to exhibit the poverty of the empirical credentials of his compromise model of parapraxes. The example involves the forgetting of a pronoun in a Latin quotation. It was discussed preliminarily in the Introduction, Sections 2C and 3B. It is quite inessential for our purposes to pass judgment on the merits of the sensational recent claim of Swales (1982: Sections III-VI) that the memory slip in question was committed by Freud himself, when his sister-in-law was allegedly pregnant by him. Hence I shall take Freud's text at face value.

On one of his trips, Freud became reacquainted with an academically trained young man who was familiar with some of his psychoanalytic writings. The young man, an Austrian Jew whom we shall call "AJ," conveys to Freud that he resented the social and career handicaps resulting from religious discrimination. To vent this frustration, he *tries* to quote the line from Virgil's *Aeneid* in which the despairing and abandoned Dido exclaims: *Exoriare aliquis nostris ex ossibus ultor* ("Would that someone arise from our bones as an avenger!"). But AJ's memory is defective, and he not only inverts the word order of *nostris ex* but altogether *omits* the indefinite pronoun *aliquis* ("someone"). Aware that something was missing in the line, AJ asks for help, whereupon Freud quotes the line correctly (S.E. 1901, 6: 9).

The young man then asks Freud to explain the memory lapse. Being glad to oblige, Freud then enjoins him to associate freely, whereupon AJ begins by decomposing *aliquis* into *a* and *liquis*. After a series of intermediate associations, the young man comes up with the thought of St. Januarius, the Christian martyr who became the patron saint of Naples, and brings up the purported miracle of this saint's clotted blood. Freud points out that St. Januarius and St. Augustine, whom AJ had mentioned earlier, "both have to do with the calendar." Then Freud asks: "But won't you remind me about the miracle of his blood?" After responding that this relic is kept in a vial stored in a Neapolitan church and liquefies at regular intervals, AJ pauses. Thereupon Freud says, "Well, go on. Why do you pause?" After AJ responds, "Well, something *has* come into my mind...but it's too intimate to pass on....Besides, I don't see any connection, or any necessity for saying it [ellipsis points in original]," Freud assures him in a schoolmasterly manner, "You can leave the connection to me" (S.E. 1901, 6: 10-11).

When AJ then volunteers that his intimate sudden thought was "of a lady from whom I might easily hear a piece of news that would be very awkward for both of us," Freud asks rhetorically, "That her periods have stopped?" He explains reasonably enough that he had interpreted the young man's prior association to the miracle of St. Januarius' blood as an allusion to a woman's period.

AJ did actually have good reason to fear that his paramour was pregnant by him. The anxiety he had felt because of this ominous possibility had indeed emerged, however tortuously, from the process of association in which he had engaged. Moreover, AJ himself was well aware of these facts. Yet he was prompted to query the alleged *causal bearing* of his genuine worry on his *aliquis* lapse: "And you really mean to say that it was this anxious expectation that made me unable to produce an unimportant word like *aliquis*?" With sovereign confidence, Freud retorted, "It seems to me undeniable." For Freud was convinced that AJ's repressed wish *not* to have any progeny from his sexual liaison had interfered with his Latin rendition of his desire to have descendants who would avenge the adversity suffered by the Jews.

Judging by Freud's account, it is unclear whether AJ had actually *repressed* his fear of pregnancy rather than merely relegated it to his own so-called preconscious by diverting his attention to other stimuli. But let us assume that this thought had been in a repressed state, at least prior to the time t_1 when AJ committed the parapraxis of forgetting *aliquis*. Soon after Freud restored this forgotten word to AJ's awareness, the young man used the restored word as the point of departure for associations, which he began to generate at time t_2. Then the anxiety-laden thought of a confirmed unwanted pregnancy emerged at time t_3. For brevity, I shall say that there was a "memory lapse" at time t_1, a "triggering restored awareness" at time t_2, and a (tortuously) ensuing "terminal emergence" of repressed anxiety content at time t_3.

As Timpanaro (1976: 51) has noted, Freud did not hesitate to intervene occasionally in the flow of AJ's associations. Hence, Timpanaro has charged that Freud thereby subtly steered the associations in a manner akin to the Socratic method of eliciting answers to leading questions.

But let us grant here, at least for argument's sake, that there is some kind of *uncontaminated causal linkage* between the restored awareness of *aliquis* at time t_2, which triggers the labyrinthine sequence of associations, on the one hand, and the emerging anxiety thought with which this sequence terminated at time t_3, on the other. Yet we must now ask the following *first question*: on what grounds does Freud, or anyone else, take *this* assumed causal linkage to be *evidence* at all for the further claim that the repressed thought harbored by AJ before t_1 was the *cause* of his memory lapse at time t_1? More explicitly, why should the ultimately ensuing elicitation of AJ's previously repressed pregnancy fear, via circuitous intermediate associations starting from the restored *aliquis*, bespeak that this very fear—while as yet being repressed—had *caused* him to forget this word, as well as to invert *nostris ex*? Why indeed should the *repressed* fear be held to have caused the *forgetting* of *aliquis* at the outset just because meandering associations starting out from the restored memory of *aliquis* issued in the conscious emergence of the fear? To endow the unconscious with cunning, uncanny powers of intrusion upon conscious actions is only to baptize the causal fallacy by giving it an honorific name. True, AJ's repressed wish not to have sired progeny from his paramour at that time *may*, though need not necessarily conflict with his conscious desire to have avenging descendants. But this fact does not show that his repressed wish caused the *aliquis* lapse in his *Latin rendition* of his supposedly contrary desire. And even if "common sense psychology" had the epistemic resources to authenticate such a causal linkage, the terminal emergence of AJ's fervent hope (that his paramour not be pregnant) from his associative chain provides *no* grounds for reaching such a causal verdict. Yet the provision of just such grounds is the epistemic burden of Freud's method of free associations in this context!

It would be untutored, besides being uncharitable, to suppose that Freud did not draw on some auxiliary hypotheses to fill the prima facie glaring inferential gap to which our questions have called attention. Indeed, he *extrapolated* from his repression etiology of neuroses, much as he had already done quite explicitly when claiming to explain manifest dream content (S.E. 1900, 4: 101 and 5: 528). Thus, he postulated that the compromise-formation model of neurotic symptoms—in which *repressed* contents are deemed *causally necessary* for symptom forma-tion—may also be legitimately extrapolated to cover parapraxes. Once these bungled actions had thus been conceptualized as mini-neurotic symptoms, Freud felt entitled to make a further assumption: if a repres-sion emerges into consciousness via free associations triggered by the subject's awareness of his parapraxis, then the prior presence of *that* repression was the cause of the parapraxis. *Mutatis mutandis*, he had already taken both of these hypotheses to apply to manifest dream contents, as we shall see in some detail later on.

Yet I maintain that the reasoning by which Freud thought he had supported these important postulates is grievously flawed. Note first that it was Freud's correct statement of the quotation from Virgil, but *not* the undoing of AJ's repression of his pregnancy fear, which served to *remove* the mnemonic lacuna of *aliquis* in the young man's awareness. Hence, it would plainly be altogether wrongheaded to credit the lifting of the repression of AJ's fear with filling the quite *different* memory gap constituting AJ's "slip." Indeed, let us suppose that Freud had *not* filled this gap for AJ by supplying the omitted *aliquis* to him. Assume further that AJ had taken *other* words in his defectively recalled Latin line as the point of departure for his associations. Then let us even postulate *without* evidence that the *latter* associations would have eventuated in AJ's recall of the forgotten word *aliquis* only *after* the conscious emer-gence of his repressed fear of the pregnancy. Even then, it would be quite unclear that the posited unaided filling of AJ's memory gap can be credited causally to the lifting of his repressed fear! In any case, Freud did not adduce any evidence that the permanent lifting of a repression to which he had attributed a parapraxis will be "therapeutic" in the sense of enabling the person himself to correct the parapraxis *and* to avoid its repetition or other parapraxes in the future. While the hypothesized repression "etiology" of parapraxes thus lacked "therapeutic" support, it was precisely such prima facie impressive support that Breuer and Freud had marshaled to show that the removal of neurotic symptoms is attributable to the lifting of repressions, so that repressions are presum-ably pathogens. In short, there is a striking disparity in regard to the adduced evidential support between the hypothesis that parapraxes are the result of repressions, on the one hand, and that repressions are the pathogens of neurotic symptoms, on the other.

Yet once Freud's postulational abandon was no longer daunted by Breuer's known theoretical restraint, Freud unabashedly enunciated his repression theory of parapraxes. He did so despite the lack of any counterpart to the evidential support from therapeutic outcome on which Breuer and he had emphatically grounded their repression etiology of neurotic afflictions. Instead of taking pause in this patent discrepancy, in 1900 and 1901 Freud assimilated manifest dream content, and then also parapraxes, to neurotic symptoms by construing them alike as compromise formations engendered by repressions (see S.E. 1900, 4: 144). Hence, I view his theory of parapraxes and of dreams as *misextrapolations* of the generic repression etiology of neurotic symptoms, which had at least had prima facie therapeutic support.

But, as I argued in chapter 3, this very etiology, with its compromise model of symptoms, is itself devoid of adequate clinical credentials. We saw that, by the same token, Freud failed to sustain the investigative cogency of lifting repressions (via "free" associations) in the conduct of etiologic inquiry. *A fortiori*, he has given us no *cogent* reason to infer that lifting repressions is a means of certifying the causes of parapraxes and of dreaming, for the repression "etiology" of parapraxes just turned out to be a gratuitous extrapolation from the compromise-formation model of neurotic symptoms. Thus, even bona fide repressions uncovered by means of free associations can be presumed to be causally *irrelevant* to parapraxes and dreams, at least until and unless *additional* grounds for such relevance are shown to exist in particular cases.

This presumption of causal irrelevance has recently been further strengthened by the detailed and well-supported *alternative* causal explanations of parapraxes that have been put forward by Timpanaro (1976) in his important book *The Freudian Slip*. The highly instructive *non*-Freudian psychological hypotheses employed by him were evolved by philologists to carry out textual criticism. The various "etiologic" categories of errors he employs fully allow for causation by unconscious mechanisms. But instead of having the status of Freudian *repressions*, these hypothesized mental processes qualify technically as "preconscious" in the vocabulary of psychoanalysis. Timpanaro (1976: 95) expects a deepening of his non-Freudian psychological explanations of slips from the currently developing study of the physiological mechanisms underlying memory, forgetfulness, and concentration as well as of their liability to emotional influences. Let us give a digest of the rival explanations of parapraxes proposed by Timpanaro.

One task of textual critics is to investigate the conditions that contribute to the corruption of a text in the course of its successive written transcriptions or oral transmissions, including quotations learned by heart. Furthermore, philologists are concerned to delineate the linguistic patterns of the errors that result from these tendencies to make alterations. The various "etiologic" categories of such errors that they have evolved include the following:

1. "Banalization," which is the unconscious replacement of a word or group of words by an actual or supposed synonym whose usage is *more familiar* to the copyist in the context of his or her linguistic and cultural patrimony (Timpanaro 1976: 21). This kind of error takes various forms. One of these is just the sort of syntactic and stylistic alterations that AJ effected when quoting from Virgil (chap. 3), for the construction of the original line is highly anomalous in Latin, and virtually untranslatable into the native German spoken by AJ, who was hardly a professional Latinist. Again, AJ's inversion of *nostris ex* is a banalization both with respect to Latin usage and German word order, although this transposition may have been induced by his attempt to cope with his memory gap, as Freud himself points out. The tendency to banalize may well be a matter of mental economy (p. 97). Incidentally, the word *aliquis*, which AJ omitted, is relatively superfluous, since its omission does not destroy the polemical message that AJ wished to express by means of the line, whereas the deletion of *exoriare, nostris ossibus,* or *ultor* would have done so. The tendency to omit the superfluous may well be a matter of mental economy no less than banalization.

2. Errors inspired by influences from the *context* in which they occur: unlike banalizations, they are the result of assimilations to preceding or subsequent words belonging to the same phrase, rather than to the subject's linguistic patrimony (p. 97). Thus, a speaker or writer who is preoccupied with what he is *about* to say or write can readily distort a given word or phrase under the influence of his anticipation of a succeeding one. Furthermore, other preoccupations or loss of interest may tax our finite mnemonic capacity and issue in forgetting or omissions.

3. The common substitution of words of an equal number of syllables that also have a strong phonetic similarity, such as rhyming, and that refer to conceptually alike items (chap. 6). The case of Freud's trying to remember the name of the Renaissance painter Signorelli and thinking instead of Botticelli (S.E. 1901, 6: 2), who is another such painter, falls into this category. Freud had no sooner thought of Botticelli when he rejected it as incorrect and then thought of the name of the lesser painter Boltraffo, which he also knew at once to be wrong. As Timpanaro explains (pp. 70-71), in the catalog of errors familiar from textual criticism, the second error is no less recognized than the first. In the philological perspective, the second error—unlike the first—is *not* a memory slip. Instead, it is an unsuccessful attempt to correct the first error: having failed to pinpoint his initial substitution of "Bottic" for "Signor" in "Signorelli," Freud had mistakenly retained the syllable "Bo" from that initial substitution, but he then compounded or "disimproved" his error by dropping the authentic "elli," thereby coming up with

nothing better than "Boltraffo." German textual critics call such disimprovements *Schlimmbesserung*, and French philologists refer to them as *fautes critiques*.

4. "Polar errors," consisting in the substitution of words having an opposite significance. Freud attributed such errors to the id's getting even with the mendacious ego (S.E. 1916, 15: lecture 3). But non-Freudians, such as the linguist Rudolf Meringer, whom Freud cites (e.g., S.E. 1901, 6: chap. 5), have held (Timpanaro 1976: 147-150, 151-153) that conceptual complementarity—such as between the words "omitted" and "inserted"—of itself can be the source of erroneous word substitutions.

5. Haplography and haplology: the coalescing of double letters or sounds in writing or speaking, respectively. Repeated instances of haplography in typesetting by the same printer may betoken a personal penchant to commit such errors (Timpanaro 1976: 136-137, 141).

6. Omissions effected when the glance of a copyist jumps from one group of letters, typically at the beginning or end of a word, to a similar group of letters in an adjacent or nearby word, as in mistranscribing the Italian word *teleologico* to become *teologico*. This sort of error is known as *saut du même au même* (p. 36).

7. Dipthography, the common, seemingly mechanical mistake of improperly *repeating* parts of words, whole words, or entire sequences of words (pp. 143-145). For example, a writer's thoughts and his putting them on paper do not always remain coordinated, so that he may mistakenly write down something that he has already written; copyists or printers may look back to a point in the text that is further back than the one at which they left off.

In largely much more sketchy form, "etiologic" categories of this sort were used by some psycholinguists and physiologists during Freud's time to give nonpsychoanalytic explanations of "slips." But, as Timpanaro stresses, textual critics are much more alert than these students of errors to the complex joint operation of a variety of such "etiologic" factors in the production of a particular slip. The "textual critic... demands an effort to understand how various general tendencies contribute on any given occasion to the production of a single and particular error" (p. 84). Yet Timpanaro (1976: 98-99) acknowledges that, at least in the current state of knowledge, such explanations are stochastic or, at any rate, yield only statistical predictions.

Thus, it is quite impossible to predict that, for example, a given text will be corrupted by a given error at a given point in a given copy. But the situation is very different at the statistical level. While I can in no way commit myself to the prediction that the word *cultuale* will be banalized to *culturale* by a particular typist or printer, I am able to predict that in all probability if the passage is given to a hundred typists or printers to reproduce, the majority of them will fall into the error. The same can be said of the banalization of *teleologico ["teleological"]* to *teologico ["theological"]*. Here the *saut de même au même* operates as an additional cause in conjunction with the tendency towards banalization, while the latter is further assisted by the fact that the two adjectives, though their meanings are significantly different, are often appropriate enough to the same context: belief in a finalism of nature is obviously related to a conception which can loosely be termed religious or "theological."

Additional non-Freudian psycholinguistic explanations for errors in linguistic performance are offered in Fromkin (1980).

Freud discusses some of the nonpsychoanalytic approaches to an understanding of slips made by his own contemporaries, but he belittles the causal factors singled out by them as merely generic and shallow (S.E. 1901, 6: 21-22, 80-81). Indeed, he indicts them for being satisfied with accepting factors that merely *favor* the commission of a parapraxis in lieu of causally necessary or sufficient conditions (S.E. 1916, 15: 45-46, 61). Scornful of the stochastic causation inherent in mere tendencies, he declares:

Such psycho-physiological factors as excitement, absentmindedness and disturbances of attention will clearly help us very little towards an explanation. They are only empty phrases, screens behind which we must not let ourselves be prevented from having a look. The question is rather what it is that has been brought about here by the excitement, the particular distracting of attention. And again, we must recognize the importance of the influence of sounds, the similarity of words and the familiar associations aroused by words. These facilitate slips of the tongue by pointing to the paths they can take. But if I have a path open to me, does that factor automatically decide that I shall take it? I need a motive in addition before I resolve in favour of it and furthermore a force to propel me along the path. So these relations of sounds and words are also, like the somatic dispositions, only things that *favour* slips of the tongue and cannot provide the true explanation of them. [S.E. 1916, 15: 46]

Prompted by this, I say: whatever the incompleteness or other defects of the more recent nonpsychoanalytic explanations of slips offered by Timpanaro or by psycholinguists, their deficits are not remedied at all by the psychoanalytic explanations. Thus, these deficits do not redound to the credibility of Freud's thesis, that all parapraxes whose causes are unknown to the subject are the result of repressions. For, to take Freud's earlier example, let it be granted that AJ's chain of associations from his corrected parapraxis issued causally in the disclosure of the repressed anxiety afflicting him, *and* that this unconscious fear of pregnancy had been clamoring for overt expression. How, then, does this assumed motive serve to explain even probabilistically why AJ suffered any memory loss at all, let alone why he forgot *aliquis*? *A fortiori*, how does

Freud's claim that AJ's unconscious anxiety is the *"sense"* or *intention* behind his slip (S.E. 1916, 15: 40) even match, let alone excel, Timpanaro's explanation, which invoked the tendencies to effect mental economies by syntactic and stylistic banalization, coupled with the elimination of the superfluous? Yet Freud downgrades psycholinguistic explanations generically. He remarks that, after such explanations were offered, "on the whole . . . we were further than ever from understanding slips of the tongue" (S.E. 1916, 15: 34), and he claims that the purported motives of parapraxes are "more interesting than . . . the circumstances in which they come about" (S.E. 1916, 15: 40). Furthermore, he maintains that, unlike psychophysiological accounts, his motivational elucidations address the question of "why it is that the slip occurred in this particular way and no other" (S.E. 1916, 15: 32; see also p. 36).

More fundamentally, suppose that Freud did use AJ's repressed anxiety to give a hypothetico-deductive explanation of his slip. Then the *causal nexus* between the repression and the slip asserted in its *explanans* would have been *epistemically unacceptable*. For, as I have argued above and also indicated elsewhere (Grünbaum 1980: 377-378), Freud has offered nothing better than *post hoc ergo propter hoc* toward the evidential support needed for *that* causal nexus, even if we grant him that the sequence of AJ's associations was an uncontaminated causal chain. In particular, the purported causal nexus is not warranted by the mere *thematic affinity* between the antiprogenitive content of the repressed wish, on the one hand, and the Latin avowal of a desire for avenging progeny, on the other. As we saw in the Introduction (Sections 3B and 3C), mere thematic affinity alone simply does not bespeak causal lineage.

The *aliquis* example is representative of other cases in which Freud fallaciously trades on the genuineness of a fear (or wish) with which the subject is preoccupied, and on its elicitation by associations initiated by a given parapraxis, to gain plausibility for the causal attribution of that parapraxis to the elicited fear (or wish). Even the unique elicitation capacity presumed for these particular associations can be spurious. As Timpanaro (1976: 143) has rightly stressed, genuine preoccupations or obsessions tend to be evoked by a great *many* stimuli, even or especially when they are devoid of any foundation. Unmindful of these pitfalls, Freud compounds the logical defect of the *aliquis* case by reporting Jung's brief analysis of a corpulent German male who was not a student of German literature and omitted the words *mit weisser Decke* ("with a white sheet") when reciting a well-known poem by Heine. The man told Jung that the white sheet made him think of a shroud, and thereby of an acquaintance who had recently succumbed to a heart attack, which in turn evoked his fear that he himself might meet the same fate. Here again, there is not the slightest reason to attribute the parapraxis to the evoked fear (of death), even if the anxiety was unconscious in Freud's dynamical sense. In a similar vein, Timpanaro (1976: 90) has aptly remarked: "Nor is it enough, in order to substantiate an avowed determinism, to assert that every 'slip' has a cause and thereupon present extravagant causal connexions as certain." It is noteworthy that, in the case of reciting from Heine, the thematic affinity between the fear of death and a white sheet is considerably more tenuous than between AJ's fear of pregnancy and his *aliquis* lapse. As Jung's Heine example illustrates, for any emerging repression it will be possible to find some thematic thread, however, farfetched, such that there will be *some* topical kinship with the given lapse. Thus, even if *strong* thematic affinity alone were to bespeak that the repression engendered the lapse, it would be unavailable in the typical run of parapraxes to warrant the causal nexus asserted by Freud.

The psychoanalytic theory of slips, which offers explanations based on repressions unearthed via free associations, ought *not* to be allowed to benefit from such credibility as is possessed by other explanations having only a spurious similarity to them. One species of such different explanations features mental states of which the subject who committed the slip was clearly *conscious*. Another species features mental states that, though not at the *focus* of the subject's consciousness, were readily available to his conscious awareness. These states were "preconscious" in Freud's parlance, as opposed to being repressed (*dynamically* unconscious). Being the adroit pedagogue and even deft expository promoter that he was, Freud exemplifies both of these sorts of slips by way of *didactic prolegomena* (e.g., in S.E. 1916, 15: 64-65). But neither of these two species can be credited to psychoanalytic theory because, as Timpanaro (1976: 122) put it concisely:

The truly Freudian "slip" or instance of forgetting presupposes the existence of psychic material which my conscious ego has repressed because it proved *displeasing*—or, given it was desirable from a hedonistic point of view, because my moral inhibitions prevented my confession of it even to myself, let alone to others.

Thus, suppose that in the course of giving a lecture on human sexuality, a person misspeaks himself by saying "orgasm" instead of "organism." It is *not* a bona fide "Freudian" explanation to remark that conceptual preoccupation with the overall topic of the lecture combined with phonetic similarity to generate the slip. By the same token, Freudians should not trade on cases in which a slip may be plausibly held to bespeak the presence of a *conscious* thought that the subject wishes to conceal; nor on instances of slips in which there is little evidence for the prior repression of a thought that a speaker tried unsuccessfully to hide. An example of this, which I owe to Rosemarie Sand, would be the man who turns from the exciting view of a lady's exposed bosom muttering, "Excuse me, I have got to get a *breast* of *flesh* air!"

Since these embarrassing losses of control appear to have psychological causes, they do call for corresponding psychological explanations. Hence, they indeed militate *against* the view, which Freud decried as widely avowed, "that a mistake in speaking is a *lapsus linguae* and of no psychological significance" (S.E. 1901, 6: 94). To the contrary, these cases of misspeaking do qualify as "serious mental acts; they have a sense [motive]" (S.E. 1916, 15: 44). Furthermore, as Benjamin Rubinstein has pointed out illuminatingly, these sorts of "slips"—though *not* bespeaking repressions—share two significant features of the genuinely "Freudian" ones: (1) they exhibit intrusions upon the agent's control of his own behavior, and (2) the intruding element is a wish or an affect. But despite being psychologically revealing, such cases are not supportive of the psychoanalytic theory of parapraxes, in which repression is held to play the cardinal explanatory role. For, in the concluding chapter of his magnum opus on slips, one of the three necessary conditions laid down explicitly by Freud for inclusion of a given slip in the purview of his theory is as follows: "If we perceive the parapraxis at all, we must not be aware in ourselves of any motive for it. We must rather be tempted to explain it by 'inattentiveness,' or to put it down to 'chance'" (S.E. 1901, 6: 239). Indeed, the avowed contribution of Freud's theory to our understanding of various sorts of "slips" is to explain those species "in which the parapraxis produces nothing that has any sense of its own" for either the subject who commits the slip or for others (S.E. 1916, 15: 41). Thus, when Freud lists parapraxes *violating* his requirement that they be devoid of a sense of their own, these violations furnish mere didactic prolegomena: they serve the explicitly stated "limited aim of using the study of these phenomena as a help towards a preparation for psychoanalysis" (S.E. 1916, 15: 55).

Freud's illustrations of such propaedeutic cases include instances of nonsensical misspoken words such that the speaker who uttered them knows at once, when asked, "what he had really meant to say" (S.E. 1916, 15: 42; see also p. 47). In fact, "the disturbing purpose is known to the speaker and moreover had been noticed by him before he made the slip of the tongue" (S.E. 1916, 15: 64). More generally, as Freud explains, "we shall find whole categories of cases in which the intention, the sense, of the slip is plainly visible" (S.E. 1916, 15: 40). In such instances "the parapraxis itself brings its sense to light" so as to be perspicuous to the subject no less than to others (S.E. 1916, 15: 41; see also p. 47). Emphasizing the propaedeutic role of all such perspicuous cases, Freud declares: "My choice of these examples has not been unintentional, for their origin and solution [motivational explanation] come neither from me nor from any of my followers" (S.E. 1916, 15: 47).

One such example features a German-speaking anatomy professor who misspoke in a lecture as follows: "In the case of the female genitals, in spite of many *Versuchungen* ["temptations"]—I beg your pardon, *Versuche* ["experiments"]..." (S.E. 1901, 6: 78-79; 1916, 15: 33). When the anatomist himself thus corrected his slip, he patently required no lifting of a repression to disclose to him that *erotic interest* was a possible contributing motive for his use of a sex-oriented term instead of the phonetically similar neutral term he had expected to utter. Yet in an article entitled "On the Freudian Theory of Speech," the psycholinguist A. W. Ellis (1980: 124) overlooks the propaedeutic role of the anatomist's slip and of all the other motivationally perspicuous illustrations given by Freud. Drawing an exegetically incorrect conclusion from these transparent examples, Ellis asserts: "It is not necessary that the speaker should be unaware of the activity of the disturbing purpose [motive] within him before it reveals itself in the slip." But, qua characterization of the scope of the *psychoanalytic* theory of slips, this formulation contravenes Freud's aforecited restriction as to the purview of this theory, for he demanded that the speaker *not* be aware of any motive for his slip (S.E. 1901, 6: 239, condition C). Hence, the inferred perturbing intention had to be sequestered in the speaker's unconscious. Having overlooked Freud's restriction, Ellis violates it anew when he proceeds to give purported illustrations of "Freud's mode of explanation" (1980: 124). Thus, his *prime* example is the anatomist's perspicuous temptation slip rather than one "in which the parapraxis produces nothing that has any sense of its own" (S.E. 1916, 15: 41).

Yet Ellis does inquire as to whether "depth-analytic explanations are needed in addition to the mechanical-psycholinguistic explanations proposed more recently" (1980: 123). His domain of inquiry consists of fifty-one word-substitution slips, which he selected from Freud's 1901 index of speech lapses. The closest he comes to considering whether *repressed* ideation might generate slips is in his remarks on word-blend errors, which result from the blending of two words (1980: section 5). Ellis notes that the speaker can attest introspectively to the prearticulatory presence of thoughts that he wished to conceal, and Ellis allows that the word the speaker intended to utter blended with a lingering phonemic trace of the disturbing thoughts, thereby betraying their presence.

But, as he hastens to point out, "those thoughts could not have been truly unconscious prior to manifesting themselves in the slip" (1980: 129). Indeed, since he took a word-blend example in which the subject's unaided introspection did disclose a prearticulatory disturbing motive, it was evident from the start that this motive did not qualify as repressed.

Unfortunately, Ellis does not reveal whether *any* of the fifty-one word-substitution slips examined by him were of the *opaque* sort required by Freud's restriction. But unless this requirement is demonstrably met, it is at best unclear whether Freud's repression theory of parapraxes is damaged by Ellis's findings. Yet Ellis claims such damage in virtue of the feasibility of giving psycholinguistic explanations of a *non*motivational kind for the fifty-one substitution slips he had selected. Thus, he notes that the erroneously substituted words are either phonetically similar to the target words, semantically closely related to them, or perseverations from prior utterances in the given lexical context.

Even psychoanalysts have rightly complained that the theoretically sympathetic experimental psychologist Saul Rosenzweig simply failed to test Freud's 1915 conception of repression when Rosenzweig claimed to have found experimental support for it in 1934 (see the first chapter, Section B). Alas, the same type of complaint is appropriate to M. T. Motley's (1980) interpretation of his ingenious laboratory investigations. He did furnish telling experimental evidence for the *causal relevance* of cognitive-affective mental sets, and even of personality dispositions, to the production of verbal misreadings. These influences acted via prearti-culatory semantic editing of the words to be read. Thus, semantic influences external to the speaker's intended utterance effected verbal slips that were "closer in meaning to those semantic influences than to the originally intended utterance" (Motley 1980: 145). The pertinent misreadings were phoneme-switching errors of the sort known as "spoonerisms" (Fromkin 1980: 11; Motley 1980: 134).

But, like Ellis, Motley misconstrues the probative relevance of his otherwise valuable findings to Freud's psychoanalytic theory of slips. In Motley's case, the crucial question is whether the cognitive-affective mental sets and/or personality dispositions he manipulated as the independent variable in his experiments qualify as *repressed*, rather than as focally conscious or preconscious. I shall argue that, in all three of his experiments, the answer is plainly negative. The semantic prearticula-tory editing manifested in these experiments occurs at three correspond-ing levels as follows: consonance with the immediate verbal context in experiment 1, with the speaker's sociosituational context in experiment 2, and with one of the speaker's specified personality traits in experiment 3. Motley (1980: 136) views these three experiments sequentially as *ascendingly* qualified to serve as bona fide tests of Freud's own theory of parapraxes. By contrast, I claim that none of them reaches even the threshold of being a test of psychoanalytic theory, as distinct from a rival theory that *denies* the causal relevance of repressed ideation. For Motley's findings could *all* be explained by the sort of rival psychological theory that countenances *only conscious* motivational influences as generators of slips. To substantiate my claim that Motley's results are probatively irrelevant in the stated sense, let me comment briefly on the pertinent salient features of his three experiments in turn.

1. Motley himself describes experiment 1 as only a partial realization of Freud's initial conditions (1980: 138-139), but he nonetheless invokes it as generic support for psychoanalytic theory. And his grounds for this tribute are that, in Freud's account, the adduced motives operate in the production of slips via prearticulatory editing of a kind that is *generically* semantic rather than just phonological (p. 136). But note that the semantic interfering stimuli in this experiment are word pairs, each of which is presented tachistoscopically for one second. Such exposure is long enough for conscious, not to mention preconscious, cognitive registration. Furthermore, Motley gives no evidence at all for the prearticulatory *repression* of these interfering semantic stimuli.

True enough, his experiment 1 does attest that semantic influences from the immediate verbal context of a slip are causally relevant to the commission of the slip. But, as we just observed, in this experiment these influences are preconscious, if not outright focally conscious. Hence, I deem the causal relevance demonstrated in Motley's first experiment to be probatively unavailing as distinctive support for the psychoanalytic theory of slips, in the sense of being support for those of its consequences that are *not* likewise consequences of *any* rival theories eschewing repressed motives. For brevity, I shall speak of such distinctive support as support for psychoanalytic theory "*as such.*"

2. Motley regards experiment 2 as "virtually a direct test of Freud's theory" (p. 139). Yet in this second experiment no less than in the first, the cognitive-affective situational sets Motley manipulated in the treatment groups can hardly be claimed to have been repressed by the subjects. In one group, the situational mental set was a conscious anticipation of experiencing an electric shock on the part of subjects who had been told explicitly to be prepared for it, and who were *ostensibly* connected to electrodes (p. 139). In another group, there was no electrical set, but the male subjects were pointedly stimulated sexually by "a female confederate experimenter who was by design attractive, personable, very provocatively attired, and seductive in behavior" (p. 140). The ensuing arousal was all too present in the subjects' conscious awareness. (There was a third "neutral set" control group.)

True enough, "Experiment 2 demonstrates that subjects' speech encoding systems were sensitive to semantic influence from their situational cognitive set [electric or sex stimulation]" (p. 141). And, as in Freud's theory, that influence originated *outside* the total semantic context of the intended utterance. All the same, since the influence was not repressed, the results of experiment 2, no less than those of experiment 1, are seen to be probatively unavailing as support for psychoanalysis as such. Hence, there is no foundation for Motley's conclusion that "Experiment 2 provides strong support for Freud's view of verbal slips" (p. 141).

3. Motley sees experiment 3 as the best of his three purported tests of Freudian theory. Male heterosexual anxiety was manipulated as the independent variable, and the experiment did succeed in exhibiting the influence of the subject's personality on his verbal slips. But, qua support for Freud, that demonstration is futile, unless the relevant personality disposition bespeaks the operation of repressed ideation. Motley gives us every reason to claim that it does not.

As Motley explains, the personality trait of sex anxiety "was operationalized as Mosher Sex-Guilt Inventory scores" (p. 142). Using these scores, Motley selected three treatment groups of high, medium, and low sex anxiety. But Mosher used a sentence-completion questionnaire filled out by the subjects *themselves* to develop scales for sex guilt, hostility guilt, and morality guilt. Thus, if the subjects who rate high, medium, and low on the sex-guilt scale are to furnish responses probatively relevant to the repression theory of parapraxes, these ratings would need somehow to betoken degrees of (sexual) repression, perhaps inversely or directly.

Yet I submit that the true-false and forced-choice answers given by the subjects on the questionnaire fail as a gauge of (sexual) repression. Plainly one reason for this failure is that a person with guilt feelings that qualify psychoanalytically as repressed will not consciously know of or admit the presence of such feelings when simply asked. Indeed, he or she will even deny such feelings in good faith, sometimes vehemently! Motley seems to have overlooked that insofar as the Mosher scores can be held to measure "psychodynamic conflict," what they measure is *conscious* conflict, *not* psychoanalytically pertinent conflict. It is as if one had devised a questionnaire to measure the *conscious* "income-tax conflict" experienced by a person torn between the conscious temptation to cheat on his tax return and the equally conscious fear of legal prosecution for having done so. By contrast, Freudian psychodynamic conflict is a clash between a repressed thought clamoring for conscious recognition, on the one hand, and the ego or superego, which denies that thought entry into awareness, on the other. When depicting Mosher sex-guilt scores as measures of "psychodynamic conflict," Motley (1980: 144) unfortunately pays no heed to the crucially pertinent difference between the conscious and the Freudian sorts of conflict: he gives no reason at all to suppose that the subjects who scored high, medium, and low on Mosher's sex-guilt scale had repressed the sexual impulse aroused in them by the provocative, voluptuous female experimenter. Hence, by using the Mosher-scale ratings as a gauge of personality disposition, Motley forfeited the probative relevance of his otherwise valuable findings for the repression theory of slips.

Motley did find (1980: 142) that high Mosher-guilt subjects committed more sex-error spoonerisms than medium-guilt ones, whose errors, in turn, exceeded those of the low-guilt subjects. And, as he rightly maintains (p. 143), he has thereby shown that—within the given situational cognitive set of sex arousal—personality disposition can issue in verbal slips via semantic prearticulatory editing. Thus, Motley's results emerge as quantitatively modulated instances of the same motivational genre as the speech error of the consciously aroused man who declared that he wanted "to get a *breast* of *flesh* air." By the same token, Motley's findings are just as probatively unavailing for buttressing the psychoanalytic theory of parapraxes as this "breast-flesh" slip. Indeed, despite claiming support for Freudian theory from the outcome of experiment 3, Motley issues the following concluding disclaimer, among others: "Whereas Freud would claim that ALL verbal slips are semantic manifestations of a speaker's private cognitive-affective state, the present study makes no such claim (and this writer would expect such manifestations to be rare)" (p. 145). As I have argued, the design of Motley's three experiments lends substance to the complaint that experimental psychologists tend to overlook the initial conditions required by a genuine test of Freud's theory. Yet, in addition to yielding otherwise interesting results, these imaginative designs seem to point the way to devising genuine tests.

The restricted purview that Freud enunciated for the *psychoanalytic* contribution to the motivational elucidation of parapraxes has often been overlooked, especially because Freud genuinely psychoanalyzes only some parapraxes, as in the *aliquis* case, but essentially merely reports others and largely lets them speak for themselves, as it were. In this way, the reader is tempted to conclude incorrectly that if these others are of the plausible sort that I have exemplified, then they automatically bespeak support for Freud's theory. Thus, Freud (S.E. 1901, 6: 95) relates how a speaker in the German parliament asked for a demonstration of "unreserved" (*rückhaltlos*) loyalty to the Kaiser, but betrayed the hypocrisy of his subservience by saying "spineless" (*rückgratlos*) instead. Another case of self-betrayal of a *conscious* thought, which was reported to Freud by Theodor Reik, is that of a young girl who did not intend to reveal to her parents her antipathy toward the young man whom they wished her to marry. But when asked by her mother how she felt about him, she described him by coining the neologism *sehr liebens*widrig ("very love-repelling"), though she had meant to be insincere and say *sehr liebens*würdig ("very worthy of love") (S.E. 1901, 6: 91). As Timpanaro (1976: 151-153, 144-145, 178-179) has shown illuminatingly, Freud describes other episodes in which a slip *might* be the result of the cunning of a repression but assumes *tout court* that it definitely *must* be, especially if the interpretation depicts individual motivations as misanthropic. Hence, Timpanaro (pp. 126-127) concludes that "all the really persuasive examples" in Freud's writings are what, *faute de mieux*, he calls "gaffes":

> "Slips" of this kind certainly presuppose that something has been suppressed, but the speaker is fully conscious of, and currently preoccupied with, whatever it is that he wants to conceal from those to whom he is speaking. It is not something which has genuinely been "repressed" (forgotten) and re-emerges from the depths of his unconscious. [P. 127]

As Timpanaro remarks perceptively (p. 105), Freud's explanations increasingly forfeit cogency to the extent that the slips to which they pertain differ from the "gaffe" type, and are alleged to have a more recondite, unconscious genesis. Indeed, he points out (p. 104) that, as Freud fully appreciated, nonpsychoanalytic accounts of gaffes have long been clichés in the folklore of commonsense psychology. For instance, such expressions as "he gave himself away" betoken the recognition that, lacking complete control of what we do say, we sometimes fail to conceal from others what is not meant for them and we would even prefer not to know ourselves, although we *are* conscious of it. The vexation that often accompanies the slip may well be the result of the unexpected realization of just this incomplete control, rather than of the unconscious appreciation of the tainted origin of the slip, as claimed by Freud (Timpanaro 1976: 157n).

But the important conclusion is this: *if there are any slips that are actually caused by genuine repressions, Freud did not give us any good reason to think that his clinical methods can identify and certify their causes as such,* no matter how interesting the elicited "free" associations might otherwise be. As is apparent from my arguments, this adverse upshot seems indefeasible even if one were to grant that the analyst does not influence the subject's "free" associations. Besides, such an absence of influence would be utopian, as I shall argue in chapter 5.

The psychoanalytic explanations of other species of parapraxes by means of repressed motivations are just as tenuously founded as in the cases we have discussed. For example, the same unfavorable verdict applies to Freud's account of *misreadings*. For, as he explains:

If we want to discover the disturbing purpose which produced the misreading, we must leave the text that has been misread entirely aside and we may begin the analytic investigation with the two questions: what is the first association to the product of the misreading? and in what situation did the misreading occur? [S.E. 1916, 15: 70]

And, as he explains further:

What we ought to read is something unwished-for, and analysis will convince us that an intense wish to reject what we have read must be held responsible for its alteration. [P. 71]

I do not deny that "an intense wish to reject what we have read" *may* be "responsible for its alteration"; but I do deny that Freud's reliance on the method of free association furnished a sound reason even for making this causal attribution, let alone for concluding—as he did—that the wish to reject "must" be held responsible. Hence, I claim that his method for identifying and certifying the purported motive ought *not* to "convince us," as he thinks. Yet I *allow*, of course, that genuinely probative methods of causal inquiry may turn out to vindicate, at least in some cases, Freud's imputations of unconscious motivations for the commission of parapraxes.

Can any of the above array of doubts as to the *repression* genesis of a slip be validly gainsaid by claiming, as Freud did, that the alleged cause of the slip is established to *be* its cause by the *introspective* confirmation of the subject who committed it? As he put it: "you shall grant me that there can be no doubt of a parapraxis having sense if the subject himself admits it" (S.E. 1916, 15: 50). Thus, when an examinee attributed his own penchant to forget Gassendi's name to a guilty conscience, Freud took it for granted that this "very subtle motivation" had to be responsible, because it was one "which the subject of it has explained himself" (S.E. 1901, 6: 27). And he reports parapraxes by Storfer, himself, and Andréas-Salomé, claiming that self-observation was able to certify the actual repressed cause of the bungled action in each case (S.E. 1901, 6: 118, 163, 168; cf. Timpanaro 1976: 146, for a rival account of Storfer's slip by reference to linguistic banalization, as well as phonic and conceptual similarity). But it is probatively unavailing that AJ can confirm having put his genuine anxiety about the Neapolitan woman's pregnancy out of his mind—if indeed he had—at least temporarily, when he discussed his resentment of religious discrimination with Freud just before quoting Virgil. It is similarly unhelpful that Jung's corpulent German interlocutor can attest to the authenticity of his cardiac fear, whether repressed earlier or not. For such confirmation is patently a far cry from certifying the alleged *causal nexus* between the given fear and the slip. Even if the person who "slipped" were not under the suggestive, intimidating influence of the analyst, how could the subject possibly know any better than any of the rest of us that the pertinent unconscious fear had actually caused his slip?

On the face of it, it would seem that the privileged epistemic access that introspection afforded these subjects to the existence of their anxieties hardly extends to the certification of the wholly unvalidated causal nexus. More significantly, this indictment of Freud's appeal to introspective confirmation is well supported, for substantial evidence recently marshaled by cognitive psychologists tells against a subject's privileged epistemic access to the identification of the causes of his own behavior (Grünbaum 1980: 354-367). I had occasion above to adduce this evidence against Robert Waelder's accolade to introspection in psychoanalytic validation. True, near the very end of his career, Freud held that a subject's assent to a psychoanalytic interpretation does not guarantee its correctness. And, as will become clear in chapter 10, he thereby implied some weakening of his 1916 probative tribute to the subject's introspective confirmation of the alleged "sense" of a slip. But, in any case, there is every reason to conclude that this confirmation is spurious and hence cannot gainsay the array of objections that I have leveled against the psychoanalytic theory of slips.

So far, we have been granting, merely for the sake of argument, that the analyst does not significantly influence the patient's "free" associations. Furthermore, we took it for granted that the thought content in which the associative process issued was actually one that the subject had previously consciously entertained or registered but had subsequently repressed. But, as we saw, even if these associations actually were causally uncontaminated, it would still be unavailing to Freud. For even such undistorted associations *cannot* certify that the repressions brought to light by means of them qualify as any of the following: (1) the pathogens of the patient's neurosis, (2) the motive forces of his dream constructions, or (3) the causes of his slips.

But it now behooves us to address a *second* question: does the patient's adherence to the fundamental rule of free association indeed safeguard the *causally uncontaminated* emergence of actually existing repressed wishes, anger, guilt, fear, etc.? Or is the process of association contaminated by the analyst's injection of influence of one sort or another? Clearly, the answer will depend, at least partly, on just what the analyst does while the patient is busy fulfilling his share of the analytic compact.

This answer is also likely to depend on the antecedent beliefs that patients going into analysis bring into the analytic situation, for many an intelligent analysand is consciously aware of the sort of material that his Freudian therapist does expect from his free associations. For example, male patients are expected to have repressed castration anxiety, and females are to have unconscious penis envy. While dealing with our question, we shall need to be mindful of another, since it likewise pertains to the epistemic effects of the analyst's *intervention*: if a plethora of unconscious thoughts surface, by what criteria does the analyst decide when to call a halt to the surfeit of associations, while investigating parapraxes and dreams? Hence, let us canvass in what respects overt and subtle interventions by the analyst affect the data yielded by the patient's associations.

The limitations of the analytic hour alone require that the patient's associations not be allowed to continue *indefinitely*. But suppose that one were to disregard the epistemically irrelevant expedient of this hour and allow the patient to continue unimpeded, even if he pauses off and on. If the intelligent and imaginative analysand is permitted to associate in this way long enough, his unfettered ruminations will, in due course, presumably yield almost any kind of thematic content of which he had at least recently not been conscious: thoughts about death, God, and indeed cabbages and kings. But, if so, how does the analyst avoid an antecedently question-begging *selection* bias in the face of this *thematic elasticity* of the associations, while unavoidably limiting their duration? Thus, if the associations do flow apace and the analyst somehow interrupts them at a certain point, he is interfering in their spontaneous causal dynamics. By what criterion does he do so? But in the case of, say, a parapraxis or a given element of manifest dream content, when the associations are faltering and the analyst demands their continuation, how does he manage *not* to load the dice by ever so subtly hinting to the patient what kind of material he expects to emerge? After all, his demand for continuation will convey his suspicion that it was censorial resistance to a related repressed content that brought the flow of associations to a halt *at that particular point*, and his attempt at overcoming that resistance may well convey his expectation.

Let me illustrate the problem of selection bias resulting from thematic elasticity. Suppose that Freud had allowed AJ to continue well past the disclosure of the pregnancy fear. Perhaps it would then have emerged that AJ's parents had taught him early that the Romans had crucified Jesus, but that Christians had then unfairly blamed the Jews for deicide. It might furthermore have emerged that AJ had repressed his ensuing hatred of the Romans when Virgil, Horace, and other Roman poets were shown great respect in his Austrian educational environment. Now let us recall Freud's criterion of "suitability as a determinant," which he invoked in the study of hysteria to give *etiologic* primacy to an earlier repression over a later one, even though the *memory* of the earlier one emerged later in the chain of the patient's associations (S.E. 1896, 3: 193-196) than the memory of the subsequent one. Would AJ's hypothesized repression of his hatred for the Romans not have had greater thematic "suitability as a determinant" of his *aliquis* slip than his anxiety about the pregnancy, even though the former assumedly emerged only later in his associative chain? After all, Virgil was a Roman, and AJ was citing the line from the *Aeneid* to express his conscious resentment of Christian anti-Semitism. What a golden opportunity to punish the unconsciously resented Romans simultaneously by spoiling Virgil's line! Although the repressed hatred for the Romans is, of course, purely hypothetical in the case of AJ, it does lend poignancy to the complaint of selection bias, which is given substance generally by the thematic elasticity of the associations I have emphasized.

But could Freud's principle of causal "overdetermination" (see Introduction, Section 4 above) not serve to derail the charge of selection bias in the face of thematic elasticity? Does this principle not obviate the need to select one cause from among the various emerging repressions, precisely because the principle allows for a conjunction and/or temporal succession of *partial* causes? Such a selection is nonetheless unavoidable, unless any and every repression emerging from indefinitely prolonged associations were actually countenanced as a partial cause. And we know from Freud's theory of psychopathology and from his account of dream instigation that, in these theories, only sexual repressions and repressed wishes respectively are picked out as the causally necessary antecedents from the patient's associative output. As for the explanations of parapraxes, the *aliquis* example illustrates the following: Far from being open-endedly hospitable to deeming every emerging repression to be a partial cause, actual psychoanalytic explanatory practice is likewise *selective* when sifting the associations. Yet, qua method of causal identification and certification, the psychoanalytic method of investigation provides no basis for effecting such a selection.

Thus, as I indicated only briefly elsewhere à propos of parapraxes (Grünbaum 1980: 377-378), the clinical use of free association features epistemic biases of selection and manipulative contamination as follows: (1) the analyst *selects thematically* from the patient's productions, partly by interrupting the associations—either explicitly or in a myriad more subtle ways—at points of his or her own theoretically inspired choosing; and (2) when the Freudian doctor harbors the suspicion that the associations are faltering because of evasive censorship, he uses verbal and also subtle nonverbal promptings to induce the continuation of the associations *until* they yield *theoretically* appropriate results; for surely not any and every previously repressed thought that emerges will be deemed a *relevant* repression for the purpose of etiologic inquiry, dream interpretation, or the analysis of a slip.

Experimental studies by L. Krasner, G. Mandler, W. K. Kaplan, and K. Salzinger, which are summarized by the analyst Marmor (1970), do bear out empirically the actual contamination of the products of free association by the analyst. As will be recalled, Freud had credited free association by saying: "it [free association] guarantees to a great extent that... nothing will be introduced into it by the expectations of the analyst" (S.E. 1925, 20: 41). Commenting on precisely this statement of Freud's, Marmor (1970: 161) writes: "Clinical experience has demonstrated that this simply is not so and that the 'free' associations of the patient are strongly influenced by the values and expectations of the therapist" (reprinted in Marmor 1974: 267). He then cites an earlier article of his (1962: 291-292), where he had written:

In face-to-face transactions the expression on the therapist's face, a questioning glance, a lift of the eyebrows, a barely perceptible shake of the head or shrug of the shoulder all act as significant cues to the patient. But even *behind* the couch, our "uh-huhs" as well as our silences, the interest or the disinterest reflected in our tone of voice or our shifting postures all act like subtle radio signals influencing the patients' responses, reinforcing some responses and discouraging others. That this influence actually occurs has been confirmed experimentally by numerous observers [reference omitted]. Krasner [reference omitted] has recently prepared a comprehensive and impressive review of the evidence in this area.

Indeed, recalling a finding from that earlier article, Marmor (1970: 161) concludes:

As a result, depending on the point of view of the psychoanalyst, patients of every psychoanalytic school tend, *under free association*, "to bring up precisely the kind of phenomenological data which confirm the theories and interpretations of their analysts! Thus each theory tends to be self-validating."

This report derives added poignancy from the studies marshaled by A. K. Shapiro and L. A. Morris (1978: 384) as support for claiming that therapists may subtly and unwittingly "communicate information to patients, such as hypotheses, expectations, attitudes, cultural values, and so on." They emphasize how this state of affairs issues in the *spurious* clinical confirmation of psychological hypotheses via the effects of suggestion: "The returned communication is then regarded as an independent confirmation of the therapist's theory [reference omitted]. This increases the credulity and suggestibility of both" (p. 384). This epistemological difficulty is, of course, compounded by the operation of those phenomena that Freud termed "countertransference" phenomena after shrewdly discerning them: the distorting effects of the therapist's feelings toward the patient on the accuracy of the former's perception of the latter's behavior (S.E. 1910, 11: 144-145).

It is evident from the current literature, as I shall illustrate presently, that even nowadays *some* analysts do intervene unabashedly in the associations of their patients. And, as my illustration will show, it is then pretended that the products of the ensuing associations are the subject's previously unconscious ideas, which have surfaced in unbiased fashion. Thus, it would be wrong to suppose that Freud's own "activist" handling of a patient's associations when giving interpretations is a thing of the past in psychoanalytic research and practice. The recognized analyst Benjamin Rubinstein, however, has pointed out to me that there surely are contemporary analysts who—mindful of the effects of overt, covert, and even *unconscious* suggestions on the patient—do indeed make a conscious effort to be far less "activist" than either Freud or the authors I am about to cite. But however sincere that effort in these quarters, it is at best unclear, I submit, to what extent this endeavor can be successful in coping with the serious data contaminant of patient compliance. How, for example, can the analyst guard against *unintended* yet potent suggestive influences? Thus, unless the mere effort to avoid them is *typically* successful when actually made, the epistemic sophistication that inspires it is surely not an adequate safeguard to assure noncontamination. In any case, there is telling evidence in the current literature that the effort is not even properly made among some influential practitioners.

Thus, a rather recent book by two respected teaching analysts (Blanck and Blanck 1974), recommending how analysis ought to be practiced, instructively reveals how at least some analytic patients are currently being coaxed, if not urged, to fulfill prior theoretical expectations. These authors present their recommendation by drawing on the case history of a patient who was unduly anxious about her general appearance, notably her skin, and who was being seen by a woman psychoanalyst. The excerpt from the paradigmatic case history provided by them is noteworthy, partly because they *interpret* their portrayal as showing that the therapist is testing her analytic interpretations quite *non*suggestively at every turn, while the patient gradually comes to discover penis envy in herself after two years of analysis. Yet precisely this methodologically favorable verdict is belied throughout by their own account.

To be specific, let us even disregard that today's typical female patient, if motivated to seek out a Freudian therapist and intelligent enough to be accepted for analysis, is likely to know a fair bit about the hypothesis of female penis envy even before going into treatment. Hence, even without the patent prompting shown in the following excerpt, such a patient may well realize that she is probably expected to give evidence of resenting her phallic deficit and of envying men their anatomical endowment. Thus, if she is minded to be a good patient, she will probably wish to accommodate her analyst by reporting such feelings of deficit. But, in any case, let us see how the Drs. Blanck relate the avowedly exemplary exchange between the analysand and her therapist.

The patient says: "Today I feel that I should see a dermatologist about my skin." The therapist responds: "You think constantly about your appearance because you are not sure that your body is always as it should be" (Blanck and Blanck 1974: 320). Note that the patient neither avowed nor implied any such motivation. This assertion is not based on data furnished by the patient but originates in the envy hypothesis. The suggestion, "You are not sure that your body is as it should be" is subtly preparing the way for the penis envy notion. It is particularly insidious because many people do feel that they would like to be more attractive than they are. Hence, the patient may readily agree at this point that her body "is not as it should be." Yet her specific worries about her skin are not pursued in the analysis, which reportedly (p. 320) now proceeds like this *for two years*!

Thus, when the patient says, "Sometimes I think I look better than at other times," the therapist tells her, "You are not always certain that your body is the same." And when the patient complains, "I always feel there is something wrong," the therapist immediately concludes that "this is a classical phallic statement" (p. 321). Furthermore, when the patient dreams about one of these interpretations, the analyst considers the dream a confirmation of the interpretation (p. 321).

Finally, in response to a question from the analyst, the patient says, "Yes, men are always more admired" (p. 321). The analyst then comments beguilingly, "They have something more to be looked at," to which the patient then associates "freely": "Oh, you mean a penis." Flushed with this supposed further confirmation that women are not only anatomically envious *but also can be made ill by this unconscious feeling*, the Blancks promptly infer that their patient's two years of analysis were scientifically serendipitous. As they put it, "When the patient says, 'You mean' to her own association, it is a projection which represents the last defense against allowing the thought into consciousness" (p. 322). But once the analysand has thus been initiated into engaging in penis talk about herself, she is likely to believe in this alleged self-discovery afterward, thereby furnishing her analyst with ever more spurious confirmation.

This analytic disposition of the dermatologically discontented female patient is perhaps modeled after Freud's diagnosis of a male patient who was afflicted by a severe skin problem and had become withdrawn (schizophrenic): "Analysis shows that he is playing out his castration complex upon his skin" (S.E. 1915, 14: 199). Indeed, upon comparing the account given by the Blancks to how Freud handled the patients in many of his case histories, one can only conclude: *Plus ça change, plus c'est la même chose*. In the same vein, the present-day female analysts Bernstein and Warner (1981: 47) adduce their clinical experience and the study of the literature to conclude: "we are convinced that there is penis envy." No wonder that the renowned traditional analyst Kurt Eissler (1977) deplored the inhospitality of the current emancipatory, sexually egalitarian climate to the purported discovery of female penis envy.

Let us assume, for argument's sake, that there is cogent evidence for the existence of unconscious penis envy in women. Then we must point out that the bare harboring of such jealousy by women is hardly tantamount to the *pathogenicity* which some Freudian analysts still claim for it. Thus, the inferential slide from the bare existence of unconscious female anatomical envy to its purposed etiologic role is akin to the one we had occasion to deplore at the end of chapter 3: The illicit use of the mere existence of the psychic mechanism of repression to vouch for the protean *causal* role that Freud claimed for it, not only as a pathogen but also as a dream-instigator and as a begetter of parapraxes. Indeed, the psychoanalytic literature contains other instances of such specious reasoning. As chapter 8 will explain, it was illegitimate on Waelder's part (1962: 625-626) to think that the *causal relevance* of an experience P to a neurosis N is supported by the mere fact that anyone beset by N who suffered P instantiates the following universal retrodiction entailed by Freud's etiology: All those afflicted by N have been exposed to P. Such an inference of causal relevance will there be seen to be no better than *post hoc ergo propter hoc*.

Yet one can only applaud that there are indeed some analysts now who deplore the epistemic procedure held up as a model by the Blancks. In a critique of just their case history, the psychoanalyst Emanuel Peterfreund issues a salutary reproach as follows (1983: 35): "although the authors [Blancks] speak of hypotheses and the need for confirmation, in actuality the therapist did not treat the initial formulation as a hypothesis for which evidence may or may not be forthcoming. It was...imposed on the patient,...a belief system into which the patient was subtly indoctrinated." And he goes on to point out that this case typifies stereotyped treatment approaches in which "the 'answers' are thought to be known from the very beginning and the task of the analysis is essentially to 'interpret' the presenting material until the patient comes to recognize the 'truth' of the assumed answers" (1983: 35-36). Though Peterfreund's own "heuristic" approach to clinical investigation and therapy does avoid *some* of the pitfalls of the stereotypic one, he does not, alas, come to grips with the fundamental difficulties besetting intraclinical validation, as set forth in this book.

5.

Repressed Infantile Wishes as Instigators of all Dreams: Critical Scrutiny of the Compromise Model of Manifest Dream Content

So far, the criticism I have offered of Freud's theory of dreams has been largely just a corollary, generated *mutatis mutandis* from the failure of free associations to validate the psychoanalytic theory of parapraxes. But the psychoanalytic interpretation of dreams calls for some further scrutiny in its own right, if only because Freud regarded it as "*the royal road to a knowledge of the unconscious activities of the mind* [emphasis in original]" (S.E. 1900, 5: 608).

On the night of July 23/24, 1895, Freud (1954, Letter #137: 322) had a dream—the "Irma Injection Dream" (S.E. 1950, 1: 340-342)—which was destined to become *the* "Specimen Dream" of his clinical theory (S.E. 1900, 4: chap. II). For his attempt to interpret the Irma dream begat a "Eureka" experience yielding the idea of wish-instigation as the "Secret" of *all* dream formation (Freud 1954: 322). And in his 1895 "Project," he proposed a *neurological rationale* for the presumed secret.

That neurobiological account, and its clinical superstratum of wishful-fillment, have recently been fundamentally challenged. In two recent papers (McCarley and Hobson 1977, 134: 1211–1221; Hobson and McCarley 1977, 134: 1335–1348), these authors have provided the first theory genuinely attempting to integrate the recent discoveries in the neurophysiology of dreaming with the peculiarities of dream mentation. Distortion, outlandishness, discontinuity, and incoherence of hallucinoid imagery are striking features of that delusional ideation. Thus Hobson and McCarley offer specific neurobiological substrates, both structural and functional, for the "formal" features of the dream process: Its uniform periodicity, constant duration, spatiotemporal distortions (e.g., condensation, acceleration), and the dreamer's delusional acceptance of these hallucinoid phenomena as "real" at the time of their occurrence. True, Hobson and McCarley commend Freud for having predicated his neurobiological model of dreaming on a generic "mind-body isomorphism." But, as they point out, during the past 80 years various findings have undermined the notions of neuronal function and of the energy economy of the brain that animated his account.

Notably, neurons have been found to have their own metabolic sources of energy. Yet

Freud conceived of neurons as if they were passive elements in a power transmission network: he believed that all neural energy was entirely derived from outside the brain, chiefly from somatic sources, from instincts. Neurons acted as passive conduits and storage vessels for this energy. Freud did not conceive of the possibility of inhibitory neurons that could *cancel* excitatory signals; in his model energy could only be *diverted* or repressed. Motoric discharge was the sole method of energy dissipation. This neural model was one that left the psychic system, in Freud's words, "at the mercy" of somatic drives. [McCarley and Hobson 1977: 1221]

According to Hobson and McCarley's rival "activation-synthesis hypothesis" of dream-state generation, physiological rather than psychological processes are the primogenitors of dreams as well as the crucial determinants of their "formal" properties: "modern investigations point to autochthonous, periodic, and motivationally neutral activation of pontine generator neurons as the cause of the D dream state" (McCarley and Hobson 1977: 1219). Furthermore, "If we assume that the physiological substrate of consciousness is in the forebrain, these facts [i.e., that the trigger, the power supply, and the regulating biological clock of dream sleep are pontine] completely eliminate any possible contribution of ideas (or [of] their neural substrate) to the primary driving force of the dream process" (Hobson and McCarley 1977: 1338). As Hobson and McCarley emphasize, their activation-synthesis-hypothesis is incompatible with Freud's psychological theory of dream formation.

According to the psychoanalytic conception, forbidden repressed wishes are stirred during sleep by the residue from prior waking experience, and they seek fulfillment under the *constraint* of the desire to sleep. Not unlike the phenomenology of day dreams, the manifest contents of sleep-dreams are engendered by censored cravings, which undergo defensive transformation into disguises. Though only hallucinoid, these masquerades afford the dreamer *some* vicarious fulfillment of the unacceptable wishes harbored in his unconscious. As against this Freudian scenario, McCarley and Hobson tell us (p. 1219) that repressed wishes need not be postulated to supply the neural energy required to generate the D-state, since that energy is already available autochthonously in the nervous system. And if no instinctual wish that makes a disguise imperative furnishes the impetus for dreaming, then there is no warrant for attributing "the dream language and the dream plot" primarily to the implementation of such dissimulation. Yet these authors caution us: "This is not to suggest that day residue material or motivationally important themes do not enter into dream content; they may do so, but neither is a causal factor in the dream process" (p. 1219). Hence McCarley and Hobson conclude that recent neurophysiological discoveries have largely discredited Freud's psychological theory of dream instigation.

But the sleep physiologist Vogel (1978) has issued a major two-fold retort to them. First, he has adduced *other* neurophysiological and psychophysiological findings that impugn McCarley and Hobson's activation-synthesis hypothesis of dream generation. Furthermore, he has presented methodological considerations to animadvert upon their rejection of the psychoanalytic theory of dream-formation. In his first objection, Vogel (1978: 1533) points to experiments showing that "the instigators of most D state dreams and the determinants of their formal characteristics are not simply [pontine physiological] processes in the brain stem, where neuronal activity has no psychological correlates." As it turns out, the forebrain, whose activities can have psychological correlates, is also necessary for the instigation, maintenance, and timing of most D sleep episodes. Hence he claims that, contrary to McCarley and Hobson's hypothesis, neural structures with possible psychological concomitants are involved in the instigation and formal shaping of the D-state. Moreover, as is attested by means of the electroencephalographic identification of the pertinent physiological states, there is also bizarre, vivid, visually hallucinoid dreaming in the absence of the pontine process. In sum, according to Vogel's first objection, various findings militate against McCarley and Hobson's contentions that specific pontine physiological processes, rather than mental processes, instigate dreams and produce their distortions.

Next, speaking methodologically, Vogel (1978: 1534–1535) points out that purely neurophysiological findings cannot serve to test a posited lawlike connection between purely psychological attributes, unless an important condition is met: There must be an empirical ascertainment of the character of the *correlation*, if any, between the pertinent physiological states and the hypothesized psychological ones. But McCarley and Hobson have failed to furnish grounds for their supposition that pontine activation of the forebrain is *not* the neural correlate of emergent, archaic unconscious yearnings. Hence they are not entitled to infer, as they do, that unconscious wishes are causally irrelevant to dream instigation. Thus, Vogel's second objection denies that McCarley and Hobson have undermined the psychoanalytic theory of dream formation. In a like vein, the psychoanalyst and dream researcher Charles Fisher has argued (1978: 96) that "Freud's wish fulfillment theory of dreaming has been given a premature burial."

Labruzza (1978) acknowledged McCarley and Hobson's identification of important physiological concomitants of dreaming. But he emphasizes that the well-defined mind-body isomorphism presupposed by their unfavorable verdict on Freud's theory is still largely programmatic. Unfortunately, while raising this justified doubt, Labruzza also affirms the reasons *versus* causes thesis. However, as I have argued earlier (Introduction, Section 4), in the present context this doctrine is preeminently untenable.

In the light of Vogel's critique of McCarley and Hobson, it would seem at best premature to suppose that their significant elucidation of the neurophysiology of dreaming has obviated an appraisal of Freud's *clinical* arguments for his psychological dream theory. Hence such a scrutiny is now in order.

As Freud tells us, "the idea that *some* dreams are to be regarded as wish-fulfillments" had been commonplace in *pre*psychoanalytic psychology (S.E. 1900, 4: 134). Hence, Freud propounded a distinctive and exciting thesis about dreaming only when he *universalized* this commonsensical idea: "the meaning [motive force for the formation] of *every* dream is the fulfillment of a wish." And, as he is the first to recognize, prima facie this completely general thesis is impugned by sundry wish *contravening* and distressing manifest dream contents (e.g., anxiety dreams). Besides nightmares and examination dreams, for instance, "nonsensical" dreams also challenge Freud's account.

Even in the prepsychoanalytic dream theories mentioned by Freud, the claim that a *particular* dream is "wish fulfilling" goes beyond maintaining that the specifics of the dream's content *depict* the realization of some antecedent hope or desire. For, in the case of such a dream, these preanalytic psychological theories maintain furthermore that once the pertinent desires are not satisfied in waking life, they *cause* the formation of a dream content in which they achieve vicarious consummation. Perhaps the commonsense credibility of this preanalytic causal attribution of *some* dreams to wishes derives from those familiar *waking fantasies* in which unrequited love and other desires find vicarious consummation. In any event, Freud relies on this commonsense credibility of the motivational role of wishes in the formation of some dreams. Thus, in the case of one of his specimen dreams—the Irma dream—he plainly trades on the conviction carried by just this credibility when attempting to authenticate the trustworthiness of his method of free association as a means of certifying the motivational causes of *any and all* dreams. One reason for endeavoring to establish this trustworthiness was that free association seemed to him to yield repressed wishes as the motives of even those dreams whose manifest contents are anything but wish fulfilling. In this way, he thought he had legitimated his universalization of wish fulfillment as being the formative cause of any and all manifest dream contents.

True, in 1933, he acknowledged the existence of some exceptions to this universal claim (S.E. 1933, 22: 28-30), and he thus modified his wish fulfillment hypothesis. While retaining wish fulfillment as the impetus of dreaming, he acknowledged that it does miscarry with fair frequency. Hence, he then concluded that "the dream may aptly be characterized as an *attempt* at the fulfillment of a wish" (S.E. 1925, 20: 46n; this footnote was added in 1935). In short, the motive for dreaming is still held to be a wish, but the dream that actually ensues is no longer claimed to qualify universally as its fulfillment. But let us defer comment on this rather minor modification and deal with Freud's earlier unqualified generalization first.

Freud relies on two avenues to ascertain the purported motivational cause (or "meaning") of a dream: (1) the free associations of the individual dreamer, which originate at the separate elements of the manifest content (usually visual images), and (2) dream symbolism, whose unconscious motivational significance is claimed to be independent of individual and even cultural differences. Freud does explain that when gleaning the "sense" of a dream, the translation of interpersonal dream symbolism complements the method of free association (S.E. 1900, 5: 341-342, 359; 1916, 15: 150). But he emphasizes that the interpersonally significant symbols play only an auxiliary, subordinate role in dream interpretation vis-à-vis the "decisive significance" of the dreamer's free associations (S.E. 1900, 5: 360; 1916, 15: 151).

Indeed, in the magisterial digest of the dream theory he gave in his "Autobiographical Study," which he revised in 1935, he even seems to deny the probative value of dream symbolism by implication. True, he there makes passing mention of the role of symbolism in the dream work (S.E. 1925, 20: 45). But he does so after having told us that the "manifest content was simply a make-believe, a façade, which could serve as a starting point for the associations but not for the interpretation" (S.E.

1925, 20: 44). Thus, when interpersonal dream symbolism is present in the manifest content, its interpretative translation can yield only *bits* for the interpretation. Hence, for the purpose of examining the credentials of his interpretation of dreams, it will suffice to confine our comments to his reliance on the method of free association as an epistemic avenue to the purported motivational cause of dreaming.

As he claims, free associations setting out from the manifest content of any dream *always* yield a repressed wish and other assorted repressed content, commingled with miscellaneous thoughts that qualify as "preconscious" in his familiar technical sense (S.E. 1900, 5: 552-553; 1916, 15: 224-226; 1923, 19: 114; 1925, 20: 44, 46). Being the presumed residues of the dreamer's waking life before the dream, the emerging preconscious thoughts may well *happen* to include a *non*repressed wish. He then identifies the repressed wish, which is purportedly universally yielded by the associations, as the agency to which the dream owes its initial formation: "This impulse is the actual constructor [cause] of the dream: it provides the energy for its production and makes use of the day's residues as material" (S.E. 1925, 20: 44). Yet it is "often of a very repellent kind, which is foreign to the waking life of the dreamer and is consequently disavowed by him with surprise or indignation."

I shall now examine Freud's interpretation of his Irma dream. This scrutiny will hardly vindicate his claim that this specimen dream authenticates free association as a reliable means of certifying the formative causes of *all* dreams (S.E. 1900, 4: chap. II). Far from supplying such vindication, I shall maintain that even when commonsense psychology regards a given dream as patently wish fulfilling, psychoanalytically conducted free association does not have the probative resources to *underwrite* this verdict!

In a preamble to his own dream about his patient Irma, Freud details the events of the previous day that avowedly provided its point of departure (S.E. 1900, 4: 106). It is clear from this account that these events left him with *conscious* feelings of frustration and aggressive desires, which clamored for expression: annoyance with Irma because she had rejected Freud's conjecture as to the unconscious cause of her hysterical symptoms; frustration because, as the presumed consequence of her rejection of his "solution," her somatic symptoms had persisted; irritation by his junior colleague Otto, who had implied censure of his handling of Irma's therapeutic expectations; and the desire "to justify" his treatment of Irma for the benefit of his respected senior colleague Dr. M, who has since been revealed to be his mentor Breuer (Grinstein 1980, chap. 1).

The aggressive wishes that had remained unfulfilled by the end of the day in question are then patently acted out or realized in the manifest dream content that Freud goes on to report (p. 107); for early within the dream, Freud avowedly rebukes Irma for her resistance to his "solution," and he explicitly blames *her* for the persistence of her pains. Then, at the end of the dream, Dr. M. and he condemn Otto for negligently causing Irma to become infected by his use of a dirty syringe. Thus, after recapitulating the conscious motives specified in the preamble, and the manifest content, Freud tells us convincingly that the following motivational interpretation "leapt to the eyes" from these data: the dream *"content was the fulfillment of a wish and its motive was a wish* [emphasis in original]" (S.E. 1900, 4: 119).

Now, if a dreamer remembers on the day after a dream what *conscious* thoughts he had on the day before his dream, it is true enough that this recollection *may* occur *in the wake* of thinking of the dream, thereby qualifying as a kind of association with the dream. Yet this sort of association clearly differs from the recovery of a *repressed* thought, first achieved if the dreamer takes elements of the manifest content as points of departure *and* is careful to heed the demanding injunctions of Freud's "fundamental rule" of "free association" (S.E. 1923, 18: 238). This distinction does indeed matter in the context of Freud's attempted use of the Irma dream to authenticate free association as a trustworthy avenue for identifying repressed wishes as the formative causes of manifest dream contents; for he traded on the label "association" to insinuate the falsehood that the plainly *conscious* aggressive wishes of the prior day, which he specifies in his preamble, were first excavated associatively in the manner of a repressed thought. That this suggested conclusion is mere pretense is evident from his own report. For when speaking of the events on the day and evening *before* the dream, he says: "The same evening I wrote out Irma's case history, with the idea of giving it to Dr. M. (a common friend [of Otto's and Freud's] who was at that time the leading figure in our circle) in order to justify myself" [in the face of Otto's implied reproof] (S.E. 1900, 4: 106).

In sum, though the aggressive conscious wishes that Freud had on the day before his Irma dream were then patently fulfilled in its manifest content, free association played *no excavating role* in his recall of these wishes after the dream, for he had been avowedly conscious of them the evening before. Hence, for this reason alone, the purportedly paradigmatic Irma dream cannot serve to authenticate free association as a trustworthy avenue for certifying that *repressed infantile* wishes are the formative *causes* of manifest dream content, as claimed by Freud's theory. Yet he relies on free association to make just this claim (S.E. 1900, 5: 546, 548-549, 552-554, 567-568, 583-584). For example, he does so to make the following assertions: "*a conscious wish can only become a dream-instigator if it succeeds in awakening an unconscious wish with the same tenor and in obtaining reinforcement from it. . . . A wish which is represented in a dream must be an infantile one* [emphasis in original]" (S.E. 1900, 5: 553). Fully *thirty years* after he had had a childhood dream at about age seven whose dominant theme was anxiety, he was satisfied that his analysis of this dream warranted the following conclusion: "The anxiety can be traced back, when repression is taken into account, to an obscure and evidently sexual craving that had found appropriate expression in the visual content of the dream" (S.E. 1900, 5: 584). Since he invoked free association crucially to draw these causal inferences, I maintain that *Freud had indeed failed to sustain the major thesis of his dream theory*, a theory in which he took special pride. Yet even in a quite recent article, the analysts Frank and Trunnel (1978) describe a training procedure based on the assumption that an archaic wish is the universal motive force of dreaming.

Thus, to this day, Freudians claim that repressed *infantile* wishes are the primogenitors of *all* dreams. Yet, judging by Freud's own report on his celebrated Irma dream, there is no evidence at all that he ever carried his analysis of the dream far enough to extend to his childhood wishes (S.E. 1900, 4: 120-121). Hence, if one of his infantile wishes was to have been the instigator of the Irma dream, Freud's own published analysis of this dream cannot possibly underwrite the principal substantive tenet of his dream theory. How, then, can his disciples justify hailing it as *the* dream specimen of psychoanalysis, instead of demoting it to a mere popularized example? Over fifty years after the publication of *The Interpretation of Dreams* in 1900, Erik Erikson made a strenuous effort to rise to this challenge in an article entitled "The Dream Specimen of Psychoanalysis" (1954). In this way, *Irma* was supposed to retain pride of place as the prototype dream of psychoanalysis.

But if it was thus not until fifteen years after Freud's death that an orthodox interpretation of the Irma dream was even proposed, how did Freud himself justify using this particular dream "specimen" to *introduce* his analysis of dreams? The answer is encapsulated in the word *method* found within the title of the pertinent chapter 2 of his magnum opus on the subject: "The Method of Interpreting Dreams: An Analysis of a Specimen Dream" (S.E. 1900, 4: 96). Early in this chapter (pp. 100-102), he states clearly in what manner his "knowledge of that procedure [method of dream interpretation] was reached" (p. 100). As he explains there, it was a matter of *simply enlarging* the epistemic role of *free association* from being only a method of *etiologic* inquiry aimed at therapy to serving likewise as an avenue to dream investigation:

> My patients were pledged to communicate to me every idea or thought that occurred to them in connection with some particular subject; amongst other things they told me their dreams and so taught me that a dream can be inserted into the psychical chain that has to be traced backwards in the memory from a pathological idea. It was then only a short step to treating the dream itself as a symptom and to applying to dreams the method of interpretation that had been worked out for symptoms. [S.E. 1900, 4: 100-101]

Note here how Freud makes light of the epistemically dubious nature of this momentous extension by vastly understating its gaping pitfalls as "only a short step." Yet he apparently wanted this step to carry conviction for his readers as well.

Thus, his initial accent in the opening presentation of his dream theory was on authenticating the *method* of interpreting dreams; for even if one grants that the method of free association ("fundamental rule of psychoanalysis") can fathom and certify the pathogens of neuroses as such, it is anything but obvious that this method can reliably perform the same epistemic service in certifying the causes (motives) of our dreams. And it would beg the question to *assume outright* that any dream can be regarded as a kind of neurotic symptom. Hence, Freud's strategy was to argue first that, in the case of the Irma dream, the use of free association does yield motives independently countenanced by commonsense psychology as having patently engendered *this* dream. Thereafter, he is prepared to rest his *substantive* theory of dreams as *universally* wish fulfilling on the deliverances of the method purportedly authenticated by the analysis of his Irma dream. This order of argument is recapitulated in the very last sentences of the pertinent chapter, which read:

> For the moment I am satisfied with the achievement of this one piece of fresh knowledge. If we adopt the method of interpreting dreams which I have indicated here, we shall find that dreams really have a meaning and are far from being the expression of a fragmentary activity of the brain, as the authorities have claimed. *When the work of interpretation has been completed, we perceive that a dream is the fulfillment of a wish.* [italics in original; S.E. 1900, 4: 121]

Accordingly, as I already indicated, this dream earned its laurels as "*the* dream specimen of psychoanalysis" on methodological rather than substantive grounds. The more so since the wishes that had been *shown* to be fulfilled by it were hardly repressed infantile ones but *only* adult conscious desires! Of course, this substantive limitation does not preclude the aforementioned crucial heuristic role played by the Irma dream.

As for the substantive conclusions derived from the published analysis of this paradigmatic dream, Freud issues a disclaimer in regard to the completeness of his account of it:

> I will not pretend that I have completely uncovered the meaning of this dream or that its interpretation is without a gap. I could spend much more time over it, derive further information from it and discuss fresh problems raised by it. I myself know the points from which further trains of thought could be followed. [S.E. 1900, 4: 120-121]

Given the principally methodological basis of the exemplar status accorded to the Irma dream, it is very disappointing that psychoanalysts have not *scrutinized* its purported authentication of free association as the method of dream analysis. One's disappointment is the greater because, of all of Freud's own dreams, the Irma dream has spawned the largest literature (see Grinstein 1980: 22 for some citations). Though the aforementioned paper by Erikson (1954) is just as insouciant epistemologically as the rest of this literature, it warrants comment, for its avowed burden is to give the Irma dream the *infantile* motivational underpinning required by orthodox doctrine. Thus, Erikson sees himself as having made good on his conclusion that "the latent infantile wish that provides the energy... for the dream is embedded in a manifest dream structure which on every level reflects significant trends of the dreamer's total situation" (1954: 55). Let us examine his reasoning.

After quoting from Freud's own lengthy summary of the Irma dream, Erikson (p. 15) points out that it does not contain any *repressed* motive: "We note that the wish demonstrated here is not more than preconscious." Furthermore, the conscious wishes detailed by Freud are all adult rather than infantile ones. Indeed, nowhere in his magnum opus on dream interpretation does Freud explicitly offer a repressed wish for *this* dream, let alone an infantile one. Hence, Erikson (pp. 15-16) proposes to supply a missing latent dream motive satisfying both of these theoretical desiderata and featuring sexual themata.

Erikson develops the hypothesized sexual origin by pointing to colloquial, sexually allusive overtones ("double meanings") of several German words in Freud's original. In the 1938 English translation cited by Erikson, the rendition of these German words was "so literal that an important double meaning gets lost" (1954: 24). The original German words, he tells us, "allude to sexual meanings, as if the Irma Dream permitted a complete sexual interpretation alongside the professional one—an inescapable expectation in any case" (p. 26).

Our focus is on Erikson's quest for the purported "infantile meaning of the Irma Dream" (p. 27), *not* on the *pansexual* significance that he claimed for it as well. Hence, I shall forgo making a methodological complaint against the alleged inescapability of the expectation that "a complete sexual interpretation" of the dream is feasible. What does matter is that *only* the sexual allusion of the German word *Spritze* figures in Erikson's account as a clue to the conjectured infantile meaning of the Irma dream. Stressing the unique allusive role of this one word in Freud's original, Erikson explains: "The recognition of this double meaning is absolutely necessary for a pursuit of the infantile meaning of the Irma Dream" (p. 27).

What, then, is the presumed sexual significance of *Spritze* on which Erikson rests his entire case for an infantile interpretation? He articulates the sexual and infantile overtones of *Spritze*, in turn, before they can be seen to merge.

First he explains the phallic-urinary tinge of the word's colloquial allusion:

The German word..."*Spritze*"...is, indeed, used for syringes, but has also the colloquial meaning of "squirter"...Squirter is an instrument of many connotations; of these, the phallic-urinary one is most relevant, for the use of a dirty syringe makes Otto a "dirty squirter," or "a little squirt," not just a careless physician.

It is undeniable that this sexual overtone is one of Erikson's *own* associations to the word *Spritze*. But, according to the psychoanalytic methodology of dream interpretation, the interpretively relevant associations are those of the dreamer *himself*; for if a repressed infantile wish is to emerge as the motive for a given dream, it can be *certified* as its primogenitor only by probing the dreamer's *own* associations to elements of the manifest content. And it was Freud, not Erikson, who had the Irma dream. Hence, even according to the inferential standards countenanced by psychoanalytic theory, the sexual allusion of *Spritze* has probative merit only if it was one of Freud's *own* associations. But that is still not enough. If a thought revealed by an association is to be adduced as a motive for the Irma dream, it must be shown to be one of Freud's associations to *this* particular dream. Therefore, those of Freud's associations that he himself linked to elements of *other* dreams, as far as we know, cannot be adduced as motives for *this* dream.

Yet Erikson's phallic-urethral association to *Spritze* is conspicuously absent from Freud's own account of the associations evoked in *him* by Otto's syringe as part of the manifest content of the Irma dream. As Freud himself explains:

And probably the syringe had not been clean. This was yet another accusation against Otto, but derived from a different source. I had happened the day before to meet the son of an old lady of eighty-two, to whom I had to give an injection of morphia twice a day [footnote omitted]. At the moment she was in the country and he told me that she was suffering from phlebitis. I had at once thought it must be an infiltration caused by a dirty syringe. I was proud of the fact that in two years I had not caused a single infiltration; I took constant pains to be sure that the syringe was clean. In short, I was conscientious [emphasis in original]. [S.E. 1900, 4: 118]

So far, at any rate, Erikson has come up empty-handed. But the success of his endeavor to legitimate the Irma dream as a doctrinal centerpiece does not turn on finding a sexual overtone for the dream motive. Mindful of the theory's call for a repressed infantile theme, Erikson offers "the dream's [sexual] allusion to a childhood problem" (p. 27) as his clincher. But unfortunately, he relies on speculation instead of clear evidence that Freud himself ever linked Dr. Otto's *Spritze* associatively to the memory of the childhood episode in question.

In the section entitled "Infantile Material as a Source of Dreams" (S.E. 1900, 189-219), Freud does indeed relate the episode adduced by Erikson to a dream. But one looks in vain for a reference to the Irma dream in the whole series of dreams he interprets there. Nor is there even any passing mention of Irma, let alone of Dr. Otto's *Spritze*. When the childhood episode invoked by Erikson is discussed near the end of the section (p. 216), its explicit associative context (pp. 215-216) is a dream relating to the revolution of 1848 (pp. 209-211) in central Europe.

At best, Freud's own report of the associative linkages of the given episode to dreams allows Erikson to *speculate* as follows: Freud *may* perhaps *also* have associated that childhood scene with repaying Otto in kind by having him malpractice with a dirty syringe. Notice Freud's own wording:

When I was seven or eight years old there was another domestic scene, which I can remember very clearly. One evening before going to sleep I disregarded the rules which modesty lays down and obeyed the calls of nature [in a chamber pot] in my parents' bedroom while they were present. In the course of his reprimand, my father let fall the words: 'The boy will come to nothing.' This must have been a frightful blow to my ambition, for references to this scene are still constantly recurring in my dreams and are always linked with an enumeration of my achievements and successes, as though I wanted to say: 'You see, I *have* come to something.' [S.E. 1900, 4: 216]

It is, of course, quite true that there is a great deal of *thematic* affinity between this humiliating paternal rebuke for immodest urination and the Otto syringe motif in the Irma dream. But surely this thematic affinity alone is not evidence that the memory of the childhood scene was the motivational primogenitor of having dreamt the Irma injection dream in particular. Thematic affinity alone fails to bespeak such primogenesis, if only because it is not a reason for giving *psychodynamic priority* to the childhood memory over the actual *adult* thought of a syringe, which Freud himself gave as the explanation for the dream syringe! Flawed though it is as a method of *certifying causes*, free association does not even give epistemic sanction to Erikson's psychodynamic attribution on the flimsy basis he uses. For even if one deems the method of free association competent to certify the agencies of dream formation for any given dream, Erikson's use of Freud's reported associations is too specu-lative to sustain the hypothesized motivational origin of the Irma dream.

As if to acknowledge the tenuous character of his documentation, Erikson proceeds gingerly when he conjectures what infantile experi-ence engendered the Otto syringe motif:

> If his father told little Freud under the embarrassing circumstance of the mother's presence in the parental bedroom, that he would never amount to anything, i.e., that the intelligent boy did not hold what he promised—is it not suggestive to assume that the tired doctor [Sigmund Freud] of the night before the dream had gone to bed with a bitter joke in his preconscious mind: yes, maybe I did promise too much when I said I could cure hysteria; maybe my father was right after all, I do not hold what I promised. [P. 42]

Here the interrogative phrase "is it not suggestive to assume" has a commendably tentative tenor. But ironically, Erikson himself under-mines the probative value of the childhood memory, even if its genetic relevance is granted, as he explicitly places it in the dreamer's "precon-scious mind" on the eve of the dream. Though Freud's wish to prove his father wrong meets the requirement of being a childhood vestige, it does not lend support to the *psychoanalytic* dream theory, unless it was also *repressed* when Freud was on the verge of having the Irma dream.

Yet despite having declared Freud's childhood memory to have been preconscious on the eve of the dream (p. 42), Erikson does not hesitate to transform it into a *latent* infantile wish in the concluding paragraph of his essay (p. 55). And unmindful of his initial caution in proposing *infantile* primogenesis, he goes on to affirm it categorically in the meta-psychological idiom of "energy" (p. 55): "The Irma Dream," he main-tains, "illustrates how the latent infantile wish that provides the energy for...the dream, is imbedded in a manifest dream structure." But for all of Erikson's impressive sensitivity to associative nuances, he offers nothing to justify thus giving *psychodynamic priority* to the infantile urination experience over the waking adult thought of a *dirty syringe*, which Freud reported from the day before the dream. Indeed, even as regards mere thematic affinity to the Otto syringe motif, the thoughts Freud reported having on the day before the dream seem closer than the childhood memory adduced by Erikson.

Moreover, the temporal priority of the infantile wish over the adult one hardly vouches for a corresponding *psychodynamic* primacy. Why, then, does Erikson, no less than other Freudians, insist (p. 34) that dreams owe their very occurrence dynamically to "an id wish and all of its infantile energy"? Let me suggest that this strained insistence on infantile causes becomes more intelligible—albeit *not* cogent—if one bears in mind that Freud explicitly modeled his interpretation of dreams on his repression etiology of neuroses (S.E. 1900, 4: 100-101; 5: 528). As I recounted earlier, when Breuer postulated the *adult* occasioning traumata to be the primogenetic pathogens of hysteria, this etiologic version was discredited by therapeutic failures. Yet Freud was determined to retain a repression etiology in some form. Hence, he was driven to demote the *adult* occasioning traumata etiologically to mere *precipitators* of neurosis, and to claim that childhood repressions were the *essential* pathogens. But, as he explained (S.E. 1900, 4: 100-101), he developed his theory of dreams by assimilating manifest dream content to neurotic symptoms at the outset. And having downgraded adult occasioning traumata etiologically in favor of childhood pathogens, he presumably felt entitled, by analogy, to give repressed *infantile* wishes psychodynamic primacy over adult ones as dream instigators.

Perhaps we should assume that the conclusion of this rationale was a tacit premise of Erikson's account, for in the absence of such an assumption, Erikson's entire case for attributing the occurrence of the Irma dream to the "energy" from a childhood motive dangles ever so precariously from the thin thread of the colloquial *Spritze* allusion. Indeed, it appears as a product of scraping the bottom of the epistemic barrel, unless infantile motives *generically* have psychodynamic primacy over adult ones. But, as I have argued, Freud's analogical rationale is not viable. Hence, it cannot serve to underwrite the psychodynamic primacy of infantile wishes. So much, then, for Erikson's imaginative but abortive attempt to provide a doctrinally orthodox infantile underpinning for Freud's own interpretation of the Irma dream.

It so happens that in the case of the Irma dream, there are actually grounds from commonsense psychology for regarding the aggressive motives reported in Freud's preamble as having engendered the manifest dream content. But free association did not first uncover these motives. Hence, their commonsense causal credentials cannot serve at all as evidence that, for any and all dreams, if certain repressed wishes reentered consciousness via a tortuous causal chain of free associations initiated by the manifest content, then *the latter emergence* would *itself* reliably certify these wishes as the initial motivational causes of the dream. Yet it is presumably just this probative reliance on free association that Erikson extolls, in the context of interpreting the Irma dream, by speaking breezily of "the necessity to abandon well-established methods of sober investigation (invented to find out a few things exactly and safely to overlook the rest) for a method of self-revelation apt to open the floodgates of the unconscious" (1954: 54).

Nor did Freud offer a *cogent* reason, in the case of dreams, for resting the *interpretive* use of free association on an extrapolation from the repression etiology of neuroses. The reasoning he does offer begs the question as follows: "We might also point out in our defense that our procedure in interpreting dreams [by means of free association] is identical with the procedure by which we resolve hysterical symptoms; and there the correctness of our method is warranted by the coincident emergence and disappearance of the symptoms" (S.E. 1900, 5: 528). More specifically, as we saw in detail in chapter 3, Freud had *hypothesized* from the *therapeutic* results of the cathartic method that affect-laden, conflict-ridden *repressed* thoughts are the pathogens of the neurotic disorders. Hence, he saw the excavation of the pertinent repressed ideation as the *sine qua non* of discovering the specific etiologies of the neuroses, and, besides, as indispensable to their therapeutic conquest. But once he became convinced that repression is the hallmark of pathogenesis, he was willing to postulate further that even the parapraxes and dreams of "normal" people are the telltale outcroppings of particular repressions. In brief, he viewed even such episodic events in the lives of healthy persons to be symptoms of (temporary) *mini-neuroses*, initiated and sustained by a repression. Thus, in his compromise model of manifest dream content, that content is seen as a compromise between the repressed (forbidden) wish and the mind's censorship, which distorts its expression in the dream (S.E. 1900, 4: 144).

But this assimilation of manifest dream content and parapraxes to the status of "compromise formations" had an important corollary: their adequate *causal explanation*, no less than that of full-fledged neurotic symptoms, could be furnished only by ferreting out the repressions that had purportedly engendered them. And, as Freud had argued, the method of free association is unmatched in achieving just such fathoming. Hence, it was the protean causal role he had bestowed on repression—generating "slips," actuating dream construction, and being generically pathogenic—that secured pride of place epistemically for free association in his theory.

But, as I have already explained in conjunction with my criticism of Freud's repression theory of parapraxes, his compromise model of manifest dream content rests on a *misextrapolation*; for he does not even try to adduce any counterpart to the *therapeutic* support that Breuer and he had claimed to have for the repression etiology of hysteria and for the *investigative cogency* of lifting repressions via free associations to fathom the pathogens. Therefore, I conclude that *Freud's reliance on free association as a means of certifying the causes of dreams is just as grievously flawed epistemically as his use of free association to certify the causes of parapraxes.* In sum, by virtue of the extrapolative justification given for the repression-models of dreams and of parapraxes, their epistemic fortunes are dependent on those of Freud's theory of *psychopathology* (S.E. 1925, 20: 45; 1900, 4: 149). As a consequence of just this epistemic dependence, the ravages from the demise of Freudian psychopathology and of free association as a tool of etiologic certification extend, with a vengeance, to the psychoanalytic theory of dreams and of sundry sorts of "slips."

One must deplore some of the transparent inconsistency demonstrated by Freud in offering the Irma dream to underwrite his epistemic trust in free association as a *causally* probative tool of inquiry. Thus, first he tells us (S.E. 1900, 4: 107) that the Irma dream is *unusual* in the sense that "it was immediately clear [from his preamble] what events of the previous day provided its starting point." And three chapters later, he acknowledges: "the connection with the previous day is so obvious as to require no further comment" (p. 165). Having himself pointed out this transparency, he declares all the same: "Nevertheless no one who had only read the preamble and the [manifest] content of the dream could have the slightest notion of what the dream meant" (p. 108). One is immediately taken aback by this puzzling declaration of obscurity precisely because, as we saw, the preamble clearly reveals that the events of the preceding day had left Freud with *conscious* aggressive desires (wishes), which are then patently fulfilled in the manifest dream content reported by him. Even on the heels of claiming that without free association, the dream's wish motives would be utterly obscure, he belies this claim as follows: "the words which I spoke to Irma in the dream showed that I was specially anxious not to be responsible for the pains which she still had" (p. 108). But worse, he waits until after he detailed his associations to *contradict* flatly his declaration of *initial* obscurity as to the dream's motive. For he then tells us convincingly that the wish character of that motive had "leapt to the eyes" (p. 119) from the conscious motives specified in the preamble and the description of the manifest content.

A second specimen dream discussed by Freud is one whose manifest content clearly depicts the *thwarting* of the very wish consciously felt by the dreamer in the dream itself (S.E. 1900, 4: 146-149). Freud presents the analysis of this dream to illustrate his contention that the manifest content of the dream is wish fulfilling despite its distressing content.

The dreamer, "a clever woman patient," challenged Freud to show how his wish-fulfillment theory can accommodate the thwarting of just the desire she felt within the dream itself. She dreamed that on a Sunday afternoon, she found herself wishing to give a dinner party. Having nothing but a little smoked salmon in the house, she had to buy some food. Yet, since it was Sunday, the stores were closed. The attempt to enlist the service of some caterers failed, since the telephone was out of order, thus aborting the plan to give the dinner party.

The frustrated hostess reported to Freud that in her waking life, she had had a long-standing craving to "have a caviare sandwich every morning but had grudged the expense" (p. 147). On the day before the dream, she had asked her husband *not* to indulge this desire of hers, although he would readily have done so. Allegedly, she had made this request "so that she could go on teasing him about it," as she was wont to do generally. Furthermore, as Freud relates:

The day before she had visited a woman friend of whom she confessed she felt jealous because her (my patient's) husband was constantly singing her praises. Fortunately this friend of hers is very skinny and thin and her husband admires a plumper figure. I asked her what she had talked about to her thin friend. Naturally, she replied, of that lady's wish to grow a littler stouter. Her friend had enquired, too: "When are you going to ask us to another meal? You always feed one so well." [P. 148]

When Freud asked her how she would account for the presence of the smoked salmon in the manifest dream content, she replied that this delicacy is her female friend's favorite dish.

Initially, Freud identified the dream motive as the wish to lessen the rival's chances of becoming plumper, since that would have made her still more attractive to the dreamer's husband. Thus, the inability to give a dinner party is conducive to the fulfillment of the patient's aim. But Freud appreciates that this account has not dealt with an uncomfortable detail: since the rival had expressed the wish to gain weight,

it would not have been surprising if my patient had dreamt that her friend's wish was unfulfilled; for my patient's own wish was that her friend's wish (to put on weight) should not be fulfilled. But instead of this she dreamt that one of her *own* wishes was not fulfilled. [P. 149]

How, then, does he propose to deal with this recalcitrant datum?

An auxiliary hypothesis is brought to the rescue. Freud postulates that instead of being the patient herself, the person who figures in the dream is actually her rival, with whom she had "identified" herself to the extent of putting herself into the rival's place. He seems to be well aware that a rescuing auxiliary can be indicted as *ad hoc*, unless it is buttressed by *independent* evidential support. Thus, he goes on to claim at once (p. 149) that just such support is supplied by the patient's request to her husband in waking life *not* to cater to her craving for caviar. For, under the collateral hypothesis that the patient can assume her rival's identity even in waking life, her avowed conscious desire to deprive the rival of food would make sense of her renunciatory request to her husband.

In this way, Freud believed he had shown that even a dream depicting the *thwarting* of a wish felt in the dream does qualify, after all, as the fulfillment of another wish, which is only latent, being a residue from the day before. As he sees it, his auxiliary hypothesis of interpersonal identification contributed to an understanding of a datum from the patient's behavior in waking life, besides enabling his major postulate of wish fulfillment to explain the initially refractory feature of the manifest dream content.

Glymour (1983) has discussed the aborted dinner party dream as an illustration of Freud's device "to confirm an interpretation by finding two or more elements of the dream which are independently associated with a key figure in the interpretation of the dream." This dream illustrates such a device, because after Freud had inferred the aim to thwart the dreamer's rival as the dream motive, he said: "All that was now lacking was some coincidence to confirm the solution" (S.E. 1900, 4: 148). When his patient reported her rival's fondness for smoked salmon, he had seized on the role of this delicacy in the manifest dream content as the confirming coincidence.

Glymour challenges this claim of confirmation as spurious. As he points out, Freud's conclusion as to the motivational cause had asserted an order of cause and effect that is the *reverse* of the causal order exhibited by the free associations, for associations generated by two manifest dream elements (the dinner party and the salmon) had *each* prompted his patient to think of her rival. But Freud took this to be evidence that the affect bound to that rival was the motivational cause for the thematic occurrence of both a dinner party and salmon in the manifest dream content. Glymour objects that "evidence for the first causal model is not necessarily evidence for the second," a causal reversal he indicts as "one of Freud's favorite fallacies." Hence, Glymour (1983) rejects Freud's invocation of the "coincidence" that both a dinner party and salmon figured in the manifest dream content: "the coincidence is manufactured: one associates, at Freud's direction, until one thinks of something which has connections with several elements in one's dream; the several elements cause the common thought, not vice-versa, and the coincidence requires no further explanation. The method of manufacture is all the explanation required." Indeed, Freud thus argues fallaciously from the confluence of associations to a causal reversal in *explicitly generalized* form (S.E. 1900, 5: 528).

As the reader will recall from chapter 4, it was in the context of my critique of Freud's theory of parapraxes that I argued for the rejection of his inference of causal reversal, *and emphasized its fallacious origination in his repression etiology of the psychoneuroses*. As a corollary to my historico-logical discreditation of his causal inference, I objected to his commission of the same fallacy in his theory of dreams. Glymour independently uncovered the fallacy in the context of Freud's dream theory by pointing out illuminatingly that it lurked behind Freud's reliance on a coincidence in the manifest dream content to *confirm* his analysis of the dream. But, as I showed in chapter 4, Freud's fallacious causal inference is not quite the glaringly crude blunder that it appears to be. This flagrant appearance results from seeing that inference in the context of the dream theory alone, as Glymour did.

Such an *isolated* appraisal neglects that Freud speaks of dreams as being "like all other psychopathological structures" (S.E. 1900, 4: 149). Twenty-five years later, he stressed this assimilation of manifest dream content to his compromise model of neurotic symptoms: "dreams are constructed like a neurotic symptom: they are compromises between the demands of a repressed impulse and the resistance of a censoring force in the ego" (S.E. 1925, 20: 45). Thus, as I explained earlier, Freud did believe that the legacy of Breuer's method vouches for free association as an avenue to the certification of repressed dream motives. And, as I showed furthermore, Freud was led to this conclusion by misextrapolation from a flawed repression etiology of the neuroses. All the same, it emerges that Freud's causal reversal inference in his dream theory is not quite as devoid of a plausible rational motivation as Glymour makes it appear to be.

It might seem that Freud's assimilation of manifest dream content to mini-neurotic symptoms has a consequence that either discredits his account of dream instigation or disqualifies free association even as a means of lifting presumed repressions. Just as sexual repressions are deemed causally necessary for neurosogenesis, so also sundry sorts of repressed infantile wishes are avowedly the *sine qua non* of dream instigation. Thus, just as the therapeuticity of lifting pathogenic repressions is the corollary of the former, so also the latter may seem to entail the following: To the extent that the *analyzed* patient achieves conscious awareness of his previously repressed infantile wishes, that conscious mastery robs these very wishes of their power to engender dreams! Hence, in proportion as the analysand's buried infantile wishes are brought to light, he should experience, and exhibit neurophysiologically (e.g., via REM sleep), a striking reduction in dream formation. But what if this decrease fails to materialize? It would then seem to follow that, unless the typical analysand is chronically unsuccessful in retrieving his buried infantile wishes, Freud's account of dream instigation is false. Yet, as Philip Holzman has told me, Freud may well avert this consequence by his claim (S.E. 1900, 5: chap. 7 (C) and (D)) that the (biological) impulse behind the emerging wishes remains undiminished in the unconscious. But this obviation may be problematic: If the repressed wishes are, at bottom, enduring instincts, in what sense are they also genetically *infantile*, as avowed?

The objections I have raised so far against Freud's dream theory would hold, even if the method of free association were not flawed epistemically by the analyst's overt and covert interventions. But this method is considerably impaired by the defects I have charged against it: manipulative adulteration as well as selection bias. In fact, these liabilities vitiate it, regardless of whether the repressions it yields are deemed the pathogens of neurotic symptoms, the causes of slips, or the motives for dream constructions. Indeed, as we shall see in chapter 10, this conclusion bespeaks the spuriousness of the consilience of clinical inductions that Freud adduced late in life (S.E. 1937, 23: 257-269) to validate analytic interpretations.

Clark Glymour (1983) has rightly complained that the contrived manner of selecting from the products of free association has enabled Freud's method to function *ad hoc* when generating the elements belonging to the purported *latent* dream content. For, as Glymour argues cogently, Freud so selected the latent content as to preserve his wish-fulfillment hypothesis from refutation by such prima facie counterexamples as nightmares and diffuse anxiety dreams. Freud gave no justificatory criteria in advance for weaving *particular* associations together to make *one* sort of story. Instead, he begged the question by tailoring his selections from the patient's associative output *ad hoc* to the preservation of his wish-fulfillment hypothesis, whenever the manifest dream content was anything but wish fulfilling. A suitably different set of selections from the associations could have been made to yield other motives, such as fear or disgust. Thus, Freud failed to sustain his account of the latent content by *warrantedly* selected evidence. But since this account was *essential* to evading refutation by anxiety dreams, Glymour concludes reasonably enough that the universal wish-fulfillment hypothesis of psychoanalytic dream theory ought to be presumed false rather than unfalsifiable.

Even more censoriously, Timpanaro (1976: 115) points especially to Freud's lecture "The Dream Work" (S.E. 1916, 15: 179-183) as evidence for the following indictment: "Perhaps most capricious and scientifically dishonest of all is Freud's 'proof' that all dreams, even anxiety dreams, are the expressions of a repressed wish." Timpanaro (1976) illustrates his accusation:

Does someone have an anxiety dream about the death of a beloved person? Have no fear; this too is a wish-fulfillment, for it represents a resurgence of archaic psychic material which reveals that at some point in the infantile life of the dreamer the death of that person was indeed desired. The anxiety dream is concerned with the dreamer's *own* death? Another case of a wish—this time for self-punishment because of a guilt complex. [p. 218]

Freud did not come to grips with any of the array of objections to his dream theory that we have put forward so far. These were of three sorts: (1) his infantile wish genesis of all dreams is causally unfounded; (2) equally unfounded is his claim that the motivational cause of dream construction, if unconscious, must be present among the free associations triggered by the manifest content; and (3) the method of free association yields probatively defective data. But, to his credit, Freud did address another epistemic challenge to his dream theory.

The latter misgiving leaves aside the methodological pitfalls of free association. Instead, it arises from the presumed likelihood that patients compliantly produce corroborative dreams under the analyst's suggestive influence (S.E. 1911, 12: 96; 1923, 19: 115). In essence, Freud is being called upon to rule out that the patient obligingly generates repressed wishful impulses, because he is aware, at least unconsciously, of the analyst's belief in their presence. Freud optimistically denied just such adulteration in 1923 (S.E. 1923, 19: 114-115).

He first points out that since the *manifest* contents of dreams are indeed susceptible to the influence of waking life, it is small wonder that those powerful impressions of waking life that the patient obtains from his analyst likewise affect what will be the foci of his manifest dream content (p. 114). Also, as he tells us, even thoughts that *happen* to be unconscious at a given time but that might readily become conscious— i.e., "preconscious" thoughts as *contrasted* with *repressed* wishes—may ingress into the latent dream content in response to the analyst's suggestive influence (p. 114). But Freud then emphasizes that the dream also "contains indications of the repressed wishful impulses to which it owes the possibility of its formation" (p. 114). Having said this, he is adamant that their latency and egress is immune to the analyst's expectations. Freud rebuffs the skeptic: "The doubter will reply that they appear in the dream because the dreamer knows that he ought to produce them—that they are expected by the analyst. The analyst himself will rightly think otherwise" (pp. 114-115).

But why is the analyst right in thinking otherwise? Freud gives a mere analogy in which the interpretative task in psychoanalysis is likened to solving a jigsaw puzzle that has a *unique* solution (p. 116). Yet astonishingly, he concedes on the very next page that "most of the dreams that can be made use of in analysis are obliging dreams and owe their origin to suggestion." For there, he explains first that one of the patient's unconscious motives is "compliance towards the analyst which is derived from his parental complex—in other words, the positive portion of what we call the transference" (p. 117). Then he goes on at once to say quite serenely:

In fact, in many dreams which recall what has been forgotten and repressed, it is impossible to discover any other unconscious wish [than obliging the analyst] to which the motive force for the formation of the dream can be attributed. So that if anyone wishes to maintain that most of the dreams that can be made use of in analysis are obliging dreams and owe their origin to suggestion, nothing can be said against that opinion from the point of view of analytic theory. [P. 117]

Thus, here Freud concedes that the key repressed wish to which the patient's dreams purportedly owe their formation is indeed often induced by "compliance toward the analyst." But he does not let on that only a couple of pages earlier he had denied that the analyst wields just such suggestive influence. He sidetracks this unacknowledged inconsistency at once by moving on to invoke the (defunct) Tally Argument in support of the following claim: the patient's unconscious wish to oblige the analyst by dreaming only mobilizes the uncontaminated disclosure, via the emerging *latent* dream content, of "what has been forgotten and repressed," largely from the patient's preanalytic life (p. 117).

Freud also maintained repeatedly that the "dream *work*" is impervious to any kind of outside influence, be it from the analyst or any other quarter (S.E. 1916, 15: 238; 1923, 19: 114). Jones (1955: 221) relates Freud's reactions to a telling criticism of this thesis:

He discussed the objection raised that the dreams of a patient often depended on which analyst he attended, that there was a similarity in the dreams of a given analyst's patients. This also may happen, but the inference sometimes drawn from it was again due to the same confusion between manifest and latent content. Remarks made by an analyst could often be the stimulus to a dream, just as those made by anyone else or, for that matter, any bodily stimulus. But how the patient's dream-making activity worked up such stimuli was a purely internal matter that was not susceptible to any outside influence.

But, as Rosemarie Sand has remarked, the immunity of the dream work to outside influence claimed by Freud and Jones is incompatible with the avowed malleability of the *manifest* dream content by external influences; for the dream work is the machinery that produces the manifest dream from the latent content, and any outside influence on the manifest content must clearly be effected by means of the dream work. Thus, even if the latent content were entirely endogenous, this would not assure that its transformation into the manifest content is similarly endogenous.

We can now conclude our appraisal of the clinical credentials of the dream theory by making a deferred comment on the qualification to which Freud was driven in his "Revision of the Theory of Dreams" (S.E. 1933, 22: 28-30). As he sees it there, he had "completely disposed of" the ever-recurring "lay" objection that anxiety dreams refute his wish-fulfillment hypothesis. He adds that "punishment-dreams, too, are fulfillments of wishes, though not of wishes of the instinctual impulses but of those of the critical, censoring and punishing agency in the mind [the superego]" (p. 27). But then he notes that two, and "only two," serious difficulties have arisen for the wish-fulfillment theory. Of these, only one seems insurmountable to him, and it is posed by the dreams of the victims of traumatic hysteria.

Those afflicted by this neurosis—for example, soldiers who endured a severe psychical trauma in combat—*regularly* relive their traumatic experiences in their dreams. "What wishful impulse," Freud asks, "could be satisfied by harking back in this [recurrent] way to this exceedingly distressing traumatic experience?" Hence, he acknowledges: "According to our hypotheses about the function of dreams this should not occur" (p. 28). Furthermore:

> We should not, I think, be afraid to admit that here the function of the dream has failed. . . . But no doubt the exception does not overturn the rule. You can say nevertheless that a dream is an *attempt* at the fulfillment of a wish. In certain circumstances a dream is only able to put its intention into effect very incompletely, or must abandon it entirely. Unconscious fixation to a trauma seems to be foremost among these obstacles to the function of dreaming. [P. 29].

From the standpoint of our earlier strictures on the wish-fulfillment hypothesis, this important, if limited, modification is only to be welcomed, for the dreams of the war neurotics are chronic and intense anxiety dreams. And, for the reasons I have stated, I claim that Freud never succeeded in rebutting the "lay" objection to his handling of ordinary, nonchronic anxiety dreams. One is all the more disappointed by Ernest Jones's (1957: 269) lame attempt to show that even the dreams of the war neurotics may well not require Freud's qualification after all:

It may be pointed out, however, that none of these dreams were quite confined to an accurate presentation of the traumatic experience. One always found in them some other irrelevant feature which called for analysis, and which may well have signified a tendency to manipulate the traumatic memory in the direction of a wish-fulfillment, even if the patient waked in terror before this could be accomplished. Indeed it would seem possible to bring all the examples mentioned above under the broad tendency of abreaction.

So much for the clinical credentials of the dream theory, which was predicated epistemically on the purported imperviousness of the products of free association to the analyst's suggestive influence.

6.

Appraisal of Freud's Further Arguments for the Emergence of Unadulterated Repressions Under "Free" Association

Besides attributing such freedom from adulteration to the analysand's associative output, Freud maintained that there is even some safeguard against the patient's compliant assent to the analyst's interpretations: "in general the arousing of resistances is a guarantee against the misleading effects of suggestive influence" (S.E. 1923, 18: 251). But what is Freud's evidence that the patient's resistance is actually a guarantee against the regimentation of the analysand's responses by suggestion from his doctor? It can readily be granted that the patient's resistance prevents his uncritical, *automatic* acceptance of *all* of the analyst's interpretations. But, as Freud himself conceded some years later (S.E. 1937, 23: 257-265), this fact can hardly assure that when there is such acceptance after the resistance has been *overcome*, the given interpretation may be presumed correct and hence uncontaminated; for after resisting initially, the patient may acquiesce in a false interpretation after all. Besides, the docility of patients *even under free association*, which the analyst Marmor (1970: 161) adduced to argue for the *self-fulfilling* function of clinical hypotheses, likewise impugns Freud's reliance on patient resistance as a safeguard against spurious validation.

That the patient's acceptance can hardly vouch for lack of distortion by the analyst is attested by the following summary:

Research evidence has consistently indicated that a patient's belief in interpretations and his consequent anxiety reduction do *not* depend on the accuracy of the interpretations. Investigators have found that individuals will enthusiastically accept bogus interpretations as accurate descriptions of their own personalities. [Fisher and Greenberg 1977: 364]

For example, aggressive people accept descriptions of themselves as being shy. As these authors note further:

In fact, Heller [reference omitted] points out that therapy systems emphasizing ambiguity and limited therapist responsiveness (such as analysis) create situations that are the most susceptible to the subtle interpersonal influence described in the studies of verbal conditioning. [Pp. 363-364]

This seems to me to belie what I call "the myth of catalyticity" espoused by those analysts who conceptualize themselves as quite *non*directively interpretative: they see themselves as mere catalysts, expeditors of the unadulterated emergence of repressions previously bottled up by the walls of censorship.

The spuriousness of clinical confirmation in psychoanalysis is *not* lessened by the now well-recognized fact that epistemological distortions are definitely *not* confined to the responses of patients undergoing psychotherapy. Expectations entertained by *experimental* psychologists can strongly color their purported observational findings even in tests of the learning skills of laboratory rats (Shapiro and Morris 1978: 382-383). Yet psychologist Robert Rosenthal (1976: part 2, sec. 19-24) and others have provided careful accounts of how to *control* for experimenter expectancy effects. Nonetheless, the need for vigilance in regard to expectancy effects has been heeded less often than one would like. Thus, as Merrilee Salmon has pointed out to me, Bertrand Russell (1960: 32-33) declared himself discouraged because studies of animal learning have yielded the following results:

All the animals that have been carefully observed have behaved so as to confirm the philosophy in which the observer believes before his observations began. Nay, more, they have all displayed the national characteristics of the observer. Animals studied by Americans rush about frantically, with an incredible display of hustle and pep, and at last achieve the desired result by chance. Animals observed by Germans sit still and think, and at last evolve the solution out of their inner consciousness.

In any case, one wonders how Freud could have persuaded himself to put much stock in patient resistance as insurance against adulteration by suggested compliance. For he himself maintained that when the patient's transference toward the analyst is positive, "it clothes the doctor with authority and is transformed into belief in his communications and explanations" (S.E. 1917, 16: 445). Interestingly, Freud's aforecited reliance on patient resistance is introduced by the following tribute to the analyst's purported ability to winnow the bona fide memories from the fancied ones: "Any danger of falsifying the products of the patient's memory by suggestion can be avoided by prudent handling of the technique" (S.E. 1923, 18: 251). But this particular assurance is especially unconvincing. Clearly the clinical authentication of the etiologically relevant early history in the lives of psychoneurotics must largely rely on the adult patient's memories of *infantile* and *childhood* experiences, and such early memories are surely more fragile epistemically than ordinary recollections from adult life! This is so especially since the analyst is doing exactly what a cross-examining attorney is forbidden to do in the courtroom: leading the witness. Freud makes no bones about this particular feature of analysis:

The treatment is made up of two parts—what the physician infers and tells the patient, and the patient's working-over of what he has heard. The mechanism of our assistance is easy to understand: we give the patient the conscious anticipatory idea [the idea of what he may expect to find] and he then finds the repressed unconscious idea in himself on the basis of its similarity to the anticipatory one. This is the intellectual help which makes it easier for him to overcome the resistances between conscious and unconscious. [S.E. 1910, 11: 141-142; see also 1910, 11: 225-226, for further details]

Freud does not specify just how the "prudent handling of the technique," which he claims to have exercised in the psychoanalytic quest for the recovery of repressed memories (S.E. 1923, 18: 251), actually provided a safeguard against the suggestive elicitation of pseudo-memories ("paramnesias").

It can be granted, of course, that requirements of consistency or at least overall coherence do afford the analyst *some* check on what the patient alleges to be bona fide memories. But Freud's own writings attest to the untrustworthiness of purported adult memories of early childhood episodes that had presumably been repressed in the interim and then retrieved by analysis (see the documentation in Grünbaum 1980: 353). And as we had prior occasion to note, he conceded that even reliance on the slender reed of the patient's recall is sometimes disappointingly unavailable: "The patient cannot remember the whole of what is repressed in him, and what he cannot remember may be precisely the essential part of it" (S.E. 1920, 18: 18; see also 1937, 23: 265-266). To fill just this lacuna, the patient simply has to take the analyst's word for the soundness of the reconstruction of his past. Indeed, the malleability of adult memories from childhood is epitomized by a report from Jean

Piaget (Loftus 1980: 119-121), who thought he vividly remembered an attempt to kidnap him from his baby carriage along the Champs Elysées. He recalled the gathered crowd, the scratches on the face of the heroic nurse who saved him, the policeman's white baton, the assailant running away. However vivid, Piaget's recollections were false. Years later the nurse confessed that she had made up the entire story, which he then internalized as a presumed experience under the influence of an authority figure. Yet, writing about Leonardo da Vinci's memories from childhood, Freud declared:

What someone thinks he remembers from his childhood is not a matter of indifference; as a rule the residual memories—which he himself does not understand—cloak priceless pieces of evidence about the most important features in his mental development. [S.E. 1910, 11: 84]

The early Freud had even been sanguine enough to declare that if he ever were to alter or falsify the reproduction of memories, or the connection of events, "it would inevitably have been betrayed in the end by some contradiction in the material" (S.E. 1895, 2: 295). Hence, he concluded insouciantly: "We need not be afraid, therefore, of telling the patient what we think his next connection of thought is going to be. It will do no harm"! Yet my discounting of early childhood memories, purportedly retrieved by the adult patient under the analyst's tutelage, is not at all a wholesale derogation of adult memories in daily life.

Apparently the analyst cannot justly claim to be a mere neutral expeditor or catalyst for the recovery of memories that can be *intra*clinically certified as authentic by virtue of his "prudent handling of the technique." Indeed, the help-seeking patient may well sense that the analyst expects confirmation of a conjecture by a memory, and the knowledge, authority, and help-giving potential he attributes to the analyst may well serve to make him compliant, no less than his desire to gain the analyst's approval qua parental surrogate. Such approval or disapproval manifests itself through the myriads of subtle nonverbal cues present in human communication.

That psychoanalytic treatment ought not to be regarded as a bona fide *memory-jogging* device emerges more generally as a corollary of at least three sets of recent research findings elaborated by Loftus (1980): (1) the remarkable extent to which human memory is malleable, (2) the interpolative reconstruction and bending of memories by theoretical beliefs or expectations, and (3) the penchant, under the influence of leading questions, to fill amnesiac gaps by confabulated material. As for the first point, people have pseudomemories for events that never occurred

(Loftus 1980: chap. 3). For example, under the influence of racial stereotypes, some experimental subjects who were shown a picture of several people on a subway car—including a black man with a hat and a white man with a razor in his hand—claimed to remember seeing the razor in the hands of the black man (Loftus 1980: 39).

The tendency characterized under the second point arises from taking various fragments of experiences and filling in details under the guidance of all sorts of suppositions, so as to create a new distorted or even fictitious "memory" (pp. 40, 76). As Loftus summarizes the evidence:

Human remembering does not work like a videotape recorder or a movie camera. When a person wants to remember something he or she does not simply pluck a whole memory intact out of a "memory store." The memory is constructed from stored and available bits of information; any gaps in the information are filled in unconsciously by inferences. When these fragments are integrated and make sense, they form what we call a memory. [P. 163]

Finally, Loftus's discussion (chap. 8) of confabulation in response to leading questions is likewise germane. For example, when people are asked to point out a previously seen culprit in a police lineup, worthless identifications can result in this *recognition test* unless care is taken *not* to steer them suggestively to a particular individual in the lineup. I claim that such pitfalls of memory-based recognition tests lurk even more when an analytic patient is asked to draw on his memory to *test* an interpretation offered him by his analyst. Such a memory test normally does *not* match the features of a *well*-designed police lineup recognition test, for the therapist tends to favor his own interpretations of the analysand's past, and this attitude will typically not be lost on the patient.

One of the questions we have been addressing in Part II was: "Are clinical data probatively cogent *even if uncontaminated*?" Let us pause to recapitulate the results obtained so far from our endeavor to deal with that issue. In the first place, I argued that even if "free" association were actually free, the clinical responses yielded by it could validate neither the repression etiology of the psychoneuroses, nor the psychoanalytic theory of dreams, nor even Freud's theory of parapraxes. Yet Freud claimed just such clinical validation for these core hypotheses of his entire psychoanalytic enterprise, each of which is founded on the notion of compromise formations engendered by repressions. But in the second place, I canvassed solid evidence for the considerable epistemic contamination of three major kinds of clinical findings that Freud deemed either initially exempt from such adulteration or certifiably unmarred by it because of due precautions: the products of "free" association, the patient's assent to analytic interpretations that he or she had initially resisted, and memories recovered from early life.

Indeed, the epistemic adulteration I have documented seems to be *ineradicable* in just those patient responses that are supposed to lay bare repressions and disguised defenses after resistances have been overcome. Yet Freud attributed pride of place to these very data in the validation of his theory of repression. Thus, generally speaking, clinical findings—in and of themselves—forfeit the probative value that Freud had claimed for them, although their potential heuristic merits may be quite substantial. To assert that the contamination of intraclinical data is *ineradicable* without extensive and essential recourse to *extra*clinical findings is *not*, of course, to declare the automatic falsity of any and every analytic interpretation that gained the patient's assent by means of prodding from the analyst. But it *is* to maintain—to the great detriment of intraclinical testability!—that, in general, the epistemic devices confined to the analytic setting cannot reliably *sift* or decontaminate the clinical data so as to *identify* those that qualify as authentic.

7.

Remarks on Post-Freudian Defenses of the Fundamental Tenets of Psychoanalysis

Though I have given an epistemic critique of the basic pillars of psycho-analysis, one might ask: why does my critique anachronistically focus on Freud's reasoning to the exclusion of the modifications and elaborations by those post-Freudians whose doctrines are recognizably psychoana-lytic in content rather than only in name? Latter-day psychoanalytic theoreticians that come to mind are the very influential Heinz Kohut, who pioneered the so-called "self-psychology," and the so-called "object-relations" theorists, who include not only the leading Otto Kernberg but also Harry Guntrip, W. R. D. Fairbairn, Donald Winnicott, and others. Thus, Heinz Kohut's "self-psychology," for example, down-grades Freud's Oedipal, *instinctual* factors in favor of even earlier, *environmental* ones as the sources of the purported *unconscious* deter-minants of personality structure (see Ornstein 1978; Meyers 1981; Basch 1980: chap. 11). More generally, insofar as these post-Freudian neo-revisionist theories are indeed recognizably psychoanalytic, they do of course embrace some version of the repression etiology. Furthermore, they rely epistemically on free association in the clinical investigation of purported pathogens and other unconscious determinants of behavior, and lift repressions as *one* means to effect therapy (Eagle 1984).

But, I submit, precisely to the extent that these outgrowths of Freud's ideas are thus recognizably psychoanalytic in content as well as in method of inquiry and therapy, my epistemic critique of Freud's original hypotheses applies with equal force to the etiologic, developmental, and therapeutic tenets of these successors. How, I ask, for example, can Kohut possibly claim better validation for his species of unconscious determinants than Freud can for the sexual ones? Moreover, it is just ludicrous to pretend with Flax (1981: 564) that my focus on Freud in appraising psychoanalytic theory epistemically is akin to the anachronistic procedure of "throwing out physics because there are unresolved problems in Newton's theory," for this purported analogy suggests misleadingly that the epistemic difficulties that beset Freud's original formulations have been overcome by the much-vaunted post-Freudian formulations of neo-revisionist theory (Grünbaum 1983). It overlooks, as well, the logical incompatibility of the most influential of these versions: as Robbins (1980: 477) points out, Kohut's and Kernberg's views are "fundamentally antagonistic" to one another, being rooted in a schism between Melanie Klein and W. R. D. Fairbairn.

Indeed, there is not even agreement among the post-Freudians in regard to the probative value that may be assigned to *the same case-study material*: while Kohut claimed clinical support for his theory from his reanalysis of Mr. Z.—a patient whose prior analysis had been traditional—the contemporary Chicago analyst Gedo (1980: 382) harshly discounts the scientific quality of Kohut's case-study material, and he concludes that the "theoretical inferences" drawn by Kohut from his clinical observations "fail to carry scientific conviction." A similarly negative assessment is reached by the psychoanalytic psychologist F. J. Levine (1979), an ardent exponent of psychoanalytic methods of investigation and therapy. Ferguson (1981: 135-136), however, believes that Kohut's case history of Mr. Z. is "a crystalline example of the *fact* that a progressive theory change [in L. Laudan's sense] has taken place in psychoanalysis." But Ferguson then seems to damn it with faint praise, saying "the case of Mr. Z. provides something of a 'confirming instance' of the new theory." For all of the fundamental defects of Freud's clinical arguments, their caliber and amenability to scrutiny is mind-boggling as compared to the reasoning of these neo-revisionist epigoni, let alone of their apologists (Eagle 1983*a*).

No wonder that the psychodynamically oriented psychologists Fisher and Greenberg (1977: ix) reached the following verdict: "The diversity of the secondary elaborations of Freud's ideas is so Babel-like as to defy the derivation of sensible deductions that can be put to empirical test." For this reason alone, it will be most useful to focus the remainder of this essay on Freud's own formulations. Besides, my examination in the Introduction of the so-called hermeneutic construal of psychoanalysis has obviated further concern with this reinterpretation altogether, I believe, although there are also hermeneutic versions of neorevisionist theory (see Flax 1981).

One must admire the strenuous and ingenious efforts made by Freud to legitimate his psychoanalytic method by arguing that it could *sift* clinical data so as to identify reliably those that are authentically probative. As we saw, these efforts included the attempt to vouchsafe the probity of free associations by secluding their *contents* in the bastion of *internal* causal relatedness, and his dialectical exertions culminated in the generic underwriting of clinical investigations by the Tally Argument. The NCT premise of this argument, we recall, was also to furnish the basis for a fundamental differentiation in regard to the *dynamics* of therapy between psychoanalysis, on the one hand, and *all* purely suggestive therapies, on the other. Hence, I submit that Freud's explicit avowal of this premise in his famous 1909 case of phobic Little Hans provides a *coherent rationale* for disregarding his seemingly equivocal, question-begging, and evasive handling of the suggestibility problem in that very case history (S.E. 1909, 10: 104-106, 120-121). There he *seems* to vacillate by adopting alternative postures as follows: (1) disclaiming the scientific reliability of patient assent and being content to secure practical therapeutic benefit, on the one hand (p. 104), and fairly soon thereafter, (2) excusing therapeutic failure by appeal to scientific gain, on the other (pp. 120-121).

If Freud's NCT were true, so that only veridical insight would have been dependably psychotherapeutic, that state of affairs would have been a tribute to the efficacy of human rationality fully on a par with the fact that "knowledge is power." And it would have supplied a rationale for the fact, reported by one of the pioneers of behavior therapy (Wolpe 1981), that analytic treatment still continues to dominate the clinical field in the United States, and that the teaching of psychotherapy is largely under the control of psychodynamically oriented clinicians. But the empirical untenability of the cardinal premise of the Tally Argument has issued in the latter's collapse, leaving intraclinical validation defenseless against all of the skeptical inroads from the massive evidence for the distortion and tailoring of its data by the mechanisms we have depicted.

Oblivious to the import of the whole array of doubts I have marshaled against Freud's NCT, Flax (1981: 566) sees herself entitled to reiterate NCT blithely as follows:

The only way to undo distorted relations with others is to reexperience them in a context in which the consequences of these relations are acted out [in the transference], can be interpreted [psychoanalytically!] and worked through [in the transference]. . . . But transference love and rational insight [as predicated on psychoanalytic etiology] are necessary for the patient's emancipation.

Indeed, despite my documentation of Freud's own keen appreciation of the *epistemic* challenge from suggestibility, his lifelong concern with this reproach was totally lost on Flax, who writes:

All the phenomena that Grünbaum counts as the clinical liabilities of psycho-analysis on empiricist grounds—epistemic contamination (i.e. [*sic*] intersubjectivity), suggestion, the placebo effect, etc.—are essential parts of the analytic process. Far from being liabilities, they are evidence that object-relations theory is correct. [Pp. 566-567]

Here she completely fails to comprehend that precisely by being a *therapeutic* asset, the patient's transference attachment to the analyst may well be an *epistemic* liability for the purported clinical validation of the analytic theory of personality (S.E. 1917, 16: 446-447)! As Freud himself put this ominous challenge:

There is a risk that the influencing of our patient may make the objective certainty of our findings doubtful. What is advantageous to our therapy is damaging to our researches [i.e., damaging to the clinical validation of the general psychoanalytic theory of personality]. [S.E. 1917, 16: 452]

Believing he had met just this challenge by means of his NCT, Freud thought that he was warranted in confining the therapeutic role of suggestion in psychoanalytic treatment to that of a mere *catalyst* ("vehicle"). Hence, he declared: "It is perfectly true that psychoanalysis, like other psychotherapeutic methods, employs the instrument of suggestion (or transference). But the difference is this: that in analysis it is not allowed to play the decisive part in determining the therapeutic results" (S.E. 1925, 20: 43). Yet, as I was at great pains to explain in an earlier article (Grünbaum 1980: section 2), just this reply of Freud's to the charge of placebogenesis was gravely undermined by the demise of his NCT. Astonishingly enough, Flax simply ignores this damaging fact.

To boot, Flax (1981: 563) makes light of epistemic contamination by claiming that, in *every* field of inquiry, "All data are epistemically contaminated." But this reliance on a *tu quoque* argument is specious: while all data are indeed more or less theory-laden, their mere theory-ladenness hardly assures their *spurious confirmation* of the pertinent theory *in the manner of a self-fulfilling prediction* (see Grünbaum 1983). Thus, Flax simply equivocates on the term "epistemic contamination," for she pretends that the mere theory-ladenness of a perceptual datum in any of the sciences is on a par with the spurious kind of confirmation by suggestion employed for psychoanalytic hypotheses, which even the analyst Marmor (1962: 289) decried as "self-validating." As will be recalled, Marmor did so by pointing to the striking effects of the analyst's communicated expectations on the character of the patient's clinical responses. Von Eckardt (1981: 572) has offered further telling objections to Flax's shoddy arguments.

In any case, since no viable substitute for the Tally Argument appears to be in sight, it is *unavailing* to take contaminated findings from the psychoanalytic interview more or less at face value, and then to try to employ them probatively in some testing strategy whose *formal* structure is rational enough as such. Indeed, the seeming ineradicability of epistemic contamination in the clinical data, adduced as support for the cornerstones of the psychoanalytic edifice, may reasonably be presumed to doom any prospects for the cogent intraclinical testing of the major tenets espoused by Freud. Moreover, as we are about to see, the clinical testing of *etiologic* hypotheses has *further* difficulties of its own. For, as will emerge in the next chapter, *the clinical vindication of the repression-etiology without reliance on the dynamics of Freud's therapy is no less a fiasco than his attempted therapeutic validation.*

These considerations can now be brought to bear in scrutiny of Glymour's defense of clinical testability, which was outlined in chapter 1, Section A, of this book.

8.

Can the Repression Etiology of Psychoneurosis be Tested Retrospectively?

Glymour gives an illuminating reconstruction of Freud's account of the Rat Man case by means of the logical pincer-and-bootstrap strategy, which Glymour had teased out of that account. I have no reason to gainsay this strategy in general as far as it goes. But I shall now argue that, with or without it, strong reasons militate against the intraclinical testability of the specific etiologic hypothesis at issue in the case of the Rat Man, Paul Lorenz, who suffered from an obsessional fear of rats.

At the time of the Rat Man case, Freud had postulated that premature sexual activity, such as excessive masturbation, subjected to severe repression is the specific cause of obsessional neurosis. As will be recalled from chapter 1, section B, in his carefully defined usage of "specific cause," the claim that X is the specific cause of Y entails unilaterally that X is causally *necessary* for Y. The latter, in turn, unilaterally entails that all cases of Y were Xs. Thus, if *this particular consequence* of the conjectured sexual etiology is to get confirmation from Lorenz's psychoanalysis, the intraclinical data yielded by it need to be able to certify the following: Lorenz, who was an adult victim of obsessional neurosis, engaged in precocious sexual activity that was then repressed. Hence, let us inquire, first, whether intraclinical data produced by the adult patient can *reliably* attest the actual occurrence of a childhood event of the stated sort. But, as I shall argue, even if the answer to this question were positive, this much would be quite insufficient to support Freud's etiologic hypothesis that repressed precocious sexual activity is *causally relevant* to adult obsessional neurosis.

As Glymour (1980: 272) notes, "Freud had...arrived at a retrodicted state of affairs, namely, the patient's having been punished by his father for masturbation." Indeed, "the crucial question is whether or not Lorenz was in fact punished by his father for masturbation" (p. 273). But Freud's specific etiology of adult obsessional neurosis as such calls only for an early childhood event in which precocious sexual activity was repressed. Why, then, should it be probatively "crucial" whether it was the patient's *father* who was involved in the sexual event required by the hypothesized etiology?

As is clear from Freud's account, the elder Lorenz's involvement became probatively weighty, because of the unconscious significance that psychoanalytic theory assigns to the patient's recollection of recurring fears of his father's death, at least after the age of six. While having these fears, the child Paul bore his father deep conscious affection. Freud derived the presumed unconscious origin of the fears from a theoretical postulate of so-called precise contrariety, which he took pains to communicate to the patient, who then became "much agitated at this and very incredulous" (S.E. 1909, 10: 180). Freud both explains his reasoning and revealingly relates his indoctrination of the patient:

He was quite certain that his father's death could never have been an object of his desire but only of his fear.—After his forcible enunciation of these words I thought it advisable to bring a fresh piece of theory to his notice. According to psycho-analytic theory, I told him, every fear corresponded to a former wish which was now repressed; we were therefore obliged to believe the exact contrary of what he had asserted. This would also fit in with another theoretical requirement, namely, that the unconscious must be the precise contrary of the conscious.—He was much agitated at this and very incredulous. He wondered how he could possibly have had such a wish, considering that he loved his father more than any one else in the world. . . . I answered that it was precisely such intense love as his that was the necessary precondition of the repressed hatred. (S.E. 1909, 10: 179-180)

Having thus theoretically inferred the patient's deep childhood grudge against his father from the recurring fears of losing the father, Freud also conjectured that the grudge remained so durably unconscious only because it was a response to the father's interference with the patient's sensual gratification.

This conclusion was, then, serendipitous by suggesting that there had been an early event satisfying the specific etiology that Freud had hypothesized for Lorenz's obsessional neurosis. Since this etiology required precocious masturbation events, Freud retrodicted that the patient had been punished by his father for masturbation "in his very early childhood...before he had reached the age of six" (S.E. 1909, 10: 183). Clearly, the actual occurrence of an event having these attributes would *simultaneously* satisfy the initial condition of the postulated etiology and explain Lorenz's early dread of his father's death via Freud's principle of precise contrariety.

Let us now suppose, just for argument's sake, that Freud's avowedly well-coached adult patient had actually reported having a memory of the very early childhood event that Freud had retrodicted. Then I ask: could such a clinical event have reliably attested the actual occurrence of the distant event? I have framed this question hypothetically, because it so happened that Lorenz actually had no *direct* memory of any physical punishment by his father, let alone of a punishment for a *sexual* offense. He did remember having been *told* repeatedly by his *mother* that there had been *one* incident of angry conflict with his father at age three or four, when he was beaten by him. When the mother was consulted about whether this beating had been provoked by a misdeed of a sexual nature, her answer was negative. Furthermore, this was apparently the *only* beating the child had ever received from the father.

But for the purpose of our inquiry, we are positing that, at some point in his analysis, the patient had claimed to remember just the kind of early childhood event that Freud had retrodicted via his specific etiology of obsessional neurosis. Then I am concerned to show that, taken by itself, such a finding would be quite insufficient to lend any significant support to the hypothesized etiology of obsessional neurosis. My reasons for this claim will then enable me to argue quite generally for the following conclusion: given the demise of the Tally Argument, the intraclinical testing of the causal assertions made by Freud's specific etiologies of the psychoneuroses, and by his ontogenetic developmental hypotheses, is *epistemically quite hopeless*!

Let "N" (neurosis) denote a psychoneurosis such as the syndrome of obsessional neurosis, and let "P" (pathogen) denote the kind of sex-related antecedent event that Freud postulated to be the specific cause of N. Thus, I shall say that a person who had a sexual experience of the sort P "is a P," and if that person was then afflicted by N, I shall say that he was both a P and an N, or just a PN. It is taken for granted, of course, that *there are* both Ns and non-Ns, as well as Ps and non-Ps. To support Freud's etiologic hypothesis that P is causally necessary for N, evidence must be produced to show that being a P *makes a difference* to being an N. But such causal relevance is *not* attested by *mere* instances of N that were Ps, i.e., by patients who are both Ps and Ns. For even a large number of such cases does not preclude that just as many *non-P*s would also become Ns, if followed in a horizontal study from childhood onward! Thus, instances of N that were Ps may just *happen* to have been Ps. Then being a P has no etiologic role at all in becoming an N. A telling, sobering illustration of this moral is given by the following conclusion from a review of forty years of research (Frank 1965: 191):

No factors were found in the parent-child interaction of schizophrenics, neurotics, or those with behavior disorders which could be identified as unique to them or which could distinguish one group from the other, or any of the groups from the families of the [normal] controls.

Hence, it is insufficient evidence for causal relevance that any N who turns out to have been a P does instantiate the retrodiction "All Ns were Ps," which is entailed by Freud's specific etiology. Thus, to provide evidence for the causal relevance claimed by Freud, we need to *combine* instances of Ns that were Ps with instances of non-Ps who are *non-Ns*. Indeed, since he deemed P to be causally necessary for N—rather than just causally relevant—his etiology requires that the class of non-Ps should not contain *any* Ns whatever, and the class of Ps is to have a positive (though numerically unspecified) incidence of Ns.

One can grant that since "All Ns are/were Ps" is logically equivalent to "All non-Ps are/will be non Ns," any case of an N who was a P will support the latter to whatever extent it supports the former. But this fact is unavailing to the support of Freud's etiology, for the issue is *not* merely to provide evidential support for "All non-Ps are/will be non-Ns," or for its logical equivalent, by some instance or other. Instead, the issue is to furnish evidential support for the (strong kind of) *causal relevance* claimed by Freud. But, for the reasons I have given, the fulfillment of that requirement demands that there be cases of non-Ps that are non-Ns, no less than instances of Ns that were Ps. Yet *at best*, the Rat Man could furnish only the *latter* kind of instance. In other words, if we are to avoid committing the fallacy of *post hoc ergo propter hoc*, we cannot be content with instances of Ns that were Ps, no matter how numerous. Analogously, suppose it were hypothesized that drinking coffee is causally relevant to overcoming the common cold. Consider, too, the case of a recovered cold sufferer who turns out to have been drinking coffee while still afflicted by the cold. Then such an instance, taken by itself, would hardly qualify as *supportive* of the hypothesized causal relevance.

Psychoanalytic theory and therapy have encouraged the disregard and even flouting of the elementary safeguards against the pitfalls of causal inference familiar since the days of Francis Bacon, not to speak of J. S. Mill. Yet even informed laymen in our culture are aware that such safeguards are indeed heeded *in medicine* before there is public assent to the validity of such etiologic claims as "heavy tobacco smoking causes cardiovascular disease." This double standard of evidential rigor in the validation of etiologic hypotheses even makes itself felt in current criminal law. Thus legal prohibitions—and so-called expert psychiatric testimony in courts of law—are sometimes predicated on such hypotheses even when they are no better than articles of faith, given credence through blithe repetition. The recently publicized reiteration of the purported pathogenicity of child molestation in opposition to its decriminalization is a case in point. (A wealth of *other* documentation on the *unwarranted legal use* of purported psychiatric expertise, predicated on theories of unconscious motivations, is given by S. J. Morse [in press; 1982].)

In our society, the sexual molestation of children is often alleged to be pathogenic, even when it is affectionate and tender rather than violent. This allegation has been invoked to justify making such behavior illegal and fraught with substantial penalties. Yet recently, a number of sexologists have maintained that very young children should be allowed, and perhaps even encouraged, to have sex with adults, unencumbered by interference from the law. In their view, such activity itself is harmless to the child and becomes harmful only when parents raise a fuss about it. Indeed, *some* of these advocates have made the daring and quite unfashionable etiologic claim that unless children do have early sex, their psychological development will go awry. Even the less daring champions of harmlessness are opposed to jailing affectionate pedophiles.

Reasons of elementary prudence and also of humaneness make it a good policy, in my view, to put the burden of proof on those who maintain that affectionate and tender child molestation is *not* distressing to the child, let alone pathogenic. But a cautionary basis for a legal prohibition is a far cry from the confident assertion of demonstrated pathogenicity, and the difference between mere caution and authenticated causation of neurosis may, of course, be relevant to the severity of the punishment appropriate for violations of the interdiction.

In a recent issue of *Time* magazine, John Leo (1981: 69) inveighs etiologically *against* the demand to legalize tender pedophilia, which he sees as a thinly disguised manifesto for child-molesters' liberation. The justification offered by him for his indictment is as follows:

Unfortunately, few responsible child experts have reacted . . . so far to the radical writing on child sex. One who has is Child Psychiatrist Leon Eisenberg of Children's Hospital Medical Center, Boston: "Premature sexual behavior among

children in this society almost always leads to psychological difficulties because
you have a child acting out behavior for which he is not cognitively or emotionally ready."

Psychotherapist Sam Janus, author of a new book, *The Death of Innocence*, says
that people who were seduced early in life "go through the motions of living and
may seem all right, but they are damaged. I see these people year after year in
therapy." U.C.L.A. Psychiatrist Edward Ritvo also says that much of his work is
with children who have been involved in catastrophic sexual situations. His
conclusion: "Childhood sexuality is like playing with a loaded gun."

But the etiologic reasoning of those whom Leo cites to document the
pernicious effects of child molestation is just as shoddy as the causal
inferences of those advocates of pedophilia who claim dire psychological
consequences from the *failure* of infant boys to act on their erections, and
of infant girls to utilize their vaginal lubrications. For the findings
adduced by Leo do not answer either of the following two questions:

1. Is the occurrence of childhood seduction not equally frequent
among those who are well enough never to see a psychotherapist? In the
parlance of John Stuart Mill, this question calls for the use of the *joint*
method of agreement and difference, rather than just the heuristic
method of agreement.

2. Would a representative sample of those who were *not* seduced in
childhood have a significantly *lower* incidence of adult neurosis than
those who *were* seduced? By the same token, we must ask those who
claim seduction to be *beneficial* psychologically to show that those who
were indeed seduced *fared better* psychologically than those who were
not sexually active in this way. Without the appropriate answers to these
questions, the respective assertions of causal relevance remain gratuitous.

Thus, we must ask those who *condemn* childhood seduction the
foregoing questions, because it may be that childhood seduction just
happens to be quite common among neurotics, even though it has no
etiologic role in the production of neurosis. In that case, the same people
would have become neurotics anyway, without early seduction. Without
answers to these questions, the evidence given by those whom Leo
invokes as authorities merely suggests the bare *possibility* that childhood
seduction is pathogenic. By the same token, certain analysts have overlooked that repressed homosexual feelings cannot be shown to be the
pathogen of adult paranoia by merely pointing to the frequency of
homosexually tinged themes in the associative output of paranoiacs
during analysis. This finding does not tell us whether homosexual
themes would not likewise turn up to the same extent in the so-called
free associations of nonparanoiacs who lead well-adjusted lives and who

never see a therapist. Here, no less than in the case of the Rat Man, the invocation of J. S. Mill's heuristic method of agreement is not enough to lend support to the hypothesis of etiologic relevance.

Hence, even if the Rat Man did in fact have the sexually repressive experience P retrodicted via Freud's etiology of obsessional neurosis, this alone would hardly qualify as evidential support for that etiology. And there is a further reason for concluding that even if the child Paul Lorenz had actually been punished by his father for masturbating, as retrodicted via Freud's etiology, this putative occurrence would confer little, if any, support on this etiology. For, as Ronald Giere has remarked (private communication), the occurrence of this sort of event is to be routinely expected in the Victorian child-rearing culture of the time on grounds *other than* psychoanalytic theory.

Moreover, Freud had made the adult Rat Man patient well aware, as we saw, of the inferences that Freud had drawn about his childhood via psychoanalytic theory. Given the massive evidence I adduced earlier for the notorious docility of patients in analysis, I submit that one ought to discount Lorenz's *putative* early childhood memory as too contaminated to attest reliably to the actual occurrence of the retrodicted early event. Such discounting is hardly a general derogation of the reliability of adult memories in ordinary life, but in the clinical context, the *posited* memory is simply not sufficiently dependable to qualify as evidence for the retrodicted event. Thus, the retrospective intraclinical ascertainment of the actual occurrence of the retrodicted distant event is just too unreliable. Furthermore, in general, the patient's memory may simply fail to recall whether the pertinent event did occur, as Freud himself stressed (S.E. 1920, 18: 18; 1937, 23: 265-66). Indeed, even in survey studies of lung cancer patients who are asked about their prior smoking habits, and of heroin addicts who are questioned about previous use of marijuana, the retrospective ascertainment of the actual occurrence of the suspected causal condition is epistemically flawed (Giere 1979: 216, 265).

Have I provided adequate grounds for maintaining that long-term *prospective* studies, which employ control groups and spring the clinical confines of the usual psychoanalytic setting, must supplant the *retrospective* clinical testing of etiology defended by Glymour? Not just yet. For suppose that analysts could secure reasonable numbers of patients who, though presumed to need analysis for some affliction or other, are certifiably free of the *particular* neurosis N (say, obsessional neurosis) whose etiology is currently at issue. Since neuroses usually occur in mixed rather than pure form, this is a generous assumption. All the same, let us operate with it. Then, if we are given such patients who, though neurotic, are non-N, Freud's pertinent specific etiology does *not* retrodict whether patients of *this* sort were Ps or non-Ps. For his hypothesized pathogenesis allows given non-Ns to have been Ps no less than to have been non-Ps, although it does require any non-P to become a non-N. Now postulate, for argument's sake, that, though retrospective, psychoanalytic inquiry *were* typically able to ascertain *reliably* whether a given case of non-N was indeed a non-P or a P. If so, then non-Ns who putatively turn out to have been Ps would merely be compatible with Freud's etiologic hypothesis instead of supporting it, since this hypothesis allows these instances without requiring them.

But what of patients who are *neither* N's nor Ps? Would such people, together with other persons who are both Ns and Ps, jointly bespeak that P is pathogenic for N (*obsessional* neurosis) within the class of all persons?

Note that the clinical testing design I have envisaged for scrutiny is *confined* to the class of neurotics. For even the non-Ns of this design are presumed to be afflicted by some neurosis other than N. The reason is that persons who have practically no neuroses of any sort are hardly available to analysts in sufficient numbers to carry out the putative retrospective determination of whether they were non-Ps or Ps. But, as Mr. Blake Barley has noticed, the confinement of this retrospective clinical determination to the class of neurotics has the following consequence: Even if every observed non-N (non-obsessive neurotic) is a non-P while every observed N is a P, these combined instances lend credence only to the hypothesis that, *within* the class of *neurotics*, P is etiologically relevant to N. But these putative combined instances do not support the Freudian claim of such etiologic relevance within the wider class of persons.

In short, the Freudian clinical setting does *not* have the epistemic resources to warrant that P is *neurosogenic*! And this unfavorable conclusion emerges even though it was granted, for argument's sake, that the retrospective methods of psychoanalytic inquiry can determine *reliably* whether adult neurotics who are nonobsessives were non-Ps in early life. But is it reasonable to posit such reliability? It would seem not.

For clearly, even if the patient believes he has the required memories, the retrospective clinical ascertainability of whether a given non-N was actually a non-P is epistemically on a par with the psychoanalytic determination of whether a given N was a P. And, as we saw, the latter is unreliable. Moreover, as Freud himself acknowledged: "The patient cannot remember the whole of what is repressed in him, and what he cannot remember may be precisely the essential part of it" (S.E. 1920, 18: 18).

Now contrast the stated epistemic liabilities of the retrospective psychoanalytic inference that a given adult patient was or was not a P

during his early childhood with the assets of *prospective* controlled inquiry: a *present* determination would be made, under suitably supervised conditions, whether children in the experimental and control groups are *P*s and non-*P*s, respectively; again, during long-term follow-ups, later findings as to *N* or non-*N* would be gathered and would pertain to the then state.

Recently, experimental validations of therapeutic efficacy have been carried out by using the response history of single individuals *without* control groups drawn from other individuals (Hersen and Barlow 1976; Kazdin 1981; Kazdin forthcoming). Thus, in these validations, the *causal* claims inherent in the pertinent assertions of therapeutic efficacy have been validated by single-case experimental designs. Hence, it behooves us to ask whether these "*intra*subject" validations could become prototypic for using a given analysand to test *intra*clinically the causal assertions made by the long-term *etiologic* hypotheses of psychoanalytic theory and by such claims of efficacy as are made for its avowedly slow therapy. To answer this question, let us first look at situations in physics in which the *probative equivalent* of controlled experiments is furnished by other means.

When a billiard ball initially at rest on a billiard table suddenly acquires momentum upon being hit by another billiard ball, we are confident that the acceleration of the first ball results from the impact of the second. Even more strikingly, astronomers made sound causal claims about the motions of planets, binary stars, etc., before they were able to manipulate artificial earth satellites, moon probes, or interplanetary rockets. What took the probative place of control groups in these cases? In the case of the billiard ball, Newton's otherwise well-supported first law of motion gives us background knowledge as to the "natural history" of an object initially at rest that is not exposed to external forces: such an object will remain at rest. This information, or the law of conservation of linear momentum, enables us to point the finger at the moving second billiard ball to furnish the cause of the change in the momentum of the first. A similar reliance on otherwise attested background knowledge supplies the probative equivalent of experimental controls in the astronomical cases.

Turning to the *single*-case validations of therapeutic efficacy, they pertain to the following sort of instance:

A seven-year-old boy would beat his head when not restrained. His head was covered with scar tissue and his ears were swollen and bleeding. An extinction procedure was tried: the boy was allowed to sit in bed with no restraints and with no attention given to his self-destructive behavior. After seven days, the rate of injurious behavior decreased markedly, but in the interim the boy had engaged in over ten thousand such acts, thus making the therapists fearful for his safety. A punishment procedure was subsequently introduced in the form of one-second electric shocks. In a brief time, the shock treatment dramatically decreased the unwanted behavior. [Erwin 1978: 11-12]

Here the dismal prospects of an untreated autistic child are presumably known from the natural history of other such children. In the light of this presumed background knowledge, the dramatic and substantial behavior change ensuing shortly after electric shock allowed the attribution of the change to the shock without control groups, for, under the circumstances, the operation of *other* causal agencies seems very unlikely. More generally, the *paradigmatic* example of an *intra*subject clinical validation of the causal efficacy of a given intervention is furnished by the following *variant* of using the single patient as his own "historical" control: (1) the natural history of the disorder is presumably otherwise known, *or* (2) the therapist intervenes only in on-off fashion, and this intermittent intervention is found to yield alternating remissions and relapses with dramatic rapidity.

Can the causal validation designs employed in these intrasubject clinical tests of therapeutic efficacy become prototypic for using an individual analysand to validate Freud's *long*-term etiologic hypotheses, or to furnish evidence that an analysis whose typical duration extends over several years deserves credit for any therapeutic gain registered by the patient after, say, four years? To ask the question is to answer it negatively. The natural history of a person *not* subjected to the experiences deemed pathogenic by Freudian theory is *notoriously* unknown! As for crediting therapeutic gain to analytic intervention on the basis of an intrasubject case history, how could such an attribution possibly be made in the face of Freud's own aforecited acknowledgment of the occurrence of *spontaneous* remissions? At best, Freudians can hope to show that the incidence of therapeutic gain in groups of patients who undergo analysis exceeds the spontaneous remission rate in untreated control groups belonging to the same nosologic category (Rachman and Wilson 1980). In short, the stated intrasubject validation by means of dramatic therapeutic gains can hardly be extrapolated to underwrite the prospective single-case evaluation of slow analytic therapy, let alone to vindicate the *retrospective* testing of a Freudian etiology in the course of an individual analysis. Similarly for other variants of this design.

Though Freud's specific etiologies did not specify numerically the percentage of Ps who become Ns, it is noteworthy that only prospective investigation can yield the information needed for such a statistical refinement. For let us suppose that retrospective data confirm the retrodiction of Freud's specific etiology that the incidence of Ps within the sample group of *N*s is 100 percent; then this incidence clearly does not permit an inference as to the percentage incidence of *N*s within the class of *P*s. Yet such information is clearly desirable, if only in order to estimate the probability that a child who was subjected to *P* will become an *N*. More generally, when *P* is not deemed causally necessary for *N* but merely causally relevant, retrospective data simply do not yield any estimates of *P*'s degree of causal effectiveness (Giere 1979: 274, 277).

Our inquiry into the Rat Man case so far has operated with a *counterfactual* posit in order to discuss the reliability of clinical data in the context of this case. The *hypothetical* clinical datum we used was that the patient *had* reported having a memory of the early childhood event retrodicted by Freud. As against Glymour's generic thesis that the specific psychoanalytic etiologies can be cogently tested "on the couch," I have argued that, at least typically, such testing is epistemically quite hopeless. Hence, it would seem that Paul Lorenz's actual psychoanalysis would have completely failed to furnish evidential support for the *etiologic relevance* of childhood sexual repression to obsessional neurosis, even if Paul's father had reliably reported having repeatedly punished his young son for masturbation. Incidentally, when Waelder (1962: 625-626) defended the clinical confirmation of the psychoanalytic etiologies, he overlooked precisely that their substantiation requires evidential support for the *causal relevance* of the purportedly pathogenic experience, and not merely the historical authentication of the bare occurrence of that experience. It emerges that the proposed clinical vindication of the repression-etiology *without* reliance on the dynamics of Freud's therapy is no less a fiasco than his attempted therapeutic validation. I gave two main reasons for this additional failure: (1) the testing design of the analytic setting appears incompetent to warrant that the retrodicted childhood experience *P* was, if actual, also pathogenic, and (2) the retrospective methods of this clinical inquiry cannot even reliably authenticate the bare occurrence of *P*.

This *major clinical fiasco* resoundingly belies the following ambitious claim, made by Brenner (1982: 5): "what a psychoanalyst does with the data which derive from applying the psychoanalytic method is no different from what any scientist does with his or her data. An analyst postulates the same cause-and-effect relationships with respect to psychoanalytic data as a physicist, for example, postulates with respect to the data available to him or her."

Let us return to Glymour's account of the testing strategy in Paul Lorenz's analysis, which was predicated on Lorenz's failure, in fact, to have any *direct* recall of receiving a punishment from his father, let alone a castigation for a sexual offense. Therefore, let us now see how Glymour evaluated the probative significance of this finding. I shall be concerned to stress the scope that Glymour does give to *essential* reliance on *extra*clinical data for probative purposes. Indeed, it will turn out that the entire testing procedure in the Rat Man case comes out to be probatively *parasitic* on an extraclinical finding. Hence, I wonder how Glymour imagines that he has rebutted Eysenck's denial of intraclinical testability, although he does succeed in impugning the demand that all extraclinical disconfirmation be *experimental*.

By Glymour's own account of the Rat Man case, the probatively "crucial" datum came from the *extra*clinical testimony of the patient's mother. On Glymour's reading of Freud, at the time of Lorenz's analysis, Freud still postulated *actual* rather than fancied early sexual experiences to be the pathogens of obsessional neurosis (Glymour 1980: 274-275). As Glymour explains lucidly, what made Lorenz's case a *counterexample* to this etiology was *not* the mere failure of the patient to recall the event retrodicted by Freud. Instead, it was the *extra*clinical testimony from the *mother* that had this negative probative import (p. 273). For it was her testimony that supplied the probatively crucial datum by contravening Freud's retrodiction when she answered the question that Glymour characterized as "the crucial question." He himself characterizes "the memory of an adult observer"—in this case that of the mother—as "the most reliable available means" for answering this decisive question as to the character of the offense for which the child Paul had been punished (p. 273). How, then, in the face of the *extra*clinical status of the *decisive* datum, can Glymour justify his description of the testing rationale used in the Rat Man case as "a strategy that relies almost exclusively on clinical evidence" (Glymour 1974: 287)?

It is true enough that, as we know from the case history of the Wolf Man, Freud regarded stories told by older members of the family to the patient about the patient's childhood to be generally "absolutely authentic" and hence, admissible as data (S.E. 1918, 17: 14, n. 2). But Freud completes this assertion by cautioning that responses by relatives to pointed inquiries from the analyst—or from the patient while in analysis—may well be quite contaminated by misgivings on their part:

So it may seem tempting to take the easy course of filling up the gaps in a patient's memory by making enquiries from the older members of his family; but I cannot advise too strongly against such a technique. Any stories that may be told by relatives in reply to enquiries and requests are at the mercy of every critical misgiving that can come into play. One invariably regrets having made oneself dependent upon such information; at the same time confidence in the analysis is shaken and a court of appeal is set up over it. Whatever can be remembered at all will anyhow come to light in the further course of analysis. [S.E. 1918, 17: 14, n. 2]

In the same vein, the present-day analyst W. W. Meissner (1978: 155) writes: "Parental recollections are noteworthy for their propensity to distortion."

Even if one were to discount Freud's and Meissner's caveat, several facts remain: (1) It is misleading to claim intraclinical testability if, as in the Rat Man case, the avowedly crucial datum does *not* come from "the couch." (2) What makes the reliance on extraclinical devices important is that, far from being marginal epistemically, its imperativeness derives from the typically present probative defects of the analytic setting, defects that are quite insufficiently acknowledged by Glymour. And, in my view, it does not lessen the liabilities of intraclinical testing that the compensations for its deficits from *outside* the clinical setting *may occasionally* be available *in situ* (e.g., from family records) and thus do not necessarily have to require the experimental laboratory. For even when supplemented by such nonexperimental extraclinical devices, the thus enlarged "clinical" testing procedure is not adequate or epistemically autonomous. For example, when it becomes necessary to resort to extraclinical information for the sort of reason that was operative in the Rat Man case, it will be a matter of mere happenstance whether suitable relatives are even available, let alone whether they can *reliably* supply the missing essential information. Why, then, dignify as a "clinical testing strategy" a procedure of inquiry that depends on such contingent good fortunes and hence, when luck runs out, cannot dispense with experimental information? (3) The real issue is whether the clinical setting *typically*—rather than under contingently favorable circumstances—does have the epistemic resources for the cogent validation of the etiology at issue in the Rat Man case, and of other analytic etiologies. In dealing with that issue, Glymour's otherwise illuminating account has not demonstrated the existence of a cogent intraclinical testing strategy, even if he succeeded in showing that extraclinical compensations for its lacunae need not be wholly experimental.

Indeed, the extent of his essential epistemic reliance on extraclinical findings can now be gauged from his view of the effect that Freud's modifications of the specific sexual etiology of obsessional neurosis (and of other neuroses) had on the *testability* of these evolving etiologic hypotheses. Glymour (1980: 276-277) recounts this evolution:

After the turn of the century and before 1909, . . . there is no statement of the view that sexual phantasies formed in childhood or subsequently, having no real basis in fact, may themselves serve *in place of* sexual experiences as etiological factors. . . . Yet after the Rat Man case the view that either infantile sexual experiences *or* phantasies of them may equally serve as etiological factors became a standard part of Freud's theory. In *Totem and Taboo*, four years after the Rat Man case appeared, Freud emphasized that the guilt that obsessional neurotics feel is guilt over a happening that is psychically real but need not actually have occurred [footnote omitted]. By 1917 Freud not only listed phantasies themselves as etiological factors alternative to real childhood sexual experiences, but omitted even the claim that the former are usually or probably based on the latter [footnote omitted]. The effect of these changes is to remove counterexamples like that posed by the Rat Man case, but at the cost of making the theory less easily testable. For whereas Freud's theories, until about 1909, required quite definite events to take place in the childhood of a neurotic, events that could be witnessed and later recounted by adults, Freud's later theory required no more than psychological events in childhood, events that might well remain utterly private.

Thus, Glymour attributes the diminishing testability of Freud's modified etiologies quite rightly to the lessening *extra*clinical ascertainability of the sorts of events that Freud successively postulated as etiologic. But if the testability of the psychoanalytic etiologies is in fact "almost exclusively" intraclinical, as Glymour told us, why should it be *vital* for their testability that the etiologic events required by Freud's later theory are just mental states of the patient to which only the patient himself and his analyst become privy within the treatment setting?

Incidentally, the problem of testing Freud's sexual etiology of the neuroses—either clinically or extraclinically—became less well defined after he gave up the quest for qualitatively *specific* pathogens of nosologically distinct psychoneuroses in favor of a generic Oedipal etiology for all of them. In fact, he used the analogy of explaining the great qualitative differences among the chemical substances by means of quantitative variations in the proportions in which the same particles were combined. But having thus dissolved his prior long-standing concern with the problem of "the choice of neurosis," he was content to leave it at vague metapsychological remarks about the constant intertransformation of "narcissistic libido" and "object libido" (S.E. 1925, 20: 55-56).

What of Glymour's reliance on *intra*clinical data? In that context, he seems to have taken much too little cognizance of even the evidence furnished by analysts that intraclinically the suggestibility problem is radically unsolved, if not altogether insoluble, because there is no viable substitute for the defunct Tally Argument. Can we place any stock in Glymour's aforecited aspiration that "clinicians can hopefully be trained so as not to elicit by suggestion the expected responses from their patients"? In view of the evidence for the *ineradicability* of suggestive contamination, it would now seem that this hope is sanguine to the point of being quite utopian. In an afterword to his 1974 article published in a second edition (1982) of the Wollheim book in which it first appeared, Glymour has reacted to some of these particular doubts as follows:

I do not see . . . that the experimental knowledge we now have about suggestibility requires us to renounce clinical evidence altogether. Indeed, I can imagine circumstances in which clinical evidence might have considerable force: when, for example, the clinical proceedings show no evident sign of indoctrination, leading the patient, and the like; when the results obtained fall into a regular and apparently law-like pattern obtained independently by many clinicians; and when those results are contrary to the expectation and belief of the clinician. I do not intend these as *criteria* for using clinical evidence, but only as indications of features which, in combination, give weight to such evidence.

To this I say the following:

1. I do *not* maintain that any and all clinical data are altogether irrelevant probatively. Instead, I hold that such findings cannot possibly bear the probative burden placed upon them by those who claim, as Glymour did, that psychoanalysis can *typically* be validated or invalidated "on the couch," using a clinical testing strategy that is mainly confined to the analytic setting.

2. The existence of *some* circumstances under which we would be warranted in not renouncing clinical evidence "altogether" is surely not enough to sustain clinical testing as a largely cogent and essentially autonomous scientific enterprise. As for Glymour's illustrations of such circumstances, I cannot see that absence of evident indoctrination, or regular concordance among the results obtained independently by many clinicians, exemplifies circumstances under which "clinical evidence might have considerable force." For—apart from the arguments I gave against these illustrations, if only à propos of "free" association—it seems to me that their utopian character as a step toward solving the compliance problem is epitomized by the following sobering results, which are reported by the analyst Marmor (1962: 289):

Depending upon the point of view of the analyst, the patients of each [rival psychoanalytic] school seem to bring up precisely the kind of phenomenological data which confirm the theories and interpretations of their analysts! Thus each theory tends to be self-validating. Freudians elicit material about the Oedipus Complex and castration anxiety, Jungians about archetypes, Rankians about separation anxiety, Adlerians about masculine strivings and feelings of inferiority, Horneyites about idealized images, Sullivanians about disturbed interpersonal relationships, etc.

3. I do not deny at all that *now and then* clinical results "are contrary to the expectations and belief of the clinician." But as a step toward vindicating clinical inquiry qua epistemically autonomous testing strategy, I can only say, "One swallow does not a summer make."

What seems to me to emerge from Glymour's interesting reconstruction is that, on the whole, data from the couch *acquire* probative significance when they are independently corroborated by extraclinical findings, or when they are inductively consilient with such findings in Whewell's sense of joint accreditation. Thus, I do not maintain that any and all clinical data are altogether irrelevant probatively. But this much only conditionally confers *potential* relevance on intraclinical results beyond their heuristic value, and surely this is not enough to vindicate testability on the couch in the sense claimed by its Freudian exponents, and countenanced by Glymour heretofore.

PART III
EPILOGUE

9.

The Method of Free Association and the Future Appraisal of Psychoanalysis

Even some recognized analysts have largely conceded that the clinical method of investigation cannot be credited with normally yielding the kinds of veridical insights that analysts have traditionally been wont to claim for it in concert with Freud. Thus, in an avowedly "irreverent" article about the future of analysis, both as a theory and qua therapy, Kurt Eissler (1969: 462) writes:

As the model of what analysis of a neurosis should be, *qua* analysis of the infantile neurosis—the dissolution of which remains the ultimate goal of classical analysis—Freud's record of the Wolf Man's analysis has always impressed me as paradigmatic. The crux of that analysis was the reconstruction of the chief events and processes taking place during the infantile period. It is not a question here of speculating as to whether Freud was right or wrong in his reconstruction in that particular instance (he himself was ready to withdraw one part of it), but rather of the requirements that an analyst would have to fulfill if he were to attempt to live up to what Freud there outlined as a goal.

I am certain that a significantly high percentage of the interpretations offered today to patients in all parts of the world have to do with the infantile period. But I doubt that they are true reconstructions, in the sense in which Freud meant that activity. . . . When they have to do with a later stage of the infantile period, they are, I fear, in most instances either intellectualizations on the part of both the analyst as well as the patient, or else generalizations obtained by way of screen memories. It is not difficult, of course, to demonstrate to a patient that he once harboured aggressive feelings against a beloved father; but a true reconstruction goes beyond the mere unearthing of a hidden impulse and includes those specific details of time, place, environment and inner processes that conjoined to produce a trauma. Yet to take hold of these is a formidable task.

As Eissler emphasizes, this epistemic task is nearly Sisyphean, even if one abjures the usual ambitious therapeutic objectives, i.e., "even if the task of psychoanalysis is not considered—as the tendency is at present— extensive enough to include the restructuring of the personality, but is instead limited to the uprooting of the neurosis, with its deepgoing ramifications" (p. 462).

Speaking of the dream *laboratory*, Eissler points out that it is one of the *extra*clinical sources that has yielded "data that do not fit psychoanalytic theory in its present form" (p. 467). Then he gives another example bearing on the poverty of clinical data as *dis*confirmations:

Masters & Johnson [reference omitted] have proven that, during clitoridean orgasm, vaginal spasms occur that are identical with those that occur during vaginal orgasm. For obvious reasons, the psychoanalytic theory has been that absence of vaginal orgasm is caused by lack of vaginal responsiveness. In view of the new data, however, one has to say that such a lack is not due to any defect in physiological functioning but rather to a suppression of sensations that the organ itself is quite ready to provide. . . . Once again we encounter the situation we encountered in relation to the new data about the dream. The error in the previous theory was by no means caused by erroneous observation, for the relevant data could never have been derived from the psychoanalytic situation. [P. 468]

The moral he draws from these cases of extraclinical disconfirmation goes well beyond the particular analytic hypotheses to which they pertain: "The fact that observations that cannot be expected to be made in the psychoanalytic situation and are gained outside the psychoanalytic situation lead to data that require new psychoanalytic paradigms is of the greatest historical importance" (p. 467). Prognostically, Eissler sees this historical importance as follows: "The fact that the dream laboratory has introduced a paradox makes me more certain that the next phase of progress in psychoanalysis will come about through the supply of data obtained from outside the psychoanalytic situation proper" (p. 470). In short, the limitations of clinical *dis*confirmations are portentous and are even more significant than the liabilities of clinical confirmations.

Despite these exhortations to expand the investigative horizons of Freud's theory well beyond the clinical setting, the lesson that Eissler derives from the limitations of clinical findings acknowledged by him does not go nearly far enough. Thus, he hails the epistemic yield from the use of Freud's method of free association in wanton terms:

I shall be discussing the methodology of psychoanalysis only in terms of the method of free association. This method is one of those glorious inventions that can hold its own with Galileo's telescope [p. 461]. . . . It is breathtaking to review what Freud extracted, during the course of four decades, from the free associations of eight subjects who each lay on a couch for 50 minutes per day. [P. 465]

Here Eissler depicts the yield of Freud's eight case histories as results that Freud "extracted . . . from the free associations" of these eight patients. In this depiction, Eissler is undaunted even by Wilhelm Fliess's 1901 challenge that Freud had no safeguard against reading his own thoughts into those distilled from his patients' "free" associations (Freud 1954, letter #145: 334; letter #146: 337).

Similarly, Eissler no less than our present-day psychohistorians is unchastened by the need to provide adequate evidential validation of psychoanalytic principles before their *application* to other fields can be creditable. Unencumbered by such hesitations, Eissler (1969: 461) claims that

if society, science and research were organized in accordance with the principle of maximal investment returns, then an Academy of Man would long since have been founded along the lines indirectly suggested by Freud. It is apparent that all the various branches of the humanities have to be rewritten in accordance with the new knowledge that psychoanalysis has brought to light about man's psychic existence.

In a similarly exuberant vein, Eissler disregards his initial misgiving that "there are many reasons" for concluding that "psychoanalysis as a therapy . . . does not have a bright future" (p. 462). For nonetheless, he states, "I believe the psychoanalyst of the future may have to devote a large portion of his practice to the repair of the damage that is done in psychotherapy and drug treatment" (p. 463, n. 3). But Eissler gives no hint of how he knows that analysis is generally far less psychonoxious than rival interventions.

In sum, one can only welcome Eissler's refreshing anticipation that the future validation and/or disconfirmation of Freudian theory will come very largely from extraclinical findings. But one may not gloss over the serious epistemological liabilities of intraclinical testing that were set forth in chapters 2–8. The import of these fundamental drawbacks for the current credibility of psychoanalysis is dismal, for its credentials are avowedly almost entirely *intra*clinical, and hence quite weak. Yet, as we pointed out in chapter 1, section A, Freud, Ernest Jones, and a host of other orthodox spokesmen claimed their theory to be well supported precisely on the strength of data from the psychoanalytic interview. So much so that Freud claimed "certainty" for the *clinically* inferred etiology of a patient's affliction, and then relied on that very etiology to: (1) *explain* therapeutic failure (S.E. 1920, 18: 147, 152, 156-157, 164, 168), and (2) justify dismissing the patient's dissent from an etiologic interpretation as unquestionably the result of neurotic resistance, which will be conquered, he says, "by emphasizing the unshakable nature of our convictions" (S.E. 1898, 3: 269).

10.

Critique of Freud's Final Defense of the Probative Value of Data from the Couch:
The Pseudo-Convergence of Clinical Findings

As we saw in chapter 1, section B, Freud explicitly assured the potential falsifiability of his etiology of anxiety neurosis in his 1895 reply to Löwenfeld. To the further detriment of Popper's mythological exegesis, Freud was no less alert to the need for safeguarding the falsifiability of the analyst's interpretations and/or reconstructions of the patient's past. Indeed, this methodological exigency and its implementation is the theme of his very late paper "Constructions in Analysis" (S.E. 1937, 23: 257-269), because it might seem that patient *dissent* from an interpretation could always be *discounted* as inspired by neurotic resistance. Hence, it is Freud's aim to show just how the analyst deals with patient assent and dissent such that "there is no justification for accusing us of invariably twisting his remarks into a confirmation" (S.E. 1937, 23: 262). He had already adumbrated this problem by reference to the etiology of paranoia (S.E. 1915, 14: 265-266), as we saw in chapter 1, Section B.

Freud begins his paper by reporting that "a certain well-known man of science," who treated psychoanalysis fairly at a time when most of the people felt themselves under no such obligation, had nonetheless been "at once derogatory and unjust" on one occasion as follows:

He said that in giving interpretations to a patient we treat him upon the famous principle of "Heads I win, tails you lose" [footnote omitted]. That is to say, if the patient agrees with us, then the interpretation is right, but if he contradicts us, that is only a sign of his resistance, which again shows that we are right. In this way we are always in the right against the poor helpless wretch whom we are analysing, no matter how he may respond to what we put forward. [S.E. 1937, 23: 257]

Yet Freud grants that this charge of nonfalsifiability of analytic interpretations by dissent from the patient needs to be addressed, because "it is in fact true that a 'No' from one of our patients is not as a rule enough to make us abandon an interpretation as incorrect." He therefore proceeds "to give a detailed account of how we are accustomed to arrive at an assessment of the 'Yes' or 'No' of our patients during analytic treatment— of their expression of agreement or of denial" (p. 257). This evaluation is to be carried out as an essential step in the quest for "a picture of the patient's forgotten years that shall be alike trustworthy and in all essential respects complete" (p. 258).

Since the analysand "has to be induced to remember something that has been experienced by him and repressed," the analyst's task of *reconstruction*

resembles to a great extent an archaeologist's excavation of some dwelling-place that has been destroyed and buried or of some ancient edifice. The two processes are in fact identical, except that the analyst works under better conditions and has more material at his command to assist him, since what he is dealing with is not something destroyed but something that is still alive—and perhaps for another reason as well. [P. 259]

In Freud's view, the material at the analyst's disposal that "can have no counterpart in excavations" includes "the repetitions of reactions dating from infancy and all that is indicated by the transference in connection with these repetitions" (p. 259). But this does not exhaust the decided epistemic advantages that the psychic researcher enjoys over the archaeologist:

it must be borne in mind that the excavator is dealing with destroyed objects of which large and important portions have quite certainly been lost. . . . No amount of effort can result in their discovery and lead to their being united with the surviving remains. The one and only course open is that of reconstruction, which for this reason can often reach only a certain degree of probability. But it is different with the psychical object whose early history the analyst is seeking to recover. . . . All of the essentials are preserved; even things that seem completely forgotten are present somehow and somewhere, and have merely been buried and made inaccessible to the subject. Indeed, it may, as we know, be doubted whether any psychical structure can really be the victim of total destruction. It depends only upon analytic technique whether we shall succeed in bringing what is concealed completely to light. [Pp. 259-260]

Freud tempers this paean to retrodictability in psychoanalysis only to the following extent:

There are only two other facts that weigh against the extraordinary advantage which is thus enjoyed by the work of analysis: namely, that psychical objects are incomparably more complicated than the excavator's material ones and that we have insufficient knowledge of what we may expect to find, since their finer structure contains so much that is still mysterious. [P. 260]

But this qualification, though sobering, does not go nearly far enough for at least two reasons: (1) on the whole, the physical regularities on which the archaeologist relies to make his retrodictions are incomparably better tested and supported than the etiologies and other hypotheses invoked by the analyst retrodictively to vouchsafe his reconstructions, and (2) the archaeological data secured from the excavated relics are uncontaminated by any epistemic counterpart to suggestion in analysis. Freud's comparison of psychoanalytic and archaeological reconstruction is disappointingly silent in regard to these two major drawbacks to his theory. But in the next section of his paper, just before turning to the central issue of how false constructions allegedly "drop out" in the course of the analysis, he plays down the problem of suggestibility by appealing to the analyst's good character:

The danger of our leading a patient astray by suggestion, by persuading him to accept things which we ourselves believe but which he ought not to, has certainly been enormously exaggerated. An analyst would have had to behave very incorrectly before such a misfortune could overtake him; above all, he would have to blame himself with not allowing his patients to have their say. I can assert without boasting that such an abuse of "suggestion" has never occurred in my practice. [P. 262]

Freud now proceeds to explain (pp. 262-265) that the analyst no more takes a patient's assent to a construction at face value than he accepts without question a dissent from it. He does so in the course of giving two main reasons for contending that "there is no justification for accusing us of invariably twisting his [i.e., the patient's] remarks into a confirmation" (p. 262):

1. Though a patient's verbal assent may indeed result from genuine recognition that the analyst's construction is true, it may alternatively be spurious by springing from neurotic resistance as readily as his dissent. Assent is thus "hypocritical" when it serves "to prolong the concealment of a truth that has not been discovered." The criterion of whether assent is genuine or hypocritical is that there be *inductive consilience* of the

patient's verbal assent with new memories as follows: "The 'Yes' has no value unless it is followed by indirect confirmations, unless the patient, immediately after his 'Yes,' produces new memories which complete and extend the construction" (p. 262).

2. Just as assent may be *either* genuine or a mere cover for resistance, so also dissent. Though the analysand's dissent thus "is quite as ambiguous as a 'Yes'" (p. 262), his "No" is of even less face value; for a "No" response may betoken the *incompleteness* of a construction rather than that the patient is actually disputing it. In fact, incompleteness may prompt apparent dissent just as frequently as neurotic resistance does. Therefore, "the only safe interpretation of his 'No' is that it points to incompleteness" (p. 263). It is only "in some rare cases" that avowed dissent "turns out to be the expression of legitimate dissent." Hence, "a patient's 'No' is no evidence of the correctness of a construction, though it is perfectly compatible with it" (p. 263). The criterion of genuineness or legitimacy for dissent, no less than for assent, is that there be *inductive consilience* with other pieces of evidence.

Indeed, as Freud explained, he placed very much greater epistemic reliance on patient responses *other than* verbal assent or dissent as "indirect confirmations" or disconfirmations of analytic constructions. For after concluding that "the direct utterances of the patient after he has been offered a construction afford very little evidence upon the question whether we have been right or wrong," Freud declares that "it is of all the greater interest that there are indirect forms of confirmation which are in every respect trustworthy" (p. 263). As one illustration of these allegedly dependable clinical data, he mentions the patient's having a mental association whose content is similar to that of the construction. Moreover, he claims that such *content*-related associations are good predictors of "whether the construction is likely to be [further] confirmed in the course of the analysis" (p. 264). As a particularly striking example of a further clinical datum that is thus inductively consilient, he recalls a case in which the patient committed a parapraxis as part of a direct denial. Indeed, when a masochistic patient is averse to the analyst's therapeutic efforts, an incorrect construction will not affect his symptoms, but a correct one will produce "an unmistakable aggravation of his symptoms" (p. 265).

Freud sums up by denying any pretense that "an individual construction is anything more than a conjecture which awaits examination, confirmation or rejection," and insisting that the subsequent course of the analysis has epistemic prospects that are decidedly upbeat (p. 265).

It is patent that Freud appealed to a consilience of inductions from *other* clinical data to assess the probative value of the patient's acceptance or rejection of his analyst's interpretations. In particular, he invoked the patient's neurotic resistance to discount the latter's dissent *only* when the analyst had what he took to be consilient support that the interpretation was nonetheless true. Hence, the epistemic conduct of an analyst who follows this recipe for testing his constructions intraclinically can certainly not be accused of simply having immunized them against falsification by the facile device of pleading that the patient is being neurotically resistant.

Alas, as shown by Peterfreund's critique (1983: 20-27) of a "Case Report by Greenson," there are well-known practicing analysts who do invoke patient resistance on just the principle *rejected* by Freud (S.E. 1937, 23: 257), when he spoke of "Heads I win, tails you lose." And prima facie, the requirement of consilience would *seem* to provide some hedge against so crude a begging of the question.

Nonetheless, I submit that in view of the demise of the Tally Argument, the purported consilience of clinical inductions has the presumption of being *spurious*, and this strong presumption derives from the fact that the *independence* of the inferentially concurring pieces of evidence is grievously jeopardized by a *shared* contaminant: the analyst's influence. For *each* of the *seemingly* independent clinical data may well be more or less alike confounded by the analyst's suggestion so as to conform to his construction, at the cost of their epistemic reliability or probative value. For example, a "confirming" early memory may be compliantly produced by the patient on the heels of giving docile assent to an interpretation. But, more fundamentally, it is precisely in the context of the claimed consilience that the epistemic defects of free association that I have discussed come home to roost; for these liabilities *ingress alike* into *each* of the three major areas of clinical inquiry in which *free association serves to uncover purported repressions*: etiologic clinical investigation of the pathogens of the patient's neurotic symptoms, and the interpretation of his dreams as well as of his parapraxes. By depending alike on free association, the clinical data from these three areas forfeit the independence they require, if their prima facie consilience is to be probatively cogent. Thus, the consilience among the seemingly distinct sets of data is likely to be spurious, or at least cannot justly be deemed genuine. But even if the emergence of repressions were genuinely consilient, it would *not* show that such repressions are pathogenic or are the primogenitors of dreams and slips. This probative failure was one moral of Part II above.

In a very recent article on reconstructions in analysis, the analyst Greenacre (1981) recapitulates Freud's 1937 paper and emphasizes the fundamental epistemic role of free association in effecting psychoanalytic reconstructions. Avowedly, Greenacre wrote her article to help young analysts understand the task of retrieving the patient's past, but she gives no hint of awareness that the problem to which Freud addressed his 1937 paper remains unsolved, if only because of the liabilities of free association. Nor is there any appreciation of the epistemic failings of that paper in Walter Kaufmann's journalistic treatment of Freud's ideas (Kaufmann 1980: 87-88, passim).

Three major conclusions emerge from the appraisals I have given in the preceding chapters.

1. Insofar as the evidence for the psychoanalytic corpus is now held to derive from the productions of patients in analysis, this warrant is remarkably weak.

2. In view of my account of the epistemic defects inherent in the psychoanalytic method, it would seem that the validation of Freud's cardinal hypotheses has to come, if at all, mainly from well-designed *extra*clinical studies, either epidemiologic or even experimental (see Masling 1983; Eysenck and Wilson 1973). But that appraisal is largely a task for the future.

3. Despite the poverty of the clinical credentials, it may perhaps still turn out that Freud's brilliant theoretical imagination was actually quite serendipitous for psychopathology or the understanding of some subclass of slips. Yet, while psychoanalysis may thus be said to be scientifically alive, it is currently hardly well, at least insofar as its clinical foundations are concerned. Nor is there a favorable verdict from such *experimental* findings as we had occasion to canvass in chapter 3 (pp. 188-189), chapter 4 (pp. 202-205), chapter 5 (pp. 217-219), and chapter 9 (p. 270).

11.

Coda on Exegetical Myth-making in Karl Popper's Indictment of the Clinical Validation of Psychoanalysis

Popper ignores that the inductivist legacy of Bacon and Mill gives no methodological sanction to the ubiquitous "confirmations" claimed by some of those Freudians and Adlerians whom he had encountered by 1919 (Grünbaum 1977: sec. 2; 1979a: 134). As he describes these partisans, they "saw confirming instances everywhere: the world was full of *verifications* of the theory. Whatever happened always confirmed it" (Popper 1962: 35). Indeed, Popper claims that, by *inductive* standards, both Freud's and Adler's psychology "were always confirmed" (p. 35). He then adduces this alleged universal confirmation of these theories, *come what may*, to indict both them and the inductivist methodology that purportedly countenances their credibility; for he characterizes them as follows: "It was precisely this fact—that they always fitted, that they were always confirmed—which in the eyes of their admirers constituted the strongest argument in favour of these theories. It began to dawn on me that this apparent strength was in fact their weakness" (p. 35). Having deemed it to be a "fact—that they always fitted, that they were always confirmed," he feels entitled to chide inductivism for probative laxity qua method of scientific theory validation, and to advocate its abandonment as a criterion of demarcation.

That Popper did regard inductivism as probatively promiscuous because he believed the ubiquitous confirmations claimed for psychoanalysis to be sanctioned by it is clear from his account of how he was led to enunciate his new criterion of demarcation in 1919-1920 (p. 36). In that account, he formulates the differences that he sees between his falsifiability criterion and its inductivist predecessor in a manifesto of seven theses, after explaining what considerations led him to them. The first of these theses was: "It is easy to obtain confirmations, or verifications, for nearly every theory—if we look for confirmations" (p. 36). But the most emphatic of the considerations that avowedly led him to the tenets espoused in his manifesto was the following: whereas Einstein's gravitational theory is falsifiable, Freudian and Adlerian theory are not, *because* "it was practically impossible to describe any human behavior that might not be claimed to be a verification of these theories" (p. 36).

It is ironic that Popper should have pointed to psychoanalytic theory as a prime illustration of his thesis that inductively countenanced confirmations can easily be found for nearly every theory, if we look for them. Being replete with a host of etiological and other causal hypotheses, Freud's theory is challenged by neo-Baconian inductivism to furnish a collation of positive instances from *both* experimental and control groups, if there are to be inductively *supportive* instances. But, as we recall from our discussion of the Rat Man case in chapter 8, if such instances do exist, the retrospective psychoanalytic method would find it extraordinarily difficult, if not impossible, to furnish them. Moreover, to this day, analysts have not furnished the kinds of instances from controlled inquiries that are *inductively required* to lend genuine support to Freud's specific etiologies of the neuroses. Hence, *it is precisely Freud's theory that furnishes poignant evidence that Popper has caricatured the inductivist tradition by his thesis of easy inductive confirmability of nearly every theory!*

Yet Popper concluded that *because* they are always confirmed, come what may, the two psychological theories "were simply non-testable, irrefutable" (p. 37). Then he hastens to add: "This does not mean that Freud and Adler were not seeing things correctly. . . . But it does mean that those 'clinical observations' which analysts naively believe confirm their theory cannot do this any more than the daily confirmations which astrologers find in their practice" (pp. 37-38). To this last sentence, Popper appends a very important footnote in which he gives his appraisal of the *clinical* confirmations claimed by analysts. Since I now need to scrutinize this appraisal thoroughly, let me cite it *in toto*:

"Clinical observations," like all other observations, are *interpretations in the light of theories* [reference omitted]; and for this reason alone they are apt to seem to support those theories in the light of which they are interpreted. But real support can be obtained only from observations undertaken as tests (by "attempted refutations"); and for this purpose *criteria of refutation* have to be laid down beforehand: it must be agreed which observable situations, if actually observed, mean that the theory is refuted. But what kind of clinical responses would refute to the satisfaction of the analyst not merely a particular analytic diagnosis but psycho-analysis itself? And have such criteria ever been discussed or agreed upon by analysts? Is there not, on the contrary, a whole family of analytic concepts, such as "ambivalence" (I do not suggest that there is no such thing as ambivalence), which would make it difficult, if not impossible, to agree upon such criteria? Moreover, how much headway has been made in investigating the question of the extent to which the (conscious or unconscious) expectations and theories held by the analyst influence the "clinical responses" of the patient? (To say nothing about the conscious attempts to influence the patient by proposing interpretations to him, etc.) Years ago I introduced the term *"Oedipus effect"* to describe the influence of a theory or expectation or prediction *upon the event which it predicts* or describes: it will be remembered that the causal chain leading to Oedipus' parricide was started by the oracle's prediction of this event. This is a characteristic and recurrent theme of such myths, but one which seems to have failed to attract the interest of the analysts, perhaps not accidentally. (The problem of confirmatory dreams suggested by the analyst is discussed by Freud, for example in *Gesammelte Schriften*, III, 1925, where he says on p. 314: "If anybody asserts that most of the dreams which can be utilized in an analysis... owe their origin to [the analyst's] suggestion, then no objection can be made from the point of view of analytic theory. Yet there is nothing in this fact," he surprisingly adds, "which would detract from the reliability of our results.") [P. 38, n. 3]

This series of charges prompts me to offer several corresponding comments:

1. Popper asks what sorts of clinical responses would count for Freud as adverse to his general theory. In chapter 1, section B, I itemized a number of episodes of significant theory modification that eloquently attest to Freud's responsiveness to *adverse* clinical and even extraclinical findings. I can now add the lesson that Freud learned from the failure of his Rat Man case to bear out his etiological retrodiction. Furthermore, we need only recall the very theme of Freud's 1937 paper "Constructions in Analysis," namely, just how he assures the intraclinical falsifiability of those clinical reconstructions that are avowedly the epistemic lifeblood of his whole theory! When Popper asks, "what kind of clinical responses would refute to the satisfaction of the analyst... psychoanalysis itself?" I ask in return: what is "psychoanalysis itself"? Is it the theory of unconscious motivations, or the psychoanalytic method of investigation? As to the former, Freud stressed its conjectural nature by espousing Poincaré's view that the postulates of the theory are evidentially undetermined free creations of the human mind (S.E. 1914, 14: 77, 117). As to the latter, he stated explicitly that when his seduction etiology of hysteria collapsed, he considered giving up the psychoanalytic method of investigation itself as unreliable (S.E. 1914, 14: 17; 1925, 20: 34).

The bulk of the pertinent textual evidence was available to Popper in the German edition of Freud's collected writings from which he cited in the passage above. Popper's deplorable neglect of this telling evidence has issued in exegetical mythmaking. Indeed, the myth has crept even into elementary textbooks, where it is untutoredly repeated as if it were a matter of well-documented exegesis (Abel 1976: 162). Though its burial is long overdue, I fear that it has become so widespread that its ravages may well continue.

2. Does the psychoanalytic employment of Eugen Bleuler's concept of ambivalence epitomize a family of theoretical notions that make for nonfalsifiability? Here, too, I can refer to chapter 1, section B, where I have argued that this complaint of Popper's boomerangs.

3. Popper characterizes the analyst's suggestive effect on the patient's clinical responses as being a matter of "the influence of a theory or expectation or prediction *upon the event which it predicts* or describes." Then Popper makes the incredibly uninformed and grossly unfair claim that such self-fulfillment of predictions via mechanisms akin to suggestion "seems to have failed to attract the interest of the analysts, perhaps not accidentally." He reports, to boot, that it was he who, years earlier, had recognized the epistemic danger of specious validation by spurious data when he coined the generic term "Oedipus effect." Thus, he chides the Freudians for not having been aware, as he was, of the relevant moral of the Oedipus legend.

As against this, I must point out to begin with that as early as 1888—fourteen years before Popper was even born—Freud gave a sophisticated, incisive account of several kinds of suggestion and of their effects (S.E. 1888, 1: 75-85). In that year, he published a long preface to his German translation of H. Bernheim's book on the therapeutic use of suggestion. There Freud called attention to the *epistemic havoc* that may be wrought in psychiatry by the doctor's suggestive intervention, if one fails to allow for the potential suggestive production of *spurious* symptoms that are *not* characteristic of the syndrome under investigation. Bernheim charged precisely such a failure against J.-M. Charcot's report of a symptom complex called "major hypnotism." Charcot contended that unlike normal hypnotized subjects, *hysterical* patients exhibit *three* stages of hypnosis, each of which is distinguished by highly remarkable characteristic *physical* symptoms. But, as Freud explains, if the symptomatology of hysteria under hypnosis were first *generated* by mere suggestion as charged, then those students of hysteria who thought they were investigating an objective syndrome would have been duped as follows:

All the observations made at the Salpêtrière are worthless; indeed, they become errors in observation. The hypnosis of hysterical patients would have no characteristics of its own. . . . We should not learn from the study of major hypnotism what alterations in excitability succeed one another in the nervous system of hysterical patients in response to certain kinds of intervention; we should merely learn what intentions Charcot suggested (in a manner of which he himself was unconscious) to the subjects of his experiments—a thing entirely irrelevant to our understanding alike of hypnosis and of hysteria.

It is easy to see the further implications of this view and what a convenient explanation it can promise of the symptomatology of hysteria in general. If suggestion by the physician has falsified the phenomena of hysterical hypnosis, it is quite possible that it may also have interfered with the observation of the rest of hysterical symptomatology: it may have laid down laws governing hysterical attacks, paralyses, contractures, etc., which are only connected with the neurosis through suggestion and which consequently lose their validity as soon as another physician in another place makes an examination of hysterical patients.

Here we should have a splendid example of how neglect of the psychical factor of suggestion has misled a great observer into the artificial and false creation of a clinical type as a result of the capriciousness and easy malleability of a neurosis. [S.E. 1888, 1: 77-78]

As Freud notes, Bernheim's stricture of spuriousness against Charcot's major hypnotism will have the salutary effect that "in every future investigation of hysteria and hypnotism the need for excluding the element of suggestion will be more consciously kept in view" (p. 78). But Freud relates that, in this case, the bogus character of the symptomatology had been ruled out by telling evidence that Charcot had gathered; for this evidence shows that "the principal points of the symptomatology of hysteria are safe from the suspicion of having originated from suggestion by a physician" (p. 79).

Thus, even as early as 1888, Freud patently had a sophisticated grasp of the *epistemic* problem of spurious data as posed by the patient's susceptibility to the doctor's influence. Thereafter, in 1901, Freud broke with his longtime close friend Wilhelm Fliess when the latter objected that the psychoanalytic technique of free association was vitiated by its inability to prevent the production of specious findings. And, as we saw, Freud's 1917 Tally Argument was a brilliant effort to come to grips with the full dimensions of the challenge of epistemic contamination by adulterated clinical responses. Freud had remained alert to this challenge in the interim by addressing it in his 1909 case history of Little Hans. Thus, by the time Popper came on the philosophic scene in 1919, Freud's writings had long since resoundingly undercut Popper's accusation that analysts are oblivious to the contamination problem. Thereafter, the writings of such other distinguished analysts as Glover (1931) have continued to undermine it.

Popper compounds his exegetical legerdemain by the slur that the purported obliviousness of the Freudians occurred "perhaps not accidentally," thereby intimating that they are being intellectually evasive if not emotionally unable to face the challenge.

To *justify* a disparaging verdict on Freud's handling of the suggestibility problem, Popper ought to have impugned the *empirical* credentials of the NCT premise in the Tally Argument, as I have done here. What *is* fair to say, I claim, is the following: Freud unswervingly, brilliantly, but *unsuccessfully tackled* the contamination issue in his "Analytic Therapy" paper, though he failed pathetically for *empirical* reasons rather than for want of methodological sophistication.

4. Popper comments on Freud's explanation of why suggestively induced dream content does not spuriously confirm analytic interpretations. Very unfortunately, Popper's citation from Freud borders on a sheer travesty. Popper cites only an excerpt from the pertinent Freudian passage in his own translation from the German text in Freud's *Gesammelte Schriften* (1925, vol. 3: 134). The full passage is given in S.E. 1923, 19: 117. And in chapter 5, we saw that, in this context as well, Freud explicitly enlists his *Tally Argument* to deny spurious confirmation.

Upon comparing Popper's excerpt to this original German wording or to S.E. 1923, 19: 117, it becomes evident that Popper simply truncated Freud's crucial sentence in a highly misleading way *without* any indication of this omission. Freud was responding to the criticism implied by the claim that most of the dreams that are interpreted in the course of an analysis are compliant dreams whose occurrence was induced by the analyst's expectation, and his response was as follows: "Then I only need to refer to the discussion in my 'Introductory Lectures [#28],' where the relation between transference and suggestion is dealt with, and it is shown how little the recognition of the effect of suggestion in our sense detracts from the reliability of our results." Amid expressing surprise, Popper purports to be rendering this sentence in the following words: "Yet there is nothing in this fact [of compliant dreams] which would detract from the reliability of our results."

Thus, in just the initial portion of the sentence, which Popper mysteriously omits, Freud refers to his Tally Argument to contend that the role of suggestion in compliant dreams and analysis generally is *not* epistemically confounding after all. Having given no hint that Freud had *argued* for this conclusion, albeit unsuccessfully, Popper misrepresents him as having offered a mere *ipse dixit.* Thereupon, Popper declares himself puzzled by Freud's allegedly unreasoned assertion. Yet it would strain charity to attribute this weighty omission to the constraints imposed on Popper by writing within the confines of a footnote.

Since Freud's Tally Argument failed and no substitute for it is in sight, Popper is quite right that contamination by suggestion does undermine the probative value of clinical data. But I have argued that insofar as his case against the clinical confirmability of psychoanalysis *is* sound, it does *not* redound to the discredit of inductivism qua method of scientific theory validation. And I have documented that Freud had carefully addressed—albeit unsuccessfully—all of Popper's arguments against clinical validation well before Popper appeared on the philosophic scene.

Bibliography

Abel, R. *Man Is the Measure*. New York: Free Press, 1976.

Baier, K. *The Moral Point of View*. Ithaca, N.Y.: Cornell University Press, 1958.

Basch, M. *Doing Psychotherapy*. New York: Basic Books, 1980.

Bernstein, A. E., and Warner, G. M. *An Introduction to Contemporary Psychoanalysis*. New York: Jason Aronson, 1981.

Bird, B. "Notes on Transference: Universal Phenomenon and Hardest Part of Analysis." *Journal of the American Psychoanalytic Association* 20 (1972):267-301.

Blanck, G., and Blanck, R. *Ego Psychology: Theory and Practice*. New York: Columbia University Press, 1974.

Blight, J. G. "Must Psychoanalysis Retreat to Hermeneutics?" *Psychoanalysis and Contemporary Thought* 4 (1981):147-205.

Brenner, C. "Psychoanalysis and Science." *Journal of the American Psychoanalytic Association* 16 (1968):675-696.

———. "Psychoanalysis: Philosophy or Science." In *Psychoanalysis and Philosophy*, edited by C. Hanley and M. Lazerowitz. New York: International Universities Press, 1970.

———. *The Mind in Conflict*. New York: International Universities Press, 1982.

Brown, D. "Tchaikovsky." In *The New Grove's Dictionary of Music and Musicians*, vol. 18, edited by Stanley Sadie, pp. 626-628. London: Macmillan, 1980.

Campbell, L. A. "The Role of Suggestion in the Psychoanalytic Therapies." *International Journal of Psychoanalytic Psychotherapy* 7 (1978):1-22.

Clark, R. *Freud: The Man and the Cause*. New York: Random House, 1980.

Colby, K. M. "On the Disagreement Between Freud and Adler," *American Imago* 8 (1951):229-238.

Considine, D. M. *Van Nostrand's Scientific Encyclopedia*. 5th ed. New York: Van Nostrand Reinhold Co., 1976.

Cooper, A. M., and Michels, R. "An Era of Growth." In *Controversy in Psychiatry*, edited by J. P. Brady and H. K. H. Brodie. Philadelphia: W. B. Saunders, 1978.

Dorian, F. "Tchaikovsky's Death a Suicide! A Biographical Correction." *Pittsburgh Symphony Orchestra Program Magazine* (October 23, 1981): 224-227.

Duhem, P. *The Aim and Structure of Physical Theory*, translated by P. P. Wiener. Princeton: Princeton University Press, 1954.

Dywan, J., and Bowers, K. "The Use of Hypnosis to Enhance Recall." *Science* 222 (October 14, 1983):184-185.

Eagle, M. "Validation of Motivational Formulations, Acknowledgment as a Criterion." *Psychoanalysis and Contemporary Science* 2 (1973):265-275.

———. "A Critical Examination of Motivational Explanation in Psychoanalysis." *Psychoanalysis and Contemporary Thought* 3 (1980):329-380. This article was preprinted from *Mind and Medicine: Explanation and Evaluation in Psychiatry and the Biomedical Sciences*, edited by L. Laudan, Pittsburgh Series in the Philosophy and History of Science, vol. 8. Berkeley, Los Angeles, London: University of California Press, 1983.

———. "Symposium on G. S. Klein's *Psychoanalytic Theory*." *The Psychoanalytic Review* 67 (1980*a*):179-194.

———. "The Epistemological Status of Recent Developments in Psychoanalytic Theory." In *Physics, Philosophy, and Psychoanalysis*, edited by R. S. Cohen and L. Laudan, pp. 31-55. Dordrecht and Boston: D. Reidel, 1983*a*.

———. "Psychoanalysis and Modern Psychodynamic Theories." In *Personality and the Behavior Disorders*. Rev. ed., edited by N. S. Endler and J. McV. Hunt. New York: Wiley, forthcoming (1984).

Edelson, M. "Is Testing Psychoanalytic Hypotheses in the Psychoanalytic Situation Really Impossible?" *The Psychoanalytic Study of the Child* 38 (1983):61-109.

Efron, A. "Magnetic Hysteresis." In *The Harper Encyclopedia of Science*. Rev. ed., edited by J. R. Newman. New York: Harper & Row, 1967.

Eissler, K. R. "Irreverent Remarks About the Present and the Future of Psychoanalysis." *International Journal of Psycho-Analysis* 50 (1969):461-471.

———. "Comments on Penis Envy and Orgasm in Women." *Psychoanalytic Study of the Child* 32 (1977):29-83.

Ellenberger, H. F. *The Discovery of the Unconscious*. New York: Basic Books, 1970.

Ellis, A. W. "On the Freudian Theory of Speech Errors." In *Errors in Linguistic Performance: Slips of the Tongue, Ear, Pen, and Hand*, edited by V. A. Fromkin, pp. 123-131. New York: Academic Press, 1980.

Erdelyi, M. H., and Goldberg, B. "Let's Not Sweep Repression Under the Rug: Toward a Cognitive Psychology of Repression." In *Functional Disorders of Memory*, edited by J. F. Kihlstrom and F. J. Evans. Hillsdale, N.J.: Lawrence Erlbaum Associates, 1979.

Erikson, E. H. "The Dream Specimen of Psychoanalysis." *Journal of the American Psychoanalytic Association* 2 (1954):5-56.

Erwin, E. *Behavior Therapy*. New York: Cambridge University Press, 1978.

Eysenck, H. *Uses and Abuses of Psychology*. Baltimore: Penguin, 1963.

Eysenck, H., and Wilson, G. C. *The Experimental Study of Freudian Theories*. London: Methuen, 1973.

Fancher, R. E. *Psychoanalytic Psychology*. New York: Norton, 1973.

Fenichel, O. *The Psychoanalytic Theory of Neurosis*. New York: Norton, 1945.

Ferguson, M. "Progress and Theory Change: The Two Analyses of Mr. Z." *Annual of Psychoanalysis* 9 (1981):133-160.

Fisher, C. "Experimental and Clinical Approaches to the Mind-Body Problem Through Recent Research in Sleep and Dreaming." In *Psychopharmacology and Psychotherapy: Synthesis or Antithesis?*, edited by N. Rosenzweig and H. Griscom, pp. 61-99. New York: Human Sciences Press, 1978.

Fisher, S. "The Scientific Vitality of Freud's Theories." *Contemporary Psychology* 27 (1982):680-681.

Fisher, S., and Greenberg, R. P. *The Scientific Credibility of Freud's Theory and Therapy*. New York: Basic Books, 1977.

Flax, J. "Psychoanalysis and the Philosophy of Science: Critique or Resistance?" *Journal of Philosophy* 78 (1981):561-569.

Frank, A., and Trunnell, E. E. "Conscious Dream Synthesis as a Method of Learning about Dreaming: A Pedagogic Experiment." *Psychoanalytic Quarterly* 47 (1978):103-112.

Frank, G. H. "The Role of the Family in the Development of Psychopathology." *Psychological Bulletin* 64 (1965):191-205.

Freud, S. *Gesammelte Schriften*. Leipzig: Internationaler Psychoanalytischer Verlag, 1925.

———. *The Origins of Psychoanalysis*. New York: Basic Books, 1954.

———. *Standard Edition of the Complete Psychological Works of Sigmund Freud*, translated by J. Strachey et al. London: Hogarth Press, 1953–1974.

Fromkin, V. A., ed. *Errors in Linguistic Performance: Slips of the Tongue, Ear, Pen, and Hand*. New York: Academic Press, 1980.

Fromm, E. *The Crisis of Psychoanalysis*. Greenwich, Conn.: Fawcett Publications, 1970.

Gadamer, H. G. *Truth and Method*. New York: Seabury Press, 1975.

Galton, F. "Statistical Inquiries into the Efficacy of Prayers." *The Fortnightly Review* 12 (New Series, August 1, 1872):125-135.

Gauld, A., and Shotter, J. *Human Action and Psychological Investigation*. London: Routledge & Kegan Paul, 1977.

Gedo, J. E. "Reflections on Some Current Controversies in Psychoanalysis." *Journal of the American Psychoanalytic Association* 28 (1980):363-383.

Giere, R. N. *Understanding Scientific Reasoning*. New York: Holt, Rinehart & Winston, 1979.

Gill, M. M. "Metapsychology Is Not Psychology." In *Psychology Versus Metapsychology: Psychoanalytic Essays in Memory of George S. Klein*, edited by M. M. Gill and P. S. Holzman, pp. 71-105. New York: International Universities Press, 1976. (This volume is Monograph #36 of *Psychological Issues*, vol. 9, no. 4.

——— . "The Analysis of the Transference: Discourse on the Theory of Therapy." In *Psychoanalytic Explorations of Technique*, edited by H. P. Blum, pp. 263-288. New York: International Universities Press, 1980.

Glover, E. "The Therapeutic Effect of Inexact Interpretation." *International Journal of Psychoanalysis* 12 (1931):397-411.

Glymour, C. "Freud, Kepler and the Clinical Evidence." In *Freud*, edited by R. Wollheim, pp. 285-304. New York: Anchor Books, 1974. An *Afterword* appears in a second edition entitled *Philosophical Essays on Freud*, edited by R. Wollheim and J. Hopkins. New York: Cambridge University Press, 1982.

——— . *Theory and Evidence*. Princeton, N.J.: Princeton University Press, 1980.

——— . "The Theory of Your Dreams." In *Physics, Philosophy, and Psychoanalysis*, edited by R. S. Cohen and L. Laudan, pp. 57-71. Dordrecht and Boston: D. Reidel, 1983.

Goldberg, A., ed. *The Psychology of the Self: A Casebook*. New York: International Universities Press, 1978.

Greenacre, P. "Reconstruction: Its Nature and Therapeutic Value." *Journal of the American Psychoanalytic Association* 29 (1981):27-46.

Grinstein, A. *Sigmund Freud's Dreams*, 2nd ed. New York: International Universities Press, 1980.

Grünbaum, A. *Philosophical Problems of Space and Time*. 2nd enlarged ed. Dordrecht and Boston: D. Reidel, 1974.

——— . "Is Falsifiability the Touchstone of Scientific Rationality? Karl Popper Versus Inductivism." In *Essays in Memory of Imre Lakatos*. Boston Studies in the Philosophy of Science, vol. 38, edited by R. S. Cohen, P. K. Feyerabend, and M. W. Wartofsky, pp. 213-252. Dordrecht and Boston: D. Reidel, 1976.

——— . "How Scientific is Psychoanalysis?" In *Science and Psychotherapy*, edited by R. Stern, L. Horowitz, and J. Lynes, pp. 219-254. New York: Haven Press, 1977.

——— . "Is Freudian Psychoanalytic Theory Pseudo-Scientific by Karl Popper's Criterion of Demarcation?" *American Philosophical Quarterly* 16 (1979*a*): 131-141.

——— . "Epistemological Liabilities of the Clinical Appraisal of Psychoanalytic Theory." *Psychoanalysis and Contemporary Thought* 2 (1979*b*):451-526.

——— . "Epistemological Liabilities of the Clinical Appraisal of Psychoanalytic Theory." *Noûs* 14 (1980):307-385. (This is an enlarged version of Grünbaum 1979*b*.)

——— . "The Placebo Concept." *Behaviour Research and Therapy* 19 (1981):157-167.

——— . "Is Object-Relations Theory Better Founded than Orthodox Psychoanalysis? A Reply to Jane Flax." *Journal of Philosophy* 80 (1983):46-51.

——— . "Freud's Theory: The Perspective of a Philosopher of Science." 1982 Presidential Address to the American Philosophical Association (Eastern Division). *Proceedings and Addresses of the American Philosophical Association* 57 (1983*a*): 5-31.

——— . "Explication and Implications of the Placebo Concept." In *Rationality in Science and Politics*, pp. 131-157, edited by G. Andersson. Dordrecht and

Boston: D. Reidel, 1983*b*. To be reprinted in *Placebo: Clinical Phenomena and New Insights*, edited by L. White, B. Tursky, and G. F. Schwartz. New York: The Gilford Press, 1983*b*, forthcoming.

Habermas, J. *Zur Logik der Sozialwissenschaften*. Frankfurt: Suhrkamp Verlag, 1970.

———. *Knowledge and Human Interests*, translated by J. J. Shapiro. Boston: Beacon Press, 1971.

———. *Theory and Practice*. Boston: Beacon Press, 1973.

Hersen, M., and Barlow, D. H. *Single-Case Experimental Designs*. New York: Pergamon Press, 1976.

Hobson, J. A., and McCarley, R. W. "The Brain as a Dream State Generator: An Activation-Synthesis Hypothesis of the Dream Process." *American Journal of Psychiatry* 134:12 (1977): 1335-1348.

Holt, R. C. "A Review of Some of Freud's Biological Assumptions and Their Influence on His Theories." In *Psychoanalysis and Current Biological Thought*, pp. 93-124, edited by N. S. Greenfield and W. C. Lewis. Madison: University of Wisconsin Press, 1965.

———. "Drive or Wish? A Reconsideration of the Psychoanalytic Theory of Motivation." In *Psychology Versus Metapsychology: Psychoanalytic Essays in Memory of George S. Klein*, pp. 158-197, edited by M. M. Gill and P. S. Holzman. New York: International Universities Press, 1976. (This volume is Monograph #36 of *Psychological Issues*, vol. 9, no. 4.)

———. "The Death and Transfiguration of Metapsychology." *International Review of Psycho-Analysis* 8 (1981):129-143.

———. "The Manifest and Latent Meanings of Metapsychology." *The Annual of Psychoanalysis* 10 (1982):233-255.

Holzman, P. S. "Psychoanalysis: Is the Therapy Destroying the Science?" *Journal of the American Psychoanalytic Association*, forthcoming (1984).

Hook, S., ed. *Psychoanalysis, Scientific Method and Philosophy*. New York: New York University Press, 1959.

Jahoda, M. *Freud and the Dilemmas of Psychology*. London: Hogarth Press, 1977.

Jaspers, K. *Allgemeine Psychopathologie*. 9th ed. New York: Springer Verlag, 1973.

Jones, E. "The Theory of Symbolism." Chapter 6 in his *Papers on Psycho-Analysis*. London: Baillière, Tindall & Co., 1938.

———. *The Life and Work of Sigmund Freud*, vol. 2. New York: Basic Books, 1955.

———. *The Life and Work of Sigmund Freud*, vol. 3. New York: Basic Books, 1957.

———. *Editorial Preface to S. Freud, Collected Papers*, vol. 1. New York: Basic Books, 1959.

Kanzer, M. "Two Prevalent Misconceptions About Freud's Project." *The Annual of Psychoanalysis* 1 (1973): 83-103.

Kaplan, A. H. "From Discovery to Validation: A Basic Challenge to Psychoanalysis." *Journal of the American Psychoanalytic Association* 29 (1981):3-26.

Kaufmann, W. *Discovering the Mind*, vol. 3, *Freud Versus Adler and Jung*. New York: McGraw-Hill, 1980.

Kazdin, A. "Drawing Valid Inferences from Case Studies." *Journal of Consulting and Clinical Psychology* 49 (1981):183-192.

————. "Single-Case Experimental Designs." In *Handbook of Research Methods in Clinical Psychology*, edited by P. C. Kendall and J. N. Butcher. New York: Wiley, forthcoming.

Kazdin, A. and Hersen, M. "The Current Status of Behavior Therapy." *Behavior Modification* 4 (1980): 283–302.

Kerlinger, F. N. *Behavioral Research*. New York: Holt, Rinehart & Winston, 1979.

Klein, G. S. *Psychoanalytic Theory*. New York: International Universities Press, 1976.

Kline, P. *Fact and Fantasy in Freudian Theory*. 2d ed. London: Methuen, 1981.

Kohut, H. "Introspection, Empathy, and Psychoanalysis." *Journal of the American Psychoanalytic Association* 7 (1959):459-483.

Labruzza, A. L. "The Activation-Synthesis Hypothesis of Dreams: A Theoretical Note." *American Journal of Psychiatry* 135:12 (1978): 1536-1538.

Laplanche, J., and Pontalis, J. B. *The Language of Psychoanalysis*. New York: Norton, 1973.

Leo, J. "Cradle-to-Grave Intimacy." *Time* (September 7, 1981):69.

Levine, F. J. "On the Clinical Application of Heinz Kohut's Psychology of the Self: Comments on Some Recently Published Case Studies." *Journal of the Philadelphia Association for Psychoanalysis* 6 (1979):1-19.

Loftus, E. *Memory*. Reading, Mass.: Addison-Wesley, 1980.

Luborsky, L., and Spence, D. P. "Quantitative Research on Psychoanalytic Therapy." In *Handbook of Psychotherapy and Behavior Change*, edited by S. L. Garfield and A. E. Bergin, 2d ed. New York: Wiley, 1978.

MacKinnon, D. W., and Dukes, W. F. "Repression." In *Psychology in the Making*, edited by L. Postman. New York: Knopf, 1964.

Macmillan, M. B. "Freud's Expectations and the Childhood Seduction Theory." *Australian Journal of Psychology* 29 (1977): 223-236.

Malan, D. H. *Toward the Validation of Dynamic Psychotherapy*. New York: Plenum, 1976.

Marmor, J. "Psychoanalytic Therapy as an Educational Process." In *Psychoanalytic Education*. Science and Psychoanalysis Series, edited by J. Masserman, vol. 5, pp. 286-299. New York: Grune and Stratton, 1962.

————. "New Directions in Psychoanalytic Theory and Therapy." In *Modern Psychoanalysis*, edited by J. Marmor, pp. 3-15. New York: Basic Books, 1968.

————. "Limitations of Free Association." *Archives of General Psychiatry* 22 (1970):160-165.

————. *Psychiatry in Transition, Selected Papers of Judd Marmor*. New York: Brunner/Mazel, 1974.

Martin, M. *Social Science and Philosophical Analysis*. Washington, D.C.: University Press of America, 1978.

Masling, J., ed. *Empirical Studies of Psychoanalytical Theories*. Vol. 1. Hillsdale, N.J.: The Analytic Press, 1983.

Masson, J. M. *The Assault on Truth*. New York: Farrar, Straus & Giroux, 1984.

Maxwell, G., and Maxwell, M. L. "In the Beginning: The Word or the Deed." A review of Ricoeur's *Freud and Philosophy*. *Contemporary Psychology* 17 (1972):519-522.

McCarley, R. W., and Hobson, J. A. "The Neurobiological Origins of Psychoanalytic Dream Theory." *American Journal of Psychiatry* 134:11 (1977):1211-1221.

McCarthy, T. *The Critical Theory of Jürgen Habermas*. Cambridge: MIT Press, 1978.

————. "Translator's Introduction." In J. Habermas's *Communication and the Evolution of Society*. Boston: Beacon Press, 1979.

Meissner, W. W. *The Paranoid Process*. New York: Jason Aronson, 1978.

Meyers, S. J. "The Bipolar Self." Reporter, panel report, *Journal of the American Psychoanalytic Association* 29 (1981):143-159.

Möller, H. J. *Methodische Grundprobleme der Psychiatrie*. Stuttgart: W. Kohlhammer Verlag, 1976.

————. *Psychoanalyse—Erklärende Wissenschaft oder Deutungskunst?* Munich: W. Fink Verlag, 1978.

Moore, M. M. "The Nature of Psychoanalytic Explanation." *Psychoanalysis and Contemporary Thought* 3 (1980):459-543. This is an earlier version of Moore (1983).

————. "The Nature of Psychoanalytic Explanation." In *Mind and Medicine: Explanation and Evaluation in Psychiatry and the Biomedical Sciences*, edited by L. Laudan. Pittsburgh Series in the Philosophy and History of Science, vol. 8. Berkeley, Los Angeles, London: University of California Press, 1983.

Morse, S. J. "Failed Explanations and Criminal Responsibility: Experts and the Unconscious." *Virginia Law Review* 68 (1982):971-1084.

————. *The Jurisprudence of Craziness*. New York: Oxford University Press, forthcoming.

Motley, M. T. "Verification of 'Freudian Slips' and Semantic Prearticulatory Editing via Laboratory-Induced Spoonerisms." In *Errors in Linguistic Performance: Slips of the Tongue, Ear, Pen, and Hand*, edited by V. A. Fromkin, pp. 133-147. New York: Academic Press, 1980.

Munby, M., and Johnston, D. W. "Agoraphobia: The Long-Term Follow-up of Behavioural Treatment." *British Journal of Psychiatry* 137 (1980):418-427.

Ofstad, H. "Recent Work on the Free-Will Problem." In *Recent Work in Philosophy*, edited by K. G. Lucey and T. R. Machan, chap. 2, pp. 39–84. Totowa, New Jersey: Rowman and Allanheld, 1983.

Ornstein, P. H., ed. *The Search for the Self: Selected Writings of Heinz Kohut: 1950-1978*. 2 vols. New York: International Universities Press, 1978.

Page, L., and Adams, N. I. *Electrodynamics*. New York: Van Nostrand, 1940.

Perrez, M. *Ist die Psychoanalyse eine Wissenschaft?*, 2nd revised edition. Bern: Verlag Hans Huber, 1979.

Peterfreund, E. *The Process of Psychoanalytic Therapy*. Hillsdale: The Analytic Press, 1983.

Popper, K. R. *Conjectures and Refutations*. New York: Basic Books, 1962.

————. "Replies to My Critics." In *The Philosophy of Karl Popper*, edited by P. A. Schilpp, Book 2. LaSalle, Ill.: Open Court, 1974.

Pribram, K. H., and Gill, M. M. *Freud's 'Project' Re-Assessed*. New York: Basic Books, 1976.

Prioleau, L., Murdock, M., and Brody, N. "An Analysis of Psychotherapy Versus Placebo." *The Behavioral and Brain Sciences* 6 (1983):275-285.

Rachman, S. J., and Wilson, G. T. *The Effects of Psychological Therapy*. 2d enlarged ed. New York: Pergamon Press, 1980.

Rapaport, D. *The Collected Papers of David Rapaport*, edited by Merton M. Gill. New York: Basic Books, 1967.

Rhoads, J. M., and Feather, B. W. "Application of Psychodynamics to Behavior Therapy." *American Journal of Psychiatry* 131 (1974):17-20.

Ricoeur, P. *Freud and Philosophy*. New Haven: Yale University Press, 1970.

————. *The Conflict of Interpretations*, edited by Don Ihde. Evanston, Ill.: Northwestern University Press, 1974.

————. *Hermeneutics and the Human Sciences*. Translated by J. B. Thompson. New York: Cambridge University Press, 1981.

Robbins, M. "Current Controversy in Object Relations Theory as Outgrowth of a Schism Between Klein and Fairbairn." *International Journal of Psychoanalysis* 61 (1980):477-492.

Robinson, A. L. "Nuclear Evidence That Neutrinos Have Mass." *Science* 208 (1980):697.

Rosenthal, R. *Experimenter Effects in Behavioral Research*. Enlarged ed. New York: Irvington Publishers, 1976.

Rosenzweig, S. "An Experimental Study of Memory in Relation to the Theory of Repression." *British Journal of Psychology* 24 (1934):247-265.

————. "The Experimental Study of Psychoanalytic Concepts." *Character and Personality* 6 (1937):61-71.

Rubinstein, B. B. "On the Role of Classificatory Processes in Mental Functioning: Aspects of a Psychoanalytic Theoretical Model." *Psychoanalysis and Contemporary Science* 3 (1975):101-185.

————. "On the Possibility of a Strictly Clinical Psychoanalytic Theory: An Essay in the Philosophy of Psychoanalysis." In *Psychology Versus Metapsychology: Psychoanalytic Essays in Memory of George S. Klein*, pp. 229-264, edited by M. M. Gill and P. S. Holzman. New York: International Universities Press, 1976. (This volume is Monograph #36 of *Psychological Issues*, vol. 9, No. 4.)

————. "Freud's Early Theories of Hysteria." In *Physics, Philosophy and Psychoanalysis*, edited by R. S. Cohen and L. Laudan, pp. 169-190. Dordrecht and Boston: D. Reidel, 1983.

Russell, B. *An Outline of Philosophy*. Cleveland, Ohio: Meridian Books, 1960.

Sand, R. "Confirmation in the Dora Case." *International Review of Psycho-Analysis* 10 (1983): 333–357.

Schafer, R. *A New Language for Psychoanalysis*. New Haven: Yale University Press, 1976.

Schaffner, K. F. "Clinical Trials: The Validation of Theory and Therapy." In *Physics, Philosophy, and Psychoanalysis*, edited by R. S. Cohen and L. Laudan, pp. 191-208. Dordrecht and Boston: D. Reidel, 1983.

Schöpf, A. *Sigmund Freud*. Munich: C. H. Beck Verlag, 1982.

S.E. *See* Freud, S., *Standard Edition* . . .

Sellars, W. "Actions and Events." *Noûs* 7 (1973):179-202.

Shapiro, A. K., and Morris, L. A. "The Placebo Effect in Medical and Psychological Therapies." In *Handbook of Psychotherapy and Behavior Change*, 2d. ed. Edited by S. L. Garfield and A. E. Bergin. New York: Wiley, 1978.

Sherwood, M. *The Logic of Explanation in Psychoanalysis*. New York: Academic Press, 1969.

Shope, R. K. "Freud on Conscious and Unconscious Intentions." *Inquiry* 13 (1970):149-159.

———. "Freud's Concepts of Meaning." *Psychoanalysis and Contemporary Science* 2 (1973):276-303.

———. "The Significance of Freud for Modern Philosophy of Mind." To appear in *Contemporary Philosophy*, vol. 4, *Philosophy of Mind*, edited by G. Floistad. Boston: Nijhoff, in press.

Slater, E., and Roth, M. *Clinical Psychiatry*, 3d ed. London: Baillière Tindall, 1977.

Smith, M. L., Glass, G. V., and Miller, T. I. *The Benefits of Psychotherapy*. Baltimore: Johns Hopkins University Press, 1980.

Stannard, D. E. *Shrinking History*. New York: Oxford University Press, 1980.

Steele, R. S. "Psychoanalysis and Hermeneutics." *International Review of Psychoanalysis* 6, (1979): 389-411.

Strupp, H. H., Hadley, S. W., and Gomes-Schwartz, B. *Psychotherapy for Better or Worse: The Problem of Negative Effects*. New York: Jason Aronson, 1977.

Sulloway, F. J. *Freud, Biologist of the Mind*. New York: Basic Books, 1979.

Sutherland, N. S. *Breakdown*. New York: Stein and Day, 1977.

Swales, P. J. "Freud, Minna Bernays, and the Conquest of Rome." *The New American Review* (Spring/Summer 1982): 1–22.

Thomä, H. "Psychoanalyse und Suggestion." *Zeitschrift für Psychosomatische Medizin und Psychoanalyse* 23 (1977):35-56.

Thomä, H., and Kächele, H. "Wissenschaftstheoretische und methodologische Probleme der klinisch-psychoanalytischen Forschung." *Psyche* 27 (1973):Part I: 205-236, Part II: 309-355. A sometimes defective English translation appeared under the title "Problems of Metascience and Methodology in Clinical Psychoanalytic Research." *The Annual of Psychoanalysis* 3 (1975):49-119.

Timpanaro, S. *The Freudian Slip*. Translated by Kate Soper. Atlantic Highlands, N.J.: Humanities Press, 1976.

Toulmin, S. "The Logical Status of Psycho-Analysis." In *Philosophy and Analysis*, pp. 132-139, edited by M. MacDonald. New York: Philosophical Library, 1954. Reprinted from *Analysis* 9 (1948).

Vogel, G. W. "An Alternative View of the Neurobiology of Dreaming." *American Journal of Psychiatry* 135:12 (1978):1531-1535.

von Eckardt, B. "On Evaluating the Scientific Status of Psychoanalysis." *Journal of Philosophy* 78 (1981):570-572.

———. "The Scientific Status of Psychoanalysis." In *Introducing Psychoanalytic Theory*, edited by S. L. Gilman. New York: Brunner/Mazel, 1982.

———. "Adolf Grünbaum and Psychoanalytic Epistemology." In *Beyond Freud: A Study of Modern Psychoanalytic Theorists*, edited by J. Reppen. Hillsdale: The Analytic Press, 1984 (in press).

von Wittgenstein, L. *Lectures and Conversations on Aesthetics, Psychology and Religious Belief*. Berkeley: University of California Press, 1967.

von Wright, G. H. *Explanation and Understanding*. Ithaca, N.Y.: Cornell University Press, 1977.

Waelder, R. Review of *Psychoanalysis, Scientific Method and Philosophy*, edited by S. Hook. *Journal of the American Psychoanalytic Association* 10 (1962):617-637.

Wallerstein, R. S. "Psychoanalysis as a Science: Its Present Status and Its Future Tasks." In *Psychology versus Metapsychology: Psychoanalytic Essays in Memory of George S. Klein*, edited by M. M. Gill and P. S. Holzman. New York: International Universities Press, 1976. (This volume is Monograph #36 of *Psychological Issues*, vol. 9, no. 4.)

Watkins, J. W. N. "Corroboration and the Problem of Content-Comparison." In *Progress and Rationality in Science*. Boston Studies in the Philosophy of Science, edited by G. Radnitzky and G. Andersson, vol. 58, Dordrecht and Boston: D. Reidel, 1978.

Weitzman, B. "Behavior Therapy and Psychotherapy." *Psychological Review* 74 (1967):300-317.

Winokur, G. "Heredity in the Affective Disorders." In *Depression and Human Existence*, edited by E. J. Anthony and Teresa Benedek. Boston: Little, Brown, 1975.

Wittgenstein 1967. *See* von Wittgenstein, L.

Wolpe, J. "Behavior Therapy Versus Psychoanalysis." *American Psychologist* 36 (1981):159-164.

Indexes

Name Index

Abel, Reuben, 282
Adams, N. I., 17, 18
Adler, Alfred, 103, 107, 108, 114-116, 279, 280
Andréas-Salomé, Lou, 207

Bacon, Francis, 47, 104, 105, 254, 279
Baier, Kurt, 69, 70
Barley, Blake, 258
Barlow, D. H., 259
Basch, Michael, 134, 148, 246
Beard, Charles, 118
Bernheim, Hyppolite, 156, 157, 282, 283
Bernstein, A. E., 214
Bird, Brian, 145
Blanck, G. and R., 212-214
Bleuler, Eugen, 282
Blight, James G., 15
Bowers, K., 132
Brenner, Charles, 52, 94, 100, 189, 261
Breuer, Josef, 7, 10, 13, 39, 45, 62, 74, 93, 117, 119, 123, 132, 146, 148-151, 153, 156, 158, 163, 164, 167, 170, 175, 177-185, 193, 221, 229, 231, 234
Brody, N., 161
Brown, David, 38

Brücke, Ernst Wilhelm, 6, 84, 85, 89
Bryant, Anita, 39

Campbell, Linn A., 133, 134
Charcot, Jean-Martin, 131, 282, 283
Clark, R., 124
Colby, K. M., 116
Considine, D. M., 19
Cooper A. M., 100

Dilthey, Wilhelm, 91, 93
Dorian, Frederick, 39
Duhem, Pierre, 35, 36, 41, 99
Dukes, W. F., 6, 101, 102
Dywan, J., 132

Eagle, Morris, 27-29, 77, 81, 83, 91, 180, 181, 246, 247
Edelson, Marshall, 94
Efron, Alexander, 19
Einstein, Albert, 99, 280
Eisenberg, Leon, 255
Eissler, Kurt R., 34, 185, 214, 269-271
Ellenberger, H. F., 188
Ellis, A. W., 201, 202
Erdelyi, Matthew H., 188
Erikson, Erik, 223, 225-230

299

Subject Index

156; free association for, 230; Freud on, 62, 117, 155, 157, 158, 159, 282-283; hereditary, 155; hypnosis for, 282-283; Kaplan on, 155-156; occasioning trauma for, 182; as psychoneurosis, 170; repression etiology of, 150; Rubinstein on, 81-82; seduction etiology of, 49-50, 117, 155, 157, 158, 159; suggestion in, 282-283; symptoms of, 62

Id, 4, 6, 165, 196, 229

Inductions, consilience of, 32, 33, 129, 275-276, 277

Inductivism, 128, 129, 280, 285; confirmation and, 279; as demarcation criterion, 103-104, 105-106; Popper on, 103-104, 105-107, 279. *See also* Confirmation

Inference, of forgotten events, 26, 27, 32-33

Intentionality, 51, 53, 69, 77-83, 89-90, 93. *See also* Meaning; Practical Syllogism

Intentions: of analysand, 27-28, 29-30, 77-80; dreams as, 82-83; repressed, 55, 77, 78. *See also* Motives

Interpretations: analysand as arbiter of, 21-26, 27, 28, 29, 33, 37, 38, 40; analysand resists, 36-37, 240, 241-242; analyst as arbiter of 27, 28, 32; assent/dissent to, 28, 240-241, 273-274, 275-277; confirmed, 31, 37, 38; discredited, 37; falsified, 33-34, 35-36, 37-38; general, 15-16, 21-23, 33-34, 35-36, 37, 38; Habermas on, 15-16, 21-23, 34, 36-37; incomplete, 276

Interview, psychoanalytic, 43, 45, 271; contaminated, 248-250 (*see also* Suggestion; Transference); observations in, 44; reliability of, 261; testability in, 97-99, 128; validity of, 248-250; value of, 97, 99-101 102, 107, 273; verbal production in, 43-49; vindicated, 127-128. *See also* Extraclinical data; Psychoanalysis

Introspection, 29-31, 147-148, 207-208. *See also* Access, privileged

Irma Injection Dream, 82, 216, 220-231

Joint accreditation, 266. *See also* Consilience, inductive

Law(s): contextual dependency of, 17-18, 19, 20; Coulomb's 18; Kepler's, 88; Newton's gravitational, 17, 18, 88, 115; Newton's on motion, 88, 259; of physics, 16-20

Lesbianism, 40, 112

Little Hans, case of, 99, 139, 248, 283

Marxism, 103, 106, 107-108

Master Proposition, 140. *See also* Necessary Condition Thesis

Masturbation, 251-252, 261

Meaning: in dreams, 55, 57; Freud on, 63-64, 66, 67; latent, 90; quest for, in psychoanalysis, 52-53, 54-57

Medicine, somatic, 11, 12, 13

Memory: of analysand, 25, 26-27, 32, 33; childhood, 242-243, 257; false/unreliable, 33, 242-243, 257; Freud on, 26, 27, 32-33, 242-243; Habermas on, 25-27; and inference, 26, 27, 32-33; lapse of, 30, 58-59; repressed, 26, 30, 33, 178; slip of, 58-59, 190-191 (*see also* Parapraxes); traumatic, 178. *See also* Paramnesia

Mental apparatus. *See* Mind, model of

Mental state, latent, 78, 79

Metapsychology, 5, 91, 100; vs. clinical theory, 5-9, 67, 69, 81-82, 84-89; criticized, 81; Freud on, 5-6, 84, 86-87

Mind, model of, 3-5, 165

Minineuroses, 230; dreams as symptoms of, 64, 65, 176, 193, 194, 234; parapraxes as symptoms of, 58, 59, 61, 176, 187, 193, 194

Mosher Sex-Guilt Inventory, 204-205

Motives: acknowledged by agent, 27-29; as cause, 70-72, 75; conscious, 29, 56, 203, 205-206; denied, 27-28; for dreams, 71, 83, 175-176, 225-226, 227, 228, 229, 230; explanation by, 73; Freud on, 70-71; 167; Haber-

Designer: UC Press Staff
Compositor: Trigraph, Inc.
Printer: Vail-Ballou
Binder: Vail-Ballou
Text: 10/12 Palatino
Display: Palatino